Telling Liv
Telling Hist

A Sumatran village boy today, in the 1990s. This child lives in the Sipirok
area, which is located about halfway between Toba and Minangkabau.

Telling Lives, Telling History

Autobiography and Historical Imagination in Modern Indonesia

Aku dan Toba by P. Pospos
and
Semasa Kecil di Kampung
by Muhamad Radjab

Edited, translated, and with an
Introduction by Susan Rodgers

UNIVERSITY OF CALIFORNIA PRESS
Berkeley   Los Angeles   London

The publisher is grateful to Balai Pustaka, Jakarta, for permission to publish translations of *Aku dan Toba: Tjatatan dari Masa
Kanak-Kanak* by P. Pospos, and *Semasa Kecil di Kampung
(1913–1928): Autobiografi seorang Anak Minangkabau* by
Muhamad Radjab; both were originally published in 1950.

University of California Press
Berkeley and Los Angeles, California

University of California Press
London, England

Library of Congress Cataloging-in-Publication Data
Rodgers, Susan.
    Telling lives, telling history: autobiography and historical
        imagination in modern Indonesia / edited, translated, and with
        an introduction by Susan Rodgers.
            p.   cm.
    English translation of Aku dan Toba and Semasa kecil di kampung.
    Includes bibliographical references and index.
    Contents: Aku dan Toba / by P. Pospos; and, Semasa kecil di
kampung / by Muhamad Radjab.
    ISBN 0–520–08546–9.—ISBN 0–520–08547–7 (pbk.)
    1. Pospos, P.   2. Radjab, Muhamad.   3. Indonesia—History—20th
century.   I. Rodgers, Susan, 1949–   . II. Pospos, P. Aku dan Toba.
English. 1995.   III. Radjab, Muhamad. Semasa kecil di kampung.
English. 1995.
DS643.T45   1995
959.803—dc20   94–30282
                                                                      CIP

Printed in the United States of America

1 2 3 4 5 6 7 8 9

CONTENTS

ACKNOWLEDGMENTS

The idea for this book came from a chance comment by one of the re-
viewers of my article "*Me and Toba*: A Childhood World in a Batak
Memoir" when that essay was being considered for publication in Cornell
University's journal *Indonesia*. The unknown reviewer wrote that a *comparative* study of the several Sumatran childhood memoirs (the two at issue
here, and Nur Sutan Iskandar's *Pengalaman Masa Kecil*) published directly
after the Indonesian Revolution of 1945–49 would prove to be a valuable
exercise, although such an undertaking would go beyond the scope of
that early *Me and Toba* essay. The larger field of autobiographical literature beyond Pospos's *Aku Dan Toba* did turn out to be a wonderful context for considering that memoir: thus, this book. William Frederick of
Ohio University's History Department urged me to speculate about the visions of history embedded in these childhood biographies. In fact, it was
our many conversations together over cups of coffee about what images of
time, person, and society might lie hidden in *Me and Toba* and *Village
Childhood* that allowed me to tackle this book project in the first place.
Many of the assertions in my introductory essay derive from my work with
Bill Frederick; his stylistic guidance for my translation strategy was also in-
valuable, especially for our work together on the first several chapters of
the Radjab memoir.

After I moved to Holy Cross, a number of colleagues there served as
sounding boards for my interpretations of these texts: Classicist Deborah
Boedecker (now at Brown University) and our mutual Honors student
Sara Broaders used an early version of the Pospos translation in Sara's
fine senior thesis on concepts of self and the transition to literacy; anthropologist Christine Greenway and historian Karen Turner, as always,

forced me to refine my points and have fun doing it. My Holy Cross students who read short excerpts of the translations of these childhood memoirs provided welcome proof that these distant Sumatran texts have a literary and emotional immediacy for young people from as far away as America.

Stan Holwitz of the University of California Press was in on this project from its early stages, always offering his generous help and enthusiasm. Michelle Nordon, also of the University of California Press, provided additional expert editorial support, and Linda Benefield, my painstaking and patient copyeditor for this complex text, kept me on track stylistically with good cheer throughout. The Radjab family and P. S. Naipospos and his daughter Elisabeth were also indispensable colleagues in this translation project, going on to give their kind permission for us to publish my translations of the memoirs. They provided abundant biographical detail about the two authors' extraordinary later lives, after childhood times.

Finally, our department secretaries Ann Papagni and Catherine Pojani devoted many hours of care to typing and helping me revise the manuscript, work for which I am deeply grateful.

MAPS

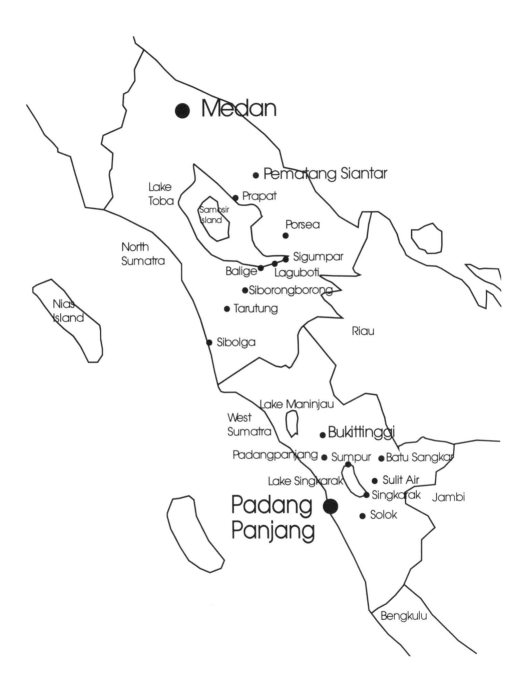

GLOSSARY

adat: 'Ancient, inherited custom.' In Minangkabau and Toba, adat is often thought of in terms of ceremonial practices, oratory, 'ancient words,' heirloom treasures, and ethnically distinct marriage practices and inheritance rules.

ambtenaar: (Dutch) A government civil servant.

bale-bale: (Toba Batak) A modest village house, in contrast to the much grander 'adat house' with its swoop-backed, thatched roof and carved, painted sides.

bendi: (Indonesian) A two-wheeled horse carriage with space behind and beside the driver for several passengers.

benggol: A Dutch colonial-era monetary denomination, two and a half cents.

Confession, the: The profession of faith in Islam.

datuk: (Minangkabau) Nobleman. Also, a person's matrilineal ancestor.

delman: (Indonesian) A horse carriage.

duku: Lanseh fruit (*Lansium domesticum*).

dukun: Folk healer, diagnostician, spellcaster or remover.

Fasting Month: Ramadan, the Fasting Month, the ninth month of the Arabic calendar.

gaba-gaba: (Toba Batak) A Christmas tree, a European importation enthusiastically used in Batak Christian churches.

Gouvernements-Vervólgschool: (Dutch) Government Link School, a sort of advanced elementary school that allowed students to continue on to secondary schools.

haji: A person who has made the pilgrimage (the haj) to Mecca.

hikayat: Tale, story, and also history, account.

H.I.S.: (Dutch) Hollandse Inlandse School, a prestigious elementary school that held some of its lessons in Dutch.

homang: (Toba Batak) A scary, ghostly spirit, although one less frightful and dangerous than *begu* (evil spirits).

horja: (Toba Batak) "An undertaking, a work," an adat feast involving meat sacrifice and hundreds of celebrants.

Huria pagaran: (Toba Batak) One of the small Christian church congregations "in the neighborhood" of a major church building. A small village congregation.

imam: Leader of communal prayer, in Islam.

jambak: A fruit (*Eugenia jambus*).

kiai: A Muslim religious scholar.

kweekschool: (Dutch) A high-prestige, Dutch-language teacher training institute for young people from indigenous Indies ethnic societies. The Kweekschool Bukittinggi was one of the most highly regarded schools in colonial Sumatra.

Lebaran: The feast day ending the Fasting Month, Ramadan.

lenggak: (Minangkabau) The second story of the *surau*.

marga: Patrilineal clan, in Batak societies.

martandang: (Toba Batak) Old-fashioned Batak courtship practice involving whispered conversations between girls in their houses and boys sneaking up under the floorboards. The young pairs would trade sly rhymed verses with each other until dawn.

martarombo: (Toba Batak) To recite clan genealogies to each other, or to relate clan or lineage histories in the context of an adat feast, or *horja*.

M.L.S.: Middelbare Landbouw School, a kind of high school using Dutch.

MULO: Meer Uitgebreide Lagere Onderwijs, a high-status Dutch-language secondary school that gave some students access to further higher education.

orangkaya: (Minangkabau) A nobleman, a ceremonial adept. The same word is used in the southern Batak societies for the chief ceremonial spokesman of a village's "ancestral wife-receivers," *anakboru pusako*.

Padri movement (also *Paderi*): A militant Islamic movement that spread the Muslim religion north from Minangkabau into the southern Batak lands during the Padri Wars, 1816–1832.

Puasa: (Indonesian) The Muslim Fast.

Ramadan: The Fasting Month.

rambutan: A kind of fruit similar to the lychee.

randai: Traditional Minangkabau drama.

rantau: (Indonesian) The realms outside one's own home ethnic domain.

ringgit: (Dutch) Two and a half rupiah, in the colonial era.

sanding: (Toba Batak) A Toba speech-avoidance practice.

santri: Boys and young men studying the Arabic texts, living together in a Muslim dormitory community.

schakelschool: (Dutch) A "wild school," a proprietary school. In Toba, parents would send their children to such institutes to supplement the sometimes-meager education they were getting in the regular public and mission schools.

Schoolopziener: (Dutch) The inspector of public schools.

selamatan: A ceremonial meal held to secure safety from supernatural dangers.

sikola guru: (Toba Batak) Teachers' school.

sikola metmet: (Toba Batak) Elementary school, often grades one through three. (*Metmet* means "little.")

sikola panonga: (Toba Batak) Middle school.

sintua: (Toba Batak) A church elder, a member of the governing board of married men that helped the Protestant ministers superintend the Batak congregations.

sunat prayer: Special prayers used in the circumcision ritual.

surau: The Muslim dormitory community for young male religious scholars and recitation students.

sutan: An honorific title for aristocratic men in Minangkabau and the southern Batak lands.

syech: An Arabic prayer and Koranic recitation teacher, in Minangkabau village Islam.

tadarus prayer (or *tedarus*): Group recitation of the Koran, performed by taking turns. Typically performed during the Fasting Month.

takbir: Recitation of "God is great" at the beginning of Muslim prayers.

tarwih prayers (also *taraweh*): Nonobligatory evening prayers during Ramadan.

Tuan: The appellation used during colonial times to address male Europeans, as in "Tuan Pendeta" (Tuan Minister, in the churches).

Zendings-Seminarie: (Dutch) The seminary run by the Protestant mission church in Toba.

PART ONE

Two Sumatran Childhood Memoirs

Imagining Modern Indonesia
via Autobiography

Personal narratives have deep public resonance in twentieth-century Indonesia, where the process of growing to adulthood and traversing a life is often recalled in terms similar to those used to think about society and the past in a more general sense. In the cosmopolitan, city-based national culture and in many Indonesian ethnic minority societies (the country has over three hundred of these, based in rural, village regions), telling a life unavoidably also involves telling history in terms of passages through ages of time and transitions between levels of consciousness and social awareness. Indonesian narrators of both public and private histories tend to draw on the same lode of symbols about eras, times of darkness and light, maturation, and growth toward greater intellectual awareness from an earlier age of social obtuseness and ignorance. In other words, Indonesian historical memory and personal memory are both animated by certain closely related key scenarios and social images, and societal histories and personal narratives interpenetrate. They also draw on each other's storehouses of aesthetic richness and emerge as deeper, more meaningful social texts because of that. Put another way, art animates the telling of history at both the public and personal levels in unusually thoroughgoing ways in this uncommonly time-conscious country.

This interpenetration of autobiographical memory and public history seems to be particularly acute for Indonesians who were born during the first two and three decades of this century. These men and women often attended Dutch-administered elementary and secondary schools in the 1920s or 1930s—a bittersweet experience that gave them their first personal taste of life in the European-dominated, colonial Indies. As young adults these men and women saw the archipelago abruptly seized by the Japanese forces in 1942; this extraordinary generation then went on to help the Indonesian national revolutionary effort in the late 1940s in their individual ways, in their diverse ethnic societies, or in more cross-culturally mixed cities. If they enjoyed a long life, they then went on to suffer or savor other major eras of Indonesian time: the Sukarno years of prideful nationalism and political chaos, and since 1965, the more stable, Jakarta-focused, fervid economic developmentalism of the Soeharto regime. Indonesians born early in the century know well that their individual lives and their family memories hold these larger eras' historical imprints deep within them in vibrant ways.

Taking advantage of this situation, this book presents the first English translations of two modestly phrased yet superbly insightful childhood memoirs from Sumatra, both published soon after the Indonesian Revolution (1945–49), which liberated the island chain from Dutch control. The memoirs, which are both written in the national language, Indonesian, are P. Pospos's *Aku dan Toba: Tjatatan dari Masa Kanak-Kanak* (*Me and Toba: Notes from Childhood Times*) and Muhamad Radjab's *Semasa Kecil di Kampung* (*Village Childhood*). Both published in 1950 and written outside Sumatra, in Java, during the Revolution, the autobiographies recall childhoods spent in late colonial times, from roughly 1915 through the 1930s. The Pospos book is set in Toba (one of the rural home regions of the Batak peoples in North Sumatra) while the Radjab memoir is set in Minangkabau, in West Sumatra. In reconstructing their boyhood selves and in writing about their remembered passage from childhood to maturity in the colonial Indies' final, unsettled decades, the authors of these two small books were also writing about much larger issues, such as national Indonesian society's own journey toward revolution and independence from an age of colonial subjugation and what these memoirists portray as an era of pervasive intellectual naïveté clouding the lives and social perspectives of Indonesian villagers and townspeople. Recalling the personal past, for these memoirists, becomes a witty but bitter effort of actively creating the public future, and trying to imagine an Indonesian national society of deep self-consciousness, social awareness, and religious sophistication. The extent to which the nascent Indonesian national society surrounding them in 1950 actually conformed to these ideals the authors leave as an open topic.

Writing of themselves, though, the two writers chronicle Sumatran childhood worlds and states of Toba and Minangkabau village consciousness which lead (by the time the remembered children reach the threshold of adulthood) to mature selves who hold strikingly cosmopolitan, self-critical, and *socially* critical views of their village ethnic universes. By the time they are seventeen or so, the boys have almost become ethnographers of their home ethnic realms and also of those Sumatran worlds' senses of time, place, language, society, and person. By the end of each narrative, the stories' new almost-adults look toward the *rantau* (the social and moral precincts outside the Sumatran rural ethnic home regions) with a sense that these polyglot areas contain a future that will bring personal and public liberation from the shackles of "unthinking traditionalism." Modern Indonesia lies out there, the memoirists aver, in the hearts and minds of young people. That is, among sophisticated school graduates like the two authors and their implied readers, all of whom live away from a village home and the past, in Indonesia and the future. One of the great strengths of these autobiographies, in fact, is their catalysis of very common twentieth-century Sumatran assumptions about history and place (about the past and the future, about an ethnic village home counterposed to a cosmopolitan, distant rantau) into the publically accessible aesthetic form of the printed boyhood memoir about personal, seemingly modest journeys to adulthood.[1]

At the same time they are chronicling these changes in their remembered childhood selves (and advocating, although, they know, hardly guaranteeing similar changes for Indonesian society as a whole), the memoirists also write by implication about the challenging linguistic task of recording personal memories and larger social portraits in print and prose. The authors do this in a knowing way, against a background of Sumatra's long-established, eloquent traditions for orally evoking the past. For centuries, Sumatran ethnic societies (see maps) have employed such genres as sung or droned chronicles, oral epics, and chanted clan genealogies to recreate a supernaturally powerful past. Some of these histories are recited in association with magically charged script texts, barkbooks, bone reliquaries, funerary obelisks, or sacred clan heirlooms. Pospos and Radjab are quite self-conscious about writing *printed* personal narratives in a modernist key, against this sometimes oral, sometimes sacred-text–oriented and certainly much more communal background. They invite their readers to share in their linguistic "maturity" in this effort. The memoirists' consistently self-deprecatory and often ironic tone is central to their vision of writing in general, and to their understanding of Indonesian historical writing in particular. The authors know they are writing "minor lives," not chronicles of prominent nationalist figures; propagandistic prose and hortatory history become impossible in this prose climate.

Beyond presenting my translations of these books in part 2, I also offer an interpretive reading of them in this introductory essay. As an anthropologist concerned with issues of modernity and tradition as these ideas have been constructed in twentieth-century Sumatran social thought (and particularly via popular media forms such as printed leisure-time literature),[2] I am convinced that these memoirs should be appreciated as gentle but nonetheless quite profound texts about revolutionary ways of thinking about Indonesian history. These small books can be read, I think, as building blocks in the country's effort to invent Indonesia, as an imagined community, as Benedict Anderson has set out that idea in his book *Imagined Communities* (1983).

Anderson asserts that modern printed popular literary forms such as novels and newspapers can foster new ways of thinking about social community in societies fragmented into separate ethnic worlds, in colonial empires. Modern literature allows readers and writers to imagine new national communities, with greatly expanded social horizons and more secular time frameworks than those available in oral media forms such as clan genealogies, or in written, script texts such as court chronicles, which themselves have heavy oral residues. Newspapers and novels encourage readers (Anderson asserts) to imagine a complex but interactive social world surrounding them, full of diverse planes of discourse and their correspondingly diverse moral worlds. These publication forms also lead readers to think of themselves as existing in so-called real, secular time, from which vantage point they can 'look back' to their society's earlier 'more mythic' modes of apprehending and telling history. The latter mythic forms emerge as entertaining (or sometimes, ethnographically diverting) forms of older "oral literature," in this new, 'more knowing' perspective. The self-consciously sophisticated reader of newspapers or novels, Anderson goes on, is also able to stand back from the flow of simultaneous events occurring at different spots in the world and work to integrate this variegated timescape into a single consistent realm, in relation to his or her own perspective, as reader. Finally, the imagined time and place of novels and newspapers makes the imagined community of the nation thinkable (1983, 31). Both worlds (the one in leisure-time print literature and the one imagined in a nascent national society) are essentially fictional ones, being composed of persons the reader or citizen will never be able to actually meet in person.

Popular literature forms such as the childhood autobiographies at issue here seem to me to promote the same variety of innovative social thought, and a special, almost seditious critical perspective (cloaked inside innocuous-looking boyhood memories) in cultures such as Revolutionary-era ethnic worlds like Toba and Minangkabau, and in their overseas diaspora communities in cities in Java. Pospos and Radjab seemed to have intuitively grasped the fact that childhood memoirs about the 1920s and 1930s were perfect vehicles for imagining a nation through print literature.

I assert all this, well aware of the fact that some deconstructionist critics of Indonesian literature might prefer to see texts such as the two translated here as bereft of larger social meanings, and as examples of the play of language per se, independent of hidden social semantics of the sort I perceive.[3] I also make my admittedly ambitious claim that these memoirs are "about history" and about the Indonesian national enterprise despite the fact that previous commentators on these two particular autobiographies (such as G. W. J. Drewes, in his 1951 essay "Autobiografieen van Indonesiers") have considered these books to be well written but fairly limited, minor portraits of recollected childhoods. In other words, most other researchers have seen these books as being more in the nature of reminiscences of childhood per se than important historical statements. In my reading (and I would speculate that this would also be true for the books' authors and for some of their more thoughtful readers), these tales of 1920s and 1930s childhood days spent in out-of-the-way Sumatran villages and school towns point beyond the surface meanings of their texts toward wider arenas of Indonesian social thought. The autobiographies seem to me to be about large issues of language, meaning, religious speech and action, public memory, private lives, "ethnic tradition," and "Indonesian modernity"—although on the surface the books are indeed simple chronicles of childhood experiences.

These autobiographies are also deeply political, despite the fact that the narratives do not mention major national figures such as Sukarno or Mohammad Hatta (Indonesia's first president and vice president, the latter a Minangkabau man), nor do they dwell on the nationalist movements of the 1920s and 1930s (which had Sumatra as a major regional base),[4] nor do they deal to any extent with Holland/Indies political relations in the late colonial decades. This period, which of course provided the time frame for the authors' stories, was the time when student political clubs, Islamic unions, merchants' groups, and loose-knit communities of intellectuals were attempting to lay the organizational groundwork for the Indies' eventual independence from the Dutch. Much nationalist activity along these lines took place in Toba and Minangkabau during this period. But, most of the action in the two memoirs is concerned with the minor emotional dramas of two village boys' lives as they navigate successively larger and larger realms of familial, religious, and schoolroom experience. Nevertheless, by describing such minor journeys, the books are about the very heart of Indonesia's effort to create itself as a modern nation. That is, these memoirs are records of individual passages toward states of consciousness in which people can question the ideological givens of village life, the received truths of organized religion, and village notions of time and society, and then go on to "migrate toward" (a major image for Sumatran writers) the new imagined community of Indonesia, as a multiethnic nation created by the conscious cooperative work of patriots drawn from these two authors' own exact generation. Note how this vision of "growing up toward Indonesia" and toward the rantau and toward critical forms of consciousness goes far beyond some simple political or military resistance to Dutch oppression. Revolution for these authors means a revolution of the spirit, an *invention* of modern Indonesia—and resistance to and overthrow of the Dutch colonial state is only one constituent part of this larger, deeper transformation of thought and "revolution of eras." It is also important to note that this action takes place not in mythic time but in secular time, with people actively intervening in history to channel its course and control its pace—and to astutely record its passage, in print. Few artists' efforts could be more revolutionary than this; few could be more deeply Indonesian.

It seems to me that much important Indonesian thought about nationhood and about the critical late colonial decades in places like North and West Sumatra is often phrased in just such personalized terms as these. My own life history interviews with elderly rajas (ceremonial chiefs) and retired schoolteachers in the Angkola Batak area near Sipirok, for instance, often include a similar evocation of revolutionary national history through personal recollections of life journeys very similar to those Pospos and Radjab write about. Public evocations of certain poignant, painful emotional states relating to individual lives as they were lived during these pivotal decades may work, I suspect, as a sort of coded language for talking about the larger and more overtly political transformation of the colonial Indies into an independent Indonesia. This convergence of personal and public memory is of course what makes the study of twentieth-century autobiography in the country so important. (And what makes oral history work so crucial today, before this older generation of men and women born between 1910 and 1920 dies without telling their stories. Few of these people had access to print publication, as Pospos and Radjab did.)

It is intriguing, also, to see that there are striking parallels between the emotional worlds of childhood created in these two autobiographies and the childhood lives described in other personal memoirs of late colonial and early nationalist times. Moreover, there are marked similarities between the emotional terrain of our two childhood biographies and the fictional world of Indonesia's finest modern writer, Pramoedya Ananta Toer. This is particularly true of his short stories about the Japanese occupation and the national revolution in his collection *Tjerita dari Blora* (Stories from Blora, 1952). A reading of the social, personal, and temporal imagery of the Pospos and Radjab memoirs will provide a means to begin to suggest reasons for these concordances across the literary scene of 1930s–1950s fiction and nonfiction in the country, although a deep consideration of the parallels between Indonesian fiction and these two memoirs is much beyond the scope of this essay. But first, some background to my reading of the memoirs' imagery: a short discussion of the texts and their authors, and the ethnic societies surrounding them, and then a consideration of autobiographical writing within Indonesian and Malay historical traditions. This is already a well-researched topic (see, for instance, Sweeney

1980a, 1980b, 1990; Reid 1972; Watson 1989. Drewes's 1961 *Hikayat Nakhoda Muda, De Biografie van een Minangkabausen Peperhandelaar* [The biography of a Minangkabau pepper trader] offers a useful comparative text, although the piece is a biography, not an autobiography).

THE TEXTS AND THEIR AUTHORS

P. Pospos's *Me and Toba: Notes from Childhood Times* was published by the government printing house Balai Pustaka in 1950. Muhamad Radjab's *Village Childhood* appeared, as noted, in the same year, again under Balai Pustaka auspices. The very existence of this publishing house was itself part and parcel of the political and artistic creation of Indonesia (Teeuw 1967:13–15; Drewes 1981). Begun in 1908 by the Dutch colonial administration as an organ for publishing high-quality works of fiction and folklore in refined, grammatically elegant Indonesian, by the 1920s Balai Pustaka had developed into a major venue for popular literature, particularly "journey novels" turning on love-story themes. In their Indonesian-language book list, the house published works that directly engaged issues of Indies modernity: the strains and pressures of life in big multiethnic cities; love marriages versus arranged matches, based on family alliance considerations; and the emotional turmoil of educated young people caught between village tradition and cosmopolitan school experiences and careers in the more Europeanized sectors of society. A number of Balai Pustaka novels (most of them by Minangkabau authors) enjoyed wide circulation among the educated classes in both Java and Sumatra. These novels included Abdul Muis's *Salah Asuhan* (Wrong upbringing), 1928; Marah Rusli's *Sitti Nurbaya* (S. Nurbaya is a girl's name), 1922; and Nur Sutan Iskandar's *Salah Pilih* (Wrong choice), 1928. The boys in Pospos's and Radjab's childhood memoirs were presented as avid readers of such Balai Pustaka novels; these love-story books, in fact, form a constant backdrop to much later Sumatran fiction and nonfiction writing.

Both of the boyhood memoirs, as noted, were written in the rantau, outside Sumatra, during the revolution years. The volumes were published in Jakarta in Indonesia's first year of independent existence. The early 1950s saw the publication of two other similar childhood recollections, set in the same time as that of our two autobiographies. These works were the prominent Minangkabau novelist Nur Sutan Iskandar's *Pengalaman Masa Kecil* (Childhood experiences), 1948, and the Muslim religious essayist Hamka's *Kenang-Kenangan Hidup* (Life memories), 1951–52. The first volume of this latter memoir deals largely with Hamka's younger years, although the set is rarely labeled a childhood memoir per se. After this early 1950s period, childhood memoirs receded from view as an important genre of modern Indonesian letters. Why this was so is a puzzle to which I hope students of later Indonesian literary periods will address themselves. This present essay will, at least, shed some light on the fact that childhood memoir publishing emerged with special force right after the Revolution. A related topic is the remarkable similarity of all these memoirs to Indonesia's first full-blown modern autobiography, the nationalist leader Dr. Soetomo's *Kenang-Kenangan* (Memories, 1934).

This is a similarity to which we can turn momentarily. But what of the two men who wrote the two extraordinary books translated here? Pospos recently retired from a career as an editor in a Christian publishing house in Jakarta. Radjab died in 1970, after long service as a newspaperman, essayist, social commentator, and university lecturer in Jakarta. Neither man is nor was an especially prominent public figure, at least in the sense that neither was a major politician, nor is either writer seen today as an important professional historian (although Radjab did publish several popular histories and folklore books on Sumatra and Sulawesi). In 1950, each man was just launching his career in the world of print. Pospos was thirty-one years old and working in Jakarta as a high school teacher; Radjab, at age thirty-seven, was employed as a newspaper editor for *Indonesia Raya,* also in the capital.

Each of the writers had already led an extraordinarily literate and even text-obsessed life by the early 1950s. After the publication of their childhood reminiscences, each author continued this trajectory into Indonesia's print culture. In a pattern typical of many Sumatrans of their generation who were educated in colonial-era schools and who came from ethnic societies, like Toba and Minangkabau, fascinated with the printed word, Pospos and Radjab spent their careers using books and newspapers to expand literacy's scope into public intellectual discourse for the new nation. And, in a poignant way, both men succeeded in having just the sort of literate, secular career that (as we shall soon see) they were struggling toward as children.

P. Pospos, whose real name is P. S. Naipospos (Paian Sihar Naipospos) was born to a family of modest means and social standing on October 9, 1919, in Tapanuli (in the subprovince now known as North Tapanuli). His only published work is *Me and Toba.* In July 15, 1987, and August 22, 1987, letters to me, Pospos writes that after attending Schakelschool (a private, proprietary elementary school that did not use Dutch) and H.I.S. (a Dutch-language primary school) in the Balige area (a heartland Toba region) he went on to the Christian MULO school in Tarutung. This market town was an administrative and church center located on the road between Toba and the port town of Sibolga. MULO, Meer Uitgebreide Lagere Onderwijs, was a prestigious secondary school employing Dutch-language instruction; MULO worked as one of the gateway schools for further education in the colonial school system. Upon graduation from this secondary school Pospos moved to Bogor, West Java, where he enrolled in M.L.S. (Middelbare Landbouw School, a sort of high school), where he studied for two years. He moved to Jakarta and enrolled in A.M.S. (Algemeen Middelbare School, also a high school). After two years the school was closed because of the Japanese Occupation. Pospos then continued his study in S.M.T. (Sekolah Menegah Tinggi, a level of high school), graduating from this school after two years. He taught in a public high school during the first few years of national independence. During this time, he also enrolled in Faculty of Letters of University of Indonesia for three years and earned the M.O. degree (Middelbare Onderwys, a degree similar to the bachelor's). From 1952 to 1964 he was employed at the Balai Alkitab (Biblical Studies Publishing House) in Jakarta. From 1965 until his retirement in 1989, Pospos worked at the Badan Penerbit Kristen (Christian Publishing Concern), also in Jakarta. Much of his work consisted of preparing translations of exegetical and theological works for a general Indonesian audience of readers. Pospos and his wife have four children: the eldest daughter is a physician; the eldest son is a civil engineer; the second daughter is a veterinarian; and the younger son is studying political science.

Muhamad Radjab was born June 21, 1913, in the Minangkabau rural homeland in West Sumatra, in the village of Sumpur, Padang Pandjang. He spent most of his adult life and career abroad, that is, in the rantau's outlying lands in Java. He died August 16, 1970, back in West Sumatra once more, in Sumpur. At the time he had been attending a conference in Padang on Minangkabau ethnic culture. For the last two years of his life, in fact, Radjab had been concentrating his writing and research on Minangkabau literature and ethnic traditions and had planned a book on these topics. His numerous obituaries in Padang and Jakarta newspapers noted that his widow was left to raise eight children, most still at home.

Radjab's family was not among the high hereditary Minangkabau nobility. However, they had endeavored for several generations to garner social prestige of another sort: the family lines on both his father's and his mother's sides boasted many Islamic religious teachers and several *haji* pilgrims. Radjab made this Muslim family milieu a major focus of tension in *Village Childhood*.

He attended village elementary school and also local Koranic recitation schools (*suraus*), finally progressing to the Sumatra Thawalib school in Padang Pandjang (this was an Islamic middle school). In his late teens and early twenties ("escaping" from country Muslim schools, in the view put forward in his memoir) Radjab attended the teacher training institute, Sekolah Normal Islam, in Padang, from 1932 to 1934. He then migrated to Jakarta and soon after that to Bandung, where he sped headlong into a newswriting career. After brief service as a junior reporter on the Padang paper *Persamaan,* he worked on the Jakarta paper *Pembangunan* from 1934 to 1935. Radjab followed this with a job as an assistant editor on the magazine *Persatuan Hidup* in Bandung during the Japanese Occupation years 1942–45. The next two years, during the Indonesian Revolution, he worked as an editor for the news service Berita Antara in Jogyakarta, Solo, Malang, and Jakarta. In the years 1947–49 he was an editor on the daily paper *Detik* back in West Sumatra, in the small city of Bukittinggi; the next year he was an editor for the same paper in Sulawesi. The latter is a large, ethnically diverse island northeast of Java. Radjab's experiences there resulted in two books about the island's folklore and about one of its prominent ethnic societies, the Sa'dan Toraja. Balai Pustaka published his journalistic, enjoyable ethnographic volume *Toraja Sa'dan* in 1952, and his *Dongeng-Dongeng Sulawesi Selatan* (South Sulawesian folktales) in 1950.

In 1950 and the following year Radjab was an editor for the daily newspaper *Indonesia Raya.* Until 1955 he again worked as an editor for the news service Berita Antara in Jakarta. Following this, from 1955 to 1963, he served as a bureau chief for the feature wire service Antara Features. Then and until his death he headed the research section of LKBN Antara. Drawing on his extensive reporting background and supplementing this with some graduate-level coursework in the law school and the faculty of social sciences at the University of Indonesia (1959–1963), Radjab also lectured on social issues at that university, at Mahaputra University, and at Trisakti University.

Village Childhood was Radjab's second book, appearing a year after his *Tjatatan di Sumatra* (Notes on Sumatra, Balai Pustaka, 1949). This volume was a journalist's account of Sumatra during the Revolution; Radjab did the research for this somewhat meandering study while part of the team of reporters sent to the island by the Nationalist government's Ministry of Information. *Notes on Sumatra,* briefly discussed below, presents a view of the island's journey to modernity and Indonesian nationhood supplemental and complementary to that set out in *Village Childhood.*

The same year that *Village Childhood* appeared, Radjab had another book published by Balai Pustaka, the previously mentioned *South Sulawesian Folktales.* In rapid succession his *Toraja Sa'dan* and *Perang Paderi* (The Padri wars), 1954, were published. This last book was a rather heated narration of the history of the 1820s Padri wars in Minangkabau. The last book of Radjab's career marked a return to the ethnographic perspective essayed in his early works on Sulawesi societies. This work was his 1969 *Sistem Kekerabatan di Minangkabau* (The kinship system of Minangkabau).

Radjab was also a prolific translator of fiction, social science works, and law texts from English into Indonesian. His eleven major published translations include three works by Dostoyevsky (all translated from 1948 to 1949) and various volumes on law and legal history.

Pospos's and Radjab's careers show both of them to have been fascinated with issues of religion, holy texts, language, the translatability of languages, ethnic literatures, social history, and the vexing matter of how authors might best describe complex social worlds, whether they be the nineteenth-century Russian landscapes of Radjab's fiction translations or the Sumatran scenes from these authors' own lives. These same large preoccupations are found again in Pospos's and Radjab's boyhood memoirs.

Pospos and Radjab address their memoirs to a broad Indonesian-speaking audience that includes members of their home ethnic societies and residents of other ethnic locales in the country: Java, Bali, Sunda, Toraja, and so on. Both authors know that Toba and Minangkabau[5] have strong ethnic profiles in Indonesian thought: Toba as a rather rough-mannered society of smart, aggressive go-getters who assiduously maintain patrilineal clan ties in the most distant precincts of their diaspora as well as "back home" in Tapanuli rice-farming villages, and Minangkabau as a simultaneously Muslim and matrilineal society with a striking record of success in business enterprises both in Sumatra and more far-flung parts of the island chain. Though neither memoirist takes especial care to set out Toba or Minangkabau social structural arrangements in great detail, in the course of each book readers do learn certain background facts. Toba's patrilineal clans, or *margas*, for instance, trace back many generations and are fractured into quarrelsome, rivalrous lineages. The latter are linked to similar lineages of other clans through ranked marriage alliances; wife-giver lineages, or *hula-hula*, bestow their daughters as brides on their indebted, subservient, lower-ranked *anakboru* ("girl-children"), their wife-receivers. The *hula-hula* in turn are subservient to their own wife-givers, while *anakboru* will play the wife-bestowing role to yet another lineage. Ideally at least, these marriage alliances are asymmetrical (wife-givers should never receive a bride from their *anakboru*) and endure over many generations. In practice, strict upkeep of this ideal vision is mostly confined to the wealthy, "core ancestral" lineages of a region; smaller, commoner lineages such as Pospos's own have much less traffic in the exalted myths of Toba "ancient marriage alliances," although regular village families do at least try to encourage their sons to marry a daughter of the mother's brother (the perfect arrangement, within *adat*). Toba in the 1920s and 1930s had circles of rajas or chiefs claiming hereditary positions of leadership within "sacrificial communities," village settlements loosely united into ceremonial leagues and cooperative irrigation societies. However, these chiefs were already much-beholden to the Dutch administration; Toba adat chieftaincies, in fact, were weak and faction-ridden even before the colonial state penetrated Tapanuli in the 1850s and 1860s and finally established full control by the turn of the century.

A renegade, self-styled "priest king," Si Singamangaraja XII, led a guerrilla resistance to the Dutch takeover for thirty years but was finally shot to death in 1907, effectively ending organized Toba combat against the "Kompeni," the Company (a then-popular Toba way of referring to the Dutch colonial state as well as its predecessor, the Dutch East Indies Trading Company). Protestant Christianity flooded through Toba in this same era, following its expansion northward starting in 1861 from its initial mission field in Sipirok. Under the charismatic pioneer missionary Ingwar Nommensen, who converted a few Angkola and many Toba to Christianity under the German Rhenisch Mission Society auspices, Tapanuli towns like Balige and Tarutung became Protestant strongholds by the time of Pospos's birth.

Minangkabau stood in great contrast to this. West Sumatra's several distinct subsocieties (in the Tanah Datar valley near Batusangkar, the Agam valley, around the mountain town of Bukittinggi, and the Limapuluh Kota valley centering on Payakumbuh) had histories of hierarchical, statelike organization tracing back to at least the fourteenth century, in contrast to Toba's decentralized, fragile chieftaincy leagues. An important pepper-growing region and a major gold-mining area until the mines were depleted by the 1780s, the Minangkabau kingdoms had forged a series of shifting trade alliances with Aceh in the sixteenth century; over the next one hundred years West Sumatran pepper acted as a magnet for traders from India, China, and Portugal. In 1663, the Dutch established control of Padang and built a fortified trading post nearby on the Batang Aran River. Throughout the late 1600s, the Minangkabau courts, especially that at Pagaruyung, extended their influence northward into the Angkola and Mandailing Batak regions and southward into Rejang. During the Anglo-Dutch war, 1781–84, the West Sumatran coast came under British control; British administration of Padang and environs was reestablished from 1795 to 1819, during the Napoleonic Wars. After that period, Dutch control remained firm; Padang developed into an important trade city, newspaper center, and school town (as did Bukittinggi); and Minangkabau merchants became fixtures in distant Sumatran towns and cities.

Conversion to Islam had begun early, in the late fourteenth century, and by the time the Dutch established political control of West Sumatra, Islam was universally accepted. In fact, Minangkabau had become a center of Sumatran piety and Muslim learning. Powerful Muslim traders began to compete with the old royal houses for political and economic preeminence by the late 1700s, the period when the mines were depleted (the economic base of the traditional nobility). Islamic reformers, led by the puritanical Padris, condemned cockfighting, gambling, opium use, allegiance to feudal models of kingship, adat ceremonialism, and strict matrilineal inheritance of wealth and village titles. During the 1820s, the Padris had acquired military forces and pushed northward into Mandailing and Angkola, converting the population to Islam. The 1820s and early 1830s saw continued military action in heartland areas of Minangkabau, as the Dutch attempted to co-opt local leadership and defeat the Padri forces. This they eventually did in 1837, when the town of Bonjol, under the Padri leader Tuanku Imam Bonjol, fell to Dutch forces.

West Sumatra continued its role as a hotbed of religious and political dispute throughout the rest of the colonial period. The Modernist Muslim movement hit the area with full force by the 1920s, and advocates called for school reform, expanded educational opportunities for women, and a deeper knowledge of scriptural theology, shorn of the accretions of local adat (in Radjab's memoir, the boy is positioned between such a modernist faction and some adat traditionalists, and he consciously refuses to fully take sides. However, the autobiography as a whole is enlivened by the sort of social critique and commitment to a search for meaning found in the modernist Islam of 1920s Sumatra).

Many Minangkabau secondary school graduates found themselves without jobs during this period, and social dislocations of this sort spurred a communist-incited armed insurrection. This revolt failed and many participants were jailed. West Sumatra remained, however, a center for nationalist thought throughout the 1930s and the Japanese Occupation years from 1942 to 1945.

Each memoir assumes a general knowledge of this ethnographic and historical background, for Toba and Minangkabau. At the most basic level, however, each memoir has a much more intimate focus, with its action structured around the growing child's progression through a series of successively higher levels of school (secular schools for Pospos, Muslim ones for Radjab). As the remembered child graduates from one type of schooling to the next (and manages in both books to muddle his way through entrance exams and exit exams, by cramming his brain full of facts) each boy discovers larger realms of the social world outside his immediate parental household. In Radjab's case the home is quite complex, for his mother had died when he was an infant and the baby was forthwith shuttled between his father's niece, his assorted aunts, and his father's additional wives (Minangkabau Islam and adat allow multiple wives). By age six Radjab was living in the Muslim surau, or recitation school community for boys; there he was learning how to puzzle out and recite the Arabic verses of the Koran. A similar movement away from his natal household also took place at a young age in Pospos's recollected life. By age eight or nine, he had begun to board with relatives in little Toba market towns such as Balige so that he could have easy access to more prestigious schools than those available to him back home near Narumonda. Other similarities of storytelling structure will become evident in brief summaries of the action and chapter topics of each book.

Me and Toba, which is eighty-two pages long in its 1950 edition, comprises twenty-four chapters, each untitled, headed simply with a Roman numeral. The prose is spare and the tone fairly intimate. To accomplish this Pospos uses such linguistic devices as the familiar first-person pronoun *aku* instead of the more formal *saya.* In parts of Tapanuli *aku* is the sort of pronoun that family members and close friends will use to refer to themselves in comfortable, close conversations (*aku* is also a common literary usage, but the Batak oral usage of the word is an important factor here). Pospos also consistently uses additional markers of intimacy such as the word *Ayah* (Dad) for *Bapak,* father. (This is another Batak usage; in standard literary Indonesian, *Ayah* is often simply the word used in printed prose for "Father," but Toba and Angkola oral conversation employs *Ayah* as "Dad.") Such terms of address and reference immediately establish a climate of easy social closeness, which persists throughout the book. This tone is reinforced by such additional devices as Pospos's penchant for starting many chapters with a casual frame beginning with the formula, "Another time, an interesting incident occurred . . ." This gives the prose a sense of being rather like a conversation between friends, or a product of an interaction between a storyteller and his or her audience.

The memoir shows numerous other influences from Toba oral culture, although Pospos never goes so far as to employ formulaic opening and closing statements to his paragraphs or chapters (the latter are devices used in many printed Batak texts about adat matters). The writer exploits the sound quality possibilities of Indonesian to the hilt, for instance. He does this by emphasizing the repetition of syllables and playful, alliterative rushes of phrases. He adds to this certain grammatical constructions that make many of his Indonesian sentences "sound like" Batak utterances. For instance, *kubuka* for *saya buka,* "I open" something, such as a door (*kubuka* more closely resembles certain Toba Batak subject-verb constructions than does the more formal *saya buka*). He also often employs Batak-sounding possessives such as *rumahku,* for *rumah saya,* "my house." The -ku suffix is often employed in self-consciously courtly, old-fashioned Indonesian prose, but in the hands of Batak writers it often evokes a sense of the home village ethnic language, since the Batak languages employ so similar a possessive. Taken all together, these tips of the hat to a Batak oral heritage frequently result in engaging paragraphs such as the following (discussed at greater length in Rodgers 1988):

> Rumahku hanja 1 km djauhnja dari sekolah, tapi sering pula aku tidur disekolah itu, karena aku takut pulang sendirian kerumah. Meskipun guruku mengatakan padaku, bahwa tidak ada jin dan setan, tapi perkataannja itu

kurang kupercayai. Malam-malam dikampung kami (kampung itu dikelilingi rumpun bambu dan hampir semua kampung ditanah Batak demikian) se-ring terdengar suara orok menangis dari arah rumpun bambu itu. Itulah katanya suara homang (semacam jin), yang dapat melompat-lompat dengan tidak kelihatan. Pada suatu malam terdengar suara demikian dibelakang rumah kami. Ibuku dengan beberapa gadis (biasanya selalu ada beberapa gadis kampung itu tidur dirumah kami, sejak rumah kami sebuah emper) pergi menghalau homang itu. Aku ditinggalkan mereka seorang diri men-jaga rumah. Hari gelap waktu itu. Karena ditinggal sendirian itu, aku men-jadi takut, gemetar sekujur badanku. Aku berpikir: "Baiklah rumah kututup rapat-rapat, supaya jin itu jangan masuk," tapi aku teringat, bahwa homang dapat berpindah-pindah dengan tidak kelihatan, jadi dapat juga masuk rumah dengan tidak ketahuan dari mana jalannya. Sebab itu kubuka saja pintu lebar-lebar dan aku berdiri bersandar ketiang pintu menanti mereka pulang, sambil mataku kupasang benar-benar melihat kekiri dan kekanan, kebelakang dan kemuka, kalau-kalau jin itu melompat kedekatku. Badanku menggigil dan aku telah bersedia berteriak sekuat-kuatnya. Mujurlah tidak ada terjadi apa-apa. Ibuku dan gadis-gadis lain kudengar berteriak-teriak mengusir homang itu. Kudengar juga homang itu diam. Kepadaku diceri-takan mereka, bahwa mereka mendengar bambu berderes-deres. Barangkali homang itu melompat-lompat lari, tapi sesuatu machluk tidak kelihatan oleh mereka, mungkin karena hari gelap. Didekat mereka aku telah biasa kembali dan pura-pura kuperlihatkan, bahwa aku tidak takut sama sekali. Aku malu menceritakan pengalamanku selama mereka menghalau homang itu.

[My house was only one kilometer away from school, but often I slept there too, since I was afraid to walk home by myself. Even though my teacher had told me that there is no such thing as jins and devils, I did not believe him.

Like almost all Batak villages, ours was surrounded by clumps of bamboo, and at night something that sounded like the voice of a baby crying could often be heard from the direction of the bamboo thicket. This was said to be the voice of the homang, a kind of spirit which could jump about without being seen. One night such a voice was heard behind our house. My mother and several girls (girls from the village always made a habit of sleeping at our house, since it had a porch) went off to chase the homang away. They left me behind, all by myself, to guard the house. It was very dark and, all alone, I became frightened and started to tremble. I thought it would be best to close up the house tight so the spirit couldn't get in, but then I re-membered that the homang could move about without being seen and so could enter the house without anyone knowing how it got in. So I opened the door very wide and stood leaning against the door post waiting for every-one to return, peering left and right, up and down, and back to front, in case the spirit tried to leap out at me. I was shaking all over and was all ready to scream as loudly as I could, but luckily nothing happened. I heard my mother and the girls shouting to chase the homang away; I also heard the homang being quiet. They told me they had heard the bamboo canes creaking and rubbing against one another. Perhaps the homang had just hopped away, but in any case they had not seen the creature; maybe it had been too dark. With my mother and the girls close by once again, I returned to normal and pretended I had not been at all frightened. I was ashamed to tell them what had happened while they were off chasing the homang.] (Pospos 1950, 26)

The book's oral features are indeed strong, but they should not be understood to work to the exclusion of the text's deep print character. In this paragraph just quoted (one that undeniably cries out to be read aloud) a deep print character is also evident: the passage has parenthetical inserts, to add detail, rather than the Toba oratorical style tending more toward aggregative accumulations of phrases and epithets. Pospos's focus on his own personal experiences and his socially critical tone would also have been largely unthinkable in an older, more thoroughly oral Toba world. As noted in my 1988 essay, the memoir's mixture of oral and print characteristics is particularly deft and self-conscious. Pospos's basic idea of writing a childhood life is a deeply literate notion, largely unthinkable in a fully oral village world, which tended to celebrate only exemplary, noble personages, such as lineage founders (whose memory is evoked in clan genealogies, *tarombo*); Pospos's memoir includes much commentary on oral speech routines, as viewed from the perspective of print and the colonial-era schoolroom. Finally, the writer has a fine sense for the poetic sound quality of the Indonesian language itself, which he uses quite astutely with a fine writerly flair to lend a seductive oral flavor to many of his paragraphs, making the book fun to read.

Me and Toba's plot is straightforward and simple, although Pospos pursues it in a desultory and meandering fashion. This is particularly true of the first several chapters. At the beginning of the book the remembered child is about six or seven years old and not yet in school. One day, the local schoolmaster (a Toba Batak man) shows up in the house yard and informs the child's mother (Ibu, the formal term for "Mother") that it is time to put the boy in grammar school. The youngster looks forward to the first day of school with excitement mixed with fear. School does indeed turn out to validate that mix of emotions, as the boy discovers the genuine delights of book learning and mathematics but also finds that he must suffer through frightening exams and put up with ignorant, pedantic, and overly strict Batak teachers. They hit him and verbally berate him for his persistent naughtiness. Nevertheless, his various teachers do recognize him as an apt pupil and a basically smart boy. However, schoolteachers decidedly do not aim to be the children's friends, the narrator finds.[6] Some Batak instructors thoughtlessly accept the dictates of the Dutch school administrators, who run the most prestigious elementary and secondary schools in Tapanuli (that is, the Dutch-language H.I.S. and MULO schools).

As the child grows older he moves through successively higher levels of village and town schools, going from a Batak-language environment to one mixed with Malay to, finally, the Dutch-language MULO school in far-off Tarutung (a place of no little excitement to the schoolchildren, since the town is so up-to-date as to have electricity). There, the Toba Batak language is stigmatized as a quaint ethnic dialect and Malay is defined as one of the pupils' "foreign language" choices. (All this was taking place when the early nationalists were working to establish *bahasa* Indonesia [basically, the same language as Malay] as the language of Indonesian unity. The narrator does not belabor this point nor indeed even mention it.) As the child and his family scrape together the school fees that allow him to pursue this scholastic trajectory, the boy also encounters new realms of experience.

Moving beyond the constricted family world of his home village, the boy discovers the social character of larger and larger areas of Tapanuli as he moves toward MULO school in the big town to the south. In the process, he also discovers more and more sectors of European knowledge through his school textbooks, maps, and atlases. He learns about the Dutch, and about what they think of Bataks. He discovers girls; he discovers how the Dutch schoolmasters and German "susters" (missionary nurses) try to control the young people's courtship fun. He begins to chart a future to follow his graduation from MULO school, which will carry him deeper into the print world (to postsecondary education) and beyond Sumatra entirely, to a school in Java. Soon after an account of the harrowing final exams at MULO school, the book ends as the seventeen-year-old narrator says good-bye to his father at the dock in Belawan, Medan's port and the gateway to schools in distant Java.

As noted, though, this fairly strong trajectory from village to city, from Batak language environment to Dutch schoolroom, from family dependency to growing sexual independence, and from oral experience to print literacy should not be taken to imply that the book's narrative moves rapidly or in lockstep from one side of the dichotomy to the other. Far from it. The story jumps from point to point in a near-conversational way at times; sometimes the author deviates momentarily from his main storyline to insert short disquisitions on Toba kin-term usage, or Toba clan history, or colonial Indies school bureaucratic structure, or poverty in Tapanuli. These side trips are rarely if ever pedantic, fusty, or folkloric. Rather, the scenes and situations reported are sharply observed and crisply presented. These descriptive, almost sociological interludes are clearly offered to readers from the point of view of the adult Pospos writing at the conclusion of the Revolution, looking back at a troubled Tapanuli of the 1920s and early 1930s. Other parts of the book present scenes from the perspective of the remembered child, as he was experiencing them at that particular point in his life in the narrative. Throughout, without explanation, Pospos refers to his younger self as Djohanis, although his own first name is otherwise. We shall see this same device in Radjab's book, where the hero is called Ridjal, not Muhamad.

Readers learn a great deal about Tapanuli schools, teachers, the typically oppressive and highly competitive atmosphere in classrooms, and punishment strategies used by the teachers to get children like the narrator's Djohanis into line. The 'I' of the story, for instance, was forever skipping church on Sundays. This would stand him in bad stead with Schoolteacher on Mondays, when the children were interrogated about church attendance. We learn about the boy's career as a "Red Devil" in class, as a result of this church truancy and other offenses. Then, in a casual narrative turn that is quite typical, we are told about a short trip the family made to visit relatives in Sibolga, the large town on the Indian Ocean coastline down from the Toba highlands. The family goes on this journey in style, in Dad's new rented car (by this time he had changed jobs and was no longer a peddler but a chauffeur). After the family's return from this trip the child has lost his place as one of the most highly ranked children in class, a position calculated according to test scores. He bursts into tears when the other children taunt him about this fall from favor. This emphasis on the child's turbulent emotional life is also typical of the entire narrative.

The teacher too is deathly afraid of being graded, ranked, evaluated, and "marked down." He and his Toba colleagues wait fearfully for the periodic visits of the district school inspector, whom Pospos mordantly calls the School Police. A bitingly worded scene ends the chapter: the inspection visit of Tuan Preacher, one of the German Lutheran missionaries. "Tuan" is the term of address Batak would use to male Europeans. The narrator's childhood self tries desperately to catch Tuan Preacher's attention by thrusting his hand up very high, but he fails at this. The Europeans remain literally out of reach. By this early date the boy is already very much caught up in the game of trying to secure the Europeans' favor and trying to best his fellow Batak in this endeavor.

These initial chapters strike the major themes used later in the book and demonstrate the main features of the author's style. Children come from hardworking, strict, rather cold, impoverished village families; schoolhouses are places of testing and failure, with an occasional bright child who manages to squeak through the final exams and pass on to the next level of schooling. Toba is both an ethnic world and a setting for a mysterious Dutch colonial bureaucracy; most children and their parents participate wholeheartedly in the colonial world's systems of status and rank. Lying beyond Toba are other ethnic realms, with other, more highly ranked, Dutch-run schools. Toba children hunger to go there. Most fail. "Our diplomas = us," Pospos writes late in the memoir, in this same vein. School success or failure defines the youngsters' social worth. Traditional social class rankings are largely omitted from mention.

Throughout the narrative the story proceeds episodically by relating some twist or turn in the boy's school fortunes, his play experiences with other children, or his family life, and then elaborating on these core, centered events by providing further detail on the general situation that the incident suggests (e.g., poverty in Tapanuli). Often he provides further detail via a mass of similar anecdotes. This storytelling style may owe a debt to oral narrative forms in the Malay world in general.

Radjab's *Village Childhood* has basically the same narrative frame and the same wandering, comfortably paced storyline. The latter is structured once again around the child's penetration of new and successively less intimate and less village-bound types of schools as he grows older. However, with *Village Childhood* the setting has switched from Christian Toba with its patrilineal clans, hardscrabble farm villages, and modest market towns to Muslim Minangkabau, with its grander sense of traditional social class, its more prosperous mercantile ties to cities, and its matrilineality. As with Toba society, Minangkabau society stresses family alliance ties (in the West Sumatran case, between matrilineal households, their daughters' households, and the homes of origin of the men who have married into the first residential unit). However, as a society with a long history of traditional state-level political organization, Minangkabau social life involves more complex extra-village structures than is the case with Toba, which, as noted, was basically a collection of fragile chiefdoms at the time of first Dutch control in the 1850s–1900 period. Minangkabau Great Houses (long, peak-roofed affairs) contain multiple, matrilineally related, female-focused hearths or households; these houses are linked together into noble lineages. Groups of matrilineally related men make up aristocratic counsels. Young men retain their basic membership in their mothers' and aunts' houses after they grow up and marry into other houses (the latter are their wives' domains, and husbands remain social and moral outsiders). Children's mother's brothers have major financial responsibilities for raising them, at least as the situation is portrayed in the ideal adat. However, as we shall see, in Radjab's case his main emotional ties and financial connections were to his father. In fact, *Village Childhood*'s overwhelming preoccupation with the father-son relationship belies any easy assumption that Minangkabau family life de-emphasizes this parental tie in favor of the avuncular one. Both memoirs, from stereotypically patrilineal Toba but also from "matrilineal Minangkabau," are overwhelmingly about boys and their fathers.

Village Childhood evokes many of the conflict-filled fundamental ideas of Minangkabau life through a growing child's eyes as he discovers his social structural world and his religious universe, bit by bit. He does this as his own life makes what are often unhappy contacts with Islamic schools, the Fasting Month (Ramadan), his village-ified kinfolk, and various social factions in rural West Sumatra. The memoir is dominated by Islam in a much more thoroughgoing way than *Me and Toba* is colored by Protestant Christianity. In fact, it is not too much to say that Radjab's autobiography is a memoir of a Sumatran native son's early brushes with Minangkabau Islam, and his eventual critical disaffection from some of the major public forms of that religion. The growing child comes to be particularly aware of what the memoirist portrays as Islam's artificiality and rote nature. Most centrally, in a religion whose adherents are normally asked only to mouth powerful sacred prayers and Koranic verses, the boy begins to wonder about what theological significance might possibly lie behind the holy phrases. His instructors in the surau discourage him in this sort of inquiry and ask him to keep to his memorization tasks. He refuses to comply, and his search for more meaning and significance beyond the level of the surface sounds of Islam's Arabic language routines constitute the main portion of his journey of maturation. Anger, pain, and frustration accompany his growing up along this linguistic trajectory, and the author's recollections of these feelings make Radjab's memoir a much darker account than Pospos's book.

The flow of events from chapter to chapter in *Village Childhood* recalls the gently composed pastiche of incidents, impressions, and school scenes used by Pospos. Radjab's book (whose chapters have actual titles, such as "A Lake Singkarak Boy") opens with a paragraph that signals that this is an author who is not going to take himself or his ethnic society too seriously:

> Why I was born into this world, I do not know. Why I was born in Minangkabau puzzles me even more. These two things have surprised me very much and have bothered me since I was little. But I will not bother with things I do not know here; I will simply relate some of my experiences that are surprising and just itching to come out. (Radjab 1974, 5)

He was born, he goes on to write, in the year 1913—"they say." A cholera epidemic raged near Lake Singkarak at the time and the boy's mother died as a consequence, when he was only a few days old. His father departs for Mecca on the haj almost immediately, telling relatives that if Ridjal (as noted, the name given to the child) happens to die in infancy, he will take up permanent residence in the holy city. If the baby lives, the father will come back home to West Sumatra and continue his career as a village religion teacher there, which is what actually happens, we find.

The boy is bright and also his father's firstborn son, so the family decides that the child should be put in the most demanding Muslim schools so that he will eventually become a religion teacher like his parent. Ridjal spends several happy months in a lakeside village, playing with friends, exploring the natural world in a hesitant way, and feeling quite at home in his tiny familial universe. Then one day Ridjal's father comes on a visit from one of his other households and suddenly announces, "It is time for you to enroll in school."

Ridjal enjoys public school. Most welcome of all is the fact that the children can *believe* what they are taught, Radjab tells his readers. This instructional situation contrasts greatly, he goes on, with the one he soon finds in Muslim school. There, the boy and his circle of young friends are taught to recite totally meaningless strings of sounds. Close friendships among the children help to make up for this puzzling situation. A tight-knit group of sixteen little boys play ball together, study together, get in trouble together, and continually harass adult travelers just returned from the rantau. The boys ask these adults to tell them stories about their foreign adventures. These tales and the public school lessons become the boys' real education, Radjab writes. The children dream of a future when they too will be old enough to leave home for distant lands. Eventually they will become merchants, get married, and move to the rantau.

After a few years of Arabic study, the boys celebrate their circumcision ritual together. They experience the Fasting Month and its moral challenges. The boys dress up as little Arabs for an early Muslim school graduation. The village women ooh and aah at this spectacle. The boys also get to know some of the strange men who loll about the surau, without jobs, wives, or much sympathy from their matrilineal kin.

From Ridjal's father the boys learn the martial arts and some of the magic lore associated with it. Ridjal and his friends also participate in rice harvests and village feasts; they hear about such exciting things as tigers in the deep forest and ghosts who carry lighted torches. As they progress in their surau studies, they begin to lose contact with this wider world of normal village life; daily existence becomes a constant round of rote memorization and Koranic chants. This far into their religious studies the boys still have absolutely no idea what they are reciting in their Arabic language lessons. They do know, however, that less-educated villagers seek their special ritual expertise. Families begin to invite the youngsters out to funerals and near-death scenes, to chant Arabic verses to help ease the corpse's transition to the next world. Sometimes the boys get into mischief on these ritual missions. Other times they get terribly scared.

A cousin falls in love with a village girl and her family marries her off to a rich merchant. This was after the boy enlisted Ridjal's aid in writing love letters to the girl. The families find out about this and cut short the love match and the heated exchange of letters. In general, in such marriage situations, Ridjal finds, the girl turns out to be happy enough. This stands in contrast to his expectations, which he had based on the unhappy love story themes he had gleaned from Balai Pustaka novels such as *Sitti Nurbaya*. That famous Minangkabau book had painted a tragic portrait of forced marriages for young women and argued instead for personal choice in matters of passion. The heroine of *Sitti Nurbaya* is victimized by a stultified adat order and avaricious parents (*Sitti Nurbaya* is also one of the novels Pospos's remembered child had consumed in an intense period of Balai Pustaka reading). In real life, Ridjal finds, teenage girls who are forced into arranged marriages discover quickly enough the pleasures of good food, nice clothes, and big houses. Ridjal decides he only knows about love in books.

Various Lebaran feasts (ending the Fasting Month) come and go. Ridjal covets impressive new clothes for these events, although he is sometimes disappointed with the meager financial help his father "deigns" to give him to buy such finery. (Ridjal is forever complaining about how ungenerous his father is.) A massive earthquake shakes the region and everyone is terrified. Many prayers are mumbled. It turns out that the world does not come to an end, after all, although many of Ridjal's elders had feared that it would. Everyone sleeps out in the rice fields to avoid being killed by falling buildings. Things eventually get back to normal. Prayers taper off.

Exhilarating Fasting Months enliven the boys' yearly round of Arabic lessons. The boys become increasingly aware of girls, who coyly watch them play ball or recite their prayers. Lebaran days become sweeter with pretty girls around. Ridjal and his father go on interesting trips to unusual mountain villages, which have exceedingly strange adat customs. In one village, for instance, men dress up as women during one festival. The boy eventually agrees to learn more mystical lore about the martial arts, at his father's urging (the older man is a martial arts instructor himself and wishes to pass on his secret knowledge to his son, who resists him in this). Ridjal eventually gives up hope that such mysticism might have any real efficacy, after he tries to work several spells and they all fail in embarrassing ways.

The boy's much-beloved cousin Asyiah gets married, leaving him without a close emotional companion. The moral of *Sitti Nurbaya* is lost on Asyiah, too, and she settles comfortably into married life with a forty-five-year-old man who already has several wives. Ridjal goes to visit her several days after her wedding; he finds she is off in a back bedroom of her mother's house, giggling and joking around with her husband. Asyiah soon moves to the distant market center of Bangkahulu, and everyone goes down to the train station to see her off. Ridjal decides not to go to the station and wonders, Will she miss seeing me? Probably not, he answers his own question: She has probably already forgotten me anyway.

Out of sorts and now also feeling out of place in his home village what with so many of his childhood friends either married or off pursuing fortunes in the rantau, Ridjal desperately asks his father for permission to leave home. After resisting much pressure to continue his religious education and become a Muslim schoolteacher, the boy finally sets off for teacher training college in Padang. His conflicted feelings on the eve of his departure provide the final scene in the memoir:

> Hearing the wall clock strike two times, my thoughts came back to Sumpur and the surau. I found that I was just daydreaming, and sorrow flowed through me when I thought of being separated from the village. I could feel how deep my love for Father was and for the surau, the place where I'd lived both happily and sadly for fifteen years—and for Mount Four Houses, and the Sumpur River and Lake Singkarak, where I'd splashed about. But I was going to leave all of it behind because I was now an adult and such were my life's pursuits and aspirations. How very sad I was that all I had loved all this time must be left behind. Life in the rantau was calling to me.
>
> It was as if my heart was being torn to pieces by an internal struggle: the struggle between love for Father and village, and love for my aspirations.
>
> But I knew that these ties to the village were just the bonds of feeling, and that sooner or later these would be snapped by my relentless, heedless life desires. And I simply could *not* base my character and life outlook on feelings alone, if I did not wish to become a mere ball in a game between nature and the world around me.
>
> Life in the wide world was beginning to call to me; its voice was blurred, like softly rumbling thunder, audible from afar.
>
> Tomorrow I would begin, and attack this life. (Radjab 1974, 210)

This ending of course also recalls Pospos's final scene at the Belawan port, as the youth is preparing to leave Sumatra for the rantau.

The two memoirs have obvious similarities. Both autobiographies chart their diminutive heroes' growth from an early state of juvenile ignorance and moral gullibility toward acute, critical levels of self-awareness and social consciousness (in the Indonesian language, toward a state of *kesadaran*, or intellectual awareness, alertness, and consciousness, from an earlier state of *kebodohan*, or clueless ignorance). As the boys age and the decade of the twenties moves on, they acquire an ability to identify and skewer social falsehoods. They come to see their local social orders and their home linguistic worlds as human constructions, open to questioning and change. They come to discover print as a tool for intellectual liberation. They move from the sound-dominated world of early childhood to a knowing understanding of the world of Indonesian- and European-language print, newspapers and books. They come to feel cut off from adults who seek solace in predictable, magical ritual speech formulas. They grow up into a world of texts and conflicting meanings.

Both Pospos and Radjab told their life stories to a wide public audience that was quite explicitly a national one. Both authors elected to write their memoirs in the Indonesian language, the national tongue, rather than in the ethnic languages they undoubtedly knew. That is, they avoided using Toba Batak or Minangkabau, which are both languages of more limited geographical scope than *bahasa* Indonesia (Indonesian). Toba Batak is the rural home region language of North Tapanuli, North Sumatra, while the Minangkabau language is spoken primarily in the Minangkabau area in West Sumatra, and in Minangkabau diaspora communities in large cities such as Jakarta. Minangkabau is grammatically and lexically quite similar to Indonesian (although the two languages are not fully mutually intelligible by any means), while the five Batak languages (Toba, Angkola-Mandailing, Dairi-Pakpak, Karo, and Simelungun) are quite distinct from either of these two tongues. As noted, Indonesian is basically the same language as Malay, and it was selected by the early nationalists in 1928 as the common national language of the Indonesian Republic, which they hoped would grow out of the colonial Indies. In the 1920s and 1930s in Sumatran village areas, Indonesian was still something of an outsider's language, accessible largely to travelers, advanced schoolchildren, and deeply literate adults. It was also the language of interethnic discourse, and the language for young people who hoped to successfully negotiate life in the cosmopolitan Indies. Both Toba and Minangkabau had extensive print literatures and newspaper publishing activities in the ethnic languages by the 1920s, but communication with members of other ethnic societies was possible only in Indonesian or Dutch.

The memoirs are similar too in that each chronicles the author's journey toward personal discovery of the colonial Indies' structures of oppression and power (a much stronger theme for Pospos, since Radjab stressed organized Islam's oppressiveness). The books also strike similar notes in describing the Toba and Minangkabau peoples' unfortunate (in the memoirists' view) penchant for self-delusion, self-importance, and empty talk. Indeed, the two childhood autobiographies are unusual among Indonesian historical texts of either the personal or the public sort in their writers' consistent critique of *omong kosong* (empty, inane talk). The writers are also distinctive in their refusal to take themselves too seriously; each memoir has many funny passages and several forthrightly hilarious ones about formal religion. The writers, too, are similar in their subtle presentation of linguistic issues relating to social thought and print literacy. In other words, these childhood recollections are very modern histories indeed.

A short discussion of autobiographical writing in the Malay and Indonesian region will make this claim more understandable and the authors' accomplishments more striking. After that, we can go on to investigate the memoirs' temporal and social imagery in more detail.

AUTOBIOGRAPHY IN INDONESIAN AND MALAY HISTORICAL TRADITIONS

The small genre of 1950s childhood autobiography considered here participates in larger patterns of Southeast Asian print literature that extend far beyond modern popular memoirs written in the Indonesian language. *Me and Toba* and *Village Childhood* also have hidden masses of tangled roots connecting them to Malay world script literature and court histories, and to oral genres relating to the past, such as village clan genealogy narratives (prominent in the Batak cultures) and epic histories (well developed in Minangkabau court literature). The two 1950 autobiographies also tap into broad realms of Southeast Asian regional thought about the past (if only to reject many of these notions) and into very general Southeast Asian propositions about how societies should best remember and record history. Some of these broader issues can be addressed first before going on to consider the somewhat narrower and more recent history of autobiographical writing in the region.

Rhetorical form and local historiographic claims have intersected in complex ways in different periods of Southeast Asia's communications history. Indigenous, Islamic, and Western imageries of the past have jostled one another for prominence since Islam entered the region in the 1400s and since the European colonial age began in the 1500s. These diverse imageries of history have mutually shaped one another's strategies for asserting truth and for claiming aesthetic excellence. The situation is admittedly confusing, especially given that these historical philosophies have been interacting and recombining for some six hundred years in a field of quite diverse local ethnic cultures—and given that Indian models of history and polity had already been influencing local historical philosophies since at least the seventh and eighth centuries.

Throughout this area of the world, though, several recurrent ideas about history and about the oral recitation and written recording of the past are common—ideas that can be provisionally identified here at the outset.

These ideas include a sense that there is a cyclical revolution of eras and an alternation of apocalypse and renewal; a hope for heroic figures who will hasten the turn of ages and will defeat foreign intruders; a sense that ancient creator beings are linked to living people and may be beseeched via ceremonial feasts, the sacrifice of animals such as water buffalo, and ritual speeches; a near-mythological expectation of times of chaos alternating with times of fragile social order; and a pervasive respect and aesthetic fondness for eloquent, often forthrightly poetic modes of history telling. There also seems to be an area-wide fascination with heirloom objects (old ceramic jars, gold jewels, frayed textiles). These sacred treasures (along with stone obelisks and stone funeral structures) serve as power-filled contact points between the dead and the living and the past and the present. In other words, history often has a physical, tactile form in Southeast Asia. These "things of history" also often work to unlock elaborate worlds of ritual oratory, in communal feasts in which past ages and ancestors are commemorated and contacted through pyrotechnic feats of speech making. The treasure objects often work as touchstones of such rituals.

In new national societies such as Indonesia, printed histories of various sorts have drawn extensively on these older philosophical assumptions and narrative styles. However, twentieth-century print versions of the past also sometimes go beyond these older forms to portray human times and "times" (eras) in terms of various "scientific histories": in relation to Marxist frameworks, for instance, or in terms of the purportedly objective histories so often sought by conservative Western scholars.

In Indonesia, all of these several modes of history telling were present on the public stage by the 1920s and 1930s, along with Muslim and Christian historical visions as well. This complex communications system (and its resultant narrative and conceptual intricacy) was especially evident in colonial era Sumatra in the period when our authors were going to school and then later writing their memoirs. So the dense intertextual nature of historical thought was particularly complex. In the Toba Batak region, for instance, where the young Pospos was going to Dutch-language school and reading his European history textbooks in MULO school, prominent features of the social landscape were the *tugu* stone funerary monuments erected over the graves of important lineage ancestors. Village elders in Pospos's little home settlement, moreover, were still reciting verse-form *tarombo,* clan genealogical narratives that purportedly linked the living to Si Raja Batak, "the first human." What Pospos made of such mythic claims we shall soon see; in brief, he writes that such myths were "stories people used to tell."

One additional, possibly pan–Southeast Asian idea about time and history is also worth mentioning immediately. This one seems to animate both childhood memoirs at a deep level. This is the assumption that the past is not intrinsically interesting, in terms of its details, dates, and series of concrete events, but is significant only as a source of wisdom and guidance for living in the present. Indigenous Southeast Asian historical thought, that is, is imbued with what historian O. W. Wolters has called a strong "forward-lookingness" (Gungwu 1979, 40), with a moral perspective about the past which charts a course for contemporary lives. This moral appreciation of history is found in both oral and written works.

Two examples can be mentioned to illustrate the logic here. In Toba Batak clan genealogy narratives, the often-troubled relationships of one distant ancestral figure with another are recalled to contemporary audiences (through oral genealogical recitations) as cautionary tales about how the living descendants should deal with one another, in everyday political terms. The "eternal" experiences of the ancestors offer practical as well as transcendent models for living lives in the here and now. Batak written texts can work in the same way. For instance, the new, ethnically based denominations of the original Batak mission church (the HKBP: Huria Kristen Batak Protestant) are currently publishing separate church histories for themselves. In this way, break-away denominations such as the HKBP-Angkola are publishing their own histories. These are often quite combative texts, which critique the "parent church" in the north, in Toba. The books work as devices for proclaiming and then negotiating difference, among the many fissiparous Batak Protestant communities. As we shall shortly see in *Me and Toba,* ethnic insults fly thick and fast among the six Batak societies. Little boys like Pospos's remembered younger self exulted in such verbal combat, especially since the Toba Bataks could claim to be the "most ancie·it," aboriginal Batak society, which was ancestral to all the other Batak peoples.

Constructions of such socially charged pasts occur with particular intensity and creativity in times of crisis, such as the national revolution era immediately preceding the publication of our two childhood memoirs. Historians Anthony Reid and David Marr remark on this association between crisis times and the production of moral histories in their preface to *Perceptions of the Past in Southeast Asia*:

> We have seen time and again [in the essays collected in that anthology, which deal with cultures located throughout mainland and island Southeast Asia] that societies faced with fundamental and inescapable choices look at their pasts with particular urgency and insight, as a key to charting the future. This is as true of the eighteenth century Balambangan chronicles as of the nationalists of the 19th century Philippines or 20th century Vietnam. (1979, viii)

It might be added that this fundamentally hopeful perspective on the past as a template for future action (and this practice of rethinking history in light of current political challenges) also apparently inspired the writing of *Me and Toba* and *Village Childhood* during the national revolution. Remembered childhoods cast back into the 1920s and 1930s from that vantage point could hardly be politically innocent documents.

Fully modern, self-reflective, witty, even self-deprecating autobiographies such as *Me and Toba* and *Village Childhood* are a relatively rare and recent sort of literary work in Indonesia and Malaysia. These memoirs' innovative position within Indonesian and Malay world historical writing and popular literature is important to specify carefully, as are these works' ties to European genres and to European ideas of authorship and reading audiences. To begin locating the memoirs in that way we can start by exploring some of the epistemological assumptions and rhetorical styles used in telling

history in oral ritual speech forms, and then in court-based script literatures in Indonesia and Malaysia. Printed memoirs of nonprominent individuals came very late in this magnificent language history.

Village cultures in Indonesia's three hundred or so ethnic minority societies tend to have deep stockpiles of oral knowledge about the past. They
typically present such knowledge in public ritual speech performances at
such events as the dedication of new villages, funerals, stone monument
dedications, and bone-reburial ceremonies. Such occasions call for poetic evocations of a transcendent past, recalled via such spoken genres as
rhymed couplet speeches. During these special ritual times, which often
go on for several hours, orators sometimes are said to speak "with the
voice of the ancestors," and the living world of contemporary humans
momentarily touches the shadow world of dead forebears. Ancestors are
intensely concerned with the lives of their descendants, according to the
folk epistemologies that underlie such speech performances.

Ritual oratory provides a crucial venue for the living and the dead (and
the present and the past) to intersect for a moment of exceptionally por-
tentous and pleasurable aesthetic congress. Such speech-making occasions
often have extensive "invisible audiences" of spirit beings in imaginary
attendance, surrounding the world of humans and their imagined forebears. Located even more distant in time and space are the actual deities
of such cultures. These gods are often ancient creator figures, with am-
biguous male and female gender characteristics (Father Sky/Mother Earth
pairs are common). Today, Outer Island Indonesian ethnic minority societies have seen their oral heritages reshaped in significant ways through
interaction with the print culture of the national society and the holy texts,
sacred scripts, and theological claims of the world religions. Even so,
though, social place, a "rightful claim" to recite a lineage or clan genealogy, and poetic elegance still work together to lend authenticity to oral
historical narratives, many in ethnic cultures in Timor, Sumba, Flores,
Roti, and highland Sulawesi. The most highly valued talk is often phrased
in rhymed couplets (a form of parallel speech involving linked couplets,
found in many eastern Indonesian cultures). Special orations in many
eastern Indonesian and highland Sumatra cultures are traded between
marriage alliance partners (for instance, verbal duels, praise speeches, and
blessing routines). The well-modulated exchange of eulogistic speeches
between wife-givers and wife-receivers serves, in the local view, to keep the
society and cosmos in order and in good condition. The exchange of human prayers for divine blessings, moreover, serves to keep the generation
of the living in fruitful contact with the past and its ancestral inhabitants.
References to sacred sites encode large amounts of affectively powerful
knowledge about founding ancestors and their exploits in "early creation

times." Important places names often undergo a constant process of terminological change, however. Thus, crucial historical knowledge becomes hidden and must be ferreted out by lineage descendants. This entails elaborate, arcane efforts at argumentation. This combative arena of public memory allows local history experts to continually adjust the remembered past to contemporary political circumstances.

Many of these exquisitely adjustable, present-focused oral historical traditions have experienced grinding encounters with script literacy and, starting in the late 1800s, print literacy. This situation has naturally worked to reshape local ideas of history.

The prosperous mercantile trade sultanates such as those in the Bugis areas of southwestern Sulawesi and in Sumatra's Minangkabau, Aceh, and Deli coast regions had extensive court literary traditions based on the Arabic script introduced as these societies adopted Islam, starting in the 1500s. Some of these mercantile societies and others such as the Batak societies (with smaller-scale polities and relatively fewer long-distance trade contacts with outsiders) also had their own script traditions. These writing systems probably derived from Sanskrit-based scripts once used in Hindu-Buddhist courts, such as Srivijaya in South Sumatra's Palembang area. Script literacy supported a number of genres of historical writing in the Indonesian archipelago and the Malay peninsula: *hikayat* (epics), *silsilah* (pedigree, genealogy), *tarich* (record, chronicle), and *sejarah* (history). These genres were not freestanding, fully literate ones but had continued strong ties to oral modes of telling history. Case studies of Malay, Bagis, and Acehnese script histories by literary specialist A. H. Johns and anthropologists Shelly Errington and James Siegel offer detailed accounts of the sorts of historical vision one typically finds in these script traditions, with their persistently heavy oral residues. In all three cases, oral, ritual speech ways of narrating history continued to thrive alongside the script texts, and the latter themselves were generally meant to be chanted aloud in public recitation performances, rather than read silently by solitary readers in the style of deep print literacy. Oral history and script-based history continually reshaped each other conceptually and rhetorically.

In the Malay sultanates, the oral base to historical thought was exceptionally resilient, far into the age of script literacy, and oral notions of causation and author-audience relations persisted in sturdy form throughout the nineteenth century. Sweeney writes (1987), in fact, that a heavy oral residue continues to shape Malaysian rhetorical expectations and social thought today.

In his essay "The Turning Image: Myth and Reality in Malay Perceptions of the Past" (1979), A. H. Johns asserts that the court chronicles set down in the fifteenth to seventeenth centuries (chronicles such as the

Malay Annals) had especially close ties to the narrative conventions and implicit worldviews of Malay oral folk stories and myths. In both these palace annals and in village folktales, narrators would tell strange, exhilarating stories about supernatural heroes, prodigies of nature, and odd coincidences that served to advance the action. In separate retellings of the same oral tale, discrete events would sometimes be inserted at different junctures of the story. The events of the court chronicles sometimes have much this same sort of "displaceability." Both the court chronicles and the oral stories had a folksy, peasant-society flavor. This did not come, Johns writes, from any direct borrowing of motifs from one genre to another. Rather,

> court scribe and peasant, sharing a common perception of the world, shared also a predisposition to tell a story, any story, in a similar way. So a folk hero's ancestry, the auguries that attend his mother's pregnancy, the events occurring at this birth and episodes of his childhood would all be known to the court chronicler and be grist to his mill as he sets about telling the story of the court, the dynasty and the ruler he serves. (1979, 52)

Common to both oral tales and Malay court writings were such tropes as trade prosperity, full harvests, overflowing granaries, kings with many children, and fields stocked with innumerable plump water buffalo. These were all put forward as signs of a realm's power (1979, 53). These storytelling devices were animated by a common set of epistemological assumptions: that time was cyclic and the human world existed within it in a kind of steady state (1979, 55); that cataclysmic battles would occur and wreck havoc but sometimes worked to hold "dangers" and social and cosmic chaos at bay (1979, 55); that benevolent heroes would protect and nurture their indebted bondsmen, poor relations, and virtuous naifs.

In a provocative related essay called "Some Comments on Style in the Meanings of the Past" (1979), Shelly Errington makes the large claim that Malay hikayats (epics) such as the Hikayat Hang Tuah remained deeply oral in their conceptual base, although they were certainly written down in Arabic script. Errington identifies several narrative features of the Hikayat Hang Tuah which indicate a heavy oral residue. The narrative is composed, for instance, of a loose constellation of rather folksy events, such as adventures of heroes, consultations with astrologers, and interactions the human protagonists have with supernaturals. Glorious noblemen and beautiful princesses flit in and out of the story, in a style reminiscent of oral epics. The hikayat's various events are related sequentially in the script version, but Errington asserts that this does not necessarily imply that the epic's writer or readers or hearers (for like many Malay *hikayat*s this story was meant to be savored in a public recital) assumed a sequential chronological framework for the story. Rather, without firm temporal markers, the hikayat's incidents were each essentially detachable from the others. The history "of old times" related in the Hikayat Hang Tuah was not a set linear sequence of events but a collection of small times and incidents that could have occurred in other sequences, or could have been understood to have taken place in a kind of eternal simultaneity with the present, accessible through the event of the recitation performance itself.

In other words (in Errington's view), the Hikayat Hang Tuah's author had no sense of history in the linear, secular sense. For him, a hikayat recitation was essentially a heavily ritualized dramatic performance, done for the pleasure of storytelling and the world of sound such a recitation could temporarily create. Errington compares this mode of history to the production of *gamelan* or Javanese or Balinese gong orchestra music:

> The form-givir.g elements in the life of traditional Malay courts were intimately linked to ordered sounds. We have on the other hand events which happen in the world. Hikayat and other such forms convert the impermanent and transitory events of this world into something which endures, at least as it is spoken. Or rather, they do not so much convert transitory events as perpetuate them, *carry them into the present of their telling.* Hikayat do not create monuments of either stone or of literature, but only perpetuate in a form which must be continually renewed to endure. I have come to think of the relation as rather analogous to that of noise and gamelan music. Individual sounds, like individual events, are merely noise. Gamelan takes these and gives them a form which itself transforms human states, has an effect in the world. Like gamelan music, it is not a content but an arrangement and performance; like gamelan music, its end does not grow out of its beginning. The past is just like noise; for traditional Malays it did not have an objective existence which had to be investigated in itself, but it stood, rather, as the material, the raw substance, which could be converted into sensible form. (1979, 40; emphasis added)

Or, put another way, the past was important primarily as the disjointed raw substance that could be converted into concrete *moral* form, as a guide to action in the present. Hikayats do seem to have been moral histories in this sense, although Errington's thoroughgoing dismissal of the semantic content of the epics in favor of emphasizing their sound qualities and aurally tantalizing aspects seems to be a considerable overstatement.

Anthropologist James Siegel examines a complex Malay world historical manuscript situation similar to the one Errington tackles in his book *Shadow and Sound: The Historical Thought of a Sumatran People* (1979). Siegel is dealing with a hikayat tradition in a deeply Muslim society, and he attends to the historical ideas of both the epics and the world religion. He focuses on the Arabic script historical narratives of the Acehnese, the pepper-trading people organized into small states, located across the Strait of Malacca from the Malay sultanates. Siegel offers a close examination of the text of the Hikayat Pitjoet Maehamat, which was written down in court circles in the mid-1700s. He extends this analysis by drawing additionally on ethnographic information about how contemporary Acehnese think of and use written texts. Using these sources, Siegel offers a speculative account of this one Malay world culture's construction of time and language (which he insists must be studied together).

In an approach to texts reminiscent of Errington's, Siegel finds that many Acehnese historical texts written in Arabic script aim at establishing certain magical effects more than they aspire to record factual events in a linear, irreversible sequential order. In this still-resilient and deeply oral tradition, the arrangement of words on a page (often a quite artistic arrangement) and the play of sound in a chanted epic are given a privileged place over the actual semantic content of the narratives at issue. Lists of the names and titles of former rulers, for instance, have a certain talismanic power in themselves, as masses of power emblems, even though the dynasties or political elites at issue in the list may have little objective historical connection to one another. Siegel states further that Acehnese histories often have the implied aim of negating the "real history" of Aceh in its often unhappy relations with outside states (with other sultanates, the Dutch colonial state, the Japanese during World War II, the Indonesian national government centered in Jakarta).

This difficult point warrants clarification. Seen from a Western historiographical perspective, Aceh has an unflattering history of successive takeovers by these foreign states. Aceh exists today as a beleaguered "special province" of the Republic of Indonesia, largely (though uneasily) under the military and bureaucratic control of the Indonesian nation. Acehnese folk history, however, argues otherwise, by organizing the world of power relations among societies in an imagined map where Aceh lies at the center and various outside states are located at the less powerful edges of this realm. Speakers in this tradition delight in unintelligible mantras, veiled allusions, and aural or scriptural loveliness. These conventions have played a pivotal role in allowing Acehnese epic chanters and writers the luxury of "forgetting" Aceh's many defeats at the hands of outsiders and turning this political decline into majestic self-eulogy. Loveliness of exposition and the chanting of "power words" work to negate the countervening power of secular defeat and misfortune at the hands of foreign forces. The Acehnese epic tradition had essentially died out by the late 1800s, but many of the same "history-stopping" motives that were present in the hikayats continued to be pursued later on, in other literary forms. These included folktales (1979, 213–228) and popular literature versions of the holy war against the Dutch (1979, 229–266).

Print literacy stands to introduce an added dimension of secularity to these oral and script versions of history, although it must immediately be noted that print communication hardly replaces these historically older media in any totalistic way. Rather, print versions of the past add to an already complex communication system relating to memory and the past. Government-owned printing press technology and commercial publishing became major forces in outer-island Indonesian societies and particularly in Sumatra after the mid-1800s, as Dutch control was consolidated in these regions. This was also the period when a thin network of public schools was being established in the Batak areas and in Minangkabau. In Toba and Minangkabau, the earliest print publications with a public impact were elementary school primers, Christian and Muslim teaching aids such as guides to the holy texts, government circulars, and bureaucratic handbooks such as post office manuals. Also of great importance by the mid-1800s were official letters and political appointment notices given by the Dutch to local chiefs and noblemen, from the offices of the colonial government. In Toba and Angkola such titles of office were sometimes kept as part of an aristocratic family's power-laden heirloom treasures. By 1900, the southern Batak societies and Minangkabau had elementary schools in major population centers; by 1920 both regions and Toba as well had ethnic-language village primary schools, a few vocational secondary schools, and several of the highly prestigious, sought-after H.I.S. and MULO schools—the Dutch-language elementary and secondary schools so important in Pospos's early experience.

By the same decade, print publications were beginning to build a wide public readership. Sumatran commercial cities such as Medan and Padang and even smaller administrative centers and school cities such as Sibolga, Padangsidimpuan, and Bukittinggi had biweekly and weekly newspapers by 1925. Most of these papers were in the Indonesian language, with some use of local ethnic tongues and Dutch (many highly educated readers were fluent in this language). Newspapers printed trade news such as rubber and coffee prices and local political items about the activities of the Dutch administrators in Padang, Sibolga, and Medan. Advertisements were sometimes international in scope: urging readers to buy Chevrolet cars; soap, powder, and cookies from Singapore; and home remedies and potions from Java.

The newspapers also published literary works, in profusion. These included verse narratives about star-crossed lovers, prose novels (which also tended to dwell on love-story themes), print renditions of old oral folktales, and printed versions of various ritual speech genres. Newspaper readers of modest means could also gain an almost ethnographic sense of what went on in the adat feasts of their social betters, for editors dispatched stringers and special correspondents to attend particularly lavish ceremonies and then write detailed, descriptive accounts of them (the Angkola Batak-language Sibolga newspaper *Poestaha* had many of these accounts).

In the Indies world as a whole, popular literature was experiencing explosive growth in this period. Both verse and prose narratives were being composed in large numbers, for publication in newspapers and as pulp paperbacks. The Chinese-Indonesian (*peranakan*) community in Surabaya, Jakarta, and Medan was particularly active in this regard; their love stories, crime tales, and stories of business intrigue were read by a wide *peranakan* and general audience (Salmon 1981). These prewar decades (1920–1942) were also the floodtide era for Balai Pustaka's modern novels. Taken together as a body of work, these novels charted out an emotional terrain of conflict, passion, and unhappiness, via love stories and tales of growing up centered on young adults from educated circles in West Sumatra. Many of these novels are basically stories of modernization gone awry.

By this 1920s and 1930s period, oral and script-based visions of history in Sumatran societies were already beginning to engage the print world in a long negotiation for status and authoritativeness. This is a negotiation process that continues to the present. Some of John Bowen's recent work on historical thought in Gayo society over the last ninety years pinpoints the major social and rhetorical processes at work here (Bowen 1991). In Gayo, entry into world Islam, the Dutch colonial state, and the postrevolution Indonesian nation have led to a complex political world and a rhetorical universe with many voices. The latter claim different bases of authoritativeness, some citing scripture, others citing sacred persons, others invoking the military power of states. These bases of authoritativeness are often competitive with one another. Gayo orators and writers have constructed viable historical pasts for themselves within this panoply of possible texts and voices.

An additional, supremely important process was also at work in this period in Sumatran historical thought and writing. With print technology, a large reading public, and the schoolbookish view of culture gaining credence in educated circles, Sumatra's old oral histories and their script-version repositories could emerge on the printed page as *literature*. In this process, older oral and script-based claims for the authoritativeness of their visions of the past could become trivialized to a degree. Writing of a similar situation in Roti, James Fox identifies the fundamental conceptual shift at issue here (1979, 25). In Roti, *manek* are local rulers or lords, and their histories were once recounted to listening publics in lengthy poetic, parallel speech performances. Fox foresees a time when print will redact Rotinese traditions significantly:

> In the words of the fabulist Borges—whose life's work forms a profound reflection on perceptions of the past—time, place and action compose the

'dramatic unities' not just of history but of literature as well. It is possible that, once detached from specific genealogies and domains, the succession of the narratives that chronicle the history of a domain will cease to be significant. The tales, with time and place consigned to an indefinite past—when the manek ruled on Roti—may merge with other related tales. Those that continue to be told will be told for the telling itself. And those who gather these tales will consider them as folk literature rather than folk history. (1979, 25)

Toba Batak and Minangkabau were already putting into print their *tarombo* clan genealogies and *Kaba* (chronicles) in this way before the Second World War. With history emerging as a form of literature, a crucial, related development was also occurring: the emergence of the individualized, critical, reflective writer's self in Indonesian letters.

Indonesian autobiography developed in the heady atmosphere of early nationalist thought and deepening print literacy in the immediate prewar decades. The country's first modern autobiography is often said to be the nationalist leader Dr. Soetomo's *Kenang-Kenangan* (Memories, which is a better translation for the word than "memoirs," since *Kenang-Kenangan* conveys a sense of loosely arranged remembrances). The founder of the nationalist organization Budi Utomo when he was a medical student at STOVIA (School tot Opleiding von Inlandsche Artsen), Dr. Soetomo produced a restrained and powerful account of his younger years in his East Javanese village of Ngepeh. The memoir focuses largely on his life up to adulthood, although Dr. Soetomo's nationalist career for which he is famous came after this period. Most importantly, the work is a personalized account of a self-identified *Indonesian* author. However, *Memories* also has continued strong ties to Javanese cultural assumptions about time, society, and person. Benedict Anderson's "A Time of Darkness and a Time of Light: Transposition in Early Nationalist Thought" (1979) provides an extremely insightful assay of the various cultural legacies at work in Dr. Soetomo's autobiography. Several other earlier and equally transitional autobiographies from colonial-era Malaya are also well worth exploring here briefly. Luckily, two of these works (Abdullah bin Abdul Kadir Munsyi's *Hikayat Abdullah* and Mohamed Salleh bin Perang's *Tarikh Datuk Bentara Luar Johor*) have been the subject of literature scholar Amin Sweeney's careful exegesis for their imageries of author, audience, self, and society. Taken together, Anderson's article on Dr. Soetomo's memoir and Sweeney's extensive research on colonial-era Malay autobiography offer a rewarding introduction to the writing climate out of which our two 1950s childhood memoirs developed.

The themes found in all of this research on Indonesian and Malaysian autobiography are that the genre developed rather late in the history of Southeast Asian print literacy; that personal memoirs with their focus on the flawed, struggling individual had to establish their legitimacy in a literary climate more attuned to hagiography; that early autobiographies maintained close rhetorical and conceptual ties to the oral cultures of village society; and that in pre-independence days the memoir form provided writers with an arena for thinking out large issues of colonial politics and nationalism. In addition, childhood days figure importantly in the telling of life histories in print.

Malay autobiography was undeniably a product of the colonial encounter with British literary forms and ideas about authorship and audience. However, it was also a local growth attuned to Malay concepts of self and public language. Nineteenth-century Malay autobiography also partook of writing patterns developed in court circles throughout the area's Muslim mercantile world. These writing styles had been used for recording the great deeds of famous sultans (as some court leaders styled themselves) and of prominent military figures. Some of this eulogistic literature had parallels in Javanese court writing of the seventeenth and eighteenth centuries.

Autobiographical writing in colonial Malaya took a more personalistic turn, as Malay officials began to write self-portraits, at British urging, for audiences of Europeanized readers. Some of these memoirs were nonetheless deeply Malay. This was the case with Mohamed Salleh bin Perang's memoir of his life in service to Abu Bakar, the Sultan of Johor, described in Sweeney's *Reputations Live On.*[7] The memoir strikes the present-day Western reader as a somewhat dispassionate compilation of dates and events rather than a fully formed modern autobiography with rounded characters of the sort Western readers expect. The book also seems to lack a stepwise trajectory of personal development for its remembered protagonist. Amin Sweeney, however, cautions us against too easy a use of such Western categories of evaluation in reading Malay works such as this. Sweeney sees Mohamed Salleh's *Tarikh Datuk Bentaro Luar Johor* as a pivotal piece of writing in Malay letters. The *Tarikh* is also a quite self-consciously modern work as well, Sweeney advises:

> The distinctive feature of Salleh's writing is that he was the first Malay author to prepare his audience for the novel idea of autobiography, so that the postulated reader is one that a Malay is willing to become. In short, although Abdullah's *Hikayat* is the first work containing autobiographical material in Malay, Salleh's writing is the first Malay autobiography. (1980, 18)

Salleh's memoir (as compiled and translated as a single volume by Sweeney) has three parts, written respectively in 1915, 1894, and 1883. Part 1 begins forthrightly enough with the statement, "I, Mohamed Salleh bin Perang, was born on the island of Singapore at Teluk Belanga village in A.H. 1257 (A.D. 1841)." This section of the memoir is indeed a life story. Its first part details (in order) Mohamed Salleh's early services as a court clerk to various officials, his study of the Chinese language (there is only a brief mention of this), his appointment as chief of police in Johor, his education and service as a land surveyor, and his dutiful work in support of Seri Maharaja Keryku Abu Bakar, the Raja of Johor. Mohamed Salleh uses just such honorific titles whenever he mentions his employer and patron, and also refers to him as "His Highness." Much of the rest of part 1 chronicles Mohamed Salleh's administrative and land surveying work done for Abu Bakar, who appears in the narrative as a high personage who issues commands for the economic development of Johor, to which the narrator reports himself answering, "I obey."

The chronicle emerges as a carefully dated account of willing royal service and ends on a decidedly conservative, traditionalist note. This follows mention of a particularly upsetting incident and the sad denouement of the author's career, a situation that must have sorely tested his loyalty to his patron. The passage, translated by Amin Sweeney, is worth quoting at some length, for it gives the flavor of Mohamed Salleh's hoary style. This will stand in marked contrast to the irony and easy conversational style used in the two 1950 childhood memoirs, and to their much more reflective presentation of a writer's self.

> After that, I was plagued by all kinds of slanders which arose as a result of my giving land to some Japanese and allowing them to open up a plantation on the Semberung River in Batu Pahat. I declared, "The land that the Japanese were given I would not even describe as 'land'; rather it was a swamp, permanently under water, and it was only due to the effort of the Japanese that it became such a profit for the government." The lives of my children and myself were in a sorry state of confusion in Batu Pahat.
>
> On 2nd May, 1912, I was pensioned off on $300 a month. My post as "Government Commissioner" administering Batu Pahat was taken over by the Hon. Engku Ahmad bin Mohamed Khalid. My son Haji Ya'kub also had his employment terminated and was granted a pension of $33 per month. Thus was the situation of my children and myself.
>
> Though I was the victim of slander, as mentioned above, that is a matter of this world, and my heart never wavered in the slightest from the truth: the recent developments have impressed upon me that everything is from Almighty God, who has such great love for His servants: I express my thanks to Him more and more and ask forgiveness for my sins each time I pray. I most solemnly enjoin upon my children and my descendants down through the generations that they should never allow even to cross their minds the idea of wishing ill upon their own raja, or of leaving the state of Johor and its territories, for in the end their lives will not know peace. (Sweeney 1980a, 69–70)

The form of this last section is obviously indebted to family genealogies, and to larger Malay orally based ideas about public reputation. So is the writer's exalted, stilted style.

Part 2 is another life story account, written in a letter format to the author's friend Na Tian Piet, a Chinese-Indonesian reporter for the Javanese newspaper *Pemberita Betawi*. The narrative again includes genealogical detail but adds more information about Mohamed Salleh's youth and schooling and some early service he did as a schoolteacher. This section's account of the opening up of Johor is also rendered in a more personalized style, with frequent invocations of Mohamed Salleh's emotional states.

Part 3 is a diary account of Mohamed Salleh's trip to China and Japan in 1883, as Abu Bakar's clerk. This section is fairly fast-paced travelogue enlivened by small amounts of ethnographic detail about Japanese temples, village dances, and diverting Chinese scenery. The account is not formally set into a life history framework. The narrator matter-of-factly uses a first-person-style narrative, as he has in his letter-based part 2.

This memoir as a whole (disjointed though it may appear to today's Western reader) is indeed a decidedly individualized life account written at a time in Malay culture when autobiography of this sort was an unfamiliar genre. Sweeney astutely notes that the major innovative aspect of the *Tarikh* was not its attention to a personal life (for that was well acknowledged in Malay oral culture) but its author's decision to use a fairly serious and self-consciously modern form of public discourse (prose) to relate his experiences to an imagined audience of Malays, who were construed to be caught up very much like the author himself in the drama of quick social change in a modernizing social landscape.

In his review essay "Some Observations on the Nature of Malay Autobiography" (1990), Sweeney makes the additional useful point that Malaysians have not typically been averse to self-aggrandizement, although their formal written traditions of autobiography are recent, starting at the earliest in the early 1800s. What seems to be most at issue is the relatively late development of *public literary forms* of personal narrative, not some mystical lack of personal selfhood in Malay culture. Sweeney writes (1990, 21–22) that a concern with "name," with a strong reputation, has been a perennial preoccupation of Malaysians and their colonial-era forebears for many years. He cites the many court biographies of sultans as evidence of this. He goes on to note that a man's public reputation was thought to derive largely from the approval and evaluation of others, rather than the opinion of the subject of the biography itself. Sweeney also writes that Malay oral culture easily accommodates personal narrative, but that such recollected lives have generally been thought to be best confined to the less exalted genres of speech, such as nonstylized conversational talk (1990, 22). Modern autobiographies of the sort that Mohamed Salleh is obviously striving toward go beyond oral personal histories to try to publicly recollect a past life in a self-critical mode, and to make this written text open to community scrutiny. And the imagined audience for such works is conceived of as including people engaged in some of the same social transitions and personal tensions as the author.

Dr. Soetomo's *Memories* is more pronouncedly modern yet than this Malay work, although the book is also deeply attuned to the Javanese ethnic world. The autobiography's modernity lies in its simultaneous participation in Javanese concepts of time and morality *and* its use of a style of narration which presents the author as someone who can stand back from these patterns of ethnic thought and comment on them, as a watching self. Allied to this is Dr. Soetomo's presentation of this childhood self as someone who came to acquire an almost ethnographic distance from the Javanese standards of behavior and cultural expectations that surrounded him as a boy.

The narrator finds certain old, well-accepted Javanese modes of behavior "strange"—a situation that gives him a perfect vantage point from which to communicate these "customs" to a group of readers (Indonesian language readers) whom he does not know (Anderson 1979, 235). The author participates in an additional kind of strangeness as well: "The strangeness" Anderson writes, "felt by the new 'watching self' in recording the long-past experience of the inner self (*bathin*)" (1979, 235). This puts a deeply literate frame, and a quite cosmopolitan one, around the core Javanese idea of *bathin*. In this way, *Memories* has a double cultural focus. On the one hand, the narrative presents a Javanese life, while on the other, the book is about the larger issues of *writing* a life in a time of social change and nascent nationalist awareness.

As Anderson points out, Dr. Soetomo's choice of life events to include in his memoir is strongly inspired by Javanese assumptions about family heritage, fate, and personal development. The objective features of the writer's life included his birth in a village in 1888, his upbringing by his maternal grandparents, his Dutch-language primary school experiences, and his matriculation in 1903 at STOVIA, the medical school for indigenous people. After graduation he worked as a government doctor. But *Memories'* narrative thrust has little to do with any straight linear narrative about this sequence of events, or even with Dr. Soetomo's prominence as an early nationalist leader. Rather, *Memories* relates a loose collection of episodes that occurred in the remembered boy's home village and it provides fleeting sketches of the writer's family forebears. School times in Dutch-run institutions are detailed at some length. The narration ends when the protagonist is nineteen years old. Discrete events from boyhood days and memories of ancestors are recorded in a rather disjointed way,

making the memoir an altogether odd one for Western readers uniniti-
ated in the pace and structure of 1930s Indonesian literature. *"Memories,"*
Anderson notes, "is not a biography in any ordinary sense. And even when
he writes at length about his forebears, we are not given their biographies,
but simply 'excerpts' or 'pluckings' from their 'stories.' Soetomo makes no
attempt to place these ancestral figures in a maturing personal or historical context. They loom up in episodes to which no clear time can be assigned, except . . . for the significant markers *jaman dahulu* (the past era)
and *masa sekarang* (the present age)" (1979, 225–226). These two temporal designations, Anderson notes, are indelibly Javanese. Each refers to an
"age," which is often seen as an era in a cosmic cycle of times. Dr. Soetomo
also presents his early life as a time when he came to discover "the natural
bent of his fate"—another core Javanese assumption.

However, Dr. Soetomo does not halt his portrayal of time and his life at
this level of Javanese assumptions. He recollects how he learned of different apprehensions of time in the Dutch colonial schoolroom; how he continuously rebelled as a child against what was expected of him (he was a
notably *nakal,* or naughty, boy); how he discovered frameworks of social
justice which pushed him toward criticizing the colonial order; how he
grew a bit apart from the village life of his forebears. For Dr. Soetomo,
growing up became a time of active intervention in history, not just a thoroughly Javanese time for conformity to fated patterns.

Beyond this, recollecting his life became an effort of recording a change
in consciousness in himself, not simply an essay in documenting a personal revolution of eras from "the past time" to "the present age." Anderson expertly spotlights what this change of consciousness involves:

> It is clear that Soetomo understood and accepted an idea of time which
> could be either fleeting or eternal, an idea in which, indeed, that distinction
> overrode all others. In this sense he was a traditional Javanese. But he was
> also a man who had been educated in a Western-style medical school, of
> which Darwinism was the cosmological underpinning, and for which death
> was defeat. In this mode of consciousness, the cosmos no longer turned, but
> moved on, up, ahead, and death was not "return" but the real end of a man.
> Soetomo was thus fully exposed to the fundamental disjuncture of progres-
> sive Western thought—history as species development and life as individ-
> ual decay. "Memories" shows that he was not only influenced by the "new
> current" (with all the ironies sprung tight within the phrase), but saw it
> within two quite different conceptions of time—*and thereby found a recording
> self within.* (1979, 232, emphasis added)

This crucial discovery of this very modern sort of writer's self is repeated
in even more pronounced form in our two Sumatran childhood memoirs,
as we shall see. Moreover, the acute social consciousness of Pospos's and
Radjab's narrations are also prefigured in Dr. Soetomo's book. The latter

has numerous veiled references to Dutch oppression and to the remembered child's growing armament of perceptual and rhetorical weapons of resistance.

Anderson details a telling incident illustrating this pattern:

> Following his account of his clashes with Dutch schoolchildren, Soetomo describes his holidays back at Ngepeh. Returning to his grandfather's home was "living in freedom with respect to naughtiness and pleasure. There I was spoiled and praised till I felt myself a truly extraordinary child." Yet the very next thing he records is his very ordinary fear of lightning and thunder. When storms came he would run and hide his head in his grandmother's lap. But then his grandfather would take him by the hand and say to him "sweetly and gently": Ki Ageng Selo, mengko bledeg rak wedi dewe. Soetomo translates this for his non-Javanese readers thus: "Child, do not fear the lightning. Are you not the descendant of Ki Ageng Selo? Surely the lightning will come to be afraid of you." Soetomo concludes: "And because of the conviction in his world, gradually I lost my fear of thunder and lightning, however terrible their voice."
>
> It is difficult not to see in this passage, coming directly after Soetomo's defeats at the hands of the Dutch children, a veiled allusion to the struggle of Indonesians generally against the Dutch, "however terrible their voice." But in addition, we may note that courage here comes from memory—memory of one's origins. One grows up by growing back. (1979, 236–237)

And, it might be added, one grows up by learning to apply the social and perceptual insights gained from a journey back into childhood to present-day events, and to larger social horizons such as the notion of an Indonesian national community whose era "will come" not simply through some cosmic revolution of eras but through the active intervention of knowing, historically grounded actors.

Dr. Soetomo's memoirs presage a number of other images of person, society, learning, and time found in *Me and Toba* and *Village Childhood*. These concordances are too numerous to be accidental. This is almost certainly not an instance of direct borrowing from Dr. Soetomo's autobiography but rather a case of the sort of literary similarities in theme which derive from larger Indonesian patterns of thought about history, remembrance, and writing, and which animate twentieth-century Indonesian literature. An examination of the imagery of person, society, knowledge, religion, time, and narration in *Me and Toba* and *Village Childhood* will begin to show how self-reflective as well as how socially ambitious this one sector of Indonesian autobiographical writing had become by the 1950s.

IMAGES OF SELF AND SOCIETY

Much the same image of an emotionally conflicted, increasingly reflective self navigating a hesitant course through a dangerous transition to adulthood is consistently found in both *Me and Toba* and *Village Childhood*. Counterposed to this presentation of the author's remembered youthful self is a similarly structured vision of society, one that stresses tensions between some groups bound to tradition and others enamored of change and modernization. The school system and the culture of print in Toba and Minangkabau serve as the small protagonists' grand highway for moving from one of these poles to the other, and for embarking on late Indies adulthoods unfettered by the "superstitions" of Toba or Minangkabau adat, or the "false lessons" of village Christianity or Islam, as these bodies of knowledge are taught to the boys by their elders. The children's main weapon in their fight to attain this sort of modern self is their open-eyed view of the traditional givens of village society. Also crucial here is the boys' equally sharp and critical stance toward formal religion. In gaining this extra measure of insight on their old Sumatran social worlds, they become revolutionaries of the spirit. In gaining a modern self, they gain a modern vision of the world, and vice versa. Selfhood becomes permeated with political meaning.

By age seventeen, when Pospos and Radjab were leaving their home villages for the rantau, they had begun to construct their own lives in line with an imagined pluralistic future. They were going on to further schooling, to become teachers and interpreters of texts, in the multiethnic precincts of Java. All of this opened them to the possibility of imagining an Indonesian nation. Moreover, for thoughtful readers, the effort of progressing through these memoirs and witnessing these children's small journeys also laid important aesthetic and emotional groundwork for thinking about more general issues of the new postcolonial period, and about Indonesian society itself, as a bold national experiment.

This twin approach to constructing a modern self and imagining a modern society is manifested in a variety of ways in *Me and Toba* and *Village Childhood*. It can be seen in the manner in which the authors describe village life and adat custom and the Batak and Minangkabau social worlds into which village life and adat are set. It can also be seen in the authors' portrayals of the parade of characters who surround the children in rural Toba and Minangkabau. The memoirists' approach to self and society can also be seen in their portrayals of the social prestige system of late colonial Sumatra (a world where Batak and Minangkabau interacted intermittently with Dutch schoolmasters, clerks, and soldiers, but more frequently with class-conscious Batak and Minangkabau). Also important are the memoirists' presentations of the developmental journeys their earlier selves traversed on their way from birth to late adolescence. The autobiographies are remarkably similar in their treatment of all these themes, so we can look at the two books in concert. There are multiple textual examples of all the points made here, but I concentrate only on particularly telling illustrations.

In their very early childhoods both small boys live in physically cramped and emotionally constricted households. This, at least, is the way the adult Pospos and Radjab want readers to believe they remember matters, whether or not that was actually the case. Much at issue with each author is the didactic point that parents should deal warmly and openly with their young children. The writers' early family experiences are recalled in important part to show readers how close kinship worlds can go awry, to the detriment of children's emotional lives.

Pospos's father, for instance, shows affection toward his son only when the boy contracts a serious infection and lapses into a coma, causing the family to think he will die during the night. In overall terms, the cool climate in the home is recalled in terms of tightly regulated speech behavior and once-warm gift-giving practices suddenly withdrawn. Unexplained taboos also unsettle the child:

> Unless there was something I really needed, I did not speak very much with my father. He did not question me about my work at school or what I did every day. He believed he was fulfilling his duties if he just made a living for us and kept us in food. I still remember when I was very small (exactly how old I don't remember), my father would often bring little cakes for me when he came home from the marketplace; I would rush up and welcome him every evening. But suddenly, for some unknown reason, he stopped bringing me things. Perhaps he thought I had gotten too old for such treatment, that it was no longer appropriate for me to be brought little cakes.
>
> Not once did my Dad clearly show his love for me. Not because he did not love me, but probably because that was just his way. If we were eating a meal together, he always gave me advice not to eat too much curry: "Later on, no one will want you as a son-in-law," he said. If a *jengkol* fruit or a *petai* bean was still left he would joke, "Don't eat too many *jengkol,* Djohanis, or your hair will turn red," and I would believe him.
>
> There were lots of food taboos for us children. For instance, we were not allowed to eat oranges at night. Eating the head of a chicken also was not permitted; people said that your hair would turn white. But no one told us that eating oranges at night might give you a bellyache or that chicken heads were the special parts reserved for grownups. (Pospos 1950, 18)

The boy's relationship with his father was one of distant teacher and respected elder to small, dependent, usually obedient child. Djohanis resents his father's consistent stinginess (this is also a recurrent theme for Radjab):

> Often, when I was quite small my Dad would teach me how to sing songs after dinner. These were not church hymns but songs in the Malay language; even now I do not know what they meant. Maybe they were in old-fashioned Malay, I don't know.
>
> I realized that we were not rich and that my father worked hard to find us a handful of rice each morning and evening. So I did not ask him for money very often, unless it was for something I really needed. I realized that if I

asked for some clothes, for instance, he wouldn't give them to me right away. (1950, 18)

Pospos goes on in this same passage to describe his relationship with his mother. Sometimes the pair actually came to blows, he relates:

> I was not even particularly close to my mother, especially once I got into middle school. She was satisfied if I helped her out by collecting firewood, boiling the rice, washing my clothes, watching the livestock, and so on. These duties I often forgot because I was so busy playing, and Mother often got angry at me, especially when she came home in the evening from the market and found that the rice was still not cooked. Often she grabbed a cane to beat me with, but I was really too big to be hit like this and I fought back. I tried to dodge her swipes and if it hurt too much I grabbed the cane and hit her back. Then Mother would go complain to my father. He was not particularly concerned—he knew my mother was always exaggerating—so sometimes he just laughed. My mother, of course, would be put out by this and say, "You're the one who's always spoiling Djohanis. Now he's just incorrigible." (1950, 19)

The boy's family world was one which virtually excluded his small sister from serious consideration, a circumstance that Pospos recalls without any rancor. In other words, *Me and Toba* does not take a feminist slant on remembered childhood worlds, to say the least. After noting that girls were not counted as part of a family's complement of "real children" Pospos goes on to recall:

> I rarely played with my little sister, especially after I went to middle school and she entered girls' school. It was customary for a boy not to be too close to his sister; they were supposed to stay apart from each other. You could not address your sister as *engkau*, it had to be *kamu*. [Batak use *kamu* as the formal second-person pronoun.] Other little girls were closer to us than our own sisters. (1950, 19)

Pospos summarizes the overall family situation:

> Perhaps because none of them was a close friend to whom I could pour my heart out, I was not particularly close to my parents or sister. Yes, it was true that my parents fed me, bought me clothes, paid my school fees—in short, gave me everything I needed—and in return for their hard work and struggle they hoped I would keep progressing in school. My father and mother were my parents, but they were not friends or close companions. (1950, 19)

Closeness with other people would have to come in the outside world, among school friends (common victims of the school's structures of hierarchy).

Radjab's Ridjal is born into an apparently happy, boisterous, and certainly crowded Minangkabau compound household composed of multiple female-centered hearths. As the author describes it,

My mother occupied one of the cramped rooms, and there I was born. I would say it was like being born in a barracks, since there were more than forty people living in that house at the time. The seven girls all had children, half of them themselves had children, and every night seven unfamiliar men came to the house, that is, the husbands of the seven women. One can imagine how noisy the place was, what with all these individual needs, dispositions, and behaviors colliding. Morning, noon, and night it was one big hullabaloo. I was born at five in the morning, when the house was quiet and everyone else was sound asleep, except for two or three of my aunts and a midwife. (Radjab 1974, 7)

Immediately Radjab recalls the feeling of deep longing this early scene always evoked in him:

That house and its surroundings always made me feel extremely nostalgic every time I visited it after I was five years old. I do not know why, and have never been able to explain it. The sense of yearning was vague, but it penetrated to my very soul. There were various flowers of different colors and some croton plants around the house, and in the backyard some aloe plants. The crotons were large, with wide varicolored leaves of red, yellow, green, and white. They always caught my attention and heightened my sensation of longing for some unknown thing. Maybe I felt this way because I planted two crotons on my mother's grave; every time I see the plant the feeling envelopes me. (1974, 7)

The early environment of fun and emotional denseness soon dissipates for the infant, after his mother dies of cholera while he is still nursing. As mentioned, the baby then gets passed among a bewildering succession of female relatives, ending up finally in the hands of several notably unsympathetic stepmothers (as the author terms his late mother's co-wives). These women lend a chill to his familial experiences, but the very young boy is quite fond of his father, and in this case, the man reciprocates. Typically, for Radjab, he remembers this situation in terms of speech use:

I lived with my father until I was five. I was never far from him, and I considered him a playmate who just happened to be rather large. I called him *engkau*, the familiar "you." I only discovered later that this was wrong. All this time I lived with my stepmother, too, so there were three of us altogether. Father really did love me, first because I was his only male child, and second because I had no mother. I always played in the mosque where father taught, or on the grounds around it. (1974, 11–12)

As each remembered child attains the age of six or seven, he begins to discover several "outside" worlds located beyond his natal household and his tiny village realm of neighbor houses and mostly female kin. First, there are other villages "out there," which the boys sometimes visit with their parents, or where thir fathers work. Second, there are exciting subsocieties in the home village or right nearby: the coffee shop scene, for instance, where adult males lounge about, read newspapers, and discuss grown-up matters, and the village schools and their tight communities of students and their mentor-teachers. Located far beyond these local communities are the far more exciting regions of the rantau. The boys hope their futures lie out there, in exotic Java or at the very least (in Radjab's case) in the commercial coastal city of Padang, where the boy and his buddies hope to become merchants. Each of these realms is remembered as having its own emotional tone and ethos. Radjab's recollections are illustrative of the approach taken in both books.

As an infant, Ridjal (Radjab's remembered child) was totally enveloped in female care, with first his mother and then his more distant kinswomen bathing him, fussing over him, and as he grew a bit larger, disciplining him. He lived near his father until age five, as we have seen (although clearly his father was periodically moving among the houses of his several wives). One memory, of a long sojourn Ridjal spent in a lakeside village, is a particularly happy one. Ridjal and some young friends swam "in the cool, clear water of Lake Singkarak. We raced and splashed each other for an hour at a time. We did not yet dare to swim very far out, since we were still little, and we stayed near the shore, where plants grew in the shallows" (p. 14). The boy's world was a small one, where jungle foliage played a large part. And the realm of foreigners started just a few houses over:

> Our world was very small, about three hundred square meters that comprised the edge of the lake, the house, and the yard. I was afraid to go outside this area. The house that was about a half a kilometer down the road from my stepmother's might as well have been in another world as far as I was concerned. When there was a wedding there, I did not dare go. I just watched from afar, hiding behind a row of castor plants. The people who lived in that house were like foreigners to me, not the same sorts of people as my father, my stepmother, and the others who lived in the two long houses and the hut. (1974, 15)

During the same period and later, too, when they got older, the boys would feel drawn to explore the deep forest that surrounded the small habitations. They would also climb up a mysterious mountain peak called The Four Houses, look out over the surrounding countryside, and dream of life in the distant rantau. The latter was full of wonders:

> When danger threatened, especially some kind of epidemic, the people of Sumpur burned incense and slaughtered a goat for a ritual meal at The Four Houses. They asked that Sumpur be spared from the catastrophe. Old people said that in times of disaster you could sometimes see a winged horse running wild through the hills, ridden by a heroic figure.
>
> From the top of the hill you could see all of Sumpur, the rice fields around it, and to the south Lake Singkarak. When I was older and had the urge to

wander or go to the rantau, I often climbed up to The Four Houses and day-dreamed, communing silently with nature, confirming the presence of a wide and rolling world that stretched from the slopes of Mount Merapi and Mount Singgalang in the north to the foot of Mount Talang in the south. But when you turned to the west, the land looked like a deep and steep-walled ravine of nothing but wild grass, through which flowed the Sumpur River, its current barely audible as it rushed downstream. I do not know whether anyone ever fell into that ravine, but I am certain that no one ever dared climb down into it. (1974, 8)

The boy's thoughts of the distant, as yet unobtainable realms (the forest world, the rantau) were shot through with feelings of longing, or *kerinduan*.

After age six Radjab's boyhood self entered two new communities. This move caused an irreparable break with his early family life, the one located close to lakeside scenes and forest groves. He was sent to school. First there was public school, which Ridjal liked very much (a subject to be dis-cussed shortly). Then there was the formidable surau, the Muslim reci-tation community centered on a small mosque. Here, a close-knit group of sixteen boys learned to recite their Arabic prayers. This school group quickly developed into Ridjal's everyday intimate community. As the mem-oirist writes later in the book, in chapter 13, life in the surau eventually led the boy and a few of his friends to sever most of their ties to the "reg-ular" outside world. As the boys penetrated more and more deeply into Islamic studies, they took up the white robes of Arabic dress and lived at a severe monastic remove from the hurly-burly of normal Minangkabau vil-lage life. Early on, however, when the boys were still surau initiates, they were much more themselves (Radjab remembers) and much truer to their normal feelings.

The sixteen boys had entered the surau at about the same age, which made them a natural community set apart a bit from the other, older boys, and from the much younger ones (the entire student body numbered over forty). Radjab remembers his closest circle of friends in finely ob-served detail. He paints an individualized portrait of each friend, remem-bering some as suspicious, some as good-hearted, some as sports mad, and so on (p. 22).

Certain adults also peopled the boys' world. There were their Muslim instructors, of course, but also visitors staying at the surau on brief visits home from the rantau. These men would regale the youngsters with exhil-arating stories of adult life in distant lands. Also present in the surau com-munity were some flagrantly strange village characters, such as Lebai Sa-man, an odd old bachelor full of divination lore and funny stories. Radjab recalls him in entertaining, fond detail. A similar but more ribald treat-ment is paid to the "Village Privates," a ragtag group of unemployed, over-age bachelors who loll about the coffee stalls and empty houses, getting into devilment. For Ridjal and his friends, the Village Privates constitute examples of the maturation process gone zanily awry.

Radjab's technique of describing an individuated social world peopled by emotionally deep children, several vaguely sketched in and rather oppressive teachers, and a small number of spectacularly interesting odd characters like Lebai Saman is reflected also in his more general approach to "writing society," in the sense of his technique of reporting a social world.

For Radjab, and for Pospos too, the human world as a whole is made up of a multiplicity of "societies," each of which has "customs." Sometimes these traditions are quirky and unusual; this circumstance renders them worthy of mention and description in the memoirs. In almost all of these instances, the small boys look out at an ethnographic world with sympathy and balanced interest. Many of their elders, however, are so old-fashioned as to actually believe in these old customs naively and fully. The boys stand off to the side of these communities of belief, wondering about Sumatra's parade of customs, and coming up with their own, distanced perspective on particular practices.

Radjab's chapter 20, about a trip the boy and his father take out to an "odd" little mountain village called Sulit Air, shows the writer in this ethnographic mode. He portrays the remembered child as sharing this same perspective. The boy relishes the parade of customs on display for him during this visit: lavish village games, fancy costumes, special Fasting Month celebrations. Later in the chapter Radjab describes the peculiar goings on associated with *badunie* (a special ritual time when villages would show off wealth by lavishing it on entertainment): men would cross-dress as women, two village factions would hold mock battles, and special processions and dances would go on till all hours.

Pospos turns much the same ethnographic lens on Toba speech patterns, marriage customs, and inheritance rules. He details, for instance, the ethnic stereotypes held by his own and various other Batak societies about one another with reportorial flair (p. 47). Pospos also reports Toba-area poverty with similar clearsightedness:

> Anyone who has ever gone by car through Tapanuli from Pematang Siantar surely has noticed that there is nothing whatever along the roadsides except the rice fields and, way out in the middle of them, villages surrounded by clusters of bamboo; they look like green islets in a green sea. Farming is, in fact, the sole means of livelihood for people there. Over toward Silindung there are a few other activities, such as rubber farming and harvesting gum benzoin for making incense, but there is not even much of that. The area's poverty is what has kept railroads out. But farming alone eventually falls short of satisfying people's needs. If a person has many sons he surely cannot divide his rice land into enough parcels for each one of them, so Toba

people search for other means of support. People flock to Sidikalang and Kota Cane to open new farms and new villages. And that's not all. Children with schooling migrate out beyond their home region to find jobs as clerks on plantations or to become *ambtenaars* in the big city.

People in other communities often got jealous of the Toba because of this. In the Simelungun area, for instance, the Toba had come to be hated because they are the ones who look prosperous and who hold positions in offices. In East Sumatra people had begun to resent them, and indeed by that time Medan had become "Tapanuli City," Tapanuli's capital. The genuine Malays and the Simelunguns and the Karos (who are also Batak) get short shrift there and count for nothing. Disputes also break out frequently with Padang people. This is not surprising. Once there was a big dispute between West Sumatrans and Tapanuli people in East Sumatra, and no cars from West Sumatra were allowed to go through Tapanuli.

People say Lake Toba is a lovely lake, but the idea never really occurred to us. Maybe this was because we were so used to lovely scenery or because we were so thoroughly accustomed to playing in the lake. But there was another reason we paid no attention to the natural beauty of our land: we had no time for that sort of thing. After we got out of school, for instance, we were not allowed to go play but were told to fetch firewood or do some other task. "Now, don't go thinking you can be like What's-his-name. He's a rich kid." That's what we'd always hear.

True enough: the fear of having an empty belly was what pushed people to work their hardest. (1950, 47–48)

It is obvious that Pospos sees blunt ethnic stereotypes and such conditions of poverty as existing outside of his own personal self, a situation that makes these idea systems open to his critical appraisal. Radjab adopts exactly the same notion of a watching self for his protagonist: Ridjal experiences a world of old Minangkabau marriage customs, inheritance patterns, divination beliefs, and village taboos. He learns of their existence as a student would, and then he treats them with a touch of skepticism. Ridjal's approach to Minangkabau marriage customs is illustrative here. He reports that many families seek to secure rich merchants as sons-in-law; that Balai Pustaka novels would lead us to believe that young women forced into such financially astute marriages would inevitably be unhappy and would pine for their true loves; but that, finally, when we observe real marriages involving people we actually know, most young women who get married off to old shopkeepers and cloth brokers end up being quite content with their lot and pleased, too, that they have fared better in the marriage market than have their girlfriends.

Both authors also take a similar critical approach to the all-important Sumatran matters of social location and a family's position within prestige hierarchies. And again, the remembered boys position themselves at a distance from the givens of their traditional village cultures, and at a distance too from the status systems promoted by the colonial school system (a particular preoccupation of Pospos's) and from those promoted by Islam (Radjab's focus). Both boys' close brushes with family instability seem to have fostered this particularly distanced view of social life. Radjab's "normal life course" was upset early on by his mother's death and he was launched upon his career of household moves from one relative to the next. In Pospos's case, his natal family remains intact but his father careens from one job to another. The family is never far from poverty and Djohanis never knows when or if he may be withdrawn from school for lack of funds.

From such experiences of watching their parents lead unpredictable lives that clash with adat models, both boys gain the insight that social stability is a cruel chimera. Pospos shows an extra measure of bitterness here, derived from his family's poverty and from that of Toba society in general.

In *Me and Toba* traditional villages are organized into contesting factions. These have greater or lesser degrees of power. It is the individual's task, in most cases, to accommodate himself or herself to this circumstance. For instance, the lowly status of Pospos's clan (*marga*) in the family's home village necessitates a certain jaundiced realism on the part of the growing boy, so that he is not destroyed by scions of more prestigious clans. Djohanis quickly learns that he has few older-lineage-brother protectors in his village, so he must avoid fistfights or he will have to fight them alone.

When Pospos's remembered self looks beyond his intimate social world outward into the Indies (that is, into such outposts of Dutch colonial control as the government school system in Tapanuli) he sees rigidly structured status hierarchies peopled by Toba children and adults caught up in rapacious games of one-upmanship. Cutthroat competition among families to have the children with "the best degrees" from "the most prestigious schools" is the motif of this Indies world. Many Toba youngsters fail to get into the supposedly right schools, and their parents' social standing suffers in consequence. Pospos himself is an apt and cagey pupil and he does manage to keep passing his final exams at each level of this status-crazed school system. In contrast to most of the other children, though, the boy doubts the moral worth of the entire colonial school enterprise. He well recognizes that the H.I.S. schools, MULO schools, and so on serve the practical purpose of giving impoverished village children an escape route out of the farm villages into a (he thinks) stable, salaried world in the colonial bureaucracies and the plantations along Sumatra's east coast. However, Djohanis is the sort of boy who asks, What moral cost does such economic progress and prosperity exact? His fellow pupils seem to him to be enslaved to an empty competitiveness, no different in basic aim or strategy from the destructive family rivalries of premodern Toba villages, where disputes flared into flame over access to new farm land or irrigation water.

The clear implication of Pospos's characterization of the school-based competitiveness he sees around him is that there must be a more defensible avenue toward the future.

Radjab's younger self is remembered in much the same way. He notices how important differences of wealth are for his fellow Minangkabau and how social status shapes marriage choices. Prestige-conscious parents, he finds, want high-status young men as sons-in-law (one of the reasons his own family wants him to train as a Muslim schoolteacher).

Very importantly, too, the child develops a cautiously neutral mental stance toward some of the most vituperative disputes his elders engage in. Ridjal watches the Traditionalists versus Modernists (*kaum tua, kaum muda*) conflict, for instance, from a measured distance, as a prematurely wise onlooker. He notes (1974, 155) that he did not take sides in this bitter rift that split Minangkabau village society during the twenties and thirties. He simply stood off to the side of the philosophical debate, watching his elders, remembering the scenes.

How does the boy gain this special measure of insight which has vaulted him beyond the level of consciousness characteristic (he writes) of most adults in his home society? The answer is the same for both Radjab and Pospos: through the schoolroom and the school text, and via the liberating world of books to which the children thereby gain access.

BOOK LEARNING, SCHOOLS, LANGUAGE, AND KNOWLEDGE

How readers should best interpret texts and how audiences should best understand speech are matters that lie at the heart of these memoirs and the social and historical vision they propose. Pospos and Radjab denigrate surface acoustical sound and physical letter shapes on a page in favor of the semantic meanings that they feel lies beneath utterance and writing. They also recognize the rootbed of ties linking language use and political power; additionally, they fear the misuse of such associations. Both writers' small protagonists suffered from such linkages in their everyday classroom experiences. Pospos and Radjab doubt, further, that one language can be smoothly translated into another, on a word-for-word or thought-by-thought basis. Finally, they find the entire notion of teaching texts by a process of rote memorization ridiculous, and also deeply insulting to young students.

These four positions regarding language put both authors' remembered childhood selves in direct conflict with their parents, schoolteachers, religious instructors, and in fact with much of the adult social hierarchy surrounding them as colonial-era youngsters. Djohanis and Ridjal are presented to readers as linguistic revolutionaries, albeit somewhat hapless ones, since their efforts to privilege content over linguistic or textual form often meet with overwhelming resistance while they are still young. Much the same fate results from the boys' childlike efforts to renegotiate the politics of speech in their rural lives and in their schools. The implication of both books is that a full social revolution overthrowing both Dutch control and traditional Toba and Minangkabau social hierarchy would be necessary if the boys' hopes for a liberated and specifically modern linguistic world are to be realized. Colonial Sumatran society has a good deal of growing up to do on this score, the memoirists infer.

Many incidents scattered throughout the two autobiographies deal with language, knowledge, and textual interpretation pursuant to these themes. One of the most recurrent types of narrative event along these lines contrasts a magical approach to language with what these authors take to be a modern reader's stance toward texts. The latter is clearly something Pospos and Radjab approve of. This stance is one in which the reader peruses books and other printed works for their publicly accessible messages and for their personal, interpretive significance; readers are not to remain fixated on letter shape or acoustical sounds or words and chant phrases. Radjab and Pospos pursue large issues like these through the concrete, minor event or scene, minutely observed, as usual.

There are numerous, sometimes poignant, sometimes funny scenes in which the memoirists pursue the idea that semantic content should be of greater social moment than sheer sound or textual letter shape. Radjab is particularly insistent on this point, and his chapter 8, "Finishing the Koran," and his chapter 13, "Reciting Koranic Verses at the Pesantran," dwell on issues of language, sense, and semantics in detail. These chapters provide the two memoirs' strongest and certainly most heartfelt statements in this area. Here, for instance, is Radjab commenting about sense versus sound in the opening passages of chapter 8:

> When I was twelve years old, I came to the end of the Koran, which I'd been learning to read and recite in the surau for three years.
>
> At the time I was learning how to read and recite the Koran, I did not know that the sentences had any meaning at all. I only knew that the Koran was in the Arabic language and had to be read by singing it, so that the reader would store up merit and later on would get into heaven. I did not know that if it was translated into our own language we would understand what God meant with all of these verses. However, though I had completed the reading of the Koran seven times, God had not said a single thing that I could understand, because it hadn't been interpreted for me.
>
> The Koran must be read, recited, and sung, said the teachers. Each night for three years I wrestled with the manner in which it was to be read: a line over A, a line in front of U, a line under I; if there was a sloping line half a centimeter long, you'd read it in lengthened form, with three letter A's, AAA, III, UUU; if there was no such mark, you'd shorten a letter, A, I, U; and if you had the letter 'AIU, you'd have to drone out 'A, 'I, 'U. And if there was

a mark looking like a backward brush, called a *tasjdid,* the letter underneath the brush would be read double.

We had to be very careful and cautious in reading the Koran, as if we were penetrating a road strewn with thorn bushes. For, the teacher said, if we read and recited it wrong (for instance, if *Islaaam* was read *Islam*), we would have committed a great sin and would be tormented in hell, whose fires were a thousand times as hot as those on earth. Or, if the voice was supposed to come out the nose and if it was supposed to be droned, but we read it with our voice coming out of our mouth (for instance, if we read 'A as A), our chances of getting into heaven were slim indeed. (1974, 52)

Chapter 13 begins with a narrative that is even more bitter in its condemnation of the Muslim teachers' inane teaching methods (inane according to Ridjal and his friends). Apparently the boys were taught two sorts of magical knowledge: the ritual sounds of their Arabic prayers and the arcane rules of Arabic grammar. They understood not a single thing. Their exalted teacher was mouthing gibberish, they found, and chastising them whenever the boys would press him to tell them what the holy texts might possibly mean.

The boys entered a period of bafflement and frustration:

We had been reading and reciting for four years, night and day, but we could not make sense of a single word of it. We couldn't take a single word of it to heart and retain it. (1974, 82)

Ridjal's uncle, his teacher here, glories in a kind of sacred inanity:

He asked God that our verse recitation studies might be lengthy and that all of us might become pious, learned persons and enter into heaven.

Then Uncle read: "Alkalamu hual lafzu murakkabu mufidu bil wadhi."

He translated this as: "As a beginning, there was the word and what was this beginning like? What was called the word was *lafaz*, which was composed, which provided a salutary benefit and a *wadahak.*"

"Will of God!" I said to myself. "What does all this mean? Even though it has been translated, it still is pitch black."

What did he mean by "the word"? I only knew that that word was an instrument for writing the Arabic letters, made of a palm tree (rib) and sharpened at the end.

He continued further: "According to the *Nahu* people, those folks, a word is whatever, it *lafaz*, which isn't like the sound of the mosque drum, which provides some salutary benefit but has no letters to it nor is it like the *wadhak.*"

This didn't make it any clearer at all, just murkier. When he mentioned the *nahu*, I remembered a certain woman in Seberang Air whose name was Nahu. Her house was along the Sumpur River out in back of the surau of the honorable Imam Muda. Perhaps she was an Arab grammarian. And why did the Indonesian passages used for the translation here have to twist and turn so much and be so repetitive, with half of the words in Indonesian and half in Arabic but the sentence structure absolutely, totally in Arabic? Only later on, three years afterward (once I'd studied Indonesian and Dutch grammar), did I come to understand that the meaning of the holy text was the following:

"A sentence is a composition of words which can be coherently understood and purposefully pronounced." If he had only said that, we would have understood!

Or if he had gone on to say: "According to grammarians, *lafaz* are the voiced sounds that can be written out with words and whose meanings can be understood," we could also have understood.

But after reciting for some two hours, listening to his murky explanations, which repeated themselves and twisted and turned like a snake's armpit, half in Arabic, half in Indonesian, I was still totally confused. So were my friends.

Moreover, I was surprised: Why didn't we understand a single word of Arabic? Why didn't we know the words for things around us, like house, surau, school, door, window, kitchen, to eat, to drink, me, you, and him or her, in Arabic? We'd been taught the grammar and we'd been taught explanations of it in an unspeakably exalted form of Arabic—which we'd have to keep mulling over again and again and asking, does each letter have to be read with an A or a U or an I? Grammar was the science of the types of words there were and the ways to join them together into compositions—but as yet we didn't even know the words *themselves* which those types and compositional rules would apply to. So what then were we supposed to be joining together into sentences?

We barely had any acquaintance at all with the Arabic language when our heads started to spin with its grammar and all these rules that we had to memorize and know by heart. (1974, 82–84)

Ridjal finally despairs of making any sense of his lessons and simply capitulates to the prevailing standard of grading at work in his recitation classes: he memorizes the sound sequences and spits them out on command. His personal, emotional life shifts over to his sports activities with his friends and to his hopes for a possible future life in the rantau when he grows up. Eventually his father allows him to leave his uncle's recitation school and (as Ridjal sees it) to return to regular human existence. Pospos strikes similar themes: his remembered child and the boy's small pals laugh at a local crazy man who walks about the village roads spouting important-sounding but silly Christian sermons, in grand church pulpit style (chapter 4, p. 15). The children also mock a variety of adults who have learned a smattering of Dutch and strut about mouthing pretentious phrases from that language (one man, for instance, was particularly enamored of the military command, "Left, march!" [p. 15]).

Both remembered children know that something serious is wrong with the way language is used in their rural home regions, but it takes the boys a considerable process of maturation for them to discover the underlying reasons for their dissatisfaction. When they are small, they are quite befuddled by the world of language. Pospos's Djohanis, for instance, looks at the telegraph poles the Dutch have built along the main Tapanuli highway and wonders what sorts of words dwell inside:

> Sometimes we stopped and put our ears against a pole. Friends told us that if we listened really close we could find out what people were saying on the telephone, or what they were wiring in their telegraphs. Indeed, there was a sort of "ngiung-ngiung" sound that you could hear through the poles. Friends told us it was the telegrams being tapped out! (1950, 37)

Ridjal, for his part, has a hugely difficult time figuring out the whole affair of newspapers, as these strange texts relate to village speech. One time, when he was about four years old, he encounters his father and some of his father's friends at the coffee stall:

> If I was not in the mosque yard, I could always be found playing in front of the coffee stall nearby. There I once saw a person reading a large sheet of paper while other people sat around a table listening attentively, occasionally sipping their coffee or nibbling on fried bananas. I asked the oldest of my playmates what they were doing. "Just reading newspapers," he replied.
> "Oh."
> Usually I saw people talking together; one said something and then the other answered. That is how it went, they took turns. But this newspaper reading was different. It was the first time I had ever seen it. One person talked for a long time while he held a big piece of paper, and the other ten people listened without responding. Why? I was surprised, and did not understand it at all.
> After that I too listened to the newspaper being read, though I did not understand because the language was Indonesian rather than Minangkabau. I often heard the words "war," "English," and "German," but did not yet know what they meant.
> One day Father was talking with his friend Sutan Sianok. I was playing trains, crawling near him and pushing the boxes that served as cars. I listened to Father talk for a long time. Sutan Sianok listened silently and nodded his head. I was surprised because my father was not holding that big piece of paper in his hands, yet the words kept on tumbling out of his mouth.
> So I asked, "Are you reading the newspaper?"
> Father was surprised that I should ask such a thing. "No," he replied.
> "But you were talking for such a long time, and Mr. Sutan was listening so long too."
> "That's because there was a lot I wanted to tell him, and he hasn't answered yet."
> I did not understand; I was quite sure that when people talked on and on like that, they must be reading a newspaper. If not, then where on earth did the words come from?
> "Then you memorized yesterday's newspaper, didn't you?"

"No, I didn't memorize yesterday's newspaper. I was expressing my own ideas."

"Expressing your own ideas? I don't understand."

"Of course not, son. You only know how to push your toy train around. Now run along!"

Father started talking again, and I continued playing with my train. I have never quite understood why Father talked so long without holding that big sheet of paper they called a newspaper in his hands. (1974, 13–14)

As the boys grow older they discover that speech and texts can be used by one group of people to assert political control over others. An element of fear enters their consciousness of language. Pospos provides literally dozens of examples of this political edge to language. For one thing, Toba families rank each other according to how many esoteric European languages their children know (this is knowledge gained in the more prestigious schools such as the H.I.S and MULO schools). Families with many children who have graduated from such schools are said to *martua*, to glow with supernatural luck powers (chapter 9). Parents who have children studying in far off Java have even more luck powers. Pospos's parents and their circle of market-seller, shopkeeper families (and also even the village farm households) raced each other to see which family could turn out the most graduates of the most glittering academy.

Pospos writes that this competitiveness represented a capitulation of the Toba Batak to the worst aspects of Dutch colonial social hierarchy. It also resulted in a penchant for kids who could put on good public performances, by showing off their language skills.

The Dutch language was held in unbelievably high regard by people in our area. There were several H.I.S. schools: one in Sigumpulon, one in Balige, and one in Narumonda that was run by the Nommensen Schoolvereniging. Of course, people preferred the mission's H.I.S. to the others, since we were all Christians. Sometimes there were children from the huria pagaran [church congregations] who got into those schools; they were usually the children of mission school teachers or of the district head. On Christmas Eve these H.I.S. kids were often asked to recite Bible verses in Dutch, even though there were only one or two people in the whole church who could understand them. I suppose it had to be demonstrated publicly that the H.I.S. fourth graders were skilled at Dutch.

Sometimes this tendency to show off got rather silly. If an H.I.S. student was walking with his parents to the market and they happened to run into a Dutch person—it did not matter who—the parents often told the child to speak Dutch with the Dutch person. If the child, perhaps only a second or third grader and naturally still very shy, did not want to do this, the father would grumble, "Well, don't continue in that school, let's just ask for your tuition money back. It's wasting money to support you there." Or if two H.I.S. kids happened to meet, the father would tell them to speak Dutch to each other: "Okay, friends, we want to hear you two speak Dutch." What delight there was in hearing other people speaking Dutch I cannot imagine, especially if the listeners themselves did not know a single word of the language. The two children—little kids in the first or second grade!—of course felt shy and embarrassed. (1950, 34)

Pospos goes on to comment that Toba people were like sheep in this herd mentality of theirs, trying to learn the Dutch language and show it off. Djohanis and his clique of young boys, however, see through this sham, and laugh at the foibles of their elders. They also laugh at some of their teachers, who cannot pronounce the Dutch phrases very well.

Once Djohanis gets into MULO school in Tarutung (in his mid-teens), he and his friends discover another political dimension of language use.

We did not usually speak Dutch at school. Wherever we were, we always used our mother tongue, even during class. So Dutch was used only when speaking to teachers. When we did try to speak Dutch among ourselves, we got teased. Someone would say something like, "You might as well toss your Dutch over there into the sewer." Our teachers knew this, so they made a rule that whoever was reported to be speaking Batak would be fined 2½ cents. But this policy failed, since none of us wanted to squeal on a friend. Indeed, we felt undeniably calmer and more confident using our mother tongue when we conversed.

After three months in MULO we received our first report card. This report also noted how many foreign languages we were allowed to choose. Malay was counted as a foreign language. I chose German and Malay, because I had heard from my friends that there was not much demand for French speakers. German seemed to be the right language for us to take. After all, wasn't all scientific literature written in German? That is what we thought then, anyway. But maybe we also chose it because our preachers were Germans, and so we were already a bit pro-German. (Radjab 1950, 51)

The Toba boys mount a subtle linguistic campaign of their own, however, against their Dutch teachers. Pospos reports an excruciating instance of miscommunication between an earnest Dutch instructor and his willful pupils:

That first year I heard an "anecdote" at school. Not long ago there had been a Dutch teacher (he had since left the school) who had read a "funny" story to his class. Much to his surprise he noticed that when he finished reading none of the students laughed. So he angrily asked one of them, "Why aren't any of you laughing after hearing such a funny story?"

"Well, um. . . ," answered the pupil, "we didn't feel your story was very funny, actually."

"What do you mean, not funny? You just don't have a sense of humor." But the student said that the story really was not funny. Finally the teacher said, "Well, in that case, you tell a story. Then I'll be able to see what kind of sense of humor you have."

So the pupil related a story—actually, he just shouted it—as follows: "Manase, Manase ditinkgir ho lubang ni hirik, hape lubang ni te" (Manase, Manase, you dug out a cricket hole, but unfortunately it was really a wasp hole in a dung heap). There is a type of wasp that adores water buffalo or cow manure (in Dutch it is called a *mestkever*). Normally it digs its hole in a pile of dry dung, and when you go to pick up the dung to use as fertilizer, you sometimes cannot tell whether this hole has been made by a cricket (which also likes to burrow in dung) or by a wasp. The story the student told is a kind of taunt in verse form commonly used to torment kids named Manase.

When the class heard the verse they burst into paroxysms of laughter. The Dutch teacher, who did not speak Batak, was dumbfounded. He asked for a translation of the verse, but the mischievous student replied, "It really can't be translated, Tuan [Master]. It wouldn't be funny anymore in another language." But the teacher kept insisting, and finally the boy said, "Manase, Manase (the stress now falling on the *na*, not on the *se* as it had above), waar ben je?" (Where are you). The class burst into laughter once again.

His face reddening, the teacher said, "What's so funny about the sentence, 'Manase, where are you?' I don't understand you people at all." Maybe the Dutch really did not understand us. (1950, 52)

The boys struggle with another aspect of language and its stockpiles of knowledge: they attempt to understand Malay, which as we have seen, the Dutch have presented to the schoolchildren as a foreign language elective. Some of Djohanis's school friends hit upon a translation strategy of their own devising: Since Toba Batak has many "o" sounds where Malay uses "e", they zip through their Batak-to-Malay translation practice drills by simply pronouncing Batak sentences with lots of "e"s. This results in many nonsensical homework sentences.

As both boys grow into adolescence they amass larger and larger stores of schoolbook knowledge, which they use as a touchstone for evaluating the truth claims of comments by their elders in the village or the surau. Occasionally they delve into magical lore (as when Radjab's Ridjal experiments with mystical prayer formulas that he hopes will bring him great riches). In each such excursion, though, the narrators find that mystical knowledge has no real efficacy in the world. What holds ultimate sway for them is the secular book learning of the public schoolroom.

PORTRAYALS OF RELIGION

Given Radjab's unflattering view of the sorts of religious language promoted in the Muslim surau and Pospos's accounts of language in the Protestant church (where hymn singing and listening to sermons are largely social occasions), it is no surprise that the two authors figuratively raise their eyebrows at their pious acquaintances' explanations for their religious devotion. Why do Minangkabau villagers and townspeople go to the mosque on Fridays, keep the Fasting Month, and recite their Arabic prayers with such assiduousness? Why do Toba Batak rural people flock to their white clapboard, tall-steepled churches every Sunday? Why are Toba such enthusiastic supporters of the church choir? (Or, the church choirs, since Toba congregations inevitably have a women's choir, a men's choir, a children's choir, and a young-unmarried-adults' choir?) The memoirs' two small boys uncover the *real* reasons for such devotionalism: the perennial Minangkabau and Toba search for social status and magical stores of power. Needless to say, the memoirists regard this negatively.

Radjab's Ridjal and his young male friends, in one instance, celebrate the end of one phase of their Koranic lessons with a lavish ceremony, and discover that the associated village festivities, parades, and fancy dress displays are the preeminent components of this sector of Islam for their rural compatriots. The boys are drawn inexorably into such celebrations, and come to believe that Islam is a matter of personal finery and village ritualism. It takes them a few more years of experience to learn differently; some of their fellow villagers never learn that lesson, the narrators report. Chapter 8, "Graduating from the Koranic Lessons," describes the boys' enthusiastic entry into this particular rung of Muslim maturity.

Later in the book Radjab discourses at length about how wrongheaded it is for Minangkabau Islam to focus so obsessively on securing such prestigious social positions. His Ridjal rejects a future career as a village religion teacher in part because the boy suspects that his large extended family is only pushing him into this job so that they may have yet one more betitled offspring to add luster to the family line.

Puasa, the Fasting Month, proved to have some of the same extratheological dimensions. The boys discover that people seem to love the fast as much for the nighttime feasting and conviviality as for its theological rationale. The boys enjoy puasa immensely, with its big spreads of food after sunset, its lazy daytime stupors, and its rapid trajectory toward the great holiday ending the fast, *Hari Raya.* The boy and his friends observe religious devotionalism in their elders during Ramadan, and mordantly criticize the inconsistencies they find there.

Pospos's remembered child is an iconoclast in much the same mode. Why do Toba Batak love Christmas services? To get free candles.

It was the custom for us Christians to celebrate the night before December 25. At that time a lighted tree would be put up (a *gaba-gaba* in Batak, a *kerstboom* in Dutch), all decorated with strips of paper, lighted candles, and so on. Often, too, a few children would recite verses from the Bible near the *gaba-gaba,* a practice we called *liturgi.* We were given these verses to memorize three months before Christmas. The children who said their verses well were praised, while the others were criticized and made fun of. That didn't make things easier for the child who was reciting. After the ceremony on December 25 was finished, lots of folks—grown-ups as well as children—milled around in front of the tree to see if they could get a candle. Immediately the church elders would form a circle around the *gaba-gaba* to guard against anyone taking candles, but no matter how firm the protection was, someone would succeed in getting one. The next morning, the church elders' children could be seen playing with candles. (1950, 20–21)

New Year's Day had a similar attraction for the children: that was the time they were allowed to set off whole fistfuls of firecrackers. Children could also convince their parents to buy them new clothes for New Year's, so the family could make a suitable presentation of itself in church that day.

Experiences like these led the boys to realize that Islam and Christianity have very different manifest communal forms than the official theologies assert. Sacred life began to exist for the children at two levels: what the formal religious texts said, and how Muslim and Christian lives were actually experienced. The boys observe this puzzling situation, and thereby gain a certain ethnographic distance from their religious communities even as they participate enthusiastically in the yearly Muslim or Christian rounds of ritual activities.

The boys also gain insight into the oppressive character of some religious personnel, by being punished or berated for some minor infraction of sacred etiquette. The boys emerge from this as still more convinced skeptics. Pospos, for instance, recalls how unreasonably strict some German missionary sisters were toward Toba teenage girls, when the adolescents were caught talking with boys (1950, 70–71). One sister ordered the girls to stay away from Djohanis and his pals, after an innocent bicycle excursion. "This sister was a German," Pospos recalls drily. "Maybe boys and girls were allowed to see each other only in Germany" (71).

Radjab's childhood self comes under even more withering fire, as we have already seen, when he dares to ask his surau instructors what some of the Arabic passages he is memorizing actually *mean*. In one instance, Ridjal found he could not believe in the literal truth of a religious tale of which his uncle (his teacher in this case) was fond. Ridjal got called an infidel—and several other epithets—for his obstreperousness:

One day, while he was teaching about the sky and the earth, my uncle explained that the first sky was made of copper, the second sky was made of silver, the third of gold, and the fourth of diamonds. And that atop these diamonds the sun revolved, pulled by thousands of holy angels on a golden chain. According to what he said, the sun went around the earth, not the earth around the sun as they taught us in school. Each of the skies was as thick as a foot trip taking five hundred years.

"Please give me leave to inquire, Your Honor," I said to Uncle, for there was something that I didn't understand yet. "Your Honor said the first sky is made of copper, which is as thick as a foot trip of five hundred years. All right, for now let's just discuss this first sky and put the second, third, and fourth ones off to the side for a moment. What I don't understand is how can copper as thick as all that be penetrated by the sunlight, whereas the sunlight doesn't shine through roof tiles of just one centimeter thickness?"

"Because God *intends* that the copper sky as thick as all that will be penetrated by the sunlight, while he does *not* intend the same for the roof tiles," answered my uncle.

"Oh, so the difference doesn't depend on the quality of the things at hand but rather upon the will of God? All right, then! Let me go on to ask, why does God's will differ in that he wants the sunlight to come through in one case but h² doesn't want the sunlight to come through in the other case, although the rays that pour out of the sun are exactly the same in both instances?"

"That is God's own will and we are not allowed to question it." (1974, 93–94)

The dialogue continues in this heated vein for several ripostes more. The uncle winds up by labeling Ridjal a lost cause.

If teachers, elders, and older relatives have a false view of the world and stubbornly refuse, further, to relinquish it in the face of rational arguments, boys like Ridjal must learn to keep their own counsel. They become hidden critics of the religious status quo; they find they must go through life second-guessing everyday events and objects and their popular interpretations. And they must hide their stance from their fellow villagers—or leave their rural homes.

Finally, religion comes down to a matter of language, custom, and interpretation for the boys of each autobiography. Radjab offers the fullest treatment of this theme. When Ridjal and his surau-mates were about eleven or twelve years old, they had begun to be sent out to little mountain villages, to provide suitably mysterious chants for the funerals or death watches of local families. These bereaved people feel that the young recitalists' chants will ease the passage of their loved ones on to the next world. Radjab's description of one such scene (a horrific one for the boys) strikes all the main notes in his general understanding of Islam as a matter of socially created speech acts and strange customs, which first the young boy and then the adult author observe and record for their own ethnographic contemplation and for a wider, critical public reading audience. Village Islam emerges as a realm of magic and fearful acts: the boys witness old women moaning out scary laments for the dead; the boys' own Islamic chants, droned in the presence of an invalid, succeed largely in scaring the entire company; the time of death opens up a ghostly passageway to the other world. The latter awful vision has more immediacy for Ridjal than do his formal Koranic lessons:

> (At that time, old folks said, a person who was about to die would see the Angel of Death descending the stairs that extended from the doorway of the sky to the soles of the feet of the person who was going to die.) I trembled even more. In a few minutes more would the Angel of Death stand in the midst of this gathering of Koranic reciters and pluck away the soul of the person who was going to die? Would I get touched on the shirt by the Angel of Death, who'd be standing just three meters from me? Or might he look toward *me* after pulling out the soul of the sick person? Oh, maybe he's already standing right in front of me and he's just invisible! (1974, 99–100)

Organized religion and such ritualized times as the Fasting Month do have one supremely important part to play in the growing boys' conceptual lives. Islam and its calendrical rituals pull the youngsters out of their everyday states of existence and give them the opportunity to dream of a future quite different from the present. In this way, paradoxically, Minangkabau Islam ("old-fashioned" as it is) has a transformative effect on Ridjal and his friends: the religion leads them to imagine a less restrictive life. In a crucially important passage in chapter 18, "The Fasting Month," Ridjal laments the leaden atmosphere Islam fostered in terms of the youths' sexual longings. The Fasting Month fostered a great deal of daydreaming about sex and girls, but left the boys with no acceptable way to pursue their sensual desires, in real life. Surely there must be a better way to organize social life, Ridjal cries:

> We young fellows—who had gotten such a strict education based on purity of body and moral decency, who were shackled by adat and religion, who were not ever given an opportunity by society to lighten the natural urges coming from inside us by having an appropriate romantic life—we would become extremely confused when we were beset by such romantic daydreams. We hadn't conjured them up on purpose; they were just gifts from the natural world and our physical existence. During the fast our appetite for food was indeed reined in. However, in reaction to that, romantic daydreams and youthful desires ran wild, unrestrainable. Oftentimes we felt as if we were deep inside a cave that had no hole from which we might climb back out. I asked myself, wasn't there a way or a mode of life in this land which would be in closer accord with human character? So that perhaps these natural desires that were so much in motion inside us wouldn't be suppressed forever—something that could ruin our entire souls?
>
> This question was still blurred in my mind and its answer was darker and more obscure still (Radjab 1974, 144).

It would take his entire journey to maturity for Ridjal to fully formulate this question. Its answer, he found, lay in imagining a future time and place outside the past, and outside Minangkabau.

IMAGES OF TIME AND HISTORICAL NARRATION

Both Pospos and Radjab offer beguiling fictive worlds for their protagonist younger selves to inhabit and comment upon. The remembered boys grow older within rich social worlds that are peopled by casts of characters which could only have been assembled in twentieth-century Sumatra. An earlier time, readers are led to believe, would have yielded only Toba traditionalist villagers, or Minangkabau Muslim devouts, or merchant families, or adat aristocrats (the latter, according to the several eras of past Minangkabau time, Radjab tells his readers about late in his book). The present day of the remembered boyhood selves offers readers a more complex social world: one with all these old factions still amply represented, but now with the addition of school-trained children like the narrators' own younger selves. These 1920s and 1930s social landscapes also have Dutch school principals, soldiers, road inspectors, and hospital personnel. Newspapers and books provide the characters with windows on other social vistas (Java, Aceh, Batavia, Holland itself). The boys experience all these different facets of their Sumatran worlds and provide the reader with a point of integrated perspective for viewing the entire scene. The boys look back toward an outmoded, somewhat benighted past; they live in a socially insecure, morally misguided, emotionally painful present; they look forward to adult lives in a more sophisticated, literate, happy, cosmopolitan future. That future time exists in their future careers (they hope), and in the geographical precincts outside their home ethnic rural regions. In other words, the future is an imagined Indonesia of personal, intellectual, and moral liberation, and an Indonesia where narrow ethnic prejudices and religious biases have been left behind. Clearly, though, the narrators are not certain that such an Indonesia can ever exist for the full population of rural characters they met as children. Readers are left to worry about incomplete journeys of maturation for the persons they have encountered in the memoirs. And after all is said and done, the protagonists of both autobiographies are left suspended in transit toward their new adult worlds in the rantau at the end of each book. Will such an *Indonesian* future actually come about? No one knows.

A number of implied messages about time, history, and the best ways to narrate the past are embedded in these texts. Timescapes inevitably evoke certain social landscapes as well in these books, so I shall discuss time and space together.

Time in both narratives inches forward at a desultory but inexorable pace, as the boys grow from very young childhood into late adolescence. Neither text allows for any possibility of backward movement through time; the notion that moments in the present might make temporary contact with past times is also disallowed by the logic of the text. The boys grow older according to school times: they are elementary school age, then middle school age, and so on. The narrators' own vantage points as adult writers looking back on earlier childhood days in rural Toba and Minang-kabau provide the logical coherence for the texts, in terms of a time sense and a moral, evaluative gyroscope.

Both authors confidently assume that it is entirely appropriate to be writing a personal memoir, although neither man is a prominent public figure. In this way, writing a personal past is also validated. Such minor lives, though, are clearly meant to capture certain typical, common experi-ences of late colonial Tapanuli and Minangkabau life (oppressive school days; youthful experiences with reading the Balai Pustaka novels; the ex-perience of discovering how different village factions deal with Indies modernity). As the narrators relate these common experiences to their readers, however, they are decidedly not asserting that their remembered selves are maturing according to some preset, ancient pattern fated from before. These boys are living minutely individualized lives whose defining leitmotif is social change and popular social discomfort in villages and ru-ral towns because of the rapid pace of that change.

The boys exist in "real time," though they are aware of mythical eras that village people say predated them by many centuries. These eras, they find, can be learned about today through legends (*dongeng*). The two au-thors also aver that it is possible to record historically real eras, such as the Padri era, which Radjab discusses at length in his final chapter. Such his-torical material should be set down for a public audience with factual ac-curacy; details should be organized into broad sociological themes. In reporting such large trends, writers should be clear-sighted, skeptical, criti-cal, and rather pessimistic in tone. Just as turning the clock back for per-sonal convenience is wrong (Radjab's Ridjal does this one time, in order to get to the market early), writing factually or thematically inaccurate his-tory would be self-indulgent.

An important aspect of this historiographic stance is each author's care-ful avoidance of anachronistic uses of the word "Indonesia" (Radjab em-ploys the term sparingly in chapter 13, but neither book tries to convince readers that the memoir's young protagonists think of themselves as living "in Indonesia" rather than in an ethnic enclave, in their childhood years). The remembered children are decidedly not portrayed as persons who think of themselves as Indonesian. They are colonial-era Toba Batak or Minangkabau. In this way each writer avoids a nationalistic, propagandis-tic approach to remembering the prewar decades.

Finally, as each boy grows older he becomes better able to critically eval-uate the plausibility of the many histories that surround him in the village. One of Pospos's narratives will illustrate how this pattern works. In all such instances, the child or the adult narrator emerges as the better historian than his elders. Here for example is Pospos commenting on Toba clan origin myths:

> Legend has it that the Batak people are the descendants of Si Raja Batak. He was born from his mother, Si Boru Deak Parujar, and was the child of gods. In fact, the child of the highest god, Debata Mula Jadi Nabolon, whose purpose was to create the world. Once the world was created, he lived in Sianjurmulamula. This village also became the residence of Si Raja Batak and was located near the slopes of Mount Pusukbuhit, which is said to be the land of origin of the Batak and Karo peoples. The legend also held that Si Raja Batak had two sons, and from them sprang the Sumba *marga* [clan] and the Lontung *marga*. These two marga groups later broke apart to become other margas, and even today new margas are still being formed. (1950, 29)

Such passages obviously relativize the validity of the old legends in light of the presumed less naive historical consciousness of the writer. Pospos forces his readers to look at the old Toba origin myths *as stories,* as narratives that past ages of villagers may have believed but ones which we moderns can appreciate as mere legends.

What of the future, and the new society each young protagonist hopes to find there? Both of the memoirists' moral histories of the self imply at least the possibility of a liberated time and place free of Dutch control and unfettered by the shortsightedness and superstition of "old Toba" and "old Minangkabau." We can turn to this critical and painful but fundamentally optimistic kind of history writing next. We can also consider several promising possibilities for future research on Indonesian autobiography.

SUMATRAN CHILDHOOD
AUTOBIOGRAPHY AS HISTORY

Each memoir has a strong "forward-lookingness" to it (to use Wolters's term again) in the way it urges the reader to imagine a society and time free from the conceptual and social restraints that hobble the remembered child protagonists. This will be an Indonesia liberated from Dutch colonial control, but more than that, it will be an Indonesian time and place unfettered by the stultifying aspects of a Toba and Minangkabau village past. Rote ritualism will have been replaced by critical theological inquiry; book learning and substantive intellectual debate will have taken over from adat traditionalism; individuals will have gained the ability to distance themselves from the sort of fierce internecine competition found in rural villages and the colonial-era school system. But neither memoir is utopian in tone: each writer knows the journey toward such an Indonesia will be an uncertain, unpredictable one. Radjab drove home this message with particular force in his collection of Revolutionary era observations from his Ministry of Information–sponsored trip through Sumatra, published in his 1949 book *Tjatatan di Sumatra* (*Notes on Sumatra*). This informally written series of newspaperman's jottings about social conditions in Deli, Tapanuli, and Minangkabau during the 1945–49 period is intensely critical of the chaotic social conditions of the time. The author also wonders at frequent junctures in his journal whether the Indonesian populace can ever possibly overcome their local rivalries to any significant degree and join together as a single, national people. Radjab condemns what he sees as "backward thinking" on the part of Sumatran villagers throughout his trip; he leaves his reader to worry that the weight of the past may well be too heavy to make a modern Indonesia a viable possibility.

In their simultaneous "forward-lookingness" and their critical and literate vision of the village past, these two autobiographies are linked to several other publications that appeared in the same period, during the late Revolution years and the early years of Indonesian independence. Remarkably similar in tone and outlook to our two memoirs are Hamka's *Kenang-Kenangan Hidup* (1951–52), the novelist and editor Nur Sutan Iskandar's *Pengalaman Masa Kecil* (1948), and, as noted, even Pramoedya Ananta Toer's *Tjerita dari Blora* (Stories from Blora, 1952). The latter is not formally a childhood memoir but has clear autobiographical roots. It is not my intention here to provide any detailed analysis of these texts but rather to point out how similar they are to the Pospos and Radjab texts.

Volume 1 of Hamka's *Kenang-Kenangan Hidup* and the entirety of Nur Sutan Iskandar's *Pengalaman Masa Kecil* offer portraits of Minangkabau boyhood worlds structured largely around each author's educational experiences at different levels of schooling. Both volumes of reminiscences are episodic and anecdotal (proceeding via detailed descriptions of telling scenes and poignant, remembered childhood events, which often focus on Minangkabau Muslim ritual practice). Hamka's book is set in the years between his birth in 1908 and his marriage in 1929 after a 1926 pilgrimage to Mecca. Nur Sutan Iskandar's childhood memoirs refer to a somewhat earlier period, as he was born in 1893. Both books portray these times, in general, as eras of Minangkabau traditionalism, which the remembered child "grows out of" (Hamka toward a more universalistic form of scholarly Islamic consciousness, Nur Sutan Iskandar toward life as a novelist and editor in the rantau). Both books, further, have a clear "stock-taking" tone to them, as their authors look back to colonial-era childhoods from the vantage point of Revolutionary-era Indonesia. Both writers see themselves as teachers and public intellectuals; both implicitly advocate a sharing of maturation experiences across Indonesian ethnic minority borders, via Indonesian-language prose stories grounded in specific ethnic, regional contexts.

Nur Sutan Iskandar's book has a somewhat didactic flavor that sometimes turns preachy. More mannered and much more obviously bookish and structured than Radjab's memoir (in fact, Nur Sutan Iskandar's autobiography turns precious and overwritten in spots), *Pengalaman Masa Kecil* includes many of the same sorts of incidents as the ones Radjab used to tell his life story. Readers learn, for instance, of schoolroom incidents, children's games, experiences in the surau, village adat festivals, and village magical beliefs that the growing child comes to distrust. The author seems to have based some of his narrative on Dutch pedagogical texts, which may help explain some of the book's fusty tone.[8] Even with this European base to some of its passages, though, the memoir has many similarities to the Radjab and Pospos works.

Pramoedya's masterful *Stories from Blora* include what are clearly the finest literary evocations of childhood village worlds during late colonial times, the Japanese occupation, and the Revolution. A full-scale comparison of Pramoedya's short stories with the Sumatran childhood autobiographies would be very rewarding though beyond this essay's scope, so let me simply point to several parallels in the texts. In his stories concerning young children, Pramoedya often portrays the protagonist's mother, father, or other older relatives as distant, unknowable, unpredictable, inconstant, and emotionally restrained. The remembered child often looks out on his changing social world with befuddlement mixed with fear; repeatedly, new regimes sweep across the social scene outside the child's control. Issues of language, surface sound, and semantic meaning also of course figure heavily in Pramoedya's stories, as do recollections of Muslim rituals such as a boy's circumcision. The two Sumatran memoirs' preoccupation with school systems is certainly not found to such an extent in *Stories from Blora,* but on most other important counts Pramoedya's fictionalized childhood landscapes closely resemble the terrain in the Radjab and Pospos works.

Toba culture and worldviews and those of Minangkabau are normally thought to be quite dissimilar, but our two childhood autobiographies show many thematic and rhetorical concordances. And these similarities extend beyond these two books to link this pair of memoirs to the larger range of Indonesian literature, just mentioned, dealing with the late colonial-era social change issues. Why are there such pervasive similarities across this broad range of autobiographical literature? Answering that question is beyond the scope of this essay, but a partial answer, at least, can be framed by going beyond literary scholarship to draw on an insightful essay by anthropologist Robert McKinley called "Zaman dan Masa, Eras and Periods: Religious Evolution and the Permanence of Epistemological Ages in Malay Culture" (1979). In his fieldwork in Malaysia, McKinley found that biographical memory and historical narration coalesced for many of the individuals to whom he talked.

McKinley sees Malaysians' talk about and written invocations of ages or periods (*Masa*) and eras (his translation of *Zaman*) to be centrally important ways of indexing much larger ways of knowing the world in that society. That is, Malay historical ideology (as basic worldview and as social vision) is given immediacy and concreteness for individuals by being condensed into coded form in such phrases as "the period of the white people," or "the period of the Japanese" (1979, 309). An individual sees himself or herself in biographical relation to these more general periods of time, and their underlying epistemologies. In other words, in Malay thought, biography and history necessarily intersect. Additionally, older adults see themselves as resilient survivors of the various periods of time that have intersected their lives. But as McKinley points out in an important aside, these "past" periods remain accessible to the individual.

McKinley recalls a recurrent incident from his fieldwork that illustrated this mode of historical recollection:

> During fieldwork in Kampong Baharu, I often received a very standardized response to my routine questions about people's ages and about the lengths of time they had lived in various places. People in the age brackets above forty-five years would give a brief recitation of the major political events which had touched their lives. They would make a counting gesture by placing the thumb of the right hand against the little finger and then begin counting off by moving the thumb against each other finger in succession. The enumeration always stopped at the index finger, as only four times or events were named. A strict counting cadence was maintained as the verbal accompaniment to this gesture. The four period names went as follows:

> 1. masa orang puteh   "period of the white people" (before 1941)
> 2. masa Jepang   "period of the Japanese" (1941–45)
> 3. merdeka   "independence" (1957)
> 4. tigabelas Mei   "May thirteenth" (1969) (This was the date of a serious outbreak of violence between Malays and Chinese.)

> This gesture, in fact, is a slight modification of the standard Malay counting gesture. Usually the sequence "one to five" goes from the thumb to the little finger and not from the little finger to the thumb. Apparently this reversal is regarded as kinesthetically more appropriate to chronological reckoning. Accordingly, the time most distant from the present is given to the finger most distant from the thumb. Each step marked in time comes closer to the thumb. The thumb itself, which could conceivably represent a fifth period, or the present, is kept busy doing the actual counting. In a teleological sense, it supplies the movement toward itself. If the thumb in this gesture does represent the present, then I might suggest, in keeping with the main argument offered here, that it is a very nimble present. Like Malay attitudes towards past ages, it can move quickly to recontact its past. (1979, 309)

McKinley asserts that this assumption, that past ages can be invoked by speakers and writers in the present, is also a guiding idea in Malaysian thought about past "religious eras," such as "the Hindu era," or "the Islamic era," or "the early era" of spirit worship before the world religions arrived. Contemporary Malaysians (who exist very much in the Islamic era) may still access past religious eras by appropriate ritual gestures or terminological references. These older eras then break into the present momentarily, carrying along with them temporary access to their epistemological assumptions. For instance, a self-consciously modern Muslim Malay may visit a folk healer for a family medical emergency and pay the specialist to say certain mantras and manipulate appropriate ceremonial offerings. During the short course of the healing ritual, the time before Islam (when spirit worship reigned) opens up momentarily into the present. In this way all past ages are continually accessible to the present, and the richness of historical thought that this assumption fosters enlivens any talk or writing about religion.

It seems to me that *Me and Toba, Village Childhood,* and the larger circle of childhood memoirs surrounding them participate in these regional patterns of telling history while telling lives, while recounting the passage of individuals through their youthful social and religious worlds. The childhood memoirs extend the core assumption about memory which McKinley identifies in relation to religion into popular literature, which in Indonesia (when such literature is written in the national language) is accessible across ethnic boundaries. There is also an additional important feature of these texts' historiographic weightiness, so to speak. This is a feature linked to the fact that they are accounts of *childhood.*

In many Indonesian ethnic societies and in the national culture, the passage to adulthood obviously has several layers of meaning. The time of growing up marks an individual's transformation into full personhood, for infants are not yet full human beings. The passage through childhood also brings the individual into full awareness of his or her membership in the local ethnic society. That is, in growing up, a boy or girl "becomes a Toba Batak" or a Javanese or whatever the case may be. The child achieves this new "more complete" social identity primarily by learning to conform to the local adat practices and by learning to speak the local ethnic language with style and precision. As the growing child becomes more adept at using local kinship terms of address in appropriate ways, for instance, he or she is "becoming Javanese" or Toba Batak or whatever in a deep psychic and social sense.

A final layer of meaning commonly associated with Indonesian childhood has to do with the boy or girl's acquisition of a sense of self as an *Indonesian,* beyond his or her identity as a Javanese, Toba Batak, or Minangkabau. Historian William Frederick provides an excellent example of this crucial linkage in his English translation of the boyhood memoirs of Dr. Roeslan Abdoelgani, Indonesia's former minister of information and minister of foreign affairs (1974).

In an early portion of the autobiography (a work in progress in 1974), Abdoelgani recalled his very early years as a boy in Plampitan, a *kampung* (neighborhood, on the model of a village) in the east Javanese city of Surabaya. Abdoelgani recalled his circumscribed world of Javanese family talk and family relationships surrounding him as a child, in about the year 1918:

> All through my childhood, and even later, when as an adult I held various positions in the government, Mother reminded me of three duties: when you meet someone or come to a crossroads, don't forget to say "Peace be with you" (Assalam alaikum), even if you just murmur it to yourself; don't look up to the powerful and rich without at the same time looking down at the ordinary folk (rakyat) and considering their needs; and always remember God. Once I asked my mother where God was. She smiled at me and whispered, "In your heart! That is why you must never forget Him."
>
> Mother also asked that, after we were grown up and independent, we children remember to be *sing Jowo*, which translates roughly as "Javanese in thought" or simply "truly Javanese." By giving us a number of examples, Mother made clear that "sing Jowo" meant being polite, friendly and open toward others, cooperative, helpful, and so forth. All this was especially important when it came to the relationship between children and their parents, and in this regard "sing Jowo" also meant to be helpful to parents, to support them when they were no longer able to do so themselves, and give them tender loving care. I often heard my mother discussing with some of her friends the sad stories of certain children they knew who, although they had risen in society and were doing well, paid no attention to their parents. They were called *ndak Jowo*, which literally meant "not Javanese." (The same term was also used by kampung people in a somewhat different sense, meaning "crazy" [*gila*] or "cracked" [*sinting*].)
>
> It may be a little confusing to someone who didn't grow up with it, but I should explain that similar words were used to describe something rather different. Small children who weren't yet old enough to understand the danger of fire, sharp knives, broken glass, and the like, were considered *durung Jowo*, literally "not yet Javanese." Children who were a bit older but were still ill-behaved, who picked on their brothers and sisters for example, were also said to be "durung Jowo." On the other hand, the child who got along well with his family, did good deeds for his grandparents, and helped his mother, was described as being *wis Jowo*, which means that he understood how to behave properly as a member of a Javanese family. (Frederick 1974, 119)

As Abdoelgani got a bit older, he recalled, he began to discover social worlds beyond his Javanese neighborhood: other ethnic societies in the archipelago, and an indigenous pan-Indies community united through their common oppression by the Dutch. In other words, he began to discover himself as an Indonesian. Where his mother had thought of some eventual resistance effort against the Dutch in terms of near-mythic Javanese cycles of cataclysms (in which a revolution of eras would inevitably bring about the European occupiers' downfall), Abdoelgani himself came to hope and plan for an Indonesian revolution that would take place very much on the human social plane, as the outcome of concrete resistance activities.

This same idea that colonial-era children are most accurately remembered as individuals who are "growing toward Indonesia" also animates the Sumatran boyhood memoirs, Pramoedya's work, and the childhood recollections of important nationalists and writers such as Dr. Soetomo and Hamka. Within this very large context the genius of Pospos's and Radjab's books lies in their successful use of an unpretentious popular literature form focused on two "minor Sumatran boyhoods" to convey these profound themes about the invention of a revolutionary consciousness and the invention of Indonesia itself. Both memoirs imply that growing toward Indonesia is at least possible for any serious-minded and contemplative young person, living anywhere in the archipelago. Again, though, the journey is not a guaranteed success, by any means.

Seen as texts that say something about Indonesian historical memory as well as about their protagonists' own experiences, *Me and Toba* and *Village Childhood* suggest several new topics for research in Indonesian literature by anthropologists, historians, and literature scholars. For instance, do writers in other ethnic societies elsewhere in the archipelago publish childhood memoirs about youthful years spent in the 1920s and 1930s? One other Outer Island childhood autobiography that I know of (Minggus Manafe's *Aneka Kehidupan di Pulau Roti*) was published in 1967 and does not exhibit the strong evocations of journeys from a colonial past to a new society that are seen in our two memoirs. Manafe's small, effective book recounts the author's childhood in the eastern Indonesian island of Roti, and focuses primarily on the transition from animism to Christianity, as the remembered child observed religious life and religious change around him in his own family and village. Manafe's book is somewhat pedantic in tone, especially when he is describing "Rotinese traditional customs." These are sometimes presented to readers in a schoolbookish way, from the adult writer's perspective.

The Manafe book may well be an isolated case. However, after other watershed dates in Indonesian history besides the Revolution (for instance, the social unrest of 1965 that ushered in the Soeharto regime) did certain forms of autobiographical writing become unusually popular? If so, were they used to make sense of the transition from Sukarno times to the New Order period under President Soeharto? Another important question is how childhood reminiscences might relate to the more obvious genres of historical writing, in different political circumstances of the nation's history. Do childhood memoirs of the unusually perspicacious sort examined here tend to occur only in societies, like these two in Sumatra, which have traditions of ethnographic writing about their own "village ways"?

The examination of ideas about gender in relation to historical writing in an autobiographical key could also be illuminating. Several of Indonesia's most powerful literary evocations of passages to adulthood are by women: the Javanese noblewoman Raden Adjeng Kartini's letter chronicle (*Letters of a Javanese Princess*) written to a Dutch friend, on growing up in colonial times, and the Sundanese novelist Soewarsih Djojopoespito's Dutch-language, autobiography-like novel *Buiten Het Gareel.* How do Indonesian women's personal memories relate to nationalist discourse? Is the linkage between autobiographical memory and public historical memory different for Indonesian women writers than it is for men writers? How is historical prose refracted differently by women in contrast to male writers like Pospos and Radjab? These topics remain opaque and unexplored, although Mary Steedley's recent work (1993) on Karo women's oral life-history narratives certainly points to significant gender-based differences in personal memory. Steedley finds that various marginalized Karo individuals (for instance, women who work as ritual healers, invoking ancestor spirits in a rather hostile age of monotheistic belief) tell personal life-history narratives of great aesthetic power and political insight. Their current-day political standing as outsiders in an outlying ethnic minority society far from Jakarta shapes their memories of past ages of personal time and Indonesian historical experience. Might the spoken recollections of other Batak and Minangkabau individuals today demonstrate some of the same themes and social and linguistic critiques found in the two published memoirs explored here? I would suspect that thematic concordances would be there, but unless such oral history research is done very soon, this older generation of Indonesians will pass away without telling their histories to wide audiences.

A NOTE ON TRANSLATION

Both of the childhood memoirs translated here were written in unpretentious, clean-lined but mellifluous Indonesian. This is a style that I have tried to maintain here in my English versions of these modestly phrased but deeply evocative recollections of colonial Sumatran childhood days. Both P. Pospos and Muhamad Radjab are expert and unaffected writers and their Indonesian prose is pleasurable to read for speakers of bahasa Indonesia. Reading through their sentences and paragraphs, Indonesian speakers get a sense of reading *good* Indonesian. In the southern Batak areas where I do most of my fieldwork, this appreciation of the national language means that its "proper" form is largely "unadulterated" by city slang, that its word structure evokes some of the playful alliteration of spoken Indonesian, and that its vocabulary is extensive and poetic. Sumatrans in Toba, the southern Batak regions, and Minangkabau often say that they speak "the best Indonesian" in the country. Some of this pride in firmly controlling the national language is implicit in both childhood autobiographies. Pospos and Radjab were perhaps concerned to help establish a robust national language literature published in the early 1950s that would go beyond the somewhat more flowery types of Indonesian literature written in the 1920s and 1930s under earlier Balai Pustaka auspices, when the publishing house was still under colonial control.

However, despite casting their lot with unadorned and relatively "high form" Sumatran Indonesian, neither author is at all averse to having his child characters use comfortable, conversational phrases or exclamations of surprise, nor does either writer hesitate to mix Dutch or Arabic words, or Toba Batak or Minangkabau words, into his sentences. Sumatran speech often has this harlequin linguistic character to it. Both Pospos and Radjab, however, generally take pains to alert their readers whenever ethnic language phrases are used in their Indonesian sentences. For instance, Pospos has his Toba words printed in boldface type, and often follows such passages with an Indonesian translation for those of his readers who may not be Batak. He leaves many of his Dutch terms untranslated (for instance, the names of colonial-era schools). Radjab tends to do the same thing for the many Arabic words connected to the Muslim prayer conventions or ritual practices that figure so importantly in *Village Childhood.*

To help my English-language readers navigate some of these Sumatran linguistic shoals, I have used the following strategy. Whenever the memoirist himself explains a word or a phrase with the aid of a passage in parentheses, I have retained that format in my own English sentence. When Pospos or Radjab does not explain something that I feel my readers may need immediate help with, I provide a brief definition or explanation right in the sentence at issue, in brackets. Each author very occasionally uses an asterisk and an accompanying footnote on the same page. Whenever that format occurs in my translation I am following the author's original text. As a translator I prefer to work as much of the meaning of an Indonesian word or phrase into my English sentence as possible, but occasionally that approach proves unwieldy, or I feel that a reader might like to know more about a puzzling passage. In those cases, I have written endnotes for many chapters, flagged by superscript numbers in the text. I hope that this has not given these childhood autobiographies too much of a scholarly appearance, for in their original form these memoirs were clearly meant as books of popular, leisure-time literature.

As a translator, I have also tended to aim for a popular literature pace and stylistic flair here in working with these particular two books, over a strict adherence to the original Indonesian-language sentence structure. Concerned to have the quality of my English prose represent the emotional tone of the original texts to the greatest extent possible, I have avoided a translation strategy which would slavishly follow the word order of each Indonesian sentence. I wanted my translation to have a sense of "good English" that would do justice to the memoirists' evident loyalty to "good Indonesian," as they imagined that language to be when they wrote their books. So, for instance, I have avoided using passive verb constructions to quite the extent that the writers themselves do. What I have generally done is to make sure that some of the original syntactic structure of Indonesian shows through my English wording but not to the extent that this would prove off-putting to my readers. Occasionally I have rearranged paragraph breaks, particularly in Radjab's memoir, since his tendency to use very short paragraphs in some sections of his book looked distinctly odd to me as an English reader. I have kept such changes to a minimum; the most typical change in paragraph structure decision I have made has been where Radjab places each new bit of quoted dialogue in a new paragraph. Somewhat more frequently I have deviated a bit from the author's original sentence structure, to combine two sentences into one or to insert a dash followed by a phrase. Once again, I was aiming for English readability and fidelity to the overall aesthetic of the Indonesian text.

Decisions on verb tense are always a challenge for European-language translators who work with Indonesian texts, as that language has no obligatory marking of tense in some instances and much time-orientation interpretation is left to contextual clues in Indonesian sentences. Since each of these memoirs was clearly written in a secular mode as opposed to some sort of "timeless, mythic" sort of Indonesian, I have made rather elaborate use of English verb tense structure here, by incorporating the contextual clues of the original text's sentences into my decisions about English verb tense. I have followed the same strategy in writing my way along other fissures of Indonesian-to-English linguistic difference. Indonesian does not have an obligatory way to mark plural versus singular nouns, for instance. In Indonesian it is possible to mark the plural by saying a noun twice, but usually contextual information suffices to make matters clear. I obviously had to mark the plural in English. Indonesian also uses one form, unspecified for gender, for the third-person-singular pronoun. Where I could determine from context that one of the authors meant to refer to a boy or man when he uses this pronoun, I have simply written *he* in my English version. The currently popular "he or she" convention familiar from American academic usage seemed to me to miss the mark in many of these cases.

Sumatran authors writing about colonial times often pepper their prose with references to denominations of Dutch colonial-era money, such as guilders, benggols, cents, and rupiah. I have retained those original words here, along with the authors' ways of writing numbers, usually in the form of numerals (for instance, "Rp. 2 a month," from Pospos's book, although in this case I have switched his original "R.2" to "Rp. 2" for the sake of intelligibility). Pospos is fond of using numerals throughout his text, in fact, and I have followed this usage, although standard English written style would demand that small numbers be written in the form of words. Throughout the translation, if any usage of this sort looks awkward to an English-language reader, a conscious translation decision always underlies the passage.

As to spelling, I have used the old, circa 1950 spelling conventions for personal names and place names but have switched all other Indonesian words over to the new spelling employed in all Indonesian texts today. In the new spelling system the old *dj* becomes *j*, the old *j* becomes *y*, and the old *tj* comes *c*. Keeping these few proper nouns in the old spelling system seems to me to help anchor my translation in its original time framework, and I hope that this does not overtax the patience of readers.

NOTES

Two Sumatran Childhood Memoirs

1. Two other anthropological explorations of the role of Indonesian or ethnic culture art forms in the imagination of a specifically national Indonesian modernity are James Peacock's *Rites of Modernization* (1968), on east Java's *ludruk* plays, and Karl Heider's *Indonesian Cinema* (1991), on popular films and nationalist sentiment. For case studies from a Batak society on popular fiction literature and visions of Indies modernity during colonial times, see my essays "A Batak Literature of Modernization" (1981) and "Imagining Tradition, Imagining Modernity: A Southern Batak Novel from the 1920s" (1991).

2. See, for instance, Rodgers 1979a, 1979b, 1981, 1983, 1984, 1986, 1990, and 1991 on Angkola Batak print literature of various sorts.

3. See for instance Siegel 1977 and Maier 1982 as examples of poststructuralist approaches to texts. Beyond this one viewpoint, the field of literary criticism on Indonesian literature is quite extensive. Of most immediate relevance to the appreciation of these two childhood memoirs are the following studies: Drewes 1951 (on childhood biography, in part), 1961, 1981; Foulcher 1977, 1980; Anderson 1979; Freidus 1977; Maier 1987, 1988; Rodgers 1991; Salmon 1981; Sutherland 1968; Reid 1972; Tickell 1987; and Watson 1972. Teeuw's *Modern Indonesian Literature*, vols. 1 and 2, provides a basic literary historical overview, while *Cultural Contact and Textual Interpretation* (ed. C. D. Grijns and S. O. Robson) is a valuable anthology of essays on a range of Malay world literature. See especially Teeuw's essay in that collection (1986), "Translation, Transformation, and Indonesian Literary History," on the need for more theoretically grounded studies in the field. On the study of Indonesian ethnic language literatures, see especially Quinn 1983 (a particularly valuable essay since its author asks why thriving ethnic language literatures are so often invisible in the scholarly study of Malay world literatures).

4. On the rise of nationalism in Minangkabau, see Audrey Kahin's (1979) "Struggle for Independence: West Sumatra in the Indonesian National Revolution, 1945–1950."

5. A basic bibliography on the Batak peoples can be found in Siagian 1966, while especially good anthropological monographs and shorter articles on Toba include D. George Sherman's *Rice, Rupees, and Ritual: Economy and Society among the Samosir Batak of Sumatra* (1990) and his 1987 article, "Men Who Are Called 'Women' in Toba-Batak: Marriage, Fundamental Sex-Role Differences, and the Suitability of the Gloss 'Wife-Receivers'." See also J. C. Vergouwen's classic *Social Organization and Customary Law of the Toba-Batak of North Sumatra*, a 1933 adat law inquiry that includes much ethnographic observation. Rita and Richard Kipp's 1983 anthology *Beyond Samosir: Recent Studies of the Batak Peoples of Sumatra* also includes solid ethnographic essays on Batak kinship, political thought, and experiences with social change. Sandra A. Niessen's *Batak Cloth and Clothing: A Dynamic Indonesian Tradition* (1993) deals adeptly with social change and art issues. On the nearby society of Karo, see Rita S. Kipp's *The Early Years of a Dutch Colonial Mission: The Karo Field* (1990) and Masri Singarimbun's *Kinship, Descent, and Alliance among the Karo Batak* (1975).

On Minangkabau history and culture, see Joel Kahn's *Constituting the Minangkabau* (1992), which is particularly strong in placing the development of notions of "Minangkabau culture" in a Dutch colonial context, as well as Kahn's 1980 *Minangkabau Social Formations,* F. von Benda-Beckmann's 1979 *Property in Social Continuity,* Elizabeth Graves's 1981 *The Minangkabau Response to Dutch Colonial Rule in the Nineteenth Century,* P. E. de Josselin de Jong's 1951 *Minangkabau and Negeri Sembilan,* and Tsuyoshi Kato's 1982 *Matriliny and Migration.* Lynn Thomas and Franz von Benda-Beckmann's extensive anthology *Change and Continuity in Minangkabau* has a comprehensive bibliography on Western languages scholarship on West Sumatra. Karl Heider's *Landscapes of Emotion* (1991) explores the emotional world of Minangkabau, with an emphasis on children.

6. In an August 22, 1987, letter to me, Pospos wrote that he published his memoir in important part to show how young children's education can go awry and harm the youngsters emotionally. Both elementary school teachers and Batak parents were too cold and harsh with small children, he felt.

7. Beyond the basic Drewes (1951) article, insightful studies of Malay world autobiography include Sweeney and Phillips 1975; Sweeney 1980a, 1980b, 1990; see also Sweeney 1987. Also useful are Watson 1989 and Roff 1972.

8. Nur Sutan Iskandar's *Pengalaman Masa Kecil* draws heavily on a Dutch pedagogical study, Jan Ligthart's *Jeugdherinneringen* (1914, published by J. B. Wolters, Gröningen, The Netherlands). The similarities extend to specific incidents from the Dutch work which the Sumatran novelist has reincorporated into his childhood memoir.

PART TWO

The Translations

Me and Toba

P. Pospos

CHAPTER 1

Mornings are generally quite chilly in the Toba region, and this one was no exception. There was always someone burning refuse in the backyard for fertilizer, and we children, attracted by the warmth, often gathered around the fire. But on this particular morning I sat warming myself by our hearth, cooking. My little sister was still asleep, and Mother sat weaving a mat near the door, where there was more light. My father had gone out with our buffalo cart, which he hired out to carry other people's goods to market. He did this three times a week: Friday to the market in Balige, Saturday to the market in Sigumpar, and Wednesday to the market in Porsea. This was our livelihood, in addition to the rice we grew in the paddies.[1]

Our house was a *balebale*,* so we were obviously not rich.[2] It was all black inside from the smoke, and in a corner under the roof hung a basket—the kind used to carry things on one's shoulder—which had been saved as a souvenir by my father. From others I heard that when my father was young

---

*That is, no more than a hut on four poles. Its walls were made of beaten bamboo and its roof of paddy stalks (the floor was changed every year so it wouldn't get holes in it). The other sorts of houses were called *sopa* and *ruma,* which were much larger and more beautiful; they were the houses of rich people. The ruma, for instance, had eight pillars. Its walls were made of carved wooden planks and its roof was of black sugar palm fiber. These houses had a single room, in which people ate, slept, and received guests. The pillars were very tall, so that the space underneath the house could be used as a pen for livestock, which made it rather "fragrant."

There was also a new type of house, usually called an *emper* (veranda). Its structure resembled the sorts of houses we see in large numbers in the city today. In our country, this type of house often had a veranda; thus the name. [Author's note.]

he had *mangallung* (or carried things to sell at the market in Pematang Siantar) and he had hung it there as a reminder of his younger days.

My father was an elder in the church, something like an assistant Gospel teacher. This position was called *sintua* in our land, and because he held this position my father did not have to pay the corvée tax of fl. 6.60 a year.[3] Maybe this is why the title was much sought after. Anyway, my father had been sintua for so long that the title was considered part of his name; when people would call him they wouldn't just say his name but would use Sintua Ananias.

An odd custom in our region was that the given names of one's father, mother, maternal uncle, grandparents, and so on were taboo to children. Because we were forbidden to say them aloud, many of us were grown before we knew our parents' or grandparents' names. In fact, there were often fights about names, for example when a child dared to say the name of another child's father.

One time, a child was punched by another, and as revenge the child who had been hurt threatened to say the name of the other child's father. "I'm gonna . . . I'm gonna say your father's name!"[4] Finally he could not stand it any longer and cried out, "Betuel!" But what is so awful about that? Well, in fact, the name he shouted out was that of his own father rather than the other child's, so we all laughed at him. A fight could even occur if the one child said to another "Hey, I just said your father's name to myself!"

Anyway, on that particular day I was standing on the hearth in front of the fire when I heard a voice from the front yard below say, "Sintua, Sintua!" It was our guru, the village schoolteacher, the man who was also, every Sunday, our gospel teacher.

"He's gone, Guru. He just left," answered my mother from above.

When he heard that my father was not home, the teacher said, "In that case, *Inang* (Mother),[5] please tell *Sintua* that Djohanis (that was me) should be told to go to school, since he is six years old now."

"Fine, *Amang* (Father),[6]" said my mother, and the teacher went on home.

My thoughts were still directed at the pot boiling in front of me, so the significance of this conversation was not immediately clear. I was already used to cooking at home, even though I was only six. We village children were taught very early to help our parents in things like cooking, gathering firewood, fetching water, and so on.

Cooking was not difficult, for village people cooked in a very simple way. To cook rice, for instance, water was first heated in a pot. When it was hot, rice was added and left until the water came to a boil. Then the water was stirred with a spoon and the amount adjusted so that there was neither too much nor too little and the rice would be neither too soft nor too hard. Fish was usually just roasted over the fire. As for greens, cassava leaves were finely pounded and then placed in a skillet with heated water. Then they were seasoned with a bit of salt and left to simmer until done. It was indeed very useful for us children to know how to cook. Our parents were usually away from home and it was nighttime before they returned. My mother, for instance, went to market every day to sell *mobe,* a kind of fruit used to preserve fish. She would go as far as Porsea, Balige, and Sigumpar to sell the mobe, and on foot too, even though sometimes she made no more than twenty-five cents profit.[7]

I scooped out all but a little of the boiling water from the pot with a coconut shell spoon. Then I damped down the fire and lit one in another hearth to cook the greens. But my mother said: "Djohanis, you better bathe or at least wash your face at the well. Then put on your clean shirt. The teacher has come to say that you are old enough to go to school now, so you should get along. I'll cook those greens myself later."

I had wanted to go to school for a long time, since for us children going to school meant being "promoted." Now, we reasoned, we would be able to join in all the school talk instead of sitting around listening with our mouths hanging open while our friends told stories about school. We would often try to gauge our own ages, to see if we were old enough to go to school yet. Since we had no understanding whatsoever of days, months, or years, we had a general method of determining age. The usual method was to have a child stand up straight and put his hand up as straight and far as he could, then wrap it around his head to see whether he could touch his ear on the other side.[8] If he could, it meant he was old enough to go to school. I had just been tested this way a few days ago myself, but my fingertips had only just brushed the top of my ear.

As happy as I was at the thought of attending school, the news had come so suddenly that it startled me for a moment. But I soon ran off to wash at the well. After eating a little and changing my clothes, I left for school with some friends who were already quite accustomed to going. The schoolhouse was not far; indeed, the schoolyard was just behind our house. The end of our backyard was marked by a clump of bamboo, then there was a road, and then the schoolyard fence.

My heart went thumpity-thump at the thought of attending school, my fear mixed with joy. All this time I had heard my friends' stories about school, and I had often looked in from outside while the students were doing their lessons. But now I wanted to see the school from the inside. Might going to school bring happiness? The question filled my head as I awaited the great moment. The bell had already rung and the students had long since gone in to study, but we new pupils-to-be were only allowed to play in the yard. I waited and waited for us to be called inside too, to start school. But that day we did not attend school. We were only allowed to play in the schoolyard, and then when it was time for the regular pupils to go home, the head teacher told us to go home too. He said that we would start tomorrow. This disappointed me. All my hopes and dreams about school, and the joy I had felt when I left the house earlier in the morning, vanished entirely. I went home dejected.

I found this first experience bitter, and the next day I did not want to go to school any more. Over and over again my father ordered me to go, but I remained resistant. He threatened me with a beating if I did not go, but even that did not work. Then he slung me over his shoulder and carried me to school. I cried and struggled to free myself, but no matter what I did my father continued toward the schoolyard with me over his shoulder. There he put me down, moaning and groaning. Friends crowded around, watching the spectacle.

Imagine my embarrassment in front of my friends! If I had dared face up to my father then, surely I would have hit him. But how in the world could a child of six hope to fight a grown adult? After that I was no longer brave enough to play truant. I was afraid of my father and embarrassed in front of my friends. It could be said that I was among the most hardworking students after that.

CHAPTER 2

In our land, village primary school was usually called *sikola metmet* (metmet = little). This school was for three years and went on to *sikola panonga* (middle school), but the level of instruction was really about the same as that of a "Gouvernements Vervolgschool" [a government continuation school]. This also required three years of study. Then there was *sikola tinggi* (high school), also called *sikola guru* (teacher's school), for four years. The name of this school was "Zendings-Seminarie," and its level of instruction was the same as that of the government-run Institute for Village Schoolteachers (the O.V.V.O.). The Mission School actually took a little longer to complete because the teachers who graduated from it had to be trained for the additional task of being Bible teachers in the local churches.

We had two teachers in village school. One of them, the head teacher, was a graduate of the Sipoholon Seminary.[1] The other, his assistant, was a middle school graduate. This particular assistant teacher still sported a hole in his earlobe, like a woman. In our village there were still lots of men who wore gold earrings; that way, when there was an adat feast they could show that they came from a rich family.[2] The earrings were so heavy that most of the older people had big holes in their earlobes, big enough to stick an index finger through. To tell the truth, I hated the sight of my teacher's ear, with that hole in it. If he happened to be nearby I would stare at his ear, but when he looked at me I turned the other way.

This teacher with the hole in his ear taught us in second grade. Frankly, he was much smarter than the teacher who replaced him later on, but he certainly was not as smart as the head teacher. My estimation of him dropped considerably when I saw him and some other people plowing a rice paddy to prepare it for planting. In those days I considered teachers to be among society's elite, and expected that they would live like salaried workers.

The head teacher of the school was *streng*, or as Jakarta people would say, very "traditional" and a stickler for obeying the rules.[3] Sometimes we would be ordered to collect firewood for him. We were not allowed to stop until we had gathered a whole armful. Once he even ordered several of my friends to cart some of his pigs to market. They were paid only 2½ cents apiece, even though the market was a whole kilometer from our village and they had to wait almost half a day for the pigs to sell.

Every Monday when I was in the third grade, as a matter of course we would be asked who had not gone to church the day before (*Marminggu*,[4] as we called it). Anyone who had not gone would be given a punishment. I wasn't really antichurch, and from the time I was very small I normally attended whatever the case, but there was something about that punishment that brought out the stubbornness in me. Once I did not attend church for months, so each and every Monday I would be given a punishment equal to my sin—and it really was a sin, too, my teacher said—and I was called names like "Red Devil" or "Horned Devil" and so on. On Mondays whoever hadn't gone to church would be separated from the others and given various punishments: for example, our palms would be rapped hard three times with a cane. Because this did not seem to work, another punishment would be tried: we would be ordered to stand on one foot for half an hour. Whoever dared to put a leg down to rest would have it smacked three times.

I rose in status, what with my Red Devil nickname. People said that my friends just copied whatever I did. As the "leader," my portion of the punishment "gifts" was larger. I should be setting a good example for the other children, my teacher said. After all, wasn't I a church elder's son? One time my friends and I had to balance a school bench on our heads as punishment. This bench was long enough for six children to sit on, and four of us held it on our heads. When we got tired or our heads began to hurt, we were allowed to balance it on our shoulders. My shoulder was exhausted, my head ached, and my face got red, but I did not whine or complain. Stubbornly, even angrily, I would say to myself: I will not give in, I can take it!

Even though my teacher punished me severely, I was still his favorite in our daily lessons. Every week we would be asked to do sums and say our tables out loud (*Maretong di roha,* to count by heart). Whoever was the best would be allowed to sit way in back. I sat on the farthest bench.

One time I asked permission to be absent for several days (actually, with my Dad's help) because our whole household was going to visit my uncle in Sibolga. My father had sold his cart by this time and had gone in with someone to buy an automobile on installment. This was the car we took to Sibolga. We stayed about two weeks. When I returned to class and took the usual arithmetic test, my score dropped to an 8; the student who had been number two, a child who was always scheming to force me off my "throne," got a 9, and I was forced to surrender my championship to him. So I sat in the next-to-last row, because the last one was packed with kids who had scores of 9 and 8½. I pretended not to care, and sat in my place without protest, but inside I was burning with shame. I had wanted to hide all this, but the other children kept tormenting me with their victory and finally I could not stand it any longer. First one tear and then another fell from my eyes. A kid cried out to the teacher, "Djohanis is crying," intending to embarrass me further. But the teacher came up to us and said, "That's just a sign that Djohanis is a good child. By crying he shows that he is sad about the slip in his grades. Doubtless he will improve them by next week." The other kids just kept quiet.

My teacher was extremely frightened whenever the school inspector came, and for several days before the arrival of the "school police" he would show signs of anxiety and jumpiness. We would rehearse over and over again the way we were supposed to stand up and greet the inspector, sit in our seats, answer questions, and so on. The smartest children were instructed to stick their hands up high in the air when the school inspector asked a question. They were allowed to sit up front, while the dummies sat near the back. All of this was arranged beforehand. I was surprised. Why was our teacher so scared of this *schoolopziener?* But then aren't people everywhere always frightened of the police?

In addition to the school inspector, Tuan Preacher[5] (the German minister) would also pay us an occasional visit (these schools were run by the mission). Our teacher was not as afraid of the clergyman as he was of the school inspector or examiner. One time, after a class period, I deliberately hit a friend of mine in the presence of the visiting German minister. When he saw me do this he looked at me furiously and said—in Batak, of course, but with a German cadence—"Now, aren't you ashamed to do such a thing?" He told me to say I was sorry. My face reddened but I did it. My aim of making myself known to him had been achieved; earlier in class he had paid no attention to me even though I had raised my hand when he asked a question.

CHAPTER 3

We ate two meals a day, one in the early morning before I left for school, and the other in the evening at about six or seven o'clock. In between those times we children got hungry, of course. Sometimes there was left-over rice from the morning, and we ate that when we got out of school at one in the afternoon. But often there would not be any rice left over, so we were forced to search for edibles from the garden: various sorts of ripe mangoes, *kecapi*,[1] and *petai* beans[2] that could be put to use filling up a growling belly. We brought salt from home to put on the sour fruits. Often we were unable to find very many fruits, and children who were still hungry would ask for a few extras from their friends. We had a method for dealing with this: we spat on our fruit so that others would not want any. But some children ate them anyway. We never brought a knife (we were afraid it might get lost), so we took turns biting into ripe mangoes. We also had seed-swallowing competitions; whoever could swallow the big sour kecapi seed was the champion. It absolutely never occurred to us that we might get a bellyache. Grownups tried to frighten us by saying that the seeds would sprout in our bellies and come up through our chests and necks and out our mouths, but of course we paid no attention.

Because we ate so much fruit, sometimes we really did get bellyaches and that often meant loose bowels. Going to the bathroom in the village was difficult because there were no proper W.C.'s.[3] We were forced to look around for a somewhat secluded spot, but even then the dogs and pigs soon came snuffling around. You could only conclude your business by brandishing a cane in your hand. There was no water for washing up and paper was hard to come by, so we used castoff stuff or dry leaves and such to clean our behinds. Often we would rub ourselves against a big house-post, and the posts in the village got to looking sort of yellow. If two children were defecating near each other, they would have to throw something (a rock, a branch, a handful of sand) at each other and say, "On ma holang-holanghu tu ho" (Here's my distance from you). If you did not do this, it was said that the nipples on you mother's breasts would close up.

There was an H.I.S.[4] kid we played with. Every morning he took a horse and buggy to school, about seven kilometers from our village. We were a bit resentful and standoffish toward him, since we knew that they studied Dutch at his school. Sometimes we would ask him what this or that was in Dutch, but he always kept silent . . . I don't know why. He was only in the first grade, but one time he was feeling boastful and wanted to show us how good his Dutch was. He said, "In Dutch, our names change to something else." Immediately I thought of my own name and had to agree; my name at home was Djohanis but in school the teacher called me Yohannes.

When we asked him what his name was in Dutch he answered, "My name is Maningar, but in school I'm called Manginar." We just kept mum. Maybe what he said was true, we thought.[5]

When it came to games I was not entirely incompetent. For instance, when we played ball I was generally chosen to be goalie because I was the best at kicking and stopping balls. But I was skinny, so if I got bumped even slightly I tended to fall down. My mother always chided me for being so skinny. She would remark, "Indahan diallang ho, ranggas tem" ("You eat rice, but your stools are nothing but dry sticks," a saying directed at children who ate a lot but remained skinny). A soccer ball was expensive for us—a rubber ball cost at least fifteen cents—so usually we just used a big citrus fruit. Our feet got all red from kicking it.

Sometimes we played other games, such as the candlenut game. We would arrange a bunch of candlenuts in a circle on the ground. Then with another candlenut (called a *panuju,* a shooter) we would try to shoot nuts out of the circle. The nuts that went out we could take, while the nuts that stayed on the edge, or on the line, would have to be redeemed with a nut. If the shooter nut stayed inside the circle or landed on the line, it would have to be redeemed with two nuts. This game was called *marpinse* (pronounced "marpisse," that is, marbles). The shooter nut had to be heavy so that the candlenuts could be knocked out of the circle easily. It was also more fun to shoot if it was heavy. So the insides of the shooter nut would be emptied out through a little hole. It was hard to get the insides out, no matter how much you scraped it with a palm fiber. So instead, you found an anthill and placed the candlenut there with its hole pointed down so the ants would clean it out. They you filled the empty candlenut with little broken pieces of a ceramic cooking pot, and close the hole with tar, asphalt, or forest rubber. Another candlenut game was *markaulu.* Several candlenuts were placed in a row, and you tried to hit them one by one with your shooter. If the candlenut at the head of the line was hit, you had the right to take all the others behind it. Each time you hit a nut, you took the others behind it.

Often we sat on the ground playing *margaja.* The first game of this sort we learned was Hole Margaja (*margaja lombang*). A circle would be divided into four equal parts and a quarter of the arc would be rubbed out; this was the hole, the space in which no one was allowed to step. The game was played by two children. The playing pieces were bits of branches, stones, or really anything just so long as you could tell your friend's playing pieces from your own. The game was over when one player lost by having his pieces crowded along the edge of the hole, unable to move forward. There was also the game of *markansuhi.* In this one, a square would be divided into sixteen tiny squares. Each player had eight pieces, four on his left and four on his right, placed in the square located on the farthest edges. You moved your pieces from square to square, but if you were going to "eat" your friend's piece you had to step on it by moving alongside it or standing right next to it, and you could not jump over two pieces at once. You lost when all your pieces had been eaten by your opponent. There were lots of other *margaja* games such as Dutch Margaja, Tiger Margaja, and so on. So we really had no lack of games to play, waiting for mealtime.

When evening came we returned home to eat and often would not bathe beforehand. Sometimes I did not bathe for an entire week, but just washed my face in the morning before I went to school. My chest and neck would get all black from the sweat and dirt, but I still had no desire to bathe; my mother would sometimes drag me to the riverbank and give me a bath there, saying, "Anggo nisuan lasiak diandorami manigor do tubu" (Chili pepper seeds would sprout on your chest). That's how dirty I was. I also used to wipe my runny nose on my shirt-sleeve. The snot dried and my sleeve got all stiff, and my nose got red from all the wiping back and forth. As far as I was concerned, handkerchiefs simply did not exist, and even if I had carried one I probably would not have used it. Wasn't it easier just to use my hand?

We had only one water buffalo, which pulled my father's cart. When I was not collecting firewood for my mother I watched over the water buffalo. I was always happy caring for that animal because he always won when matched against another buffalo in a contest. His horns formed a circle with the arc open at the top, which meant he was called a *sitingko* in our language.[6] Sometimes when Dad was not looking, I paired the animal off against another water buffalo and hugged him happily if he won the contest. We also used our buffalo to pull a plow in the rice paddies. We really loved him. With me, he was always good. He let me sit on his back, or stand on his neck or on top of his head; he let me do anything. When he became old and was no longer so strong we did not have a heart to sell him to be butchered for meat. My Dad arranged for him to be cared for out in a village on a mountain slope and I never saw him again. Later on I heard that my buffalo had fallen into a ravine and died. Apparently he was just too old.

My father tried another line of work. He left our cart in its storage shed and became a blacksmith. When I came home from school in the afternoon I worked the bellows. I did not like this task, especially if any of my pals were playing nearby. Every moment or so, while my father was forging a piece of iron we had heated to a nice glow, I would go over to my friends. I would say to my Dad, "It's too hot near the fire," and fan my body with my shirt as I walked away. But then I would enjoy playing so much that I forgot my duties. My Dad would get angry with me and, thoroughly irritated, I would return to my work at the bellows.

Anyway, blacksmithing did not suit my father for long. He bought a cow to pull our cart. Cows are able to pull carts faster than water buffalo, but they are not as strong. Again I was the one who kept watch over our cow, but it was different from watching a water buffalo. I was not allowed to spoil the cow, and I was not supposed to ride her. What is more, the cow smelled positively rancid, probably because it was never bathed.

The death of our old water buffalo had apparently been a sad event for my father, too; he did not seem to want to hitch up the cart very often anymore. The cow cart was not used for long. He sold it and used the money to buy the car we took to Sibolga. My Dad drove it from Medan to Bukittinggi and back again, as a hired driver. But after a year of driving, he asked for his money back because, he said, "The automobile has made me forget my obligations as a church elder." But perhaps that was not the real reason my father asked for his money back. A life of driving an automobile truly had no structure to it.[7]

CHAPTER 4

In those days the language of instruction in village school was Batak. But then we learned that beginning with the next school year students would be taught in Malay, so my teacher and my father decided that I should repeat the third grade. I would not lose any time, my teacher said, because the following year I could go right into fourth grade in middle school. Since third graders from primary school were usually admitted only to third grade in middle school, if I were admitted to fourth grade after an extra year of primary school, I would not be behind at all. According to my teacher I would certainly pass the entrance exam for fourth grade. So for a whole year I emphasized Malay and did not pay much attention to the other subjects.[1]

After a second year of third grade, the time came to take exams in arithmetic and the Malay language; in the latter, we had to translate from Batak to Malay and vice versa. Batak and Malay were not the same, even though the two languages shared many words, for example "finger," "hand," "eye," and so on. Other words in Malay like "gun," "edge," and the like were somewhat different in Batak, for example the Malay "e" was often changed to "o" in Batak; thus *bedil* [rifle] became *bodil*, and *tepi* [edge, border] became *topi*. Yet other words were entirely different. So when we had to translate sentences such as "Bojak mangangkat-angkat dirodang" (The frog jumped about the swamp) and "Rongit mandoit-doit di podomanku" (Mosquitoes were biting me in my bed) from Batak to Malay, some students translated[2] them into "Bedjak beringkat-ingkat di redang" (The *bejak ingkat*-ed in the swamp) and "Rengit mendeit-deit di pedomanku" (The mosquito *deit*-ed me in my guide book), neither of which made much sense at all. I did not know what the Malay word for "bojak" (frog, *katak*) was, so I just wrote *bedjak*, which means nothing in Malay. Despite such problems,

I was accepted into fourth grade in middle school, for I had the second highest grade on the exam.

Middle school was the next educational level for students from dozens of little primary schools in the surrounding area. Middle school in Laguboti, for instance, accepted primary school graduates from a number of places, such as Lumbanbagasan, Lumbanbalian, Hutahaean, Tambunan, Baruara, Haunatas, Sampuran, Bonandolok, Sintongmarnipi, and so forth. Not all these places were near Laguboti. Some were five, and even ten stone marker posts[3] away; Sampuran, for instance, was more than ten kilometers away, so the children who came from there really had to get up early. To keep from being late for school they would take a large citrus fruit from home. They would run along kicking the fruit, and by practicing soccer in this way they managed to get to school on time. [Djohanis apparently lived in a tiny village outside Laguboti.]

Nearly every day when I was in fourth grade we came across a certain crazy person. We called him Si Lingis, but if he heard this name he would fly into a rage and threaten to pounce on the person who had yelled "Lingis." If there happened to be a stick or stone at hand, he would often throw it. But we always teased him with the name Lingis, so he would always be chasing us and hurling abuse. He dressed in a tattered soldier's uniform, and according to what school friends from Bonandolok said, one time he taught the kids in primary school how to line up in rows, military fashion. He gave the command, "Links om!"[4] So if the children saw him they yelled out "links," "lings," or "lingis," and eventually his nickname became Lingis. Si Lingis was also fond of sermonizing. Regardless of whom he was speaking with, verses from the Bible would tumble out of his mouth (that is, of course, if he was not being teased about his name at the time). He considered anyone who called him "Apostle" to be a great pal and he allowed that person to sit beside him. Unfortunately, we children were happier tormenting him by calling him Lingis.

The head teacher taught our class in the fifth grade. People said that he was the best at instructing that grade and so had been promoted to head teacher. He had been married—for the second time, as his first wife had passed away—for just a few months, so when he went home during recess we children had many naughty suspicions about what he was doing.

Our class did not have many atlases of the Netherlands East Indies, so the teacher asked us all to order atlases from Jakarta at a price of Rp. 1 per book, with an additional 10 cents in postage, for a total cost of Rp. 1.10. Within a month, he said, the atlases would be in our hands. However, the month became 5 weeks, 6 weeks, 2 months, 3 months, and still no news about our order. "Maybe the order forms or our mail order payments didn't arrive at the bookstore. Maybe they went astray," the teacher said. We believed him, too. Who among us could suspect our teacher?

Drawing and penmanship did not particularly interest me, but arithmetic—ah, that was the thing. Nevertheless, by the last quarter of third grade I ended up with an 8 in penmanship. When I compare it with my handwriting now—well, my present penmanship is not worth more than a 3.

Around this time my father bought a horse and a two-wheeled buggy called a *bendi* (in Indonesian, *delman*). Two months later he bought a second horse. Once more, of course, I was the one who tethered the horses and kept an eye on them out in the grassy pasture.

My father was rarely angry with me, but when he was, it was not unusual for him to grab a bamboo or palm rib switch to beat me with. I was the only child—well, there was my younger sister, but for us, girls in the family did not really count—but my Dad did not spoil me. He was of the opinion that "It is better not to have any children at all than to have bad children." ("Children" here meant "sons" in Batak; daughters were called *boru*.[5])

One time I was busy looking for rice paddy crickets, which we called *bangkurung* in Batak. We looked for them in the paddy fields after the harvest. The rice had already been cut with sickles, and the only things left standing were the stalks. The bangkurung made their nests in little holes in the ground; these places were easy to locate if the crickets made a sound. Walking on tiptoe, we crept up on the bangkurung as they chirped away. If they heard us, of course they fell silent, but we would already know approximately where they were. Often the noises would lead us astray, however. It would seem that a cricket was right in front or right behind us, when actually it was far away. We put the male bangkurung into a matchbox and fed him with rice and grass; we did not take females, because they did not sing. If you wanted the cricket to make a noise, you just poked him with a blade of grass and he would start singing, perhaps because he liked being tickled, or perhaps because he thought he had defeated another cricket in battle and was signaling victory, like a fighting cock that crows when it wins a contest.

Once I became so engrossed in hunting bangkurung that the horse I was watching wandered off somewhere. I looked and looked but could not find him, though it was already getting dark. What could I say to my parents if they saw me come home without the horse in tow? Because I was afraid that my father would beat me, I waited till sundown. I did not have the courage to go to a relative's house since they would surely tell my Dad that I was there. So I crept up slowly upon our house. Through the spaces in the wall I could see that my mother and sister were eating. This made me even hungrier, but I still did not dare to go into the house. My mother had been looking for me and had asked my friends where I was, but no one knew. Eventually, since it was already nighttime, they closed up the house and went to sleep. I found a place to lie down on top of a beam that joined the houseposts. There, holding on to the beam above, I dozed until daylight. Luckily my father had not come home that night, for if he had I would have gotten a whipping for sure. I went right out to search for the horse, and very fortunately, I found him. I totally forgot my exhaustion and considered it to be my punishment for neglecting my duties.

One time we went in the buggy to visit my grandparents in Narumonda. Dad and I sat up front, while Mother and my sister sat in back. Every so often I was allowed to hold the reins, but when I did so the horse slowed down and then Dad took them from me. Apparently the horse always knew who was holding the reins.

CHAPTER 5

Unless there was something I really needed, I did not speak very much with my father. He did not question me about my work at school or what I did every day. He believed he was fulfilling his duties if he just made a living for us and kept us in food. I still remember when I was very small (exactly how old I don't remember), my father would often bring little cakes for me when he came home from the marketplace; I would rush up and welcome him every evening. But suddenly, for some unknown reason, he stopped bringing me things. Perhaps he thought I had gotten too old for such treatment, that it was no longer appropriate for me to be brought cakes.

Not once did my dad clearly show his love for me. Not because he did not love me, but probably because that was just his way.[1] If we were eating a meal together, he always gave me advice not to eat too much curry: "Later on, no one will want you as a son-in-law," he said. If a *jengkol* bean[2] or a petai bean was still left, he would joke, "Don't eat too many jengkol, Djohanis, or your hair will turn red," and I would believe him.

There were lots of food taboos for us children. For instance, we were not allowed to eat oranges at night. Eating the head of a chicken also was not permitted; people said that your hair would turn white. But no one told us that eating oranges at night might give you a bellyache or that chicken heads were the special parts reserved for grownups.

Often, when I was quite small, my dad would teach me how to sing songs after dinner. These were not church hymns but songs in the Malay language; even now I do not know what they meant. Maybe they were in old-fashioned Malay, I don't know.

I realized that we were not rich and that my father worked hard to find us a handful of rice each morning and evening. So I did not ask him for money very often, unless it was for something I really needed. I realized that if I asked for some clothes, for instance, he wouldn't give them to me right away. He always dodged the question by saying that I still had lots of clothes, but if I asked him many times—at least four—he would finally take me off to the tailor's, where he always tried to get away with buying the cheapest things possible. If I had not been really stubborn about it (with the support of the tailor, naturally) I never would have gotten anything halfway decent.

I was not even particularly close to my mother, especially once I got into middle school. She was satisfied if I helped her out by collecting firewood, boiling the rice, washing my clothes, watching the livestock, and so on. These duties I often forgot because I was so busy playing, and Mother often got angry at me, especially when she came home in the evening from the market and found that the rice still was not cooked. Often she grabbed a cane to beat me with, but I was really too big to be hit like this and I fought back. I tried to dodge her swipes, and if it hurt too much, I grabbed the cane and hit her back. Then Mother would go complain to my father. He was not particularly concerned—he knew my mother was always exaggerating—so sometimes he just laughed. My mother, of course, would be put out by this and say, "You're the one who's always spoiling Djohanis. Now he's just incorrigible."

I rarely played with my little sister, especially after I went to middle school and she entered girls' school. It was customary for a boy not to be too close to his sister; they were supposed to stay apart from each other.[3] You could not address your sister as *engkau*, it had to be *kamu*.[4] Other little girls were closer to us than our own sisters.

Perhaps because none of them was a close friend to whom I could pour my heart out, I was not particularly close to my parents or sister. Yes, it was true that my parents fed me, bought me clothes, paid my school fees—in short, gave me everything I needed—and in return for their hard work and struggle they hoped I would keep progressing in school. My father and mother were my parents, but they were not friends or close companions.

Once I was very ill—I found out later from my mother that I had a bad stomachache and for half an hour solid I slept with my eyes wide open, not moving at all—and my mother cried because she thought there was no hope that I would live. My dad looked at me and was silent, as if he did not love me. Mother was angry with him. Why was he just sitting there in a daze? But Dad did not answer her. Finally he could hold back no longer and cried out in a low moan, "My son, my son, how can you have the heart to leave us like this?"[5] Luckily I came back to the world. I started to move again and a week later I was all better. Right away my mother brought me a *lele* fish—a *sibahut*, our people say. She grilled it and then sprinkled it with lime juice and salt. My mother always bought that sort of fish for me when I was sick, and in fact she said that the reason I had become sick was that I had not eaten any *lele* lately.[6]

Christmas Day and New Year's Day were joyful days for us children, special days that we waited and waited for. Beforehand, we got new clothes. For instance, I asked my father for shoes, a tie, a shirt, and a European-style straw hat or, as we often called it, a *tudung tuan* ["Master's hat"]. (Everything that was foreign or unusual would have *tuan* [master] or "Dutch" tacked onto its name. For example, big mangoes, which were hard to find in our area, were called Dutch Mangoes. All Europeans were called *tuan,* and to differentiate a Batak preacher from a German preacher, there were the terms "preacher" and "*tuan* preacher." That is also how the terms *guru* and *tuan guru* came about, to distinguish between the graduates of the teacher training school in Sipoholon and the kweekschool in Solo.)[7] In the village usually I went without shoes, so to guard against my feet hurting over the holidays I practiced wearing them at night. The first time my father bought me some rubber shoes, but the second year I asked for leather ones. My socks were made of silk and were usually called *sok,* a Dutch word. I wore short pants. The socks were held up with elastic garters, which snapped on down at the bottom. But because only one side of the sock was held up the other one fell down. The elastic garter was buttoned on above the knee, so it wouldn't fall down. This style was already outmoded, but at that time I felt myself quite the *tuan,* a little master. In addition to all this I wore a suit jacket and a shirt with a tie, with a straw hat on my head. Without fail, everyone would look at me as I passed by and say, "Just look at how dashing our Djohanis is!" But imagine how annoyed I was when I heard one of father's acquaintances say, "Can that be your son, *Sintua*? He's certainly gotten big. But he sure doesn't look like you. Nope, he looks like a Chinaman." After that I never wore the straw hat, the one that made me look Chinese.[8]

It was the custom for us Christians to celebrate the night before December 25. At that time a lighted tree would be put up (a *gaba-gaba* in Batak, a *kerstboom* in Dutch), all decorated with strips of paper, lighted candles, and so on. Often, too, a few children would recite verses from the Bible near the *gaba-gaba,* a practice we called *liturgi.*[9] We were given these verses to memorize three months before Christmas. The children who said their verses well were praised, while the others were criticized and made fun of. That didn't make things easier for the child who was reciting. After the ceremony on December 25 was finished, lots of folks—grownups as well as children—milled around in front of the tree to see if they could get a candle. Immediately the church elders would form a circle around the *gaba-gaba* to guard against anyone taking candles, but no matter how firm the protection was, someone would succeed in getting one. The next morning, the church elders' children could be seen playing with candles.

On one Christmas Eve an accident almost happened. Our teacher at the time had recently moved in from Balata to our village. The sintua who was decorating the *gaba-gaba* apparently hung the strips of paper too close to the candles, and when the candles were lit the paper caught fire and the whole thing had to be put out. From that event folks made up a ditty: *Guru i guru sian Balata, Disi ro guru i masurbu gaba-gaba* (The teacher, he's a teacher from Balata. The teacher had barely arrived when the Christmas tree went up in flames).

On New Year's[10] we were allowed to set off firecrackers. About two weeks before New Year's Day (sometimes as much as two months before, since the closer it got to New Year's the more expensive fireworks got) we bought firecrackers. These firecrackers were sold in bunches, wrapped together in packages. Some kids would buy one package, some two, three, or four, depending on their parents' wealth. There were three kinds of firecrackers: small ones, which usually had black wicks and could be held after they had been lit; regular ones, which had black and white wicks, and at least the black ones could still be held when lit; and big ones, normally called *long*.[11] Among us children, Goose brand firecrackers were the most famous, and we always looked for this kind at the market. After you bought them you did not just store them in the cabinet until New Year's Day. Rather, you laid them out in the sun every day to dry. Sometimes you also roasted them on a *para-para* (a sort of rack set on top of hearthstones that had turned black from the smoke) so they would be extra dry and make a great big noise when they were lit.

Not every child was able to buy firecrackers, so those who could not often made their own . . . out of bamboo. They took a length of bamboo more than three joints long, and removed all but the last joint, making a bamboo pipe with one end closed. Then near the closed end they scraped out a hole as big as an index finger; that was the mouth. A little kerosene was rubbed around it, and because fire was always being put into the pipe via this entry, the pipe got hot and created a sort of gas from the kerosene. It was probably this gas that made the "pang" sound when the device was lit.

We thought that whoever had the most firecrackers was tops. (This particular fact would be publicly known on the morning of New Year's Day by the number of wrappers strewn around the yard. We took a good long time sweeping the yard clean that day, so friends could see all the firecracker wrappers.) When we set off firecrackers on New Year's Eve, we were able to "lengthen" the night, that is, stay up until after midnight, when everyone in the family gathered together and prayed to God, giving thanks to Him for protecting us unto that day.

We did not set off all the firecrackers at once, but rather bit by bit. When other people had finished theirs, we set ours off with a vengeance so that all might hear that we had lots of firecrackers. If possible, we set off a quarter, a half, or even a full package all at once, so the explosion was really loud. A crackling sound would be followed by the sound of one of the *long* ones, rrrrrt . . . pang . . . rrrrrt . . . pang! Such were the joyful, splendid sounds we heard. Sometimes we did not use up all of our firecrackers on that one night but kept a few for the next day, for playing with friends.

My mother would generally get angry if I set off firecrackers in the house, but one New Year's Eve I was surprised at her. Before we went off to sleep to wait for the stroke of midnight, my mother set off several firecrackers. She threw one in the kitchen, for instance, and one into the house or into our bedroom. When I asked her why she did this, she answered, "So the *jins* [evil spirits, demons] and devils get frightened away and do not hide in there." I just nodded my head.

Just think how noisy and festive it all was on New Year's in Laguboti! It was just like "Ka·naval" week, which we had often seen in newsreels at the movie theater. The only difference was that in Laguboti there were no big puppets, but it was probably just as much fun. The little town was laid out in a long rectangle, and around it on New Year's Day there marched a gala procession of bicycles, animal carts and automobiles. All these vehicles were beautifully decked out, and people even competed with each other in creating the most beautiful decorations. It cost 5 cents to go around once, and the cost for an automobile was one *benggol*, worth 2½ cents. But to just sit there in a *delman* or a car certainly was not very interesting, even if everyone was sporting new clothes. So people would think up different things to do. For instance, men riding in a delman [buggy] would wear women's clothes, or automobile passengers would dance to the beat of a gong ensemble or play a *serunai*, a type of big wind instrument or *blaasinstrument*,[12] and so on. Firecrackers were not omitted from the proceedings, either. People never tired of going around in circles the whole day long. From all over the region people would come in to the little town to watch, to meet friends, or to say "Happy New Year!" to relatives and acquaintances. And the children, of course, came along to have fun!

CHAPTER 6

There were not many secondary schools in our land to go on to after finishing middle school. Middle school graduates could continue their education by attending a missionary-run vocational school, but even there not everyone was accepted. Anyhow, not all pupils felt called to become craftsmen, who were not held in very high regard. Then there was nursing school, and also high school, that is, the teacher training school in Sipoholon. Beyond Batakland there were other schools such as the Normal School (also an institution for training teachers) in Pematang Siantar, but it accepted very few of our people, no more than four a year. I still remember how the students from this school wore sarongs, white shirts, and *peci*[1] when they came home on vacation. They were not allowed to wear trousers, people said. It was a real "native school," an Inlandse school.[2]

Each major church congregation area in our region (or *huria sabung-an*) was divided into a number of smaller congregations (or *huria pagaran*). Each of the smaller congregations had a primary school, and each major congregation a middle school, which was a secondary school for all the primary schools around. The Laguboti huria sabungan, for example, had about ten huria pagaran, so the Laguboti middle school received pupils from about ten primary schools. If each primary school turned out 30 pupils a year, that would mean that ten of them graduated about 300 pupils every year, which was certainly too many for a single middle school, even though there were two parallel classes. If each class took 30 pupils, only 120 could be accepted altogether. So where would the other 180 students go? They were forced to return home.

There were more than twenty major congregations, and if each turned out 50 pupils a year, there would be about 1000 people leaving the benches of middle school annually. And for these 1000 people there was only one vocational school, two nursing schools (in Balige and Tarutung), and one high school (in Sipoholon). It was no great surprise that those who entered these schools felt themselves a select group, as indeed they were. A missionary school teacher's standing was high in our circle, in spite of the fact that his salary only started at Rp. 7.50 and went no higher than Rp. 30. Even a medical assistant (*mantri verpleger*) did not receive a salary higher than Rp. 30 a month, but his standing was also high in our social circle. He was called a *dostor* (doctor).

Because very few children were able to continue their schooling past middle school, many migrated outside the Batak region to become police-men or soldiers, although people held the latter occupation in low esteem: it was "selling your head," folks said. There were some who continued their studies in private Dutch- and English-language schools. But none of this could solve the problem of too few secondary schools. First of all, not everyone was accepted into police or military training, and second, there were not, in fact, very many who went to private schools, for the fees were too high.

Anyone who was an official (in Dutch, an *ambtenaar*) was held in high regard. It goes without saying that the life of an ambtenaar was manifestly more orderly and stable than that of a villager. Ambtenaars were like tuans already, and in order to become one of the ambtenaars people would even go so far as to work several months in a government office without pay in hopes of being noticed and offered a job. Mission school teachers and dostors were ambtenaars, so people tried very hard to get their children into the appropriate schools. Sometimes they did not play fair, either. For example, they might give the tuan preacher a valuable *ulos* cloth[3] so that he might exercise his influence on their behalf. Or a father who wanted to get his son into Sipoholon high school might suddenly become extraordinarily faithful in attending church on Sunday, for whether or not a child's father was "good" would also be investigated by the school admission authorities.

My father very much wanted me to become a teacher in a mission school. As a sintua he believed that his son should also work in the religious field. When we graduated from middle school we were still only twelve or thirteen years old, too young for teachers' school, which you had to be fifteen to enter, so a preparatory school was established, a night school. Anyone who taught at this school also had to teach in the daytime, and so they only had evening hours open. Usually the night school instructor was the head teacher at the regular school. We paid him tuition in the form of two hanging lamps and, each month, a can of kerosene, some of which he could use to light his own house. So, each year the head teacher got two lamps and free kerosene, for after the course was over the lamps were not returned, but were presented to the teacher as a gift.

Our lessons in night school simply repeated what we had studied in middle school, the only difference being that Bible study was added. We really had to know the Old and New Testaments and the Ten Commandments. The school was attended by pupils from the huria pagaran too, and because their homes were so far away, many of them had to spend the night. My house was only one kilometer away, but often I slept there too, since I was afraid to walk home by myself. Even though my teacher had told me that there is no such thing as jins and devils, I did not believe him.

Like almost all Batak villages, ours was surrounded by clumps of bamboo, and at night something that sounded like the voice of a baby crying could often be heard from the direction of the bamboo thicket. This was said to be the voice of the *homang*, a kind of spirit which could jump about without being seen. One night such a voice was heard behind our house. My mother and several girls (girls from the village always made a habit of sleeping at our house, since it had a porch)[4] went off to chase the homang away. They left me behind, all by myself, to guard the house. It was very dark and, all alone, I became frightened and started to tremble. I thought it would be best to close up the house tight so the spirit couldn't get in, but then I remembered that the homang could move about without being seen and so could enter the house without anyone knowing how it got in. So I opened the door very wide and stood leaning against the door post waiting for everyone to return, peering left and right, up and down, and back to front, in case the spirit tried to leap out at me. I was shaking all over and was all ready to scream as loudly as I could, but luckily nothing happened. I heard my mother and the girls shouting to chase the homang away; I also heard the homang being quiet. They told me they had heard the bamboo canes creaking and rubbing against one another. Perhaps the homang had just hopped away, but in any case they had not seen the creature; maybe it had been too dark. With my mother and the girls close by once again, I returned to normal and pretended I had not been at all frightened. I was ashamed to tell them what had happened while they were off chasing the homang.

About thirty of us attended the night school, but only two were picked to continue in school. We were being sifted through and chosen with great care. The night school failed to satisfy my expectations, so my father put me in the government school in Balige, seven kilometers away from home. This school started at 8 A.M., and since there were no horse carriages available at that hour, I was forced to walk. (Even if there had been carriages available, I would not have had the money to pay for one every morning.) I left at 5 A.M. so I wouldn't be late. The school was run by the colonial government, and most of the students who went on to the Normal School in Pematang Siantar were from its ranks. The teachers were almost all products of the Pematang Siantar Normal School too. The lessons were of a much higher quality than those of middle school, and the Malay was better as well; it was the genuine article. Even the local language used there was special. In Toba, we were forced to study Mandailing.[5]

A Normal School teacher felt himself to be much above a Mission School teacher. Mission School teachers would even pay considerable sums of money to take lessons from the Normal School teachers in hopes that they might pass the government examination, which would give them the same rights and privileges as the Normal School graduates. Sometimes the Mission School teachers would even take Dutch lessons from a government teacher's school graduate. In such ways Mission School teachers would attempt to elevate their standing, but very few of them ever succeeded.

Mission School teachers did not study the Dutch language in Sipoholon, so when they came across some Dutch words in our reader, they had a hard time pronouncing them. Sometimes the words would come out badly mangled. I still remember that when I was in middle school one of our teachers was putting on airs and teaching us how to say "'s Lands Plantentuin Buitenzorg" (the State Botanical Gardens in Bogor). He always put too much stress on the letter "s," and his *tuin* sounded more like *toin*.

It was too tiring to walk back and forth to Balige every morning, so my nephew[6] and I stayed in Baruara at the house of one of our relatives, whom we paid for room and board. We only went home on Saturdays. In the evenings we cooked our own rice, since our relative did not get home from the marketplace until after dark. But this lifestyle did not last long for me. In Sigumpar, about five kilometers from Laguboti, a "government link school"[7] opened. People said that this school was almost the same as a full-fledged government-run school, and since this one was run by the Mission and the head teacher had an excellent reputation, my dad insisted that I attend. My father promised to buy me a bicycle, so I agreed to move from Balige to Sigumpar. I was back in fifth grade again.

My dad sold his horses and the delman, and went in with someone else to open a goldsmithing business. He had to study, too, in order to learn the trade. This business prospered to some extent, so my father replaced our house with one with a porch . . . and fulfilled his promise to buy me a bicycle. At first I got a sort of broken-down bicycle to practice on, and then after I could ride I got one that was fairly new. I did nothing after school every day except ride my bike. At first my friends lifted me up onto the bike while they held it, and then gave me a push from behind (still holding the bike). Eventually they only pushed me, as I learned how to keep my balance. But this did not work well after a while because I could not always find someone to push me when I needed it. So I tried to do it myself, and finally succeeded in starting off from a standing position rather than sitting down.

I cannot relate everything about my first experiences riding a bicycle; my only clear memory is that for days and days I did not want to let go of that bike. My mother got angry at me. She said I might get too tired. One time I fell off and ran into some thorny bamboo. Not unexpectedly, the thorns scratched me all over, but at that time I felt nothing, probably because I was so enthralled with the bicycle.

Mornings I rode my bike to Sigumpar, but my mother forbade me to ride my bike every morning. She said I had to alternate it with other modes of transport. I did, but not because I was afraid of getting sick like my mother said, but because riding a bicycle every day eventually got sort of boring.

CHAPTER 7

Legend[1] has it that the Batak people are the descendants of Si Raja Batak. He was born from his mother, Si Boru Deak Parujar, and was the child of gods. In fact, the child of the highest god, Debata Mula Jadi Nabolon, whose purpose was to create the world. Once the world was created, he lived in Sianjurmulamula.[2] This village also became the residence of Si Raja Batak and was located near the slopes of Mount Pusukbuhit, which is said to be the land of origin of the Batak and Karo peoples. The legend also held that Si Raja Batak had two sons, and from them sprang the Sumba marga and the Lontung marga.[3] These two marga groups later broke apart to become other margas, and even today new margas are still being formed.

The old people in our land knew their family histories in detail, as far back as three or four generations. If someone came to visit, it would have to be ascertained exactly who he or she was (this was called *martarombo,* or investigating the family connections). Often we heard the grownups repeat the saying

Tiniptip sanggar bahen huruhuruan
Djolo sinungkun marga asa binoto partuturan.

Which meant:

The *sanggar* grass is clipped to make a little cage.
One's *marga* is asked, so as to know the family connections.

So by asking what the visitor's marga was, who the father was, and who the uncles, grandparents, and so on were, we would know what family relationships we had and in what manner we should serve this guest.[4]

Knowing the family history also meant knowing about one's *dongan sabutuha* (literally, womb companions), that is, one's lineage within the marga. Ties within the lineage were still strong, and the members of the same lineage would immediately feel themselves united against outsiders. This sometimes resulted in the desire to put the interests of one's own lineage first and foremost, before all others. If one's lineage did not get ahead, often a person would find a way (sometimes a decidedly improper[5] way) to get ahead of another lineage or bring it down. Small margas or lineages often did not have much room for maneuvering.

In our village our marga was a small one. Even though we were the village founders or "owners" (in the past, the village took the name of our marga), after a while we had for the most part gotten crowded out.[6] As a child I did not feel this too sharply. My only experience was that I had no older brother within the lineage to complain to or lean on for support if someone was trying to beat me up. One time the "other side" challenged me to a tugging match with a kid almost my age, but I was not interested. Then they told my opponent to flick my ear with his finger. It was customary for us children to do this as a sign that we were not afraid of someone; it was a kind of insult. Of course I got angry, and the two of us set to fighting. The others yelled at us, egging us on. I got so angry I forgot the proper tactics in fights of this sort. I got flopped on my back on the ground, with my opponent on top of me. I surrendered, and they shrieked gleefully. I got all red in the face, but how could I fight that many people all at once? I just remained silent and thought, So what if he flicked my ear, what good would it do to fly off the handle? After that I realized exactly where I stood. I knew that I was all alone and would have to rely solely on my own strength. From that time on, I always took care to avoid fighting; I knew how to carry myself around other children so as to avoid confrontation. My father called me a "good boy" because I never got into fights.

My dad became rather skillful at working gold, and because the business was not sufficiently profitable for him (it did not make enough to be divided two ways, [between the two partners]), my father opened his own goldsmithing outfit in Porsea. At that time I was still a night school student in Sigumpar. Because school was closer to the business than to our village, I lived with my dad, who also needed me around to do the housework. He did not tell me why he had moved to Porsea, but in fact it was not entirely because the goldsmithing business did not bring in enough profit; from others I heard that he had had a disagreement with our district headman.[7] He preferred to laugh that situation off.

All this time my father had been discussing me with the teacher from the government school in Porsea. The teacher told him that I could be admitted, but that it would be better for me to try fourth grade first. If it became apparent that I could keep up with the lessons, then I would be allowed to move to fifth grade. So I entered fourth grade in government school first (normally graduates of middle school and link school were placed in fourth grade in Government School). After several months I was asked to go on and move to fifth grade, but I did not want to do this. I thought that following a full year's course of study in just four months was too much, and I was afraid I would not be able to pass the fifth-grade final exam. But I had another reason to stay behind in fourth grade. I had great hopes of being the smartest kid in the class, and therefore great hopes, too, of taking the entrance exam for normal school.

One time our fifth-grade teacher told us to add up two sets of figures very quickly. Whoever was the fastest and got the right answer would get a prize consisting of a pencil and small briefcase. It happened that there was a kid in class who was repeating fifth grade. He was smart, and was taking fifth grade a second time because he had not passed the entrance exam for normal school. He finished a little bit before me and ran up to the teacher to show him his work. But unhappily for him one of his computations was incorrect. I was the second one to finish so the award was presented to me. Unfortunately, however, the Depression meant that neither the normal school nor the high school were accepting new students. My plans had to be changed again. But in what direction?

When I was in the link school my name because associated with that of a certain girl. Being around girls was a normal sort of thing for me, actually. Since I was little I had played with both older and younger girls. In our village, indeed, I had a fiancée, an *oroan* in Batak.[8] (According to adat, a boy could be engaged to a girl even when they were quite young, so young in fact that their stools were still milky.) My parents did this, Mother

said, following someone's recommendation that I would grow up healthy
if I were engaged. And indeed, after being seriously ill that one time, I
never got sick again. My *oroan* was older than I—six years older—so I was
shy in her presence. To tell the truth I would not have known she was my
intended if it had not been for the fact that other kids yelled it at me, or
slipped me the word quietly. Since I was shy, I moved away if I saw her
coming.

Every church had its own choir,[9] and since I had a nice voice I was allowed to sing in the choir made up of teenaged girls. I was the smallest of
the lot, and they were always pestering me. I horsed around and sometimes even traded punches with them. Apparently some of the older boys
got annoyed when they watched me playing and joking around with the
girls, and one time one of them called me over and said, "Try hitting her
breasts. You watch, you'll make her cry." I wanted to try this out, so at one
point I did punch one of the big girls in the chest. But she did not moan
with pain. Instead I heard her say, "Hey, you're naughty!" Her breast was
indeed softer than the normal chest, but I really did not have a clue why
she called me naughty.

So in the girl department I had lots of "experience," if I can use that
word here. In government school I felt rather attracted to the opposite
sex, though I did not know why. And why my friends started shouting that
girl's name along with my own, I had no idea. From the pupils in another
class—the classmates of this girl—I learned that one day when their class
had been let out, she and one of her girlfriends happened to be eating
sweets in front of the classroom window. This girl supposedly peeked at
me every now and then from the next doorway (she used a mirror), and
gestured invitingly toward the snacks she was eating. (I had no idea what
she was doing.) Anyway, the others drew the conclusion that this girl wanted
to be friends with me, and they took to shouting out my name whenever
she passed by or if I happened to be in the neighborhood. I pretended to
pay no attention to them, and anyway, what could I do to fend off that
many kids by myself? Actually, the girl had caught my eye, and me hers.
This became evident later, after we graduated. But at this point in our story
I will surrender to time constraints and move on.

In Porsea we bathed in the famous Asahan River. It was a deep river,
and anyone who did not know how to swim was forced to stay close to
shore where there was lots of mud. I learned how to swim very quickly so
that I could have fun and play tag with my friends in the water. In fact,
after school let out we did nothing but play in the water (I told the folks at
home I was going to take a bath). We splashed about for as much as four
hours at a stretch, to the point that my eyes were red when I went home.

In this river there were different places for males and females, but we
boys liked swimming at the girls' spot better. The water was clearer (be-

cause it was deeper), and in addition there were lots of girls we knew there. We bothered them, and frightened them by diving down deep and pulling their legs as we came up. The never failed to scream and squeal.

It was when I was in government school that I first discovered the Balai Pustaka books. According to the rules we were not allowed to borrow more than two books every two weeks, and since I did not like this rule I tried to make friends with the librarian. I would help him register the books and put covers on them. In exchange, I was allowed to read to my heart's content. I read a great many books. The ones I still recall were love stories like *Pertemuan* [Meetings] I and II, *Karam dalam gelombang pertjintaan* [Foundering in the waves of love], *Pertjobaan Setia* [A trial run at being faithful], *Djeumpa Atjeh* [The flower of Atjeh], and so on. I read no fewer than sixty books in that year and three months' time.

CHAPTER 8

The Dutch language was held in unbelievably high regard by people in our area. There were several H.I.S. schools: one in Sigumpulon, one in Balige, and one in Narumonda that was run by the Nommensen School-vereniging.[1] Of course, people preferred the mission's H.I.S. to the others, since we were all Christians. Sometimes there were children from the huria pagaran [church congregations] who got into those schools; they were usually the children of mission school teachers or of the district head.[2] On Christmas Eve these H.I.S. kids were often asked to recite Bible verses in Dutch, even though there were only one or two people in the whole church who could understand them. I suppose it had to be demonstrated publicly that the H.I.S. fourth graders were skilled at Dutch.

Sometimes this tendency to show off got rather silly. If an H.I.S. student was walking with his parents to the market and they happened to run into a Dutch person—it did not matter who—the parents often told the child to speak Dutch with the Dutch person. If the child, perhaps only a second or third grader and naturally still very shy, did not want to do this, the father would grumble, "Well, don't continue in that school, let's just ask for your tuition money back. It's wasting money to keep you there." Or if two H.I.S. kids happened to meet, the father would tell them to speak Dutch to each other: "Okay, friends, we want to hear you two speak Dutch." What delight there was in hearing other people speaking Dutch I cannot imagine, especially if the listeners themselves did not know a single word of the language. The two children—little kids in the first or second grade!—of course felt shy and embarrassed.

Toward the end of my time in fifth grade in government school, a Dutch course opened in Porsea on the initiative of a teacher from the teacher's school. It cost Rp. 2.50 a month, with one lesson a week. I took this class.

About ten of us at first (the number shrank to six after a month, four after two months, and then dwindled to none at all) diligently sat there in front of our teacher. One time the teacher told us to finish the sentence, "de vogel vliegt over . . ." (The bird flies over . . .). A pupil answered, "De vogel vliegt in de logulogutooi" (The bird flies in the *logulogutooi*). The day before the teacher had taught us the sentence "De vogel zit in de kooi" (The bird is in the cage). The child had apparently memorized this sentence but he had not gotten it quite right. What had apparently remained in his head was just the sound "ooi," so when the teacher told him to complete the sentence "De vogel vliegt over . . . ," he added "in de logulogutooi."

The night school for Dutch did not last long. When we heard that a Schakelschool was going to open in Parmaksian, I registered as a pupil there. Almost everywhere wild schools[3] for Dutch instruction were opening up. The first in our area was a schakelschool in Balige that was built and run by the Dutch Trade Association. Within two years this school had brought results: two of its students passed the entrance exam for MULO.[4] They got a lot of propaganda out of that one.

There is a Batak saying that goes, *Songon lombu do hajolmaon* (Humankind is like cattle). That is, people follow others, just as cows always follow their bull. I still recall how, back in the beginning, very few people owned automobiles (actually, they didn't own them, they were just paying for them on credit). But soon lots of people formed groups to buy cars on credit, to the point that there got to be too many automobiles. The same is true with mechanized rice mills. They sprang up like mushrooms, even though there was not all that much rice to mill. (People preferred to pound their rice by hand, especially since they did not always have enough money to pay to get it done.) So all because of people wanting to "keep up with the Joneses," dozens and dozens of mechanized rice mills, wild schools, churches, and so on sprang up. Indeed, North Tapanuli can hardly be conceived of without all its churches, they got so numerous.

Each church had a bell, and its sound became part of our flesh and blood, for we heard it nearly every day. The bell was rung at any and all opportunities; if there was a meeting at church, for example, or if a person died, if it was a holiday, and so on. On Sundays the bell woke us up very early in the morning, at about six o'clock. At eight o'clock the bell would remind us to eat; at nine, to walk to church; at 9:30, to gather in front of the church; and at 9:45 or 10:00, for services to begin. So on Sunday morning alone we heard the bell ring four times before church even began. Maybe after church the bell would be rung again, if some boys were practicing their hymn singing (in Batak, *marguru ende* or *margurende*). If someone died, the bell would be struck, but not continuously; it would be hit once and then it would stop. After that it was hit once, then a pause, then once more, then a series of beats with pauses between them. When it was struck, the number of beats was counted, and from the total number we knew whether it was a child who had died or an adult. If there was a fire or an accident, the bell was also rung.

At midnight on New Year's Eve (that is, twelve o'clock on the night of December 31) we children heard our church bell, along with those of all the churches nearby. The bells with the clearest and richest tones were praised, and the ones which did not sound nice were criticized as sounding tinny. Sometimes fights broke out as a result. Kids whose church bell had been called a tin can would feel insulted. Maybe that is why all the churches ordered—yes, they actually fell all over themselves ordering—nice bells from Germany.

A teacher without a diploma who taught at this wild school was called Guru Hebben. The story was that once someone happened to walk by and hear this teacher giving a lesson in Dutch, as follows: "Ik heb, wij hebben" (I have, we have). Apparently the word *hebben* stuck in his mind and, because he often forgot the teacher's name, he'd just call him Guru Heb, Guru Hebben. After that everyone called the teacher Guru Hebben, and soon the name was applied to all teachers who did not have diplomas. In fact these teachers had a variety of educations. Some were from H.I.S. or from levels one, two, or three of MULO. Some had already graduated from MULO, some had gone to teacher's school but had not graduated, and so on.

I became a pupil at the Parmaksian Schakelschool, though not with the intention of continuing my education from that point. I just wanted to know a bit of Dutch. It never occurred to me that next I might tackle the entrance exam for MULO, and even if this did somehow happen I certainly had no hope of actually passing it. There were lots of people from H.I.S., people who had studied Dutch for seven full years, who still could not pass the test and continue.

Parmaksian was about three kilometers from Porsea. We biked over there and when we got bored with our bicycles we walked and took a shortcut. Some girls we knew rented a horse carriage on a monthly basis. Sometimes we tried to tag along after them (wherever there are flowers, bees buzz around). I was rather attracted by one of these girls, so I tried as hard as I could to get near the carriage. But sometimes we pretended not to care about the carriage at all, to act as if we did not care about them in the least. That was a tactic too!

I knew the owner of this carriage well. Once, when he had no one to drive it, he asked me to do so. At school I could tether the horse and give him grass (he said), and after school I would take him home, along with the girls. I did not mind being a coachman. But when I drove the carriage, quarrels would break out between the girls and me. The way I figured it, the girl I had my eye on hated me just like the others did, since she was joining in on all the teasing. But one morning I was astonished to get a letter from her through her little brother. She said that it was not because of her that we had the quarrels in the carriage; she was not at fault in the least. I did not answer this letter, but it was a sign that she did not hate me after all. Even so, I asked the carriage owner if I could quit my job as driver.

Our studies at the Schakelschool went very quickly. This was not surprising, since most of us had already graduated from middle school. And our teacher worked really hard for us. He punished us severely if we did not study or if we did something else wrong. Nevertheless, we knew that he was doing this for us. We all studied happily under his leadership.

When we went home along the main road we did all sorts of things to amuse ourselves along the way, so we would forget how hungry we were or how long the journey home was. I had played these games when I was forced to walk home from link school in Sigumpar to Laguboti. For one thing, there were lots of telegraph poles all in a row along the road. We tried to hit them or the telegraph wires with stones we found by the roadside. Whoever could hit the wire consistently was generally considered the most accurate shot. Sometimes we stopped and put our ears against a pole. Friends told us that if we listened really close we could find out what people were saying on the telephone, or what they were wiring in their telegrams. Indeed, there was a sort of "ngiung-ngiung" sound that you could hear through the poles. Friends told us it was the telegrams being tapped out!

We stopped these games if we heard the road inspector coming along on his motorcycle. This tuan was a rather tall Dutchman, so we called him *Tuan Sibarung,* or Mr. Heron. He was really funny to look at, sitting all hunkered down, with his knees sticking up on his motorcycle, as if he were hunkered down to defecate in the river. We ran into him almost every day, so we got to know the sound of his motor. Our hearing was really sharp then, and we knew all the cars in the vicinity, for we passed them every day. We knew which auto was coming just from the sound of its motor or horn, or from its license plate number. Plates marked B.B. were from Tapanuli, and those marked B.K. were from East Sumatra.

There were lots of kapok trees along the road. Sometimes we knocked the kapok fruits off the branches with rocks. The young seeds were edible, even though some people said that if you ate too many you would come down with *tukik,* a kind of ear ailment in which your ear exudes pus. One time I ate some kapok seeds, but they did not taste very good. But of course if you are hungry you will eat anything.

The wild schakelschools in our district were always half alive, that is, existing somewhere between life and death. This was not surprising, considering our land's economic conditions at the time. The tuition fees, which at first had been Rp. 4 and were later dropped to 1 ringgit,[5] were still too high for most people. The Toba region, for instance, had no other product besides rice and there was only enough of that to eat. To buy the other necessities people had to raise one or two pigs. They cost hardly anything because they only ate rice bran and leftover cooked rice. All we had to do was sell them once they got big. Fear of losing this comfortable means of livelihood and fear of not being able to eat this delicious meat was what often pushed North Tapanuli people into becoming Christians.[6]

There was only one way out of this cramped economic situation, and that was to migrate outside the region or seek a paid position in another district. This is why parents were so competitive in trying to enroll their children in school, even if it nearly killed them to pay the bills. A great many students thus went off to Java to attend school. Without anyone really noticing, there was a huge exodus of young men, the flower of their people, from the Batak region, which thus became a kind of second Menado and Ambon![7]

Our teacher in Parmaksian Schakelschool once got into a disagreement with the administrators of the school, as a result of which he moved to Porsea and opened his own school. The old Parmaksian pupils split into two groups, and we were his first pupils. I was already in third year at the time. Our school was just a regular old house, with our teacher's house right next door. The school was at the edge of the market, so when it was market day it was really noisy. Luckily we just had a half day of classes on market day.

Our teachers here consisted of the head teacher, two male teachers who were both products of the MULO in Tarutung, and a lady teacher who was a product of the Padang Panjang Normal School. One of the men teachers taught us Dutch and arithmetic; the other one gave us elective subjects (or, as we said in Dutch, *blokvakken*) such as geography, history, and so on. This second teacher was very touchy. If someone happened to be laughing and he could not see them, he always asked why, quite angrily; he was afraid that the child might be laughing at him. When he strolled about the school, he looked quite dashing. He stood straight up, not looking left or right, gazing off into the far distance. Maybe this performance, in which he appeared so bold and tough, hid feelings of inadequacy.

The Dutch language teacher was a real braggart. He could often be seen chatting with our *juffrouw* [Dutch, "Miss": unmarried woman], our young lady teacher, the normal school graduate. One day he got angry at one of the girls in my class, the plump, dark one who had sent me the letter via her little brother. At the time, we did not know why he was angry. Later on he told the child who lived with him in his house to go fetch his album. He showed all sorts of pictures of Tarutung to this girl, telling her that he was very used to socializing with girls. The girl who had gotten him angry just kept silent. Only at recess did I find out (from the kid who lived in the teacher's house, of course) that people—and apparently especially the plump, dark girl—were linking him with our *encik*.[8] We noticed that, for her part, our encik remained quite unflustered, and in fact thought that the matter was too small to have gotten so angry with the girl about. But maybe the teacher was paying some attention to the encik after all, or else why would he have gotten all that angry?

This normal school lady teacher taught us Malay and singing. She was not all that expert at speaking Dutch, and one time we burst into laughter when she said, "Tot so feer mar eeerst."[9] One time she got angry at me because I had left my songbook at home, and she said, "Waarom laat je neus ook niet achter?" but I simply replied, "Dat kan niet, Juffrouw" [That's impossible, Miss]. She looked at me without saying another word.

Our encik was replaced by another lady teacher, a product of the Medan Home Economics School. This teacher did not have the nerve to teach us anything except reading, and even then she never explained any of the complicated words. She was too full of herself, which was especially grating since we were much more fluent in Malay than she was.

CHAPTER 9

My father was not only a craftsman, fixing or making things of gold; he also sold gold jewelry, which he obtained from a Chinese in Pematang Siantar and handled on commission with the agreement that when objects sold he would pay up immediately. So there was always a good deal of gold jewelry in my dad's storage cabinet. When the pieces were not on display in the shop window, they were stored in a box. I always felt nervous holding them, perhaps because when I did I could not help thinking about a woman's body. If I held an earring, I thought about a girl's ear; if I had a necklace in my hands, I recalled her neck. So I tried not to handle the jewelry, and whenever my dad asked me to go get a certain piece I would bring him the whole box and say, "Perhaps you should take it out of the box; I'm afraid I might break it."

After school I usually stayed at home keeping an eye on our business, because in addition to running his jewelry shop my father also sold other things. In the evenings I would play with my friends. In our town there was a person who did bicycle stunts. He could stand up, lie down, and do all sorts of other things on the bike. So we tried to copy him. We did have little accidents now and then, but that did not stop us from practicing. Often, too, a boxer would come to town, because his father happened to live there. Sometimes he showed us his skills in the ring or demonstrated his strength by lifting something heavy. We had a notion to do the same things, so not long afterward we bought the ropes for a boxing ring. But that is not all we did to get strong. We often tried to lift heavy objects (for example if someone was unloading an automobile), just as we often watched the drivers' helpers do. In fact, we kind of hankered after becoming driver's helpers ourselves because they got really, really strong from loading and unloading baggage and freight all the time.

We had great hopes of getting strong and becoming bikers or boxers. We admired the strongman very much indeed; he was tops. Because we were always working out, naturally we wanted to test our strength, to put what we had learned into action. All this pent up strength had to come out, so when we got into disputes with each other, we moved quickly to displaying our physical strength and punching, boxing, and wrestling. After all, weren't our bodies strong by now? We wanted to show off our boxing skills.

Fortunately none of this lasted very long. One day our teacher told us that whoever wanted to try taking the entrance exam for MULO would have to tell him right away and bring in Rp. 5. I told my father that we were allowed to take the exam to get into MULO, but my aim was only to let him know about it; actually planning on taking the exam did not even enter my head. It was impossible to think that someone from a wild school could pass the exam for MULO. Nevertheless, my dad advised me to take it, and I brought in Rp. 5 and gave it to the teacher. After that, I did not have time to play anymore. I had to return to the schoolhouse again in the evening, to study with the head teacher, going over the same lessons and preparing for the MULO school exam. And the closer it got to examination day, the more anxious I appeared.

The MULO exam was really a trial for me. Day and night I thought of nothing else. Lessons I had already gone over, I went over again. I groaned and moaned. What was the exam going to be like? Did I have any hope of passing? All these questions filled my brain, to the point that I started to look troubled and weak.

One day two of my friends who were also going to take the exam said to me that they no longer saw any use in taking it. They said they knew, from a dream one of them had had, that they would fail and only I would pass. When I asked what the dream had been about, they did not want to tell me. Only after the results of the exam were known did they tell me about it. One of them had dreamed that a mouse appeared in the main hall at the marketplace. The three of us were there and we tried to chase the mouse away. One of us got a length of bamboo pole to poke the mouse with it, but no matter what he did, it would not budge. The other boy took a try too, with the same result. Then I came along. I barely picked up the pole and right away the mouse ran away. The boys interpreted this dream to mean that I was the only one of us who would pass the exam. Fortunately we are not allowed to believe in dreams! [as Christians]. But maybe this dream was true after all, in another sense; those two friends of mine are no longer with us here in this transitory world.

I could hardly sleep the night before the exam. Anxiously I awaited the next day. I awoke very early, and after I washed, my father told me to eat a little something but I was not hungry. It felt just as if I were leaving on a long journey. The horse carriage we rented for that morning was going to take us to Narumonda, where the exam was to be held, only three kilometers away. It took only fifteen minutes, but it felt as if I sat in that carriage for hours.

In the yard of the Narumonda H.I.S. many pupils had gathered to take the MULO exam. Because we were from town, lots of them knew us, so we did not feel like total strangers.

All our wishes were fulfilled.[1] Out of us four students from the Hematschool [the "cut rate" school], two got into Level One and one into Level Zero of MULO. My scores were 6 in Dutch, 7 in geography, 8 in history, and 9 in counting and calculating; they said I should be especially proud of such a good score in Dutch.

A father was understandably pleased if his son got ahead in school. But in our region there was an additional facet. A household's prosperity was no longer measured simply by how extensive its rice fields were or how many animals it owned, but now especially by the kind and level of school its children attended. To denote how high-level such and such a child's school was, just mentioning Java or Betawi (old folks would say "Matau") was quite enough.[2]

In Laguboti there was a certain Mission School teacher who had a son attending the kweekschool in Solo. He was very proud of his son, and whenever he was chatting with someone at a food stall he would steer the conversation toward education in order to have a chance to relate how this son of his was going to school in Java. One day, during vacation, his son came home for a visit. His father had him teach his students to do calisthenics, and Dutch military commands spilled from the boy's mouth. After that, the father, not wanting to be outdone, also gave his commands in Dutch. "Een, twee, een, twee" (One, two, one, two), that is what we heard as he led the exercises. Once he even tried teaching Dutch to his pupils by having them say the words *Landbouwbedrijf Sibarani* (Sibarani Plantation) for one solid hour.

The social standing of a child who was in school was therefore really quite high in our area. A father of even modest means who had daughters would often offer to support a boy through school, with the firm promise that he could marry the man's daughter later on. So sometimes a boy who was not particularly well off could get ahead if, as we said, he "had a brain."

CHAPTER 10

Our people did not understand many of the ins and outs of schooling. When we were explaining something about a certain unfamiliar school to an older person or a parent, often we took the simplest path, which meant comparing it to a school or a position in our own area that they'd be familiar with. For instance, when the question was, "What's the difference between the Solo teacher's school and the Sipoholon teacher's school?" or "Why do you have to go all the way to Java to attend teacher's school?" the answer would be "The teacher's school on Java isn't like the one in Sipoholon. The teachers who graduate from this school are just the same as the tuan guru (Dutch teachers) who teach over at the H.I.S." Many children from our area went to school in Solo, so all parents knew that if a child said he was going to school in Solo he was a pupil in a teacher's school. Solo had become synonymous with teacher's school!

Also in our area was the GAIB school.[1] People knew that GAIB men went on to become *demang*s,[2] assistant *demang*s, and so on. Medical school was also getting to be known. The graduates of this school were not just "dostors," either, like pharmacists' aids or nurses; they were real *dostor manusia* [human doctors, i.e., "real" doctors].

Because our children were going to more and more kinds of schools, new terms sprung up to explain them. For instance, parents would ask, "What sort of school do you go to in Java?" The child would answer: "A.M.S. school." But the parent would not know what that was and so would ask further, "So, what are you going to become then, once you get out of there?" It was hard for a student to say he did not have a position waiting for him, so he would think up something and say, "I'm going to be a Tuan Kumis [Mr. Moustache]." Similarly, graduates of K.W.S.[3] would become road inspectors like Tuan Heron.

Law school was not held in high regard, for being a *mester* meant being a no-account unlicensed lawyer, a forked-tongued type, a dodger, and a rogue.[4] People who were leaning in that direction did not need a real education, it was thought: the most schooling they needed was government primary school. So if someone asked what you were going to be after graduating from law school, you absolutely could not say you were going to be a *mester*. People would cast about for some more respectable analogy and say, for example, "I'll be an attorney for a Tuan Controleur."[5] And of course people's jaws would absolutely drop open: wasn't the controleur virtually a demigod? People did not realize that there were post office controleurs, tax office controleurs, bus controleurs, accounting department controleurs, and so on. But the word "controleur" was in itself enough to signify a person's rank, because for ignorant people it meant the same as "Dutchman." And yes, it is true: my uncle did get a lot of respect wherever he went because he had a son who became a controleur (bus).

Schools that did not turn out civil servants (ambtenaars) were not accorded any respect. A child who said he was going to agricultural school in Java was inevitably told, "There's no way you need to go to Java to learn how to use a hoe!" The same for vocational school; people stuck their noses up in the air and said, "Why go so far away? There's a vocational school right here in Laguboti." Nor did they want to know about business school because they said you did not need to study to know how to sell things. Didn't lots of people sell merchandise at the market, despite not having gone to business school? All you needed was a bit of capital to start out with if you wanted to become a retailer or a merchant. So, to avoid this kind of talk, business school students said they were in "Bukkoning School," which meant *boekhouding* [bookkeeping] school. People thought more of bookkeepers than merchants.

A friend who had also passed the exam and I went to report and register for MULO in Tarutung. In our district we rarely saw Dutch people (that is, white people), and if there did happen to be one around it was invariably a person of high rank. So "Dutch" was synonymous with "big tuan" (*tuan besar*) as far as we were concerned. Not surprisingly, therefore, I felt a bit frightened at approaching the director of the MULO, especially since I had never spoken Dutch to a Dutchman. Back in school the teacher had instructed us in what we ought to say to the director. The sentences started with "Heb ik de eer . . ." (Do I have the honor [of addressing the director of] . . .) and so forth. I memorized these sentences and when we went to meet the director I was still muttering them to myself on the way, lest I forget them. It just so happened that the director was out taking a stroll in front of his house. We had already asked a neighbor if that was tuan director, but when I got near him I nevertheless blurted out, "Heb ik de eer . . ." and so on. When he responded that he was indeed the director, I just handed him my letter of application without saying a single word more. I totally forgot everything I had memorized so perfectly on the way there. Fortunately the director opened the letter right away and read it. Then he asked us into his house for a moment to write down our names and make the application formal. He said we would receive our official responses later on at home.

And indeed a month later we got word: we had been accepted.

CHAPTER 11

Toba is the region surrounding Lake Toba, but in common speech the word has come to mean "rude" or "rustic," like the word *uluan* (upriver people). The Angkola,[1] for instance, call all those who come from the north of them Toba, even if they happen to come from around Sibolga. And by the same token Sibolga people call Tarutung folk Toba. People from Silindung call people from the Lake Toba area "toba." The real Toba people, of course, feel insulted and say, "If it weren't for Toba, Silindung wouldn't eat." The Angkola say that the Toba are rough-mannered and greedy, and the Toba respond by saying that the Angkola are stingy. In Toba there is a funny story about the Angkola. It is said that when the Angkola make curried stew, they are so cheap that they just hang a slice of meat above the hearth so they can dip it into the pot for a second every time they boil up their vegetables, then pull it back up again.

Angkola parents did not allow their daughters to marry Toba boys. In fact, Silindung people would not let their young daughters to even socialize with Toba boys. The Toba boys who had just gotten into MULO in Tarutung were constantly teased by being called "toba." Eventually all this changed, even in the matter of marriage. In fairness perhaps it should be mentioned that, by contrast, the Toba considered themselves superior to people from Humbang and Uluan, and from Samosir as well.[2]

Anyone who has ever gone by car through Tapanuli from Pematang Siantar[3] surely has noticed that there is nothing whatever along the roadsides except the rice fields and, way out in the middle of them, villages surrounded by clusters of bamboo; they look like green islets in a green sea. Farming is, in fact, the sole means of livelihood for people there. Over toward Silindung there are a few other activities, such as rubber farming and harvesting gum benzoin for making incense, but there is not even much of that. The area's poverty is what has kept railroads out. But farming alone eventually falls short of satisfying people's needs. If a person has many sons he surely cannot divide his rice land into enough parcels for each one of them, so Toba people search for other means of support. People flock to Sidikalang and Kota Cane to open new farms and new villages. And that's not all. Children with schooling migrate out beyond their home region to find jobs as clerks on the plantations or to become ambtenaars in the big city.

People in other communities often got jealous of the Toba because of this. In the Simelungun area, for instance, the Toba had come to be hated because they are the ones who look prosperous and who hold positions in offices. In East Sumatra people had begun to resent them, and indeed by that time Medan had become "Tapanuli City," Tapanuli's capital. The genuine Malays and the Simelunguns and the Karos (who are also Batak) get short shrift there and count for nothing.[4] Disputes also break out frequently with Padang people.[5] This is not surprising. Once there was a big dispute between West Sumatrans and Tapanuli people in East Sumatra, and no cars from West Sumatra were allowed to go through Tapanuli.

People say Lake Toba is a lovely lake, but the idea never really occurred to us. Maybe this was because we were so used to lovely scenery or because we were so thoroughly accustomed to playing in the lake. But there was another reason we paid no attention to the natural beauty of our land: we had no time for that sort of thing. After we got out of school, for instance, we were not allowed to go play but were told to fetch firewood or do some other task. "Now, don't go thinking you can be like What's-his-name. He's a rich kid." That's what we'd always hear.

True enough: the fear of having an empty belly was what pushed people to work their hardest.

CHAPTER 12

I gathered together everything I needed to take to MULO. I had bought three pairs of long pants (students at the Tarutung MULO did not normally wear shorts), two pairs of shoes, a towel, a handkerchief, a toothbrush, soap, and so on. I got most of these things from our own store—my dad had given up his jewelry shop and had gone into selling variety goods. I got all these things without him knowing it, of course. This was what I would set off with for Tarutung.

A week before I left, my father held a ceremonial banquet[1] for me, to bless my departure and ask for my well-being and success at school. This was the second time such an occasion had been given for me. The first was when I was confirmed (*marguru malua* in Batak, *aangenomen* in Dutch) and thus became a full member of the church congregation. I did not particularly like these special meals, for not only did I have to pitch in and help serve the food, but I was also forced to sit there with everybody and listen while they gave speeches offering me advice. And to each of the thirty speeches of advice I had to respond with an expression of thanks. Well, the world often works backward. We exhaust ourselves serving guests food, yet we are also the ones who have to go and say thank you, too.

I had never been separated from my parents from the time I was small, so going to Tarutung frightened me a bit. How would people treat me at the place I was going to board? Living in Tarutung turned out to have its good points, however. Even though boarding costs were not very expensive, the MULO students were treated very well. You did not have to watch the landlord's kids like you would if you were in Medan, or to do this or that around the house.[2] Maybe this was because MULO students were well thought of.

When I first moved to Tarutung I took room and board in the house of a relative who ran a coffee stall on the Pahae Road.[3] It was sort of noisy there in the middle of the day, since people came in to drink their coffee. It was only at night after the stall had closed—about nine o'clock—that I could get to my studying. Of course this could not be allowed to continue because it was not good for my studies, so after living there for about three months I looked around for another arrangement.

It was not easy to find a place in Tarutung, especially since you had to find one that was cheap enough but also conducive to studying. Cheap and good could not be found quickly, quite unlike cheap and crummy, or expensive and good. Eventually I moved into the house of a veterinary assistant. There I was treated a bit better, but the atmosphere in the house was not very nice, for each evening we heard the man of the house getting angry at his wife and children, even though they had just been reading from the Bible.

From there I went to the house of the friend who had passed the exam with me back in Porsea, and I stayed there for the rest of the first year. They lived in Kampung [village] of Hutabagot, out in the middle of the rice paddies. When we went there from Tarutung we had to walk along the riverbank. It was covered in long grass, so when we walked there early in the morning our shoes would get wet from the dew on the grass. On rainy days the riverbank was full of mud and no matter how we watched where we walked every once in a while we would accidently step in some mud. Of course our shoes got dirty and we had to wipe them off with grass to get the mud off. And every morning we were forced to walk along a small ditch through the rice paddies. This ditch was soft and moist, so the bridges placed over it always sank into the mud. You could not just jump over the ditch, because of course our shoes would sink in the soggy mud. So we took off our shoes on one side and put them on again on the other. But because the water in which we washed our feet after crossing was so dirty (after all, it was muddy ditch water), our socks—or our shoes, if we were not wearing socks—got filthy.

I felt rather cooped up living there, for once we reached the kampung after school, it was difficult to leave again. Luckily the two of us were together every day, or else it would have been intolerable.

The pupils at MULO came from all corners of the Batak region, but the majority were from the area around Lake Toba and Silindung. Sometimes there was someone from South Tapanuli,[4] but that was rare. Almost all of the students were Christian; after all the school was run by the mission. It was the most advanced school in Tapanuli, which was perhaps why the students considered themselves so special.

At first it was hard for me to follow what the teacher was saying in classes where he spoke Dutch, especially if he did not pronounce his words clearly. When I was asked something I usually just responded with ya or nee [yes or no]. But eventually this changed. Maybe because I did not study hard enough, my written assignments rarely even got average grades. A five, a five and a half, at the most a six minus, was what I was earning. But this did not bother me so much, because in other subjects I was not doing so poorly.

The subject that really appealed to me was math, and in fact I came to believe that I had a talent in it. Hadn't my grades in lower school been good in arithmetic? For us kids and for the grownups in the village, the person who was best at figuring was the "expert." No one else really measured up, even if they had a talent for languages or whatever. People said that if you were good with figures you could not easily be cheated.

At school I was the one everyone came to, to ask about algebra and geometry. As a result, I started to call myself [in Dutch] a *wiskunstenaar,* a math wizard. Nowadays I am not quite so sure where my talents lie; maybe I do not possess any at all. But I can guarantee that I am no mathematician. I was simply attracted to new things, and perhaps because the various kinds of math were new to me, I intuitively moved in that direction. Other explanations I shall not seek. Indeed, not many Indonesian children know what their talents are.

We did not usually speak Dutch at school. Wherever we were, we always used our mother tongue, even during class. So Dutch was used only when speaking to teachers. When we did try to speak Dutch among ourselves, we got teased. Someone would say something like, "You might as well toss your Dutch over there into the sewer." Our teachers knew this, so they made a rule that whoever was reported to be speaking Batak would be fined 2½ cents. But this policy failed, since none of us wanted to squeal on a friend. Indeed, we felt undeniably calmer and more confident using our mother tongue when we conversed. And this represented one victory for the Dutch in our area.[5]

After three months in MULO we received our first report card. This report also noted how many foreign languages we were allowed to choose. Malay was counted as a foreign language.[6] I chose German and Malay, because I had heard from my friends that there was not much demand for French speakers. German seemed to be the right language for us to take. After all, wasn't all scientific literature written in German? That is what we thought then, anyway. But maybe we also chose it because our preachers were Germans, and so we were already a bit pro-German.

Our math teacher also taught us German. (German grammar is only good for mathematicians anyway!) Since my grades in German were good, I became increasingly certain that I had a talent for math.

CHAPTER 13

That first year I heard an "anecdote"[1] at school. Not long ago there had been a Dutch teacher (he had since left the school) who read a "funny" story to his class. Much to his surprise he noticed that when he finished reading none of the students laughed. So he angrily asked one of them, "Why aren't any of you laughing after hearing such a funny story?"

"Well, um . . . ," answered the pupil, "we didn't feel your story was very funny, actually."

"What do you mean, not funny? You just don't have a sense of humor." But the student said that the story really was not funny. Finally the teacher said, "Well, in that case, you tell a story. Then I'll be able to see what kind of sense of humor you have."

So the pupil related a story—actually, he just shouted it—as follows: "Manase, Manase ditinkgir ho lubang ni hirik, hape lubang ni te" (Manase, Manase, you dug out a cricket hole, but unfortunately it was really a wasp home in a dung heap). There is a type of wasp that adores water buffalo or cow manure (in Dutch it is called a *mestkever*). Normally it digs its hole in a pile of dry dung, and when you go to pick up the dung to use as fertilizer, you sometimes cannot tell whether this hole has been made by a cricket (which also likes to burrow in dung) or by a wasp. The story the student told is a kind of taunt in verse form commonly used to torment kids named Manase.

When the class heard the verse, they burst into paroxysms of laughter. The Dutch teacher, who did not speak Batak, was dumbfounded. He asked for a translation of the verse, but the mischievous student replied, "It really can't be translated, Tuan. It wouldn't be funny anymore in another language." But the teacher kept insisting and finally the boy said, "Manase, Manase (the stress now falling on the *na*, not on the *se* as it had above), waar ben je?" (Where are you). The class burst into laughter once again.

His face reddening, the teacher said, "What's so funny about the sentence 'Manase, where are you?' I don't understand you people at all." Maybe the Dutch really did not understand us.

Two incidents in school startled us. The first was that a level-two student pointed a knife at a teacher and threatened to kill him. The boy said he did not actually intend to stab the teacher but just to frighten him. People said that teacher was "sweet outside but a wolf inside." I never had any firsthand experience of this teacher being sneaky. I was a bit afraid of him, but maybe that was only out of prejudice. Anyway, it turned out badly for this boy. He was expelled from school. Sometimes a small matter determines the whole course of your life.

The other incident was that another child in level two was expelled because it was thought that he had insulted the statue of Tuan J. Nommensen,[2] the German preacher who had first spread the Christian religion in Tapanuli. This statue had been erected in commemoration of his services to the Batak people (spreading religion was a service, it seemed). On the one hundredth anniversary of his birth, the statue was decorated with flowers and the Dutch flag (which, indeed, he had served, by helping to establish it in the Batak region). Three days later the incident in question occurred, though in retrospect it really did not amount to much of anything. Several students living in the dormitory were playing and they took the flowers and flags from around the statue. Possibly they thought that nothing would come of it, since the ceremony was long over, but a teacher saw everything (the statue stood in a little field out in front of the place where the teachers lived). After the matter was investigated it came out that one particular student was more or less the leader. He was described as the *hoofddader* [main culprit], alias the rebel-in-charge. He was expelled from school with a bad letter inserted in his file saying that he had been expelled by the director (at the time he was teaching our class) and that his report card had been ripped up in front of him. All wrongs had to be punished, especially wrongs perpetrated on the tuan preachers.

Frequently a hawker selling *mandrek*[3] passed by the front of our school. He was a Bengali, and we called him the "komplet"[4] peddler. His coconut cakes were always good and his mandrek was always hot. He was very careful when big bunches of students came crowding in around him all at once, but no matter how careful he was, there were always some who would cheat him. He apparently discovered this when, back home, he counted up his profits, and as a result he stopped coming by our school so often. We were forced to go over to his house, and there of course we could not play our little games with him.

A peanut vendor also often came by. Peanuts were just the right thing to perk us up. The ones this man sold were not very different from plain old fried peanuts, but they tasted incredibly, incomparably delicious. I doubt there are peanuts that good anywhere else. Many of us did not always have pocket money, so we would be forced to write out IOUs. Paying them was not as easy as eating the peanuts.

We were forbidden to smoke. If a boy was found smoking, all of his cigarettes were confiscated, so the majority of children smoked in secret. We smoked in back of the classroom, but the safest spot by far was on a tennis court about 100 meters from the school building. This tennis court was actually school property, but it was rarely used because tennis was a sport for rich kids. We also went out there if we had a lot to memorize, because it was quiet and the view of the Silindung Valley was very lovely. So the tennis court was converted into a smoker and a study hall.

CHAPTER 14

The world had changed a great deal in the past few years,[1] but not the town of Tarutung. There were still MULO students with all their posturing and mannerisms; with swollen heads, as the Japanese say. They had nothing to do with the smaller kids, and only mixed with adults—indeed, many of them were already pretty much grown up themselves. I was seventeen years old when I entered the school and even though the rule was that no one over fifteen was allowed in, that was not an obstacle. Anything on paper can be adjusted, can't it?

When I first entered MULO, I was not allowed to mix with students in level three. I used this same tactic myself, when I got to be in level three. Generally the lower classes were not allowed to mix with the higher classes. This was especially the case with level-zero kids, who were forever being teased by kids sticking their hands high up in the air and forming their fingers into a zero because, they said, this was the Goose Egg Class. ("Egg" in Batak is *pira*, but *pira-pira* means testicles, so the epithet Pira-Pira Class was an insult.)

Not surprisingly, many of us were quite big. A majority had gone to other schools before going to Dutch school (H.I.S.). And since we were already nearly grown up, many of us would go courting girls in the town's neighborhoods.

Martandang was the only sort of socializing between young girls and boys that adat permitted. Girls usually slept at the house of an elderly grandparent or a widow. The boys would come over to shoot the breeze and get to know the girls. This form of socializing eventually disappeared, especially among "modern"[2] youngsters, who preferred to write letters. (In fact, the reason parents gave for not sending their girls to school did have a certain logic: they said that girls went to school just to learn how to send love letters to boys.)

Since I did not want to get married just yet, I did not go *tandang* visiting, though friends had asked me to come along. Once, however, I did go *menangi-nangi*, at the urging of some friends (*tangi* means to listen in).[3]

It had become the custom in Tarutung for MULO students to go for a stroll in the evenings between five and seven-thirty, to take a bit of air. The busiest thoroughfares, such as the Sibolga-Pematang Siantar Road, were full of MULO students making a lot of noise, laughing and joking, and jostling, pestering, and taunting each other as they walked along. When they entered a shop or a coffee stall things got rather dangerous for the owner. One of the popular snacks was a small, softish kind of sponge cake, two or three of which could be held in your hand and tossed into your mouth at once. It was possible to grab three or four of these cakes but claim you had only eaten one. Another tactic was to have one boy haggle over the price of a few cakes while the others were stuffing dozens of them into their pockets. But the funny thing was, it was these very shops and stalls where we did these kinds of things that seemed to be the most prosperous.

When a girl passed by the street, the boys invariably set to quarreling with each other. Some looked for a way to attract her attention; some were bold enough to follow her right into a shop pretending to buy something even though they just wanted to look at her. MULO kids did all sorts of things. Flowers always attract bees, it is true, but not in the way most people think, that is, with flowers existing for the benefit of bees. No, Nature has determined that bees exist for the benefit of flowers.

Like my friends, I attended church faithfully. Pearaja (the name of the place where Tarutung's church was located) was not very far from town, only about one kilometer. The road went up a hill but we did not have bikes and always walked. We were not particularly pious or headed for careers as religious teachers; we went to church simply because it had gotten to be a habit. After all, since the time we were small we had been told that we had to attend church. That is just what you did on Sunday. And besides, for us guys going to church meant a chance to watch girls. In Pearaja, for instance, the young men (and thus the MULO students) sat in the upper balcony, while the girls sat off to the side, in front of the balcony. This arrangement was the very best way to get young men and girls to go to church.

I myself did not feel right if I did not go to church on Sunday. If you think about it, going to church was worthwhile. Didn't we get a chance to gossip with friends? Couldn't we get a look at all the new and pretty clothes, all in the very latest fashion, à la the year 2000?[4]

CHAPTER 15

Tarutung was only about sixty kilometers from where my family lived. Nevertheless, I rarely went home because the travel costs were so high (50 cents one way, so Rp. 1 round trip, and villagers could live for a month on this). Indeed, Tarutung seemed more prosperous than small towns such as Porsea. There was electricity, *waterleiding* [piped water], a movie theater, and so on. Half of the town was located in the Silindung Valley, and the other half was in the foothills above the valley. There were beautiful buildings on the mountain slopes, for example the MULO building, the government resthouse, the assistant resident's house, the MULO teachers' house, and so on. When we stood in the valley in the evening and looked to the west, toward the foot of the mountain, it was like seeing a Christmas tree because of all the electric lights shining in the night.

The town of Tarutung is cool, especially early in the morning from about four to seven, when it feels truly cold. The sun's rays extend from the east and warm you up nicely at the foot of the mountain. If there were no lessons in the morning, we MULO students loved to sit on the school steps, studying and sunning ourselves. Indeed, of all the towns in North Tapanuli, Tarutung is the healthiest and most prosperous. Its residents certainly appear to be the best off. Perhaps that is because they became acquainted with the Christian religion before others did.

In level two I wanted to be in Section A, because my plan was to go straight to work after graduating from school. I told my father this, but after I explained the difference between Section A and B,[1] he said, "You'd be very foolish to pick A. If you have permission to enter B, why not take the opportunity? We don't know what the future holds; who knows, maybe a huge gold nugget will fall from the sky." So I picked Section B.

When I started level two I moved into town. I lived in the house of a relative of ours who worked as a driver. The vehicle he drove carried goods such as rubber from Tarutung to Medan, so he rented a house to use as a warehouse. He also lived there. The house was located along an alley of shops, so it was built like a shop. There was one very large room (the merchandise room), then behind this there was a bedroom, and way in the back there was a kitchen, a washroom, a toilet, and so on. They stored the goods to be transported in the big room; among other things, there was a lot of rubber. Rubber does not have a pleasant odor, to say the least, especially when it is old. So I did not sleep in that big room. The house had an upper floor, and I slept up there on a rattan mat. Early in the morning and at night it was very cool, but in the middle of the day it was pretty hot and you could not sleep well then. If I got sleepy in the middle of the day I lay down below, but the smell of rubber would annoy me and I would just have to fight off my drowsiness. Eventually I got used to the rubber and could stand it even when it was really awful, so I was able to sleep on the ground floor.

The head of the household drove to Medan often; sometimes he did not come home for three days, so his wife (my father's sister's child) would often be left alone with her two small children. They were delighted that I had joined the household. In all the time I was in Tarutung, paying room and board to this family pleased me the most. Not because of the food or the bed and so on, absolutely not. I felt happy there because they considered me a member of the family. I felt as if I were in my own house.

When I went home over holidays my mother sometimes criticized me. She said I had gotten spoiled over there at What's-her-name's house (the family I boarded with), so apparently I couldn't stand to be near her anymore. I just laughed to hear her say this, for I did not have any real reason to be derisive about the whole situation to her. It was true, in Tarutung I was spoiled, if that is the right word for it. When I left for school my food was all ready on the table and I just had to eat it. I never had to wash my own clothes, because there was a laundrywoman. My bed was made up every morning, my room swept out . . . I was treated like a tuan. But in my own house, with my father and mother, my meals were not regular (our meals weren't at set times), I had to wash my own clothes, my bed was just a single thin rattan mat on the floor, and so on. In Tarutung I was used to an ambtenaar's life, with my meals at regular intervals, my sleeping arrangements all orderly, a nice bathroom and toilet all provided—the latter being especially necessary.

From the "Rubber House" I moved to a better-looking place on Balehongstraat. This street name was known only to us MULO students. A German man lived on this street and because his name was hard to pronounce, he was just called Balehong. So the street got called that too.[2] The house was about a kilometer from school, but this was no problem. We were used to walking.

At that time level two had no more than twenty-seven people, even though level one had parallel classes. Many level one students had to stay behind a grade, but there were also a number who could not afford to pay the tuition fees without taking a break.

Farmers did not, in fact, have much of an income. At the most Rp. 20 a month, which had to be divided up among the sons in the family. So it was very difficult to ask for additional allowance from home. My pocket money was only Rp. 2 a month, and I did not get this until after I sent in my list of all expenses, such as tuition, boarding costs, books, laundry, haircuts, and so on. My mother said that this Rp. 2 was already too much. Couldn't I just wash my own clothes in the afternoons after school? I laughed, and my dad did too.

Sometimes it did occur to me to put one over on them. Why not do what other kids did and tell them, for example, that we needed to buy one book or another, or that the teacher had told us we had to go on an excursion[3] someplace? But I did not have the heart to do that, and I would likely have been found out eventually anyway.

CHAPTER 16

Several of the pupils in level two were girls. Our interactions were awkward, perhaps because we were no longer little children, but also because adat held that boys and girls did not customarily meet outside the martandang courtship places. Unless we needed something, we scarcely communicated;[1] we just stared at each other.

One of our classmates apparently liked a certain girl. She did not have a very pretty face, but she was light-skinned and had a fresh complexion. Our friend was always trying to attract this girl's attention. Every morning and at recess, after we had already gone in but before the teacher had entered the room, he was the very last one to come in. He sat on his bench, looking over at the girl. He had a wristwatch with big hands, and he made a show of raising his arm up to look at his watch, just to show that he had one; often he rolled up his shirt-sleeves too. This was love from afar, however (and maybe it wasn't even love), because the girl paid absolutely no attention to him. Probably she did not even know he existed.

One day the teacher asked this girl to read aloud. Unfortunately for her, the reading selection included the word "cicak" [a small house lizard], and no matter what the teacher did this girl could not read it except as "sissak." As a result, we nicknamed her Si Sissak.[2] We quite regularly assigned nicknames to people—even teachers—in this manner. For example, we had a teacher called Gambier[3] (because he smoked gambier cigarettes), anothe. was called Bitch-Butcher (because he was fond of eating dog meat), and so on.

Not all that many girls in our area went to school, and even fewer to Dutch-language schools. A girl who graduated from MULO could certainly hope to marry, at the very least, a teacher's school graduate or a MOSVIA graduate.[4] Rarely did you see a girl from H.I.S. with a husband who was only an H.I.S. graduate himself, or a MULO girl married to a MULO boy. Often parents would have their daughters go to school with the sole purpose of securing a husband who would hold an official position.

In level two there was a friend of mine, a boy. His eyes were a bit crossed, but that was not why we always laughed when we were around him. He was [as they say in Dutch] a *droog komiek,* a dry wit, and all we had to do was look at him to be amused. He talked like a parent giving sage advice to little children as he rubbed his beard, and he was always searching for the odd word in his speech. Instead of "piglet" (*anak babi,* which was actually a taboo thing to say) he said "circus child" (*anak ni sirkus*) and we would roll on the ground laughing. He also changed our teachers' names in funny ways, like Tekken or Si Typist for Tcekens [the teacher's real name] and Mingka for Minkhorst, and so on.

Eventually we stopped feeling ill-at-ease and out of place in level one, and by level two we felt completely comfortable. By the time we got to level three, we felt like we were at the top of the heap.

There were not all that many of us left in level three, perhaps no more than twenty-six people. Each year we lost some students. Out of sixty people in level one only about twenty-five or so made it to level three. They said it was to protect the good name of the "renowned" MULO-Tarutung. And indeed it was a good school: no less than 75 percent of Tarutung students normally passed the annual MULO final exam; in my day it was 100 percent. The MULO-Tarutung was considered to be a cramming school[5] for the exams, an idea that persisted. Middle school students did practice drills in night school in order to pass the entrance exams for high school or for normal school. In H.I.S., students were specially prepared for taking the exams for MULO or other schools. And in MULO it was the same thing. They valued tests more than a child's character and turn of mind.[6]

Our interactions with teachers were not very close, and in fact even interaction with other students was rare. In primary and middle school I was afraid of my teachers, a circumstance that did much to shape my disposition; I did not change appreciably in MULO, where to make matters worse there were Dutch teachers. We were disinclined to speak casually with them, especially since we were forced to speak Dutch, and none of them, for their part, made an effort to really engage their pupils. Maybe they just figured that they could keep drawing their government salaries whether their students liked them or not. The way we looked at it, teachers were not friends or figures to be loved; the majority of them were simply policemen or spies always on the lookout, counting our mistakes.

CHAPTER 17

When I was in level three my father bought me a pair of soccer shoes. Maybe he thought I had grown up. The shoes were not very good ones; the toes got crushed easily and when they got wet the leather wrinkled up, so finally I was forced to buy some better ones.

Normally for the MULO soccer team the level three pupils were chosen first and only after that were students from other grades taken. But in my years there, not many in our class were interested in ball games and only three people were actually in training. The three of us were chosen to play, and I took the position of back.[1] This was because no one wanted to be back; everyone wanted to play forward.

Once a year there was a soccer match in Tarutung to determine the Silindung championship. Our MULO had kept this trophy for several years running, but when I played back we were forced to surrender it to another team. In fact, that year the MULO soccer team was a team in name only.

One time on a holiday there was a soccer game between the MULO and the local military unit. People knew that this game would really be something; everyone in Tarutung knew that the MULO pupils did not get along very well with the military. There were often fights between the two groups. The soldiers saw themselves as "the Company's men,"[2] while the MULO students were totally pro-Tarutung. In such an atmosphere violence could easily break out. The soldiers were solidly built, but the MULO students were not exactly children. And the students had a way of moving around in large groups; who wouldn't be brave, if there's a lot of you?

One time a violent fight broke out, and our school director was forced to come in with his pistol and referee. We were punished by not being allowed to walk together or gather in groups larger than two people, and each group had to stay twenty meters away from all the others. It lasted for two weeks. We were not brave enough to break the rules, because we had been threatened with being expelled from school if we did. And we students were ready and willing to endure any and all punishments just so that we were not expelled from school.

Anyway, for this game with the military, the director and our teachers came to watch. Their *komandan* [commander] came too. Back at school our director had warned us that if anyone started to play rough he would be punished according to the nature of his offense. We promised not to turn the match into a fist fight.

We knew that the military types were not particularly good[3] at soccer, and we were convinced that we were going to win. The playing field was muddy at the time, but the game went on anyway. I played left back, which was really easy. All I had to do was kick the ball, because there were people out in front of me who would cover me. The game was not rough at first but rather *fors,* or vigorous.[4] They tried as hard as they could to beat us but were unsuccessful, and they trailed 2–0. They could not accomplish anything. The ball only went halfway across the field. When the ball came in from midfield, we were ready and waiting to intercept it and kick it back. The right field could just doze because the ball never got near them. This shook them up, maybe. One time the ball did come in from the center, and two of us were exactly the same distance from it. My opponent ran after it to kick it toward our goal; I ran after it to kick it back toward center field. The two of us got to the ball at almost the same time. Without a moment's thought he kicked as hard as he could with the idea of kicking me and the ball at the same time. But I made glancing contact with the tip of my shoe at the same time that I jumped to the left, at precisely the right time. His long leg kicked the air and almost got me in the rear end. But the air felt no pain—he was the one who was moaning.

We were invited by the Sibolga soccer league to play against the MULO in Padang Sidempuan.[5] The expenses for our meals and overnight lodging were paid by the league, and we had only to pay for the round-trip auto costs. We left Tarutung about nine in the morning along with several girls, since there was also going to be a basketball game. We made all kinds of noise, laughing and joking, singing, and so on. At Adian Koting we stopped a while to eat. This spot was famous for its food. Doubtless this was a good place to eat, as people said, but not so much because the cooking was good, but because the cool air whetted your appetite.

At kilometer ten we paused for a moment because the view of Sibolga Bay was lovely from there. This bay was protected by Mursala Island from the large waves of the Indian Ocean. Appropriately enough the bay was traditionally called *tapian na uli* (beautiful bathing place). This became the name of all the Bataklands, Tapanuli.

The lineup of games had been scheduled beforehand. Tarutung would play Padang Sidempuan first, then a combination of players from the two schools would play the Sibolga soccer league. The next day a basketball game would also be held, between the Tarutung and Padang Sidempuan MULOs.

I played back again. My position as back was safe, certainly, because no one else wanted it. The game got underway. It was fast paced and enthusiastic. There were a number of spectators. Tarutung took the lead by racking up a goal, but a response to that came not long afterward, so the score was 1–1. We were all young, and whenever young men play games you see some serious-minded playing. Each team tried its best to win. The reputations of our schools were at stake, weren't they? Things continued this way until half-time, with Tarutung succeeding in making one more goal. The score was 2–1.

After a break the players started in again. The pace of play was the same, but eventually it became obvious that Tarutung was yielding. Maybe it was because the weather was too hot; they seemed tired. Even so, they still managed to set down one more goal, making the score 3–1. Because they thought they had already won, the play became indolent. Maybe Tarutung thought that Padang Sidempuan would not do anything about their defeat. But Padang Sidempuan soon succeeded in changing the score to 3–2, and five minutes before the final whistle sounded they racked up another goal, bringing it to 3–3. Padang Sidempuan's playing actually had been far better and more disciplined than ours and they only failed to win outright because of the simple bad luck that we happened to take the lead first. Probably if we had played a quarter hour more we would have gone back to Tarutung in defeat.

We were not so lucky in basketball, suffering a 1–0 loss. And the combination teams match with Sibolga was not to our advantage. The fact was that they had more experience in sports than we did.

CHAPTER 18

When I was still in link school,[1] I was the one to help my father watch our store. As store clerk, I served the customers. H.I.S. kids from Narumonda often came there to buy something or other, and they often mixed Dutch words into their sentences as they chatted with their friends. They were always doing this, without even being aware of it; it had become a habit. But this habit was a real annoyance to me, a cinder in my eye, for I suspected that they only wanted to show that they were going to a Dutch school.

Maybe it was because I attended a school that also taught Dutch but was apparently not considered to be on quite the same level as theirs.

When they came to our store I really perked up my ears to listen to their Dutch, but not with the intention of learning anything from them. I wanted to know whether they were saying something nasty about me. I thought that if I heard something I would lash out and kick them straight-away. After I became a MULO student I continued to play this game. During the quarter break and the long vacation I still helped my dad, and since I was wearing my usual clothes no one suspected that I was not just the store clerk. Luckily I never did hear them say anything bad. Jealousy and envy can truly make people do things they should not.

When I was in level three in MULO, several girls arrived as new pupils. They were not aᵉ shy as the other ones, maybe because they thought them-selves modern.[2] I do not remember exactly how, but I made friends with these girls. Maybe it was predestined; we cannot always say why a boy and girl fall in love, can we? Perhaps before we met one another there was a tie between us we simply could not see, a tie that bound us to one another. For instance, a common focus of attention, a common favorite thing, or something of that sort. Getting to know one another was thus only a mat-ter of tightening the tie.

But I can recall—I can almost see it before my eyes—one particular day: we were having recess, and I was walking along down below the school along the main road. I saw several of the girls standing up above me. Playfully I lifted my hand and waved at them, certain that they would not wave back at me, for after all, where is there a Batak girl who waves her hand at a young fellow she does not know? Imagine my surprise when I saw them wave back. I was surprised and very pleased indeed to see that but was not entirely sure they were waving at me. Maybe they were waving at someone else. So I tried it again and I laughed happily. After that we got to know each other right away and became friends.

People said that one of the girls in level one was really pretty (I did not think so, but maybe I did not yet know how to gauge prettiness). To me she was like any girl, with a nose, eyes, ears, hair, and so on. My friend said this girl was the Arab type. She lived in a private dorm on Naheong Street. Her eyes were large, which was thought to make her especially attractive. I was afraid to look at her. Every afternoon after this girl got home from school lots of MULO students would amble along Naheong Street. Jok-ing and jostling with each other loudly to attract this girl's attention, they glanced up at the upper story of the house where this girl lived, but they did not catch even a glimpse of her. All this happened every evening. Naheong Street became the hub of town for MULO students. They never gave up.[3]

With some girls—that is, five girls from level one and one girl from level three—we six boys formed a club of sorts. Wherever we went, on a picnic, for instance, we went together. One time we went picnicking to Siatas Barita. We had such a good time on the way there that we were not aware that we had arrived. Indeed, when we went on picnics with girls we did not particularly care where we were supposed to be going; the important thing was being together.

We did not tell each other what was in our hearts. But we made guesses and could tell that this person liked this other person. The big word— "love" (*sinta,* we said)—we were not yet brave enough to pronounce to each other. Only two couples had their names linked together, among them me and one of the girls. The other couple, it was said, had already agreed to spend their lives together. To tell the truth there was not anything in my heart for this girl acquaintance of mine (she probably felt the same way). Even so, the two of us would always join in when the others laughed at us, teasing us as being future husband and wife. We took part in the joke, and it got to the point that we wore ourselves out laughing whenever we all got together. It brought us all closer together. Don't people drift apart if there isn't something interesting and fun to talk about? Talking about our studies would just have bored us, especially because we were in different grades.

When we gathered on Sundays at a girl's house, we never once discussed important things. Joking and laughing was the task before us. But then, who goes to a girl's house to spout philosophy? Even though we did not discuss anything important, we were quite ready and able to sit there together for hours and hours. Perhaps our common interests had developed into a common sympathy for one another. After socializing with these girls I underwent a kind of change, deep down. I was no longer as dirty as I used to be, and as much as I could manage it I tried to keep my clothes clean. I watched my friends do the same thing. From this perspective, socializing with girls did have its uses. Might it be that a girl can alter a young man's character?

CHAPTER 19

My girlfriend was not particularly good at riding a bicycle. Actually I had never seen her on a bike, but one Sunday we took a notion to ride to a spot outside town. When we checked with others about it, no one mentioned they might have a problem. Early in the morning when it was time to depart I saw my girlfriend and her friend standing there with their bikes, but when I asked them to ride alongside us, they said we should just go on ahead and they would follow. I was taken aback to hear this, but we went on ahead anyhow. There were three of us boys, and two girls. When we reached the outskirts of town we waited for them, but when they got near us one of the girls got down off her bike and said, "If you don't go first, we won't come after you." We were forced once more to bike on ahead. But finally we could not stand going on ahead like that. What is the use of riding bikes if the only companion you get is the wind? So we waited for them again, and the girls had to give in and ride along with us.

We were on a major road and automobiles came along frequently, but at that particular time there was no traffic. The edge of the road was grassy, and then there was a drainage ditch running its full length, bordering an expanse of rice paddies. We were able to bicycle along without a problem. I rode in back and the girls were in front of us. Suddenly I saw my girl-friend's bike veer off into the grass. I thought she must be playing around, for we kids often did such crazy things. But then she cried out, "Ee eeee!" and a moment later she fell into the drainage ditch and her bike went off into the rice paddy. At the moment it happened I was busy talking to another friend so I did not see exactly how she had fallen, but we stopped right away. I put my bicycle down at the side of the road and ran over to her, pulling her out of the muck.

According to adat young men were not allowed to touch a girl's body, so when I went to pull her out of the drainage ditch like that I was a bit hesitant and worried, but I screwed up my courage anyway. After all, I did not want to leave her lying there in the muck just because of adat.

My pants got muddy too, and my shoes. So did the pants and shoes of my friend who pitched in to help me with her. After she was rescued, we were able to laugh about the whole thing; even the girl joined in and laughed uproariously. After all, isn't it better to laugh about something than to cry over it? We washed out our shoes and pants so it would not be too obvious that one of us had fallen off. It was lucky the accident had happened when there was little traffic, so no one or almost no one had seen it.

We were quite far from town, so it would have been a waste not to just continue on and finish our trip. We were not worried about our clothes, since they would dry out in the sun. One of my friends pulled the girl's bike along and I let her ride sidesaddle behind me. In this way we continued our trip, laughing about the unexpected occurrence. We promised not to tell anyone about the incident; it would be our secret. Actually, we did not have the courage to discuss it, for we did not want people to dub our trip a "fiasco."[1]

CHAPTER 20

The six of us were always together. And wherever young men hang around, girls are a topic of conversation. Maybe girls do the same thing with boys. We talked about the MULO girls or the H.I.S. girls, with a great deal of side commentary. One person would say that such and such a girl was ugly and black,[1] but someone else would defend her by saying she had a nice smile, and so on and so forth. None of us boys had the same opinion about any of them.

A social unit sometimes leads to the development of smaller twosomes, threesomes, and so on. And in much the same way our group spawned several breakaway bunches. We split apart not because of fights but because of girls. Cherchez la femme.[2]

One Sunday after church a friend of mine and I got our bikes and went off to find someone to shoot the breeze with. We happened to run into three girls we knew, on two bikes. We asked where they were going and if we could accompany them, but they snapped that they were not going anywhere at all. We just stood there watching, and finally they went off to the house of one of them. We got back on our bikes and went looking for some friend or other. Not long afterward we ran into the three girls again, and once more we asked them where they were going. We got the same answer. We thought, There's no point at all to riding our bikes, because we're not going to run into a friend anyway. But several minutes after this we saw these three girls once again, going down our street and heading out of town. We were flabbergasted. These girls had never refused us permission to accompany them before. So why this time? So we grabbed our bikes and followed them. For the third time they snapped that we were not to follow them, and we felt insulted and went home. We vowed never to speak to them again. After all, an insult had to be responded to.

At the time we had absolutely no idea of what was going on, but two months later, after we all were getting along again, we found out that the girls had been distancing themselves from us on purpose. They had been warned by the Zuster [the Sister] who supervised their dorm that they would be expelled if they were seen associating with boys. The Sister was a German; maybe boys and girls were allowed to see each other only in Germany.

The next day, when we were standing around in front of the building before going into school, the three girls passed us and one of them said hello, but we refused to answer. I was even greeted twice, but I stood there like a statue. We studiously ignored (or, as we say, *sanding*-ed) each other for two months. But no one except the members of our club knew anything about the matter then, and we never told any outsiders about it later. Around other people we behaved normally but simply did not address each other, so no one else knew.

Two of the five girls chose to be in our clique. This was simply out of mutual sympathy, and because of it our group of six boys was split. Three joined our party, while the other three formed a group with the remaining three girls. In this way, with all this *sanding*-ing, we discovered our different interests and sympathies. We learned that this particular friend had his heart set on this particular girl, and that friend had his heart set on that girl. Out of every misfortune comes some good.

To be subject to *sanding*—to be given the silent treatment—was hurtful, especially if those who did it to you have been close friends before. The first day was really hard to take. Without being aware of it, you sometimes wanted to speak to the person being *sanding*-ed, and then you realized that you were supposed to be giving that person the silent treatment. I thought it would be preferable to be soundly beaten than to be treated like this. You would be paid less attention to than the wind; to your friends you were nothing but a vacuum, dead space. Then, even though no one is angry at you for a long time and they want to be on good terms again, no one wants to make the first move. Neither side says hello for fear they will not get a reply, and so, ashamed and shy, they keep *sanding*-ing each other for months on end.

Fortunately we took a trip to Sibolga. Even though we were still snubbing each other, I was unable to keep my distance from the girls I was supposed to be ignoring. I sat next to them in the car, and because there were no other friends to talk to I was forced to speak to them. I was embarrassed at first; it was like talking to a stranger. Apparently they had wanted to get back on good terms with us for a long time, so since I started things off our conversation eventually got easier. We were back on good terms again and our club flourished.

CHAPTER 21

The final exams were near. Usually we went home at the end of each quarter and during our long vacation, but this time, during the third-quarter break, none of us in level three went home. We had to study for the coming exams.

We were very frightened of the finals. We believed that they or the diploma we expected to get after them would have great significance for our future lives. To succeed in this exam meant that you would also succeed in life. Our estimation of our worth was measured with a diploma. Diplomas = us.

We had heard many stories about these final exams from pupils who had graduated. Some said that So-and-so was the smartest, but he turned out to be the one who did not pass. By contrast, What's-his-face had never studied, but he did fine. Someone else related that he had begun to review his lessons six months before the final exams and that was why he had passed. The final exams were all luck, it was said.

I began to open my books one month before the exam. To tell the truth, I was not particularly afraid of the finals. Nevertheless, every so often doubts would come to me. I knew that I was not strong in either languages or electives, but I only used my time to review the latter. Math I did not dare to avoid at all.

The girls directed their attention to our exams as well as their own. They asked us when the exams would be held. Had we started to study? Sometimes if we had been shooting the breeze for too long they reminded us that we should go home to study, but we always had one excuse or another. For instance, we were too tired to study or had gotten dizzy and headachy, so we needed a break.

Four in our group were in level three, three boys and a girl. We reminded each other that we had to really study, for if we failed the exams people would say that our friendship was the problem. Among our sort of people, especially our parents, school and girls were thought not to mix; in fact, school was considered to compete with girl chasing.

The closer the exams got the less desire I had to study and my body felt weak and tired. Privately I decided to study until one in the morning— well, at least midnight—but it remained a plan rather than reality, for usually I was sleepy at ten. I would go to bed and promise myself to get up later at four in the morning. But mornings in Tarutung were exceedingly cold, and this goal too remained just a goal. As the Bible says, the spirit is willing but the flesh is weak.

We level three students were given permission to stay home to study, and each day I confronted my books. I felt as if my life had stopped. All other work, playing ball, taking walks, and so on ceased. I lived for my "sacred" texts.[1] But every time I finished studying a book I had doubts about whether or not I really knew it thoroughly. Not once could I truly say that I had the book down pat. This feeling of dissatisfaction tormented me constantly. Finally, I got so fed up that I just left my books firmly shut and said to myself, If you don't pass it, so be it. Maybe that's just fate. Just so long as you really try, you can't fault yourself and regret the outcome.

But a moment later an inner voice would interrupt me, Have you really tried hard? There's "really" and "really," you know, differing in degree. There's half really, quarter really, twenty-fifth really, and so on. Which really is your really?

Finally I could study no more. I could not stuff one more thing into my packed brain. I determined simply to take whatever might come, not caring whether I passed or not. Doing well would be fine, not doing well would be fate. Maybe I lacked faith in my strengths, in my abilities.

For two days before the exams I didn't touch another book. I had no desire to even so much as look at a book. My friends were still studying away. That night and the following night I tried to think over all the material, reviewing what I had studied, but my brain had just gone numb. I could think no more.

People say if you are about to take an exam it is not good to go to sleep too late the night before; they say you should try not to stay up later than ten. I went to bed at 9:30 the night before, but no matter how much I tried to close my eyes I could not fall asleep before midnight. I was nervous in the face of the next day's exam.

Whenever I was about to leave on a long trip I had no appetite. It was just the same when I was about to take an exam. Perhaps there was a connection between going on a trip and exams. When I awoke very early the next morning I was extremely anxious and constantly asked myself what the exam would be like. That morning I dressed more neatly than usual. I was turned out all prim and proper just as if I had been going off to church. I gathered together everything I needed for the exam: pens, pencils, erasers, compass, ruler, triangle, and so on. With these weapons I departed for the exam hall.

At the scene of the exam all was in readiness. The seats had been placed far apart so that no one could do "cooperative work." Folio paper and lined paper had been placed on the desks.

Normally each morning there was a bell telling us to come in, and before entering we gathered in the hall. After singing one or two verses from the book of Christian hymns and praying to Almighty God (led by a teacher), we were given our mail. Fancy Dutch terms of address on the envelopes such as *Aan den Edelgeboren Heer* [To the noble master] always made us laugh out loud and made our teacher angry. He said we should still be addressed as simply *jonge heer* [young master].

On exam day we level three students did not have to wait in the hallway but were allowed to go straight into the examination room. We took our places, kept quiet, and found ourselves closely watched by the teachers.

The questions were passed around. We sharpened our wits and strained our heads answering the problems set in front of us. Some were easy, but some had to be thought about until sweat and tears poured down. We had all vowed not to leave the examination hall before the bell rang, so that others would not get anxious or panicky. But even so some students left early. Perhaps the sage advice of my teacher—"In an exam there are no friends, only opponents"—was true.

After we were tested on one subject we gathered in groups to exchange opinions on that exam and find out whether our answers were right or not. In these exchanges some people were actors. They were ashamed to say that their answer was wrong.

In level three there was a boy who was a good sort. He was always kind to his friends, a faithful churchgoer and diligent student, and so on. People said he had read many of Rutherford's books. I was not aware of what the content of these books was and only knew that the teachers forbade us to read them. After this student read these books he appeared to change. He no longer went to church regularly, and when people asked him why, he answered that people could go to church in their hearts. "Your heart is your church," he said. He did not even want to take the final exams, and it was only because of pressure from the director that he sat there with us in the examination room. But on the first day he did not answer the exam questions. Calmly he drew a picture of a mountain with a bright sun shining out from behind it. On the second day he was nowhere to be seen. The sun must indeed have shone in his heart, for our self-worth does not depend solely upon diplomas, but upon our inner selves. We all thought he had had a nervous breakdown from reading too many Rutherford books. But maybe he was laughing at us in his heart. Happy is he who can defy the world because of his conviction. Isn't it from such persons that we get the great men, such as Buddha, Muhammad, Christ, Luther, and so on? For this it takes courage, and not the sort of courage coming from wielding weapons but the courage that issues from within oneself. And we do not meet very many of these people in this transitory world.

CHAPTER 22

The written exam was over and we knew the results. All of us were permitted to proceed and take the oral exam, even though there were two or three students who had almost no hope of getting through it with even an average grade. The oral exam was to be given in Dutch and English. I realized all too well that I was not very fluent in these two languages, so I tried to compensate for it by knowing the grammar well. Maybe I could still manage a score of 6, no matter what.

We went back to working ourselves to the bone studying for the oral exam. We were divided into several groups. Each day about five people would be examined, so the others had to wait their turns. The results would be made known the same day as a person's exam, and those who passed would be given their diplomas, so by the second and third days we ran into friends who had completed all their requirements.

I had already sent a letter home saying I had passed the first part of the exam but that I still had to take the oral exam on such and such a day, at such and such an hour. I also said that they should not be concerned about me, since the way I figured it, I would pass. This conviction of mine was not really genuine. I still had doubts about my work, but to assure my parents that all was well, I could not do other than what I did.

Before the oral exam began I was told to go into a certain small room. There I was shown the lesson I was to be tested on. I was allowed to read it two or three times in order to answer questions about it. The same for English.

When I was called inside the main examination hall, I did not know how long I stayed there. I had absolutely no sense of time, perhaps because all my attention was concentrated on the examiner's questions. Only when I was given a sign that time was up did I know that I had sat for the exam for a full hour. But I felt as if I had only been in the examination room for five minutes. An hour spent working goes faster than an hour spent waiting.

Nor did I know whether the answers I had given were good ones or not. Feelings of doubt still troubled me: Would I fail or would I pass? Our names were called. The diplomas were awarded. I had passed. Doubts disappeared. My hand trembled as I took the letter giving me life. Now, this was a piece of paper I must store away carefully, said the director. But I did not value this diploma very much anymore, now that it was in my hands. It had been more valuable to me before I had it.

One of the girls I knew was crying after she came out of the examination room. She had no idea whether or not she had given acceptable answers, but she was convinced that there was no way she could not fail. We cheered her up, so she would not be so *pessimistis,* for after all, the results were not actually known yet and it was not certain that she had failed. But we were not really convinced by our own words. Imagine how delighted she was, how she wiped away her tears, when she heard that she had passed. The child we had feared had disappeared came to life again.

Apparently my father was not satisfied with the tone of my letter. Perhaps a small flutter in his heart said that my letter was not communicating what I really thought. Concerned, he departed for Tarutung to look into my affairs. But there was nothing left for him to do except hear the news that I had passed. He invited me and two friends of mine to go eat pork stew,[1] a sign of his delight. From there we went back to my boarding house, where he heard that I had not paid the bill for my meals yet. He was not mad at me, however, and simply paid the bill after asking me what I had done with that money—and receiving the answer that I had spent it on miscellaneous expenses.

Everything had a beginning and an end, and the time came for us to leave Tarutung. We exchanged pictures with the girls and promised one another that we would write no matter where we might be living. As the saying goes, far from sight but never far from the heart. But that is just theory, for we only wrote two or three times. It is human nature to direct your attention to what is nearby, not to what is distant.

CHAPTER 23

I still did not know where I was going to continue my studies. From the director I had gotten some information about a few schools on the island of Java. Once I asked my father where I should go, but he replied that maybe I should not continue my schooling at all. Nevertheless, I sent letters to two schools applying for admission, although I did this halfheartedly.

We had a two-month vacation. Whether or not I would be on vacation forever (that is, not going on in school) I did not know, but whatever the case I was determined to have a good time. I did not want to just stay home for those two months. I wanted to have some fun at a few of our relatives' houses in Sibolga, Pematang Siantar, Tinjauan, and so on. And since I was taking these trips, I was not around my dad very much.

The new school year was to begin in two weeks. Unexpectedly, my father sent a letter to me in Tinjauan, saying that a letter had come for me from Jakarta. He also asked what was happening with my school plans. Had I sent in a down payment to a school?

I went home and told my father that I had not sent in application forms to any school anywhere. He got angry at me. He said I was an ignorant child, intent on merely traveling around and having fun, forgetting all about school, and so on. But when I answered that he himself had told me I would not be going to school anymore, he replied that he had just been joking. He told me to write a letter of application immediately, and if I was not admitted he would box my ears.

I just laughed. I opened the letter from Jakarta. I was not admitted to that school. So now what was the plan? A response to my other letter had not come yet, and if I was not accepted to that school, what then? I related all this to my father and said that I would wait for a response for one or two more days. Only if the answer was no would I send out another letter.

But the next day he was already pressuring me, asking if I had gotten a response to my letter yet. Finally I said, "All right, give me five rupiah and I'll send a telegram to the director of the school and prepay a reply. Today, or at the latest tomorrow, I'll get an answer." He gave me the money. Luckily the next day the news came that I would be accepted at the school, which started on August 1. I was delighted and so was my father, but he still nagged me. Indeed, he was never satisfied with me. If my score was a six he wanted a seven, and if it was a seven he wanted an eight, and if it was an eight he wanted a nine. There is never any satisfaction in this world.

My departure day was set. I would leave from Laguboti, from our village, not from Porsea, because we had the most family there. We would just stop awhile in Porsea on the way. Many of our relatives came to escort me to the auto. They grabbed my hand to shake it but slipped me a fifty-cent piece or a whole rupiah that they had hidden in their palms. So every time I shook someone's hand I stuck my hand into my pocket afterward, to stash away what I had in my palm. In that manner, I hauled in a lot that day.[1]

The same thing happened in Porsea. My mother called me over and then she kissed me. This is the only time I remember her ever kissing me. Because I had never been kissed, and also because I was already pretty big, I felt rather embarrassed. I had never been that close to my mother, except perhaps when I was a baby.

CHAPTER 24

My father took me to Belawan. He had already bought the ticket, and as I was about to board the ship he gave me thirty rupiah. He said it would be enough money to live on for a while in Jakarta. I pretended to be astonished and said, "But how could Rp. 30 be enough to go to Jakarta with?" But he answered that I had received a lot of money from relatives. Indeed, I was just pretending to be upset, because I actually had about thirty-five rupiah more in my pocket.

We claimed our spots on the deck. I had already set out my rattan mat and suitcase, and I went down to protect my spot so that no one else would take it. I saw many school friends and so did not feel too lonely.

The ship's whistle blew twice, and my father got off the ship. The quay cables were freed and the gangplank pulled up as well. The ship started to move. At first it moved away from the dock very slowly, but soon it was headed out to sea. We all ran to the railing to say good-bye to friends or relatives left behind. Imagine how crowded and exciting it all was then! Handkerchiefs were pulled out and waved and waved. Even my dad took his handkerchief out of his pocket to wave good-bye to me. I was standing right next to the railing, pulled up straight like a soldier saluting as his commandant passed by. Just as I had been surprised at my mother kissing me, I was surprised again to see my father waving to me. He had never once been so *intiem*[1] with me before. But he was also feeling the fact that he had never been close to me. He held his handkerchief in his hand a long time, as if he did not know what to do with it. Then he waved at me, slowly at first, and awkwardly, and then in a more normal fashion like all the other people. Could he do any different?

I did not want to bid good-bye to my father in such an old-fashioned way. Calmly, I looked at him down below. Finally I just could not hold back my heart, which was full of feeling, and one tear fell and then another. I was embarrassed to be shedding those tears. I did not want to be weak and soft like a girl, so I bit my lip and forgot my tears in the pain.

My father was still waving at me from below. But I was not waving back at him, so he stopped and held his handkerchief in his fist. I felt sorry for him, because even though he had never shown his love for me, I knew that I was his favorite child. He probably thought that this day was the moment (who knew if it might be the last opportunity?) to show his love for me. Could my father see my tears?

We got farther out, and the more time passed the smaller the people on the dock became. Even though many on the boat had started to leave their places, I still stood at the rail. I wanted to show my father that I too felt sad at being separated from him, not by waving my handkerchief or my hand at him but by standing straight and tall and looking at him calmly. Could he perhaps understand that I loved him?

The dinner bell sounded, but not many of us went to get some food. We were still full from what we had eaten ashore. And we were still too tired and too full of feelings to be able to put rice into our mouths.

It was the end of July near the beginning of the new school term, and the Belawan-Tanjung Priok ship was packed with students going off to Java. They were the victims of educational politics, which had concentrated the schools on the island of Java. Because there were so many students, we did not feel lonesome on board ship. In fact, this crossing became a fond memory. Most of the students were from North Tapanuli, heading toward a variety of schools scattered between Jakarta and Surabaya; not a single school had been overlooked.

It was noisy on deck. After all, these were youngsters. Because of all the racket many of the second-class passengers thrust out their heads and gawked at us. The young people were all singing to the accompaniment of guitars or ankle bells, and when they got bored singing someone else would come along and haul out some jokes. They made a never-ending racket until it was time to go to sleep.

The moon shone brightly. Most of the students snored away, tired from the day's noisy fun. But a friend of mine and I still had no desire to sleep, and we crept up to the top deck to take in a cool breeze and gaze at the shining moon. My friend had also been a student at the MULO in Tarutung. He was one class ahead of me but had not passed the final exam and was forced to repeat level three in Kotaraja. We ran into each other on the ship, for he was also going to Java to continue his schooling.

As we looked at the bright, clear moon, our hearts were full remembering the village and the family members we had left behind, remembering school and friends there on the other shore. We told stories about our lives in the times now past. I also told him about my plans for when I got to Java. He did the same thing. But one question we were not able to answer. Would we ever return safely to our homelands² carrying the degrees we hoped for? Human beings can only make plans; it is God who determines the outcome.

NOTES TO *ME AND TOBA*

Chapter 1

1. This indicates that the family was not well off financially, as they apparently had so little inherited rice land that both parents had to supplement the family's income via peddling and transport service work. It is striking that Pospos sees fit to admit this forthrightly.

2. Toba villages in this area near Lake Toba indeed had several varieties of houses, graded by family income. Most magnificent were the large, ornate, carved adat houses, shaped like jaunty boats floating on a sea of green paddy rice. These were the homes of aristocrats, inherited through noble lineages and constructed at great cost, with many lavish public feasts. There were also simpler, plank-sided Malay-style houses, and small bamboo-walled structures, like Pospos's boyhood home. Today few new adat houses are being constructed and the older ones are falling into disrepair.

3. The Dutch colonial state's corvée taxes and corvée labor obligations extended throughout Toba, Angkola, and Mandailing.

4. Toba adat had many such name taboos between special pairs of relatives who should deal with each other with great reserve and respect. A particularly strong name taboo is found, for instance, between men and the women who marry into those men's wife-giving lineages. These men and women may not even speak directly to each other. There is much discussion about speech rules in the Batak societies.

5. Pospos often uses the Toba Batak kin term of address and then immediately translates it for his readers in Indonesian, in parentheses. In Toba and the southern Batak societies, children call their mother *Inang*; she in turn will call her daughters "Inang" and her sons "Amang" (the term of address used toward a speaker's father). That is, a reciprocal usage holds here. One's children are often said to be the replacements for one's own parents (after the parents' deaths).

6. This usage of *Amang* conveys respect for the teacher.

7. Market selling was at this time and remains today a major economic activity of Toba village and market-town women. The goods they handle include betel, spices, coffee, machine-made cloth, homespun ceremonial *ulos* textiles, and fruits and vegetables. Toba market women are reputed to be aggressive, hard bargainers.

8. This technique for guessing age shows up again in Radjab's memoir.

Chapter 2

1. This Sipoholon Seminary was locally quite famous in Toba and Angkola in late colonial times. Status-conscious families would brag about having a son who had graduated from there.

2. Adat feasts involved the slaughter of water buffalo and the politically astute distribution of its meat (so that the family hosting the feast could solidify interfamily alliances and out-compete old rivals, via an idiom of profligate generosity). Earrings, armbands, headdresses, and piles of ceremonial *ulos* cloaks were worn at these

occasions as public signs of wealth and good breeding. Toba retained the practice of earlobe holes for men longer than many other outer island Indonesian cultures.

3. Literally, "adat-strict." And *streng* is Dutch for "strong, harsh."

4. *Minggu* is the Indonesian word for Sunday, also often used in the Batak languages. *Mar-* (similar to the Indonesian *ber-*) is one of the main Toba verb particles.

5. The honorific *Tuan* was in common usage by Batak for high-status Europeans at this time. It was never used for Toba men or members of other ethnic groups.

Chapter 3

1. A sour fruit, sometimes grown commercially but more often found in home gardens.

2. The pungent, beanlike fruit of the *petai* tree, eaten raw or cooked.

3. Water closets. In Tapanuli, *W.C.* is a common term, even today, for toilet.

4. H.I.S., Hollandse Inlandse School, was a Dutch-language primary school of extremely high prestige, in the eyes of Batak commoner families. The children of Batak church officials, government workers, and school personnel could sometimes succeed in getting a son or daughter into one of these illustrious elementary schools.

5. The Dutch schoolteacher was doubtless just mispronouncing the child's name.

6. Special sorts of water buffalo all have different honorific names, in Toba.

7. Literally, "tidak teratur," said of something which has no sense of proper order to it. This is strong opprobrium in Tapanuli.

Chapter 4

1. Doubtless Malay would not have been used in the boy's home at this time, so the language took much conscious study.

2. Today in Tapanuli, translation is often referred to as "changing" or "transforming" a sentence from one language into another. That is the usage employed here in this sentence too.

3. The colonial road system had stone markers at one-kilometer intervals on major roads. Each of these named places are little villages, or *huta.*

4. A Dutch military command meaning "To the left!"

5. This contrasts with the Indonesian language, where *anak-anak* can mean children of both sexes. *Boru* is closely linked in meaning to the category of *anak-boru,* "our girl-children," and (at the same time) the men who marry our daughters. That is, our wife-receivers.

Chapter 5

1. This behavior is strikingly unusual, for Toba fathers (stereotypically at least) are quite affectionate with their young sons and daughters.

2. *Jengkol* is a sort of tree with edible beans that can be consumed raw (the *Pithecolobium*).

3. Indeed, there is a strong respect relationship between Toba brothers and sisters, according to the idealized adat at least. The two should not repeat ribald jokes around each other, or engage in rough and tumble play as children.

4. Toba apparently imagine that the formal form of the second-person pronoun is *kamu,* although standard Indonesian usage employs *kamu* as a fairly intimate form of "you." The formal and plural "you" in Toba Batak is *hamu,* which may help explain the usage (also prevalent in the Angkola region when people there speak Indonesian).

5. In Batak adat funerals and in more personal lament songs, parents of dead children sometimes angrily denounce their youngsters for "having the heart to leave us."

6. Special fish meals are indeed used in Toba village medical belief in this way. The notion that sickness can result from unrequited cravings for certain fish is also common throughout many Batak areas; it is a major theme of oral stories, too.

7. Kweekschools were very selective teacher training institutes. A degree from a kweekschool was the ultimate badge of status and educational accomplishment for a rural Batak schoolteacher. Sumatra had kweekschools in Kutaraja (Banda Aceh) and in Bukittinggi, in West Sumatra. The kweekschool in far-off Solo of course had special luster.

8. The Chinese have been stigmatized as greedy, amoral, usurious people in Tapanuli for many decades. Calling a Batak a "Cina" is an ethnic slur, or, as in this case, a pointed jest.

9. This popular practice engages the attention of children and adults for many hours, as they memorize large chunks of biblical text to recite in church on Christmas, as part of a serial recitation of the story of the birth of Jesus. Toba and Angkola Christians enthusiastically continue this practice today.

10. Toba and Angkola Christians consider New Year's Day to be a major Christian holy day. It is a time when families take care to clean off the graves of ancestors and invoke their blessings for a prosperous new year. Much praying to God also occurs, in and out of church.

11. Apparently the English word *long* is meant.

12. The *serunai* is an important part of the Toba adat ensemble of musical instruments, for ceremonial music at feasts.

Chapter 6

1. *Peci* are the black felt caps worn by men in Sumatra as part of formal dress. During the Indonesian Revolution the cap became an important badge of nationalist sentiment.

2. The implication here is that the school had an aristocratic air about it, as it was confined to the true "native elite."

3. *Ulos* textiles are hand-loomed cloaks given as gifts between families at major life-crisis events such as births, weddings, and funerals. Toba well recognize the political benefits of giving *ulos* gifts to foreigners, thus obligating them to help the givers.

4. At this time Toba teenagers would often sleep together in single-sex groups, away from home.

5. That is, the Mandailing Batak language, which is a moderately different dialect of Batak than Toba. Many of the early Batak schoolteachers were from the southern Batak societies of Angkola and Mandailing; these men gave Toba education a southern slant, still evident in the 1920s.

6. Pospos uses the Indonesian word *keponakan* here, which means niece or nephew in a rather generic sense. Doubtless he is using this word from the national language in place of a more specific Toba Batak kin term, perhaps *bere* (speaker's mother's brother's daughter's child).

7. The *Gouvernements-Vervolgschool* was intended to offer a continuation of lower schooling but at government standards, with the possibility of continuing to higher levels.

Chapter 7

1. The word used here is *dongeng*, which means a fanciful story with an air of the tall tale about it.

2. *Debata Mula Jadi Nabolon* means Great-Creator-God-of-First-Origins, while the place name *Sianjurmulamula* means Source-Spring-Spot-of-First-Origins. It is located near Pangururan, near Samosir Island.

3. *Marga* can be used to mean a single patrilineal clan, such as the Pospos clan, or an entire cluster of clans, whose origin point is said to be further back in time nearer to the era of Si Radja Batak.

4. Sometimes the *martarombo* question-and-answer conversations between new acquaintances are quite stylized and involve sly rhymed jousts and counter-jousts. A pair of speakers' marriage alliance relationship toward each other's lineage is also of great importance in determining their proper behavior (in adat) toward each other.

5. Literally, a way that was "not *halal*," which means not pure or permitted according to the tenets of Islam. This conversational turn of phrase has the sense of something "not being kosher," in English usage.

6. That is, newcomer marriage alliance partners had eventually swamped the village "owners" in political influence and number of residences there.

7. Toba village life is filled with political disputes of this sort, between men jockeying for influence and prestige. The loser in a dispute will indeed often cut his losses and leave the village for a brief or extended period.

8. The two children were probably matrilateral cross-cousins, the ideal boy-girl pair for marriage according to Toba adat. In other words, Djohanis was engaged to his mother's brother's daughter, or at least to some little girl from his mother's father's lineage. In that way, if the marriage was eventually carried out, the boy would have repeated the same sort of marriage his father made years ago by marrying Djohanis's mother.

9. Its own *Koor*.

Chapter 8

1. Ingwar Nommensen was the great missionary converter of the Toba to Protestant Christianity.

2. District head, or *Kepala negeri.*

3. Wild schools were proprietary institutes offering extra instruction to supplement the education children got in the regular schools. Parents hoped that these additional lessons would afford their children access to good higher-level schools, and after that, salaried jobs. *Schakelschool* was the Dutch term for these wild schools.

4. MULO, Meer Uitgebreide Lagere Onderwijs, was a sort of junior high school but one of high standing, since several European languages were taught there and much instruction was in Dutch.

5. One ringgit was equal to two and one-half rupiah.

6. That is, as opposed to converting to Islam, a religion that of course forbids pork consumption. Toba was something of a Christian enclave by the 1920s within largely Muslim Sumatra.

7. These areas in (respectively) northeast Sulawesi and the Moluccas were ethnic home regions that sent many migrants to Java and even the Netherlands.

8. *Encik,* a Malay usage, "young lady teacher." Often used in Sumatran school discourse.

9. Pospos conveys a Dutch phrase badly butchered in both pronunciation and meaning.

Chapter 9

1. The author actually uses a roundabout saying here, to convey the boys' surprise at doing so well on their entrance exam: "We'd hoped, you might say, for something so simple as leafy sprouts to be served, but lo and behold real vegetables were brought to the table."

2. "Betawi" was a reference to Batavia, now the city of Jakarta.

Chapter 10

1. GAIB probably stands for Gouvernements Akademie (GA) and Inlands Bestuur (IB). The Indonesian word "gaib" means mysterious and magical.

2. A *demang* was a district head, in the Dutch colonial administration in Sumatra. This was quite an exalted post from the viewpoint of village Batak.

3. A.M.S. stood for Algemene Middelbare School, while K.W.S. was Koningin Wilhelmina School, begun in 1901, where the Part B course of study was for machinists, mining engineers, and so on.

4. From the Dutch *meester,* itself a shortened form of *meester in de rechten,* or bachelor of law.

5. In colonial Sumatra, a controleur was the district administrative official.

Chapter 11

1. Angkola is the Batak subethnic region lying to the south of Toba, near Sipirok and Padangsidimpuan. Toba and Angkola have long enjoyed a heartfelt ethnic rivalry, phrased in terms of which Batak society "has the most adat," the best cooking, the best way of raising children, the greatest interest in their children's

education, the greatest fidelity to *agama* (world religion, Islam or Christianity), the best ritual dances and gong music, and so on.

2. These are subregions within Toba, said to have slight differences in adat practice.

3. A large commercial town in the Deli coast plantation belt in East Sumatra.

4. Medan is located in an old Malay ethnic enclave. The city also acted as a magnet for migrants from the nearby Batak rural regions.

5. That is, with Minangkabau.

Chapter 12

1. A *perjamuan,* clearly a reference in this Toba context to a blessing meal. These are often held, within Toba adat, to "firm up the soul" of the person being fêted.

2. Batak teenagers boarding at relatives' houses while they attend school are generally expected to do house chores.

3. This is the road up into the mountains leading toward Pahae, a gateway town near the border with Angkola.

4. That is, from Angkola or Mandailing.

5. This is a confusing comment.

6. Malay was the language soon to be established as Indonesia's national tongue, with the 1945–49 revolution. In Indonesia, the language is now called bahasa Indonesia. In 1920s Tapanuli schoolhouses, though, Malay was an outsider's language, an unfamiliar idiom to many, although it had been a widespread trade language for many centuries.

Chapter 13

1. The English word is used here.

2. The missionary converter of the Toba, Reverend Ingwar Nommensen. Pospos seems to have used the incorrect first initial here.

3. *Mandrek* is a sweet, thick drink: colored water sugared with syrup, with bits of fruit such as coconut mixed in.

4. A Dutch borrowing from French or English, applied to food and meals, meaning "complete" in the sense of "with all the trimmings."

Chapter 14

1. Literally, this phrase reads, "The world had changed a great deal." The implication here seems to be that the changes in question were the ones of the last several years.

2. The English word "modern" is used in the text.

3. That is, to listen in to all the *tandang* courtship speech going on.

4. In the text, "mode à la tahun dua ribu." Apparently a reference to fashion styles in the eminently modern, future year 2000.

Chapter 15

1. The author does not explain the difference to us. However, Section B apparently was the track that prepared students for further schooling.
2. *Straat* is "street" in Dutch.
3. An "excursie" in the text.

Chapter 16

1. In the text, "sapa-menyapa," trade inquiries with each other. This Indonesian phrase gives a sense of the Toba conception of friendly speech as a series of verbal ripostes, especially when it concerns young people's communications with each other.
2. "Si" is attached to names in many Indonesian languages to convey an air of familiarity and a sense that all users of this appelation know the person in question.
3. *Gambier* is an ingredient of betel-nut chewing.
4. MOSVIA was Middelbare Opleiding School voor Inlandse Ambtenaren, a school, accompanying OSVIA, for native officials.
5. A "drilschool."
6. The word here is "watak," character, nature, disposition.

Chapter 17

1. The words "back" and "trainen" are used in this paragraph. In the next paragraph the word "kompetisi" is used.
2. In the original, the soldiers are said to think of themselves as "anak kompeni," company guys. "Kompeni" was a popular way to refer to the Dutch colonial state, in 1920s and 1930s Sumatra. The reference is to the Dutch East India Company, whose export enterprises in the archipelago predated the establishment of the civil government of the Dutch Indies colony.
3. The author places quotation marks around the word "kuat" (strong) in this sentence.
4. "Fors," in the original (robust, massive, loud, forceful). The author uses Dutch words at several junctures to discuss soccer.
5. Padang Sidempuan is the commercial and administrative hub of the Angkola region. The town's name has several spellings.

Chapter 18

1. In schakelschool.
2. "Modern" is used in the original.
3. An idiom in the original: Their resolve and determination was like iron.

Chapter 19

1. "Fiasco" in the original, in quotation marks.

Chapter 20

1. Calling a person "black-skinned" in Toba is a way of chiding them for being ugly. However, one can also be "sweet and black" (*hitam manis* in Indonesian).

2. In French in the original.

Chapter 21

1. The word here is *kitab,* "book"—but in Sumatra it has the connotation of holy texts.

Chapter 22

1. Pork stew is the main ceremonial food in Toba adat; it is available as well for big splurges at food stalls.

Chapter 23

1. This practice continues today as a common means of slipping a relative a cash gift, usually in an adat context.

Chapter 24

1. "Intiem" (Dutch) in the original.

2. Homeland is "tanah air" here. This could refer to Toba or to Sumatra as a whole. It is not a general reference to Indonesia, in this particular context.

Village Childhood

(THE AUTOBIOGRAPHY OF A MINANGKABAU CHILD)

Muhamad Radjab

CHAPTER 1: A LAKE SINGKARAK CHILD

Why I was born into this world, I do not know. Why I was born in Minangkabau puzzles me even more. These two things have surprised me very much and have bothered me since I was little. But I will not bother with things I do not know here; I will simply relate some of my experiences that are surprising and just itching to come out.

They say I was born in mid-1913, when the cholera epidemic began to spread through Minangkabau and other areas, taking dozens of people a day to death's door. At a time when other people were dying and being buried in the ground, I was alive, given birth to by my mother. Doubtless, to fill an empty place in the world, so that the earth would continue to be filled.

My *datuk* [lineage elder, ceremonial leader in adat][1] was a farmer and a mosque official. He was the most highly regarded person in our village, both because of his religious devotion and because of his knowledge of *silat*, the traditional Minangkabau art of self-defense.[2] My datuk was also known to possess magical powers; he had formulas that could cure a sick person, make one person love or hate another, and even put a curse on someone. Village people considered him to be, as they put it, "potent," even though he was quiet, never bothered anyone, and did not boast about his powers. I do not know what my datuk looked like, since he died before I was born.

My father was stout, healthy, and muscular; he was brave and had strong desires, but he also had a quick temper. When he was angry at someone, anyone else who got in his way came under attack as well. He looked for some reason, some fault, to be upset about. My father was no longer young when I was born, so we were not really very close. He was a devoted religious teacher who was feared and respected, both because he was so knowledgeable and because he was adept at sword fighting. His outlook on life stood in contrast to that of my mother.

My mother was a good woman, with a slender body, skin the color of *langsat*,[3] and a tender heart; she was also patient and devout. When she was not cooking in the kitchen, she was crocheting or sewing. She did not much like to chat, much less gossip about others.

I was barely a week old when a friend of my father's asked him what he had named his child.

"Because he's my first boy, and the word for 'boy' in Arabic is ridjal, he will be named Ridjal." So even though I am an Indonesian, my name is Arabic, to give it a faintly Islamic ring.

I was born in Sumpur, a village at the northern end of Lake Singkarak. It was an excellent location, in a peaceful green valley between two mountain ranges running north to south. The valley was filled with irrigated rice fields, and down the middle ran the Sumpur River. Hidden in the shade of coconut palms and fruit trees, the houses of my village were scattered along the northern edge of the rice fields on either side of the river. They were fine houses, almost all of them of the traditional type, long and with steep, six-pointed roofs.[4]

What I have just described was only the village of Lower Sumpur, which was cut in two by the river. The part on the eastern bank of the Sumpur River was called the Baruh, and that on the western bank was known as Seberang Air [Over-on-the-Other-Side-of-the-Water]. That was the location of my mother's house, the place where I was born.

My mother's house was of the traditional type, but because we were not well-to-do the floor and walls were only made of bamboo. The steps, though, were made of ironwood, strong enough to last a hundred years. The house was sixteen meters long and eight meters wide, and the floor was two and one-half meters off the ground. There were two parts of the house. In the front was a large space where guests could sit when there was a gathering and where children played and slept; the back was divided into seven rooms, each occupied by one of my mother's female relations.

The house was built by the husband of my mother's grandmother, who had had to move from another house because it was full. She had two girls, who in turn had families, one of seven children (five girls) and the other of five children (three girls). In order for everyone to have a place in the house the back was divided into seven rooms for the women of the house. The men slept in the front until they were married, when they slept at their wives' homes. A woman had to have her own room because that is where she would receive her husband. She would not be taken in by her husband. That was the custom in Minangkabau. Everyone who was living under the same roof was considered part of the same family, that is, they were all grandchildren of the same woman.

My mother occupied one of the cramped rooms, and there I was born. I would say it was like being born in a barracks, since there were more than forty people living in that house at the time. The seven girls all had children, half of them themselves had children, and every night seven unfamiliar men came to the house, that is, the husbands of the seven women. One can imagine how noisy the place was, what with all these individual needs, dispositions, and behaviors colliding. Morning, noon, and night it was one big hullabaloo. I was born at five in the morning, when the house was quiet and everyone else was sound asleep, except for two or three of my aunts and a midwife.

That house and its surroundings always made me feel extremely nostalgic every time I visited it after I was five years old. I do not know why, and have never been able to explain it. The sense of yearning was vague, but it penetrated to my very soul. There were various flowers of different colors and some croton plants around the house, and in the back yard some aloe plants. The crotons were large, and wide varicolored leaves of red, yellow, green, and white. They always caught my attention and heightened my sensation of longing for some unknown thing. Maybe I felt this way because I planted two crotons on my mother's grave; every time I see that plant the feeling envelopes me.

Behind the house were the high, jungle-crowned mountains. That deep green jungle also posed an enigma for me when I was between eight and ten years old: it seemed to say, "I have an enormous secret; try to find out what it is!" And not far behind the house, within earshot but unseen, flowed the Sumpur River, whose rumbling current had for centuries played its lively, tumultuous song, carrying it far away to other continents, calling me and causing my thoughts to drift away.

The house and the village were full of emotion for me, especially the crotons, which when I was young and naive moved me very deeply. Sometimes I prayed to God that the agonized longing in my heart would cease.

But let us return to the story I started to tell.

Besides the villages of Baruh and Seberang Air, on the slope of a large hill at the top of which was a spot called The Four Houses, there was another village called Upper Sumpur or Sumpur Negeri. And here was a little mosque at which my father taught religious studies.

Old people said that the ancestors of the inhabitants of Sumpur, when they moved here from somewhere to the north, built huts—four of them—on the place now called The Four Houses. As time went on they flourished, moving to the slopes of the mountain and into the valley below. The four houses were torn down, but since that time the land on which they were built has been considered sacrosanct by the inhabitants of Sumpur. When danger threatened, especially some kind of epidemic, the people of Sumpur burned incense and slaughtered a goat for a ritual meal at The Four Houses. They asked that Sumpur be spared from the catastrophe. Old people said that in times of disaster you could sometimes see a winged horse running wild through the hills, ridden by a heroic figure.

From the top of the hill you could see all of Sumpur, the rice fields around it, and to the south Lake Singkarak. When I was older and had the urge to wander or go to the rantau,[5] I often climbed up to The Four Houses and daydreamed, communing silently with nature, confirming the presence of a wide and rolling world that stretched from the slopes of Mount Merapi and Mount Singgalang in the north to the foot of Mount Talang in the south. But when you turned to the west, the land looked like a deep and steep-walled ravine of nothing but wild grass, through which flowed the Sumpur River, its current barely audible as it rushed downstream. I do not know whether anyone ever fell into that ravine, but I am certain that no one ever dared climb down into it.

From The Four Houses you could also see two small villages located on the two northern corners of Lake Singkarak. The one to the west was called Sudut [Corner], and the one to the east Batu Beragung [Gong Rock]. Both were part of Sumpur. Sudut was so named because it really was at the northern corner of the lake; Batu Beragung got that name because on the lakeshore at that location there was a large rock that, if you hit it with another stone, made a gonglike sound. After I was older I often hit that rock, before and after going swimming. Sudut and Gong Rock were inhabited by fishermen, who caught fish in the lake every day.

Not far to the east of Gong Rock, just at the edge of the lake, was a large stone wall with Sanskrit writing on it, in other words an inscription. People seldom took their boats near it because the villagers considered it to have supernatural powers. What is more, the water in that spot was very deep and blue, and there was a whirlpool that sucked everything within reach down into it.

When I was forty days old I was "bathed," which meant that I was taken into the yard and bathed in the river. They just call it bathing; actually, I was carried down in my cloth sling, resting on my mother's hip, to be introduced to the river. My mother sat on one of the large rocks at the river's edge, and I was allowed for the first time to breathe in the pleasant, pure air. After a quarter of an hour I was taken home and given a bath in warm water.

That day my mother killed a chicken and invited a few devout Moslems to a little *selamatan*, a ceremonial meal to ensure a long and healthy existence for me. From that day onward I was taken to the river every day and bathed in its cool, clear water. Even now I can recall once being carried on someone's shoulder to the river, though I cannot remember who carried me. Perhaps my mother. I can catch a glimpse of her face in my memory, but the recollection is only of those few minutes; after that everything is murky.

Every woman who met Mother as she was carrying me around in the sling pinched my cheeks and said, "What an awful child you have!" This was because people in our village did not want to say that someone's child was wonderful; it was bad luck. According to superstition, if a child was spoken of admiringly it would catch smallpox when it was older. The women in my village were also very pleased if their child had an Arabic name, which according to their aesthetic sense[6] sounded the most beautiful. And they very much liked pointed, well-formed noses.

But I was not long happy in my sling, cuddled and loved by my dear mother. One night when I was only nine months old, she caught cholera, and the next morning, just as dawn was breaking and after she had told my aunt to take care of me, she died. I no longer had a mother. I really do not remember what she looked like. There is no picture of her, since in those days photographs were forbidden by the religious teachers.

After my mother was buried and the crotons were planted on her grave, my father carried me, crying all the way, to his mosque at Upper Sumpur. From then on that is where I lived. Father was very sad because in two weeks he was to leave for Mecca on the haj.[7] I would have been taken along, but I was still too young. So two weeks after my mother died, my father departed for Saudi Arabia with my Aunt Salamah. They took a lot of baggage: two sacks of rice, three sacks of coconuts, fifteen kilograms of dried cooked meat, and an assortment of cakes to be eaten on the ship and in the desert. They also took mattresses, pillows, and blankets, just as if they were moving.

I was left with a girl named Maimunah, one of my father's nieces. Since my mother's death, people say, I did not nurse. There was a woman who was nursing her own child and wanted to nurse me, too, but I refused. When I got thirsty I just drank tea or water, because they did not have cow's milk for babies, as they have now. People tell me that my father told the girl who was to take care of me to send a letter to Mecca to tell him whether I was dead or alive. Because if I followed my mother in death, he would remain in the Holy Land for the rest of his life. If I lived, he would come home. He said his son Ridjal was all that tied him to Minangkabau.

Because I was not nursing, I was not given a pacifier (maybe no one sold them then) and so I liked to suck my own tongue all the time. At least so I was told by my aunt.

My life was much like that of any other youngster. What my experiences

were up to age six I no longer really remember. If I had died then I would
have felt no loss and would not have been afraid of death, since I would
not have understood what it meant. It is as if I would have been fortunate
to die then, when I was still so unaware.

I do not remember when my father returned from Mecca, but when he
did, naturally he popped a date into my mouth.[8]

What I do still recall—why we remember some things and not others, I
will never understand—is that when I was four I really adored boiled eggs.
Sometimes I ate four or five a day. I called the shells "pails," perhaps because I often used them to scoop up water. When I cried for "pails" my father knew I wanted to eat an egg.

I also liked to imitate my father doing silat. Besides being a religious
teacher, he was a teacher of the arts of self-defense. Whenever he told me
to watch, I would imitate all his movements. He bought me a proper black
silat shirt and black trousers, so I could be a martial arts master too. I was
very happy, and ran laughing back and forth across the yard. What was
funny, my father told me, was that every time I practiced I touched my
gombak (a sort of forelock); other people touched their headcloth, but I
did not have one yet. This gombak was a length of hair on the crown of
the head, about five centimeters long. The rest of the head was shaved, or
at least cut short, and that part allowed to grow long. There were children
with gombak over twenty centimeters long, and braided. The Minangkabau kept the gombak on their childrens' heads so they wouldn't have their
brains sucked out by vampires. The custom of having gombak has gradually disappeared; now only real country folk have them.

I lived with my father until I was five. I was never far from him, and I
considered him a playmate who just happened to be rather large. I called
him engkau, the familiar "you."[9] I only discovered later that this was wrong.
All this time I lived with my stepmother, too, so there were three of us altogether. Father really did love me, first because I was his only male child,
and second because I had no mother. I always played in the mosque where
father taught, or on the grounds around it.

Parents in those days did not think to give their children toys, in the
way that children now are given toy cars, airplanes, dolls, and so on. We
had to make our own toys. For a train we used some boxes pulled by an
engine made from an ink bottle. That is what I pushed around the floor
of the little mosque, day in and day out, making the sounds of the engine's
whistle. I do not know how many pairs of pants I must have worn out the
knees of, crawling on the floor like that. When the knees ripped, my father got angry and said he would not buy me any more. If we wanted a
cart, we made one out of a large citrus fruit that we dragged around the
yard. If we got tired playing with that, then we dug a hole and made toy

chickens out of the clay-rich dirt. We copied what we saw around us but we thought things up and made them ourselves.

I still remember the time I saw a child who had a small toy car. I cried because I wanted one too, so when my father went to Padang Panjang he bought me a little red toy car. I was unspeakably happy. Day and night I pushed that car to and fro on the mosque floor. If you revved it up and then let go, the car sped along by itself. I liked watching it do this, and chasing after it.

But ten days later a boy who was bigger and smarter than I—his name was Djamal—asked me if I wanted to trade the car for three bananas. "You can eat bananas and they taste good, but you can't eat cars," he said. I fell for it. I ate the bananas and returned to the mosque with no car.

Father was angry, and asked Djamal to give it back in exchange for four bananas. "If you trade it again, I won't buy any more toys for you," my father told me. I did not know then that the car cost more than three nice bananas; that's why I had wanted to trade. What is more, I had started to get bored with the car.

Djamal was well known as a persuasive kid, adept at coaxing my friends to trade their toys for things of lesser value. Once he wanted me to trade a whistle I had bought at the market for five cents, for three marbles. Afraid that my father would be angry, I refused. Djamal was a smooth talker and really made the things he had to trade sound good.

If I was not in the mosque yard, I could always be found playing in front of the coffee stall nearby. There I once saw a person reading a large sheet of paper while other people sat around a table listening attentively, occasionally sipping their coffee or nibbling on fried bananas. I asked the oldest of my playmates what they were doing. "Just reading newspapers," he replied.

"Oh."

Usually I saw people talking together; one said something and then the other answered. That is how it went, they took turns. But this newspaper reading was different. It was the first time I had ever seen it. One person talked for a long time while he held a big piece of paper, and the other ten people listened without responding. Why? I was surprised, and did not understand at all.

After that I too listened to the newspaper being read, though I did not understand because the language was Indonesian rather than Minangkabau. I often heard the words "war," "English," and "German," but did not yet know what they meant.

One day Father was talking with his friend Sutan Sianok. I was playing trains, crawling near him and pushing the boxes that served as cars. I listened to Father talk for a long time. Sutan Sianok listened silently and nodded his head. I was surprised because my father was not holding that big piece of paper in his hands, yet the words kept on tumbling out of his mouth.

So I asked, "Are you reading the newspaper?"

Father was surprised that I should ask such a thing. "No," he replied.

"But you were talking for such a long time, and Mr. Sutan[10] was listening so long, too."

"That's because there was a lot I wanted to tell him, and he hasn't answered yet."

I did not understand; I was quite sure that when people talked on and on like that, they must be reading a newspaper. If not, then where on earth did the words come from?

"Then you memorized yesterday's newspaper, didn't you?"

"No, I didn't memorize yesterday's newspaper. I was expressing my own ideas."

"Expressing your own ideas? I don't understand."

"Of course not, son. You only know how to push your toy train around. Now run along!"

Father started talking again, and I continued playing with my train. I have never quite understood why Father talked so long without holding that big sheet of paper they called a newspaper in his hands.

One of my stepmothers, a woman named Ami, lived in Muara, a village not far from where the Sumpur River flowed into Lake Singkarak. One time my father told me to stay at her house for a while, maybe because she requested it, for she had no little children still at home and sometimes needed someone to take care of and spoil. The life of a childless woman was really sad because there was a kind of emptiness there, with no one to give her love to, no one to nurture, no one to talk with and whisper little nothings to. My father went to her house once a week, but for only two nights; the other evenings he had to spend with my other two stepmothers.

My days in Muara are still clear in my memory; they left an indelible impression. Every day, four or five times a day, I swam with some friends in the cool, clear water of Lake Sangkarak. We raced and splashed each other for an hour at a time. We did not yet dare to swim very far out, since we were still little; we stayed near the shore, where plants grew in the shallows. If we saw blue water beneath us our hearts quickened and we swam toward shore. It was nice hiding among the thick, tall weeds, oblivious to the possibility that there might be a dangerous animal lurking there.

My mother's [11] house was about fifty meters from the edge of the lake; it was a long house built in a clump of tall trees. At the edge of the lake was another long house, owned by her grown child who lived closest to her, and I often played there as if it were my own house. I even ate there a lot. Not far behind the house, right at the water's edge, was a hut made of bamboo and palm fronds. We often meandered down from the house to swim in front of this hut; if we tired of swimming, we sat down or stretched out on the rocks around it.

Beside the hut was a huge banyan tree that frightened me a good deal at the time,[12] but I was content to play beneath it anyway, examining its thousands of roots hanging down. When we were bored with swimming we played in its shade and hung on its roots, swinging by holding one root in the left hand and one in the right.

After swinging in the tree, we played at the side of my stepmother's house, under a tall, shady nut-tree, looking for nuts that had fallen to the ground. We cracked them open with a stone and ate them; they tasted even better than coconut. But the sap stained our shirts green. When we had eaten enough nuts, we went down to the lake again to watch the fishermen knot their nets or come in from the middle of the lake with their loads of fish, with the women waiting to buy them at the shore. Sometimes we went out into the lake with them in their boats.

Our world was very small, about three hundred square meters that comprised the edge of the lake, the house, and the yard. I was afraid to go outside this area. The house that was about a half a kilometer down the road from my stepmother's might as well have been in another world as far as I was concerned. When there was a wedding there, I did not dare go. I just watched from afar, hiding behind a row of castor plants. The people who lived in that house were like foreigners to me, not the same sorts of people as my father, my stepmother, and the others who lived in the two long houses and the hut.

The strange thing was that every day I watched brown smoke pour into the sky out of Mount Merapi. Sometimes there was a loud rumbling and hot lava came out. I did not understand why. I asked my stepmother. She said that God was angry at wicked humans.

This surprised me, because I had never seen a wicked person. One time one of my friends said "God," and I asked who God was. He said, God is a *haji* with a large turban made of silk, and he sits on a golden chair behind the blue sky. He has a golden cane and a long beard. Sometimes God descends to earth, my friend said, and hides behind doors to play tricks on little children.

When I got home I asked my mother whether God was from Sumpur.

"Don't be silly," she said. "God isn't a human being: He made human beings."

I was not satisfied with this answer and wanted to meet this God who was so terrific. I looked behind the door to see if God was there, hiding and waiting to play with me.

Every day I ate lake fish of one or another variety; they were all delicious. Sometimes I ate their eggs, which came in strings that were sometimes as long as my sleeve, cooked fried or roasted; they were even better
than the fish themselves. These fish eggs were so good, in fact, that I did
not finish them with my rice, but saved them. After my rice was gone I
took a big pile of fish eggs into the yard, where I licked them and nibbled
them bit by bit as I walked down to the water's edge.

Two days a week my father came. Every time he came he brought fruits—
*rambutan*s [lychees], *duku* [lanseh fruit], mangoes—or cakes for me. I ate
them with my friends.

For a whole year I lived there with the fishermen, learning how to be a
good swimmer and diver; it was a part of my life I will never forget. Then
one day my father came, and two days later I was taken away with him
forever to Upper Sumpur, where I was to live once more with him at the
mosque.

"Did you like it down by the lake?" Father asked me.

"Very much, Father. Why do I have to go back to Upper Sumpur?"

"You're going to school," Father said.

CHAPTER 2: GOING TO SCHOOL

Any child who could put his arm over his head and touch his left ear was
accepted in primary school. That was the rule in Sumpur and everywhere
else, or so we were told by the children who were already going to school.
We wanted to go to school tomorrow, so today we tried to see whether our
fingers touched our ears.

I could already touch the top of my ear with my index finger when my
father took me for my first day of school. I was brought before a teacher
who had a trim body, dark skin, a large head, and a strict-looking expression on his face. My heart was beating hard as he wrote down my name,
age, parents' names, and how much I was to pay for school fees. On his
desk was a rattan cane. This is what they called a teacher? I did not know
what they meant by "schoolteacher." I was acquainted with a catechism
teacher, with his Chinese-style jacket, plaid sarong, and sandals. The schoolteacher, however, wore a buttoned-up jacket, trousers, and fine-looking
shoes. And my father was going to hand me over to him.

I started to feel better when I saw the teacher laughing and talking with
my father, being respectful toward him. I thought, if that's how they get
along, then I won't be mistreated.

Father asked him to take care of me. "If he's naughty, you may whip
him." Father said.

"Fine, sir," the teacher replied. "I'll take good care of him." Turning to me, he said, "You can sit there," and he pointed to a long desk at which three other children were sitting.

"Thank you very much, in advance," said my father. Then he walked over to me at the school desk and said, "You just stay here. I'm going to go home now. Don't you leave until the teacher tells you to. And be careful, don't play on the railroad tracks."

Father went home, and I stayed there with dozens of other children whom I did not know. I was very sad, especially since I did not see any of my friends from the surau[1] or from Muara, no one whom I could talk to or walk home with. I did not know any of the three kids whom I shared a desk with. They were also quiet and did not budge. We were all embarrassed to be the first one to say a word. We all waited for the teacher to say something.

He told us to relax and sit quietly, with our hands on top of the desk. I was thinking of my father, who had already gone home. I wanted to go home too. I thought I would be freer playing at home or on the lake shore than sitting quietly at this desk.

After a few days I started to enjoy school, however, and rose happily every morning because I had many friends there to play around with and run races with, and to play soccer, jousting games, boxing, marbles, and tops with.

I was very fortunate that my father was open to sending me to school. In that era many fathers did not want to send their children to school, and certainly not their girls. The reason for this was not that they were unwilling to spend the money, which was only 15 or 25 cents per bill,[2] but that they were prevented from doing it by old superstitions that had settled in their brains. According to the superstitions handed down from their ancestors, whoever knew how to write would have his fingers sliced off in hell. That was the oldest superstition. Those who did not believe this superstition but still were averse to sending their child to school did so because they did not see the use of learning how to read and write if the child was not to be a secretary or a foreman of some kind.

Wealthy people and businessmen were reluctant to give their children schooling because, in their view, school was only necessary for learning how to earn money when you grew up; they already had a lot of money— far more than what a clerk made, for example—and on that account merchants' children learned how to make money from the time they were very little.

Serious Moslems were reluctant because they thought it sufficient if their children knew how to read and write the Arabic letters. Religion was more important than anything else, they said, because it was religion that determined one's fate in the hereafter.

Girls were not permitted to go to school because it was thought that they would just use their knowledge of writing to send love letters to boys. The girls were not supposed to be looking for their own marriage partners from among the young men they liked; marriage partners were supposed to be chosen by the parents.

So thousands of children like me in Minangkabau in those days were kept in the dark and had their futures ruined by ignorant parents, parents who provided the wrong sort of preparation for their children's future. The older generation, and the ancestors they were so proud of and tried so hard to emulate, regressed further and further because they did not know how to read and write and did not want to learn. And they prohibited the younger generation from studying precisely at a time when the school doors were wide open.

They had fallen behind the times, and they were forcing their children to fall behind too. They were not aware that they were regressing, and this was a fundamental ill that was difficult to treat. They were unable to compare their intelligence with that of other peoples; they did not want progress: this much was clear from the way they spoke back then. I heard them every day. They were satisfied if they had enough to eat and slept well at night. Every afternoon the teachers had to go to the villages and try to persuade parents to send their children school.

But, the problem was, few did.

Every morning I got two and a half cents [one *benggol*] pocket money to take to school. In those days we still had coins called *pitis*, small coins with a round hole in the middle, worth one third of a benggol. I usually bought fried peanuts for a pitis, a cool drink called *cendol* for another pitis, and a piece of sugar cane for one pitis more. On market days I got five cents, which meant I could buy more things. I really needed this pocket money, since at recess times my friends all snacked; what was I supposed to do, sit and watch? It was common practice to ask a friend for a bit of whatever it was; for example, if someone had boiled peanuts and you asked for some, you got three or four, or if someone was having a cendol you might get a couple of spoonfuls.

Some of these friends of mine were stingy and did not want to give you anything when you asked. There were also those who were generous; usually their fathers were rich. There were some who liked receiving but did not want to give. Whenever they ate something they hid behind a fence or behind someone's house, afraid that one of their friends might ask them to share. And there were those who neither received nor gave; if offered something, they refused.

In those days no one took bread and butter to school, like children do today in the cities. When children brought something to eat from home, it was fried bananas wrapped in banana leaves, or fried peanuts in a little sack. People who brought things like this usually did not get pocket money from their mothers.

Asking for pocket money was not easy because usually it had not already been put aside for us before we left for school. It was still in the father's pocket or the mother's money holder. The relative difficulty of the task depended on the father's mood at the time. If he was happy, he would see you and call you over and give you some money. But the next day he might be in a bad mood and pretend not to notice you or just keep away from you or be absorbed in his work or something. In that case you were afraid to ask for money and just trudged sadly off to school with empty pockets and an empty stomach. Even when you were down the road a bit, he did not call you and give you your pocket money. Whether or not he was simply pretending to be wrapped up in what he was doing or not, I could not say.

Sometimes you got snapped at, maybe because he was disturbed about something or because he had had a bad dream the night before. "What do you mean, money"? he would say, "Go ask somebody else."

Then you would be afraid and go off to school dragging your heavy feet along with you. At recess you hoped your friends would share. If you asked your stepmother for pocket money, she had usually been told by the father not to give you anything. But a child's real mother would generally give something, especially if she knew that the father was angry. From her *uncang* (a beltlike money holder used by older Minangkabau women and made of two folds of cloth with a pocket in the middle for money), she would take out one benggol.

My experience in school was not much different from that of any other child, so there is no sense in telling about the ordinary. Between the first and fifth grades, nothing out of the ordinary happened. We found we could easily take in all the lessons we were given, as they consisted of evident, obvious, provable material. All the lessons were clear and useful, so they did not run counter to our way of thinking. At school they did not teach superstitions or illogical beliefs that we were forced to accept, like the religious teachers did at the surau. The teachers at the school were wise, too, and knew what students liked and did not like; they knew how to hold a child's interest. They did not teach by rote, ignoring the ideas and talents of the children in the way the older generation did.

I remember an incident that occurred when I was in the third grade. One day the teacher was about to cane me because I had really misbehaved. I tried to prevent this from happening by saying, "You'd better not cane me; my father is a martial arts expert and he'll beat you up."

Much to my astonishment, I got caned anyway.

"Tell your father the martial arts expert to drop by," he said.

When I got home I complained to my father that the teacher had been impolite and brazen, and had caned me even though I warned him that my father was adept in the martial arts. I was spanked again, this time for trying to play my father off against the teacher. I decided never to do that sort of thing again, no matter what the circumstances. The next day, and for a whole month afterward, I was teased by my friends, who cried, "You'd better not cane me; my father is a martial arts expert and he'll beat you up." I was mortified.

Later it appeared that I was not the only one who had done this. There was a boy in another class whose father was a martial arts expert, and he had also tried to frighten the teacher with this. So my embarrassment was at least halved.

In the school system of those days, if you did not follow along when the lesson was being read you were told to stand in the front of the class, on top of a bench. You had to stand like that until the lesson was over, with a book in your left hand and a walking cane in the right, like a preacher reading a sermon at the mosque. What was unbearable about this punishment was the embarrassment of having everyone stare at you. But one time a daring child stood up on the bench and began to recite as loudly as he could, imitating a Moslem preacher, "Peace unto you, with the mercy and blessing of Allah!"[3] Everyone laughed, except the teacher.

CHAPTER 3: AT THE UPPER SURAU

*Surau*s are small mosques, most of them built of wood, where people would go to pray every day. Because the big mosque was used only on Fridays, people would say their regular five daily prayers at the surau.

The surau was also the place where kids and adults would learn how to read and recite the Koran, the religious laws [*ilmu fikhi*, in Arabic], and other sorts of religious knowledge. Usually the surau would be the property of the religious teacher who taught there.

After reciting the Koranic verses and saying the evening prayers, the small children (the ones under twelve years old) would go home to their parents' house; the youths from age twelve to twenty would sleep in the surau. This was because in Minangkabau it struck people as odd if youths slept in their parents' house. Then, too, the boys themselves would be embarrassed around their brothers-in-law, who's be coming in every evening to their houses.[1]

A young man over twenty customarily would have already migrated to the rantau, or if he was living back home in the village he would of course be married by then and sleeping in his wife's house.

Those who were sleeping over in the surau brought their mats, pillows, and blankets from their parents' house. They'd do this when they started sleeping there like their friends. Also sleeping there in the surau would be two or three extremely pious elderly men—just awaiting their deaths and doing nothing but bowing before God, totally ignoring this worldly life. They'd be sleeping in the surau because back home their children and grandchildren would always be pestering them.

So, the surau would be the most visited spot in the whole village: by the youths, by men and women going to say their prayers, and by old grandfathers[2] spending day and night there in diligent religious study.

The surau where Father taught was called the Upper Surau, to differentiate it from the Lower Surau, which was the one my Uncle Haji Daud had. His surau was located in a little hollow, half a kilometer from the Upper Surau. Both of these were on the northern edge of Upper Sumpur village.

Over forty people recited their Koranic verses there. Sixteen of these were my age. The others who were already pretty grown-up or who were still really small wouldn't do for us as playmates. So it was these sixteen who would always associate with one another, play together, recite the Koran together, and go to sleep together—in short, they formed a unified group that shared a single way of understanding things, the same attitude, the same pleasures, and the same worries.[3] To tell the truth, though, since there were so many of us, we'd rarely *have* any worries, for there was no time to think about personal troubles. And then, too, any troubles we'd have would be little ones, as is normally the case with children. There'd always be a pal there at every turn, engaging us in conversation, or jesting with us, or just generally annoying us.

Not all of this group of sixteen could be counted as my really intimate friends. Some were very close, some were not so close, and some were still constant friends though not terribly intimate ones, because we were all there together in the same surau. Such arrangements can't be forced, but must be determined by the givens of nature, and by our personal qualities and inner voices.[4] True, it wasn't that we directed any outright antipathy toward such and such a person: we just didn't send any particular sympathy his way either, nor would we entrust a secret to him.

This wasn't because they weren't good people, but because they didn't match up exactly with us, or have quite the same spirit. They could just go and be close to other people, whose feelings would align neatly with theirs.

The ones who were really close with me were Zainal, Bujung, Dullah, Djamin, and Saini. The six of us were inseparable—we'd go everywhere together. We'd be of a single heart, of a single thought, rarely arguing.[5] And if somebody from outside our ranks would try to bother us, we'd always defend one another. If one of us happened to come into something valuable, we'd divide it up evenly among all of us.

Zainal was short and fat, like a sack that had just been packed full. He always had a sour look on his face, as if he were going to cry. This wasn't because he was really anxious about anything; it was just his way of carrying himself. We'd often bother him by goading: "So, sure looks like in a moment or two it's going to start raining, Zainal." He was honest and on the level, but if he heard from a friend that I was going to make some suggestion or other that might entail some work to carry out (like, say, going to climb a mountain together), he would simply vanish for two or three days. If I went looking for him he'd hide. We were always kidding him. He was a rich man's son, but all that came to nothing because his father had as many as twenty-seven children from several mothers. We remained close friends throughout our childhoods.

Bujung was slim, with chocolate-colored skin and an extraordinarily congenial face. He was a descendant of aristocrats, and because of that his behavior was always nice and polite and he never interfered in other people's business. When our pals would be having a ball gossiping about someone's rottenness, he'd just go on home and climb his avocado tree, or to kick around a soccer ball by himself.

Dullah was tall, like a heron. He was the tallest one of all of us. He had a good heart and was a patient boy; no matter how much he might be teased, he'd just smile and turn his face away, or just go home. He was always a doubting sort, though: whatever a friend might say to him, if he had not seen it for himself he wouldn't believe it. Even if I knocked myself out for a quarter of an hour explaining something to him in detail, he would always just answer: "Well, it's not yet certain whether that is true or false." This was what was really annoying about Dullah's behavior. He never took other people's painstaking efforts into account.

Djamin was a sleep bug. But his mind was sharp. He had nice eyes, and a good voice, and he had a fine way of singing the Koran. He hoped to become a merchant like his maternal uncle over in Muara Aman. Most all our friends liked Djamin because of his good looks and behavior. He loved to play ball and always wanted to win.

Saini was a sloppy, careless sort. Whatever task he'd tackle wouldn't come out right; he'd guess the measurements all wrong. He'd want to finish something really quick and since he rushed the job, the results wouldn't be perfect, and finally he'd just leave it all unfinished. He was a meat merchant's son. Every morning he'd give me a cut of dried, spiced meat he'd stolen from his mother's kitchen cabinet.

Saini liked me a lot, just as I liked him. If he didn't happen to see me for a day—for instance, if his father took him to Padang Pandjang—he'd go looking for me and present me with some little cakes he'd brought back from town, or maybe a piece of spiced meat.

One time, afraid that our friends would find out if we went ahead and actually roasted the spiced meat (because the kitchen would fill up with smoke and the fragrance would pervade everything), we just ate our spiced meat half raw, sitting up there in the second story of the surau. We just laid it out to roast for a few moments on the hot zinc roof.

As to our other friends, beyond just these five, well, I'd associate with them all right, and we'd chat, but we didn't particularly place any great trust in one another, nor were we especially intimate, even though we weren't rude or cool to one another. Often, I just didn't care what was going on with them. And they were the same way toward me. But when confronted with someone from outside our group of sixteen (if someone set upon one of the group's members, for instance, at school), then we would join together to fight him as a *single* force.

Mornings from 8 A.M. to 1 P.M. we'd be in school. Afternoons we'd play ball in the soccer field, which was called Simpang Usang, or we'd bathe and swim in the lake or in the Sumpur River. Before sunset we'd eat at our mothers' houses, and after sunset we'd recite the Koran until evening. After this, if we weren't playing outdoors, we'd all fall asleep together, sometimes sharing a single mat, pillow, and blanket.

So it was no surprise that lots of us had fleas and lice. There were also many bedbugs in the spaces between the floorboards. No matter how diligent we were in combing out our hair every day and delousing our clothes, the next day there would be *more* of them—lice and fleas who'd moved in from the head or blanket of a pal.

We'd be delighted if some evening somebody would want to stay the night in the surau and serve as our conversational partner. We weren't really scared out there, for we had lots of companions (at a minimum there'd be thirty people sleeping there). But it was just that we wanted to *increase* our number of companions, because the more there were, the cheerier folks would be. So after evening prayers, there we'd be, coaxing and cajoling these people so they wouldn't go back home. Little kids we'd scare by saying there were ghosts out on the road. Sometimes this would succeed, too: the kids would get scared and sleep over in the surau. Happy at this turn of events, we'd invite them to use our own mats, pillows, and blankets.

Adults we'd coax to tell stories, and these could be any sort at all. Sometimes this tactic wouldn't work because one of them would remember his wife waiting back there at the house. But if lots and lots of us asked him to stay, often enough he'd want to sleep over in the surau and tell stories. He'd be instructed to sleep right in the middle of the group, surrounded by all of us, because he was to be the center of attention that whole night. Old people normally enjoyed being respected and happily jostled about by crowds of children, and they'd tell us lots of funny stories and jokes and we'd all laugh heartily. If we were looking at the guy avidly, he'd dispense his tales at a high price. One moment he'd be quiet, rolling a cigarette, then the next moment he'd *still* be quiet, and then he'd take a hugely long time to inhale the smoke from the cigarette. We'd wait impatiently.

One thing that caused considerable merriment back home in the village during childhood was the following.

If, say, there was a person who had just returned from the rantau, from Java, South Sumatra, or Tapanuli,[6] after evening prayers were over we'd ask him if he'd like to sleep at the surau. Or, if he wasn't going to sleep over, at least don't go home right away [we'd say]: stay and tell stories for two or three hours. We'd ask him questions about all sorts of matters relating to the other lands he had visited, and about the way folks made their living there and about the sorts of jobs they had. We'd ask all about the inhabitants of those lands, and about their food, clothes, adat, and favorite pleasures.

The village farmers would also join in and ask about this and that, and about their relatives off in the rantau. Every answer and story the newcomers provided was listened to with intense interest. In fact, it was swallowed whole and used as great food for the imagination. We'd use these stories as fuel for our own hopes and dreams. They whetted our desire to migrate to the rantau: to make money, to seek experience and knowledge. All the stories were deeply attractive to us, for they were all new. This is what added to the stock of knowledge available in the village, supplementing books. Every time we listened to these stories, we felt our stock of knowledge grow wider and bigger, and we'd be emboldened to talk about leaving the village. The soles of our feet would get itchy to start striding away from home, in pursuit of this or that visiting merchant.

But parents were still in charge of things, and as yet we had no travel funds. Half of our friends, though, could entertain themselves by saying that, anyway, they would be going to work for their maternal uncles, in just three years, off in the rantau.

Among the villagers who'd visit the surau at prayer time (and who would often sleep over with us after evening prayers) was a close friend, teacher, and adviser of mine named Lebai Saman.

He often appears in my memories.

He was perhaps forty-five years old or more, short and sturdily built, and his face—maybe his whole body in fact—was pockmarked. His eyes glinted with humor and showed just how much severity he had in him. His hair was almost totally white. From the time he was quite young he had been famous for his bravery (once he slept atop the grave of a murdered man!) as well as for his great strength and his expertise at the martial arts. Why, three youths could not down him in a fight, if we happened to be wrestling and playing around in a rough-and-tumble fashion trying to test his strength.

But really he was a thoroughly good man, and friendly and open, a person who loved to joke. His speech and behavior especially were just very funny. We loved playing with him and joking around—or, at night before going to sleep (even though the lampwick had already been put down), listening to his hilarious stories in the pitch dark—most of which couldn't be believed at all, like the ones in *A Thousand and One Nights.*

Sometimes, I'd read stories to him from Indonesian language books, ones I had borrowed from the library, although I'd have to explain them again in the Minangkabau dialect.[7] He was happy to listen, because these stories were all new to him: after all, his brain hadn't been out of the village from the time he was little.

Daytimes he was rarely in the surau, for he'd be out in the fields or the rice paddies, or he'd go off fishing in the river. He was actually a very hard worker. Every morning, after saying the dawn prayers, he'd sweep his house yard and then go out to the fields or the rice paddies and hoe the ground and the mud in the paddy until late afternoon. If it was raining, he'd knot casting nets at home or clean the kitchen utensils. All of this he'd do with great accuracy and conscientiousness. His hands and feet were never still—except when he was sleeping. Even when he was telling a story, his fingers would be rolling tight, neat cigarettes from banana leaves.

Lebai Saman was also a medicine man,[8] a healer, although people's faith in him, it has to be admitted, was rather thin. Because of this few came to ask him for magic potions. He did possess lots of magical lore, though; it was rather a shame that much of it had no efficacy. Lots of young guys asked him to go put spells on girls, so they'd fall in love with them, but these spells wouldn't leave any mark. The girl at issue would just keep right on acting as she always did, and not be at her wit's end at all. And, she'd certainly not be hankering to go meet the guy.

All his life Lebai Saman never did get married. It wasn't because he hated women but because no family ever came along and proposed to him. He had never gone out to the rantau, after all. He had always stayed right there in the village, being a farmer. Because of this, people didn't hold him in very high regard, and no young girl's parents nor any widow's parents had any desire to take him in as a son-in-law. One time he did migrate out to Lampung, to work for his nephew. But after six months there he came back. He couldn't stand living in the land of foreigners, whose language he would have to apply himself to in order to learn.

Lebai Saman was never sure of anything. He'd always act cautious or suspicious. Whatever task he did would always take him a very long time to accomplish, and he would repeat it over and over again. In taking water for the prayers, for instance, he'd swish the water around in the tub in front of him, so that the water on the bottom would come up to the surface. If he was still cautious about this (if he saw it wasn't clean enough), he'd scoop around some more. So it would take at least a half an hour for him to finish.

Going to pray was the same thing. The other folks had already said they were "humbled before God" and were almost to the kneeling down part, but there he'd be, still at the *takbir* part [reciting "God is the Greatest"], which phrase he would also be repeating over and over, because he suspected that the one who had recited it to the assembly hadn't gotten it quite right yet. When the imam [prayer leader] was already to the kneeling down part, he'd just be getting through the *takbir*, so Lebai Saman would have to kneel down too because he was forced to. What with all of this he never did get to the part drawn from the opening chapter of the Koran, or to the Kulhu.[9]

If he was fetching prayer water on Fridays at the Sumpur River, he also wouldn't want to be downstream of anyone. If he was already squatting down to wash his face in the shallow section of the river, suddenly he'd notice that someone was upriver of him and straightaway he'd go upriver of that person. Squatting down there, he'd notice someone upriver of him again, and he'd go farther up to get beyond this person. He'd behave like this so that the water wouldn't be dirtied up by the person upriver. And this went on and on, with him going upriver of each person beyond him. Sometimes he'd go upriver of folks for four full kilometers along the Sumpur River, and end up in Gunung Radja village.

When he'd go back downstream after getting prayer water in Gunung Radja, usually it would already be 1:30, and when he got to the Sumpur Bawah mosque, the people who had been to Friday services there would be coming out of the mosque to go home. Lebai Saman would say the noon prayers in the normal fashion.

One time, when he was going to say noon prayers, I told him that there was house lizard shit on his sarong, even though this wasn't true. He believed it, and he went down to the wash tub and washed his sarong until it was really clean and then he hung it out to dry. Waiting for it to get dry, he went back home to get another one. With this sarong in hand, he went on to pray.

I pitied him. After that, I didn't want to make fun of him anymore.

Lebai Saman was the first person to tell me that the sun circled the earth, and that the earth was flat, supported on the back of a cow, who was standing upon a stone, and that the stone was atop a fish and that the fish was atop the sea and the sea was atop the air. And what this air was atop of Lebai Saman didn't know.

"Walahu Alam," he'd say. [God knows best; heaven knows!]

Once I got into the fourth grade and I said that the teacher in school had taught us that the earth was round like an egg and that the earth revolves around the sun, he got angry, his mustache trembled, his eyes flashed, and his air of good humor disappeared.

"That teacher is mistaken," he said. "Such teachings come from Satan."

At first I thought he knew everything, and whatever he'd say I'd believe, but eventually all his superstitions conflicted with what the schoolteacher was teaching us—although the aforementioned had sounded all right to my mind when I first heard it.

Even though our beliefs had begun to differ, we did remain close friends, for in this matter of belief I really didn't know how to debate him further. In several other matters his thoughts were healthy and strong; this was exactly what I needed. I would often ask his advice if I was dealing with some difficulty. And if I was sick, he'd be my companion every night, sleeping near me, talking to me, and making me feel better and shoring up my confidence, all the while blowing on my forehead while reciting mantras, so that I'd recover quickly.

At just the time I felt lonely and scared, he would be right beside me, making my suffering easier to bear.

CHAPTER 4: ASCENDING MOUNT GALOGANDANG

Sundays we didn't have to go to school. For us, this was great, for this meant that on that day we could go wherever we wanted and play to our hearts' content. On that day, my friends and I would usually go on pleasure trips outside the village, such as to Batu Tebal, to Malalo, or to Mount Radja. Mothers and fathers allowed us to go only to the nearby villages, because we had to be back home before evening prayertime.

Once a month we'd go to Kubang Si Rawit, an orchard of *jambu* [rose-apple] fruit seedlings and *karamunting* fruits in the foothills of the Galo-gandang mountain chain, which stretched out along the east side of our village. We'd go picnic-style, carrying along a big leaf packet of cooked rice with all its side dishes, because the orchard was rather far away, and we were going to play there a long time. And then, too, it was just extraordinarily delicious to eat our meal outside in the open, in nature. Out there we'd normally eat three times as much as we did back home, because we were hungry or maybe because it was just more delicious eating out there all together in a big boisterous group.

At seven in the morning we'd set off as a group, about twenty people, merry as could be as we carried along our provisions and our drinking water in bottles. All along the way we'd joke and cheer, expressing whatever we felt down deep inside. That way the walk wouldn't wear us down.

We'd walk along following the dikes between the rice fields. After cutting through the paddies for a kilometer we'd cross a stream and from there we'd start the ascent.

From that point, our jokes would become fewer. Everyone would be beginning to get tired climbing up the steep incline; sweat would flow over our bodies. Even though we considered ourselves strong and sturdy (free, happy young kids), this little bit of mountain climbing would constitute a real struggle. Arriving at a level clearing, we would stop and rest and gather our strength to start climbing again. There in the clearing some of our friends would already want to eat (having lost their strength to stave off their appetites any more), but they'd be restrained by the others because we hadn't gotten to the intended place yet.

At Kubang Si Rawit, underneath the thicket of tended trees and out in the middle of the karamunting shrubs, we'd eat a big meal all together. And then we'd all struggle to be the first one up the orchard trees to pluck the sweet karamunting fruits and stick as many of them as possible into our pockets. After that we'd chase each other around and play hide-and-seek down in the bushes until the sun had set in the west.

On the way home, we'd bathe in the river, which flowed alongside the foot of the mountain. We'd take two hours at this, playing with sand and rocks. After finally getting our fill of bathing we'd go home to our separate houses, red-faced, our clothes damp from sweat. Every time we'd come back from one of these excursions Mother would be mad at us, because our clothes were dirty, our bodies exhausted—and they sure wouldn't be exhausted because we'd been helping Mother sweep out the houseyard! But her anger would not run very deep, for when we'd ask for some rice to eat, of course she would give it to us.

One time we wanted to climb up all the way to the peaks of the mountain chain that bordered the dale between our village and Luhak Tanah Datar. We wanted to find out what the area on the other side of the mountain chain looked like. Every morning we'd see the sun appear over there, and this intensified our desire to find out what was there.

On Sunday, all sixteen of us, carrying our rice meals, set off to climb Galogandang Mountain. All of us were happy, our hearts pounded hard, for we were going to see a new world.

Climbing no farther than the slope up Kubang Si Rawit, we were tuckered out already. We almost couldn't pick up our feet. Half of us didn't understand why. One of our older friends said our quick exhaustion was caused by empty stomachs. Well, true enough, not a single one of us had eaten breakfast. Try eating a bit to increase your energy, he said. After eating we did evidently become strong enough to start climbing again. Only half the rice was consumed, though, because after all, the big thing was to eat our meal up there on the mountain peak.

Near the slopes of the mountain chain no more trees appeared. Everything was bare, with short, tough grass growing there. An extremely rough wind was blowing up there. We had a hard time even standing up; it was as if the wind was going to throw us down off the mountain.

Arriving at the peak, we got a view of Luhak Tanah Datar, the place we had been dreaming about all this time. Here and there villages were visible, and between them garden fields and rice paddies. On the eastern valley of Galogandang, Galogandang Village itself was visible—the place famous throughout Minangkabau where folks made clay pots, kitchen utensils, and so on. People said it was the women who made these things. They'd work in the nude under the house, behind the posts, so that no one could espy the manner in which the pots were made.

Simambur was also visible, but not Batu Sangkar. I very much wanted to go roaming all over that area, after eleven years of living in the Sumpur valley, but, well, that would take money. It wasn't certain that Dad would give his permission. Ah, such a pity I couldn't do this, for it was a lovely region.

At the foot of the sky on the eastern side, I saw another mountain and another long mountain chain, glowing blue in the distance, full of secrets. And the sun appeared from behind that mountain chain as well. Its peaks were endless. Perhaps the ocean was located on the other side of those layers of mountains? To see the sun appear from under the earth, it looked like I'd have to go to the other side of *that* layer of mountains. Gee, imagine how far away that is.

We took a look at our own village and our individual houses, visible behind the trees. We tried guessing what our father, mother, or little brother or sister was doing inside the house at that time. And for sure, everyone could guess, too, because we already knew what each member of our families was doing at any particular time.

In a sheltered spot where the winds weren't too rough, we ate again. However, because our drinking water had run out back there on the way up, our throats were dry. After eating we were even thirstier. Water was visible in a stream of liquid jetting out from the side of the mountain, but it was very far down below on the slope. Two of our companions, Sulaiman and Zainal, descended to that spot to fetch some. While waiting we chewed on grass roots;[1] they were sweet like sugarcane.

But only halfway down to the spot below, three wild water buffaloes—and there were lots of them, roaming around, ownerless—three buffaloes nursing their young, that is, all came rushing along at us in a row, one after the other, chasing after our two friends. This was because the buffaloes thought our friends were going to loot their calfs. Sulaiman and Zainal wanted to run up a tree but there weren't any around. So the two ran toward the peak where we were, pursued furiously from behind by the three raging water buffaloes.

Without thinking all of us ran as fast as we could to the north, along the back of the mountain chain, descending and ascending over three entire peaks. And the buffaloes just kept chasing us from behind. We were really exhausted, panting, totally out of breath; some of us fell and rolled over on the ground but got right back up, from fear of being gored by the buffaloes, who had such sharp horns. When we got to the third mountain peak the water buffaloes and their calves finally came to a halt. They stood there looking at us angrily.

On the slope of the third mountain were some bushes and trees, and several farmers' garden fields. We went to the houses there, seeking shelter and drinking water. Of all of us, Sulaiman and Zainal had the palest lips.

The farmer gave us some sugarcane which grew in abundance in his fields. After resting and sleeping in his field hut for two hours, we went on down the mountain going toward Bunga Tandjung. We wanted to bathe there in the abundant local streams, which were famous for their clear, refreshing water.

When we arrived back at our village, the day had grown dark. That night our trip to climb Mount Galogandang and our misfortune to have been chased by wild buffaloes became the main topic of conversation among our friends who hadn't come along with us. In telling this story, the whole Tanah Datar area was still reflected in front of my inner eye—a Tanah Datar still new to me, and one that I did not yet know in detail. And my desire burned to go roaming through that entire area.

CHAPTER 5: HIDE-AND-SEEK

After reciting verses from the Koran and saying the evening prayers, we children (not wanting to go to sleep yet) would play out in the yard in front of the surau, or near the coffee stall close by. Whenever there was a full moon we'd go out to the playing field about half a kilometer from the surau. We'd play various games while waiting for our eyelids to get sleepy: hide-and-seek, joking with each other, tickling and teasing friends, and wrestling.

If it wasn't a rainy day, and most especially if there was a full moon, we loved playing outdoors. Normally we'd use these fine evenings, the ones when Father had already gone on back home (so we wouldn't have to be hesitant about doing such things) to play hide-and-seek. Because lots of our pals wanted to join in (often as many as sixteen people) we'd divide up into four small teams, each one consisting of four people. Three teams would go hide, while the other one would go seek. If a member of a team got found, his band would take their turn as the seekers. The places to go hide in increased in number and range because there were so many people who were trying to hide, and because we were so ardent in seeking them out. It wasn't just a matter of using the area right around the surau: the area about five houses out from there was also included. Before things would begin, we'd make a pact that no one was allowed to go outside the set boundaries (for instance, beyond So-and-so's house or a certain tree). And it was also decided that one was absolutely not allowed to hide inside a house; the roof and the space behind the house posts under the floorboards were all right, though.

The team that was going to go seek would stand in the courtyard facing the surau wall or the big water tub, so they wouldn't see the movements of those of us who were running off and hiding or see which way we headed. We'd ask Lebai Saman (who was watching us) to keep a close eye on the seekers, just in case they tried to look. They'd wait for a whistle blow from the team's chief as a sign that everyone was hidden and ready now and that they could all be looked for. We'd hide under people's houses, in trees, in ditches, on roofs—which we'd climbed up to on the trees that leaned up against the houses—and we'd hide out in the bushes. When I reminisce now, I shudder to think about the dangers that might have befallen us when we were in hiding, such as being bitten by a ground snake, or stepping on a piece of crockery, or being stung by a centipede, and so on. But at that time we didn't think about these things, in the least. The only thing that was important was finding a good hiding place.

Sometimes, when it was fruit-picking season, playing hide-and-seek was a good opportunity to get to the rambutans [lychees], mangoes, and the duku and jambak fruits[1] owned by the villagers who lived around us. During this season we'd play hide-and-seek far into the night, and everyone would be sound asleep, not hearing a thing. Once we saw that all was quiet now in the house of the rambutan owners and that they'd gone to bed, we'd climb up the rambutan tree very, very quietly and sit on a fruit-laden leafy branch. While hiding there, we'd pluck and eat rambutans one by one, or duku fruits or mangoes.

But we did not get the ripe ones because in the dark we couldn't tell which rambutan was ripe and which one was still young and green. We'd sure know once they were eaten, though. We'd feel our lips pucker and we'd toss the fruits away.

In the fruit season the ones who went and hid were quickly found because the seekers always knew where their opponents would go. In this endeavor, each was adept in guessing the other's thoughts. Upon locating a friend during the fruit season, you wouldn't cry out, "So-and-so had been found!" as you normally would. Rather, you'd climb up into the tree, catch hold of your opponent, and whisper, "Hey you, you're caught!" This was so the rambutan owner wouldn't wake up. The team member who had found the kid would whisper to his friends that he had found So-and-so from team such-and-such. By whispering, it was decided that team such-and-such would have to be the seekers now. And the team that had just been the seekers would go hide out in yet another rambutan tree.

Sometimes the rambutan owner would awaken—or rather her husband would. At first he'd shout "Who's that?"

We hiding up in the rambutan tree would fall silent. We'd stop eating and hold still and quiet, like statues, bringing our bodies close in to the tree. If the owner was overheard coming to the door we'd slide down; the ones perched down rather low in the tree would jump right down out of it, totally scared, forgetting the fact that their legs might get broken. At the exact moment that the owner opened his kitchen door, all of us would be on the ground, racing each other madly to get back to the surau. It could well be that the man heard the great thumps of our feet sliding down out of the tree and then running off.

But, really, there wasn't any such a thing as fear for us, when we were still children. Often we'd hide behind the masonry walls of a grave, which in Minangkabau are always near the surau. According to the beliefs of Muslims there, the closer a person's grave is to the surau or the mosque, the greater the good fortune of the deceased will be. The merit generated by people praying and reciting the Koranic verses there will serve to protect them and give them shelter, rather like a chilled person sleeping near the hearth and thereby gaining warmth. Because we feared being found, we'd hide atop graves, but every moment or so we'd remember that the dead person was stretched out there down below. Maybe he'd heard us up above, and what if he should pull on our leg from down underneath?

One time, oh wow! was I scared. It was when I was hiding on top of a rather old grave; maybe its wooden corpse cover had rotted away or gotten holes in it, I don't know. The packed earth over the coffin had sunk down into the ground, falling into the corpse cover, and when my right foot stepped on it my leg sank in, up to the thigh.

I was scared speechless. When I looked into the hole a white form appeared inside, like the shroud of the dead person. Immediately, I ran off toward the surau. In running, I was caught by the seeker team. "Ridjal's caught!" they cried.

Actually, it was my turn to be a seeker again but once they had heard my story, that there was a ghost down there in the grave, hide-and-seek was halted and we went into the surau to go to sleep.

One time when we were absorbed in playing hide-and-seek, a friend of mine, Zainal, hid himself inside his sister's house. According to the rules we had set before playing—rules Zainal also agreed to—no one at all was allowed to go hide inside a house, even if its location was within the set boundaries. We were allowed to hide in the space under the house, or on the roof. The roofs of all the houses were made of thick zinc sheeting so stepping on them wouldn't ruin them.

But this one time, maybe because he was very tired or didn't want to play much anymore and was afraid to ask for the game to be stopped, Zainal and his team went off to go to sleep in his older sister's house. We took great pains searching for them for over two hours. But the only ones we found were the other teams; we three teams took turns playing. Zainal's team didn't go seek and never was caught. We were all astounded: could they possibly have gone outside the boundaries? When we called them they didn't answer. We began to suspect they had gone outside the boundaries. Half of us began to get angry. Now we had the right to go search on tops of the houses. We knocked on the doors of each house asking if Zainal was there. People in each house woke up but didn't rise from their beds. With sluggish voices they answered that Zainal was definitely not in their houses. It didn't occur to us that all this might have disturbed their comfort.

After knocking on the doors of several houses (the ones we were brave enough to knock on, that is), and Zainal hadn't been found yet, finally we went to his sister's house. It could very well be that he was there. It so happened that his grandfather had just then come back from the surau. After evening prayers he usually just did the *sunat* prayer.[2] This old grandfather was extremely devoted to prayer and quite diligent at doing them. We happened to go up into the house at the same time and, sure enough, Zainal and three members of this team were sleeping away in there. They were sleeping on the floorboards, without mats, since his sister had not expected their arrival.

Hearing us come in, they awoke, quite startled and surprised. I saw Zainal turn pale. He immediately acknowledged his fault and asked to be forgiven. On the way home to the surau he was roughly advised not to do such a thing again.

"If you're tired or don't want to play any more you can just ask to stop, but don't go running off to go to sleep in secret," our friends said.

After that night, Zainal was rarely asked to play, except when he promised not to run off again, for we had begun to not trust him. He didn't have the courage to just be frank with us. If he wanted to do some certain thing without talking it over with others first, he'd just go ahead and do it, and he didn't realize that he was violating a promise and really putting other people to a lot of trouble.

Eventually we forgot his mistake and he was allowed to play without having to swear a formal oath first. Apparently he regretted things.

If we weren't playing hide-and-seek, we'd play touch field tag. The surau courtyard was rather spacious, and we'd make boundary marks out there on the ground with dribbles of water, three lines laid out lengthwise and five across. Two of the lengthwise lines would be the end lines. Between the lines there were three meters. A player was not allowed to go outside these lines. If he went out, he was "scorched," and his team would have to "hamper him," or count him out. The crosswise lines were the places where five guards would stand, and they would have to defend these lines so that no opponents passed over them.

This game taught us to keep a sharp, careful eye out, to be nimble and adroit, and to move quickly.

Whoever could pass by, over the lines, without being tagged out by the guards was in the clear. But if he got nudged slightly, he and his friends would have to change places and be guards.

So in this fashion we'd check each other from going over the lines, taking turns back and forth. If a member of one team came in from the first line and then could adroitly run straight back to line number five and still wasn't caught, he and his team were "salty," which meant that they'd won.

When there was a winner, the losers would usually begin to get a bit hot under the collar. They'd get real expert at catching their opponents, and when it was their turn to be pursued, they'd run very carefully and with extreme deftness, so they wouldn't get caught. Because if they weren't careful and fast, they wouldn't be able to mount a respectable response. That is, to wipe out their loss.

So that our clothes wouldn't wear out quickly from all the sweat (and especially so that we'd be hard for our opponents to catch), usually we'd play without our shirts on. We'd only wear trousers. And this was especially the case since wearing shirts often led to disputes, because our opponent would say he had nudged against our shirt even though we hadn't quite felt it. That is often what led to disputes. Because of this, it was better just to go shirtless. That way, if our pals touched our bodies we'd feel it for sure.

One night the villagers who'd been saying their evening prayers had all gone home. So had Father. Ten of us were playing touch tag in the light of the full moon.

Because none of us was shy around the others anymore in the surau, one of our friends named Sjarif made the proposal that we just play naked, so as to conserve our shirts and trousers and so that our opponents couldn't catch us. All of us (all between the ages of twelve and fifteen) agreed to this. Zainal said that there were still two old women saying their sunat prayers in the surau.

"Oh, there's no need to worry," answered Sjarif. "They don't know anyway, and they won't come down out of the surau, because those old grandmas and grandpas are always totally absorbed in their prayers and verse repetitions[3] anyway."

Without the least bit of shyness we striped off all our clothes. We were as stark naked as Adam after he has just descended from heaven. The ones who weren't playing (some kids our age and Lebai Saman) watched from the sidelines. They were simply dumbfounded by our recklessness.

We chased each other around, tagged each other out, and soon everything turned clamorous and high-spirited. We got damp with sweat, but no matter: we were grateful to have the chance to play naked this one time.

While we were absorbed in playing, suddenly two old women from the village came over to the surau to defecate. Seeing them come, we immediately hid behind the wall of the cement water tub, and half of us dove into the tub and started to bathe. Eventually, everyone was in there bathing. All the while the two women were in the outhouse we bathed, swam, splashed about and threw water at one another. Only after they had gone on home and had disappeared behind a house did we start playing touch tag again. Not long afterward, a man passed by. We weren't shy at this but just kept on playing. He wasn't angry; rather, he took pleasure in seeing we had such modern thoughts.

While we were still totally absorbed in chasing each other around and checking and tagging one another, without our suspecting a thing, Father approached us. We were shocked beyond words! Who had informed on us and said that we were playing naked? Or did he perhaps just want to come get a holy book? We didn't know.

We ran for our clothes, intending to run as far away as possible, but he forbade this sharply and said whoever ran off would get a severe penalty the next day. We came to a sudden halt not knowing what to do; we were afraid and embarrassed at the same time. Not long afterward, he went up into the surau and all of us were ordered up in there too. We weren't allowed to carry our clothes or put them on. The sweat of recent play trickled down our bodies, augmented by the sweat of embarrassment. But luckily, everyone was male. The old grandmothers kept on with their prayers.

Father called us in, a person at a time. We were ordered to sit down with our right foot placed up on the bookstand for the Koran. Each player was beaten twenty times with a rattan switch; Sjarif and I each got thirty switches apiece because we were considered the leaders. Then we were told to promise that we would not misbehave like this ever again in the future. If we did not want to so promise, the number of beatings would be increased. We promised, but in our hearts we did have the intention of doing it again, because playing naked was loads of fun and, after all, it did conserve our clothes.

The punishment didn't entail all that much pain. It was the embarrassment that was unbearable. Everybody laughed in great amusement to see us lined up there waiting for the rattan switch—ten stark naked people with their bodies shining with sweat.

I believe that Dad was actually laughing inside to see what we had done. But as a teacher he had to get angry about it and he had to mete out due punishment. After rattan-whipping us, he took a holy book down from the pulpit and went on home, issuing an order to Lebai Saman to make sure to tell him tomorrow if we played tag the same way again.

That night we didn't play again. It was already late at night, eleven o'clock. After bathing again and dressing, we went to sleep in an orderly and peaceful manner, afraid of being informed on tomorrow.

I've related above that we played hide-and-seek during the fruit-harvest season, while at the same time plucking off a good load of other people's lychees, duku fruits, mangoes, and jambak fruit. In short, making quite a haul of little fruits. One time there was a big one, though, a jackfruit. To get this one we weren't playing hide-and-seek, but rather we set off purposely from the surau to shake it down from its tree.

The owners of big jackfruit trees normally wrap the fruit in gunny sacks, rattan sacks, or rotten old cloth so they won't get eaten by the squirrels. One evening when Djamil was walking by underneath a jackfruit tree, he smelled the fragrance of the ripe fruit. He averred that this one was prime picking, just ready to eat. After evening prayers Djamil asked me and three other friends to go with him to pick it. At first I was a bit worried—this jackfruit was a real sizable one. The owner's anger would *also* be sizable, and she sure wouldn't forgive our taking it any time soon. But since there were so many other buddies of mine who were ready to do the deed, I just joined in anyway.

At ten o'clock, when the villagers were all asleep, the five of us crawled stealthily toward the jackfruit tree, out in back of the owner's kitchen. This was about five hundred meters from the surau. Djamil, the leader, cut through the stem of the jackfruit with a penknife, and we four caught it on its way down. Wow, we almost collapsed in a heap on the ground— kerplop!—it weighed about thirty kilograms. If we had really done so, the owner would surely have woken up.

Working together, we carried the jackfruit outside the village to an open field. Underneath a tamarin tree we cut into the fruit, but after cutting it in two it was clear that it wasn't ripe yet and it wasn't good to eat. We then came to the decision, let's not eat it yet: let's just let it sit there and ripen for three more days. And we hid it back in the bushes, covering it over with dried leaves.

The next day, the old grandma who owned it complained to my dad. She was already sure that the recitation students at the surau were doubtless the ones who had stolen it. And who would be their leader except Ridjal? Dad called me in, for he felt that I was the group's leader. In this particular matter, in truth, Djamil was the promoter at issue; I merely corroborated what he did. As usual, I wouldn't confess to anything. Because there was no proof, I wasn't reprimanded. And this case ended right there, just like that. We were surprised. We were prepared to get several whippings with the rattan switch. Apparently, Dad had advised the owner to just donate the jackfruit as religious alms. It's better that other people eat it than that you eat it yourself, maybe Dad said.

Three days later, almost at sunset, the five of us went out to the bushes where we had hidden the jackfruit. Along the way we met two pals who said they wanted to join in and help us eat it. We asked them if they were capable of bearing the burden of sin, too? Sure, they could do that, they said. The seven of us finished up all the jackfruit. We only came out of the bushes after it had gotten really dark so that people wouldn't see that our hands had sticky jackfruit juice all over them and smelled of it too.

This jackfruit was the only big fruit we ever stole. According to the terminology we used at the time, it wasn't really stealing, but rather, just adding to the fruit owner's store of religious merit, so that her palace in the World Hereafter might grow more beautiful.

CHAPTER 6: GETTING CIRCUMCISED

In my village at that time, kids were circumcised only after the age of ten, never at a younger age. I myself was twelve years old; my older first cousin, Maskur, was fourteen when he was circumcised with me.

For us boys, circumcision was an important event in our lives, one which left traces in our souls. For, at that time we began to be aware that we differed from girls, and we began to become bashful and respectful around women.

Our hearts pounded, embarrassed and scared: if say, all of it got cut off, surely we'd die. Maskur was even more scared than this—he actually ran away. Only after he was threatened with a rattan switch did he come home. If his parents would have allowed it, he would rather not have been circumcised at all. But his elders always frightened him, saying, "If you're not circumcised, you aren't a Muslim, because circumcision is one of the stipulations of Islam. Do you want to be an infidel?"

He obeyed. After all, didn't he fear being viewed as an infidel?

Usually we'd be circumcised during vacation, in the Fasting Month [Ramadan, a month of fasting from dawn till dark] when we didn't have to go to school. Mother put on a small religious meal, sacrificing two chickens to serve the circumciser and several *santris* (religious adepts). By early morning Mother had already gone to market—to the Thursday Market—to shop. All day long she had been at home cooking.

In the afternoon, at four, the circumciser arrived from Gunung Radja. His scalpel was renowned and his knife was very sharp. Three days before, Dad had summoned him. From the noon prayertime, Mother had told us to go soak in the water tub so our skin would get soft and easily cut. Upon seeing the circumciser arrive with a bag full of instruments, our hearts pounded even harder, Maskur's face went pale, and his knees shook. I made an effort at smiling, but actually my heart tightened with fear.

Mother told us to get right out of the tub and put on sarongs. We weren't allowed to wear trousers. Several of our friends watched the scene from the yard.

"Well, you know, I'm afraid maybe he'll die," said a friend who had already been circumcised, to those standing beside him.

"Maybe so," said his friend, "and, you know, I'm surprised: Why haven't graves been readied for both of them?"

We were walking by them and shrunk back in fear, even though we knew they just intended to tease and frighten us.

The circumciser was waiting at the surau along with Father and two of his students, who were going to hold us down firmly, just in case we revolted and put up a fight. The others out in the courtyard weren't allowed up into the surau because we'd be embarrassed if lots of people were standing around watching. I was told to sit on a box with my legs akimbo, while on the floor in front of me was the tray filled with ash from the kitchen hearth, to catch the blood. My sarong was rolled up; one of the two students held my hands from the back while the other one held my feet and I couldn't move anymore. The circumciser knelt down in front of me reading mantras out loud, and took out his tweezers and knife. My body trembled.

Then I was told to look outside the window at the top of the jambak tree. I had just begun to pay attention to a jambak tree whose fruits were red and ripe up near its top, when I felt a smarting sensation, and in the wink of an eye the job was done. Really skillful! Blood dripped into the ash and the part of my body that had been thrown away got buried in the ash. The pain wasn't so bad since I had been soaking for so long.

Right away I was put onto a mattress that had been made ready, in a corner of a small room in the surau. In the corner there was another one for Maskur. On top of the mattress was also some ash, placed on top of banana leaves. I was made to lie down on my back with my knees bent up in the air, and I had to keep my legs apart all the time. I wasn't allowed to stretch them out straight. While this was going on I heard Maskur scream and start calling for his mother. I was praised by Father because I hadn't cried. Later on when Maskur was laid on his back like me, he was still crying.

That night many friends came over to where we were, congratulating us and wishing us good luck.

"Now you've become real men and real Muslims," they said.

Some brought us rambutans, lychees, jambaks, duku fruits, and so on. Father didn't allow us to have roasted peanuts or young coconuts. Chicken and eggs also weren't allowed. For us, these taboos weren't much of a problem, although sleeping in the same position continually was wearying and made us quite stiff. We weren't allowed to turn to the right or the left; we always had to lie stretched out on our backs so we got very hot back there. It was lucky that the mattress was lined with banana leaves on top.

We did not have to follow the fast because we were considered invalids. It also wasn't necessary for us to say the prayers. Our joy knew no limits!

One time, an acquaintance who wasn't fasting came by for a visit, bringing along some boiled peanuts. I wasn't strong enough to withstand the desire to eat them. After all, I hadn't tasted peanuts for several days. He gave me five. Father found out. He beat me on the knees, and my whole body shook.

Eleven days afterward, we'd almost fully healed. We were allowed to go for walks, though not very far away, and we had to wear our sarongs. At this point, Maskur was allowed to go home to his mother's house. In fact, Maskur had already gone home.

The night before market day I'd asked Father, might I be allowed to go to market the next day, since all the while I was sick I hadn't gotten to go? Father did give me permission, and he gave me a quarter guilder as spending money. That was a great deal for me at the time; normally I'd only get five cents per market day.

"You go on ahead tomorrow at eight o'clock." Dad said.

All that night I could not close my eyes. My thoughts kept floating off to the market place, imagining what sorts of things I might buy tomorrow. Two and a half cents' worth of fried peanuts, two and a half cents' worth of coconut and rice syrup, sauteed along with its rice in platted little coconut leaf bundles, two cents' worth of sugar cane, two cents' worth of glutinous rice *lupis* cakes—and then I'd just save the rest of the money.

All this was reflected before my eyes along with the exact way I was going to eat all this food. And, oh yes—two cents' worth of fermented cassava, that fermented cassava with black sticky rice made by the folks out in Pitalah. That's the best. And not two cents' worth—how about three cents' worth so I'll get full. That leaves three cents. Well, let that be. Probably tomorrow something delicious will show up to spend that three cents on. For hours I dreamed about what I'd do tomorrow, all the while rubbing the quarter guilder with my finger in my pocket. How was I supposed to get sleepy?

I woke up really early in the morning, at five, and wanted to go to the market right away. I turned on the wall lamp. No one else had gotten up to go say their dawn prayers yet, for during the Fasting Month normally they'd sleep in till eight or nine o'clock. After washing up I went in search of the rice that Mother had left for me in the cabinet after the midnight meal. It was already cold, and I ate it with some delicious rind-*kerupuk* (*kerupuk* crisps made from water buffalo leather), also a leftover from the midnight meal. It tasted extraordinarily delicious this one time. Especially its oil, which was all mixed with salt and hot pepper—I even licked the plate.

I still had lots of rice left, after the oil had already run out, so I took hold of the bottle of coconut oil over in the corner of the room and threw all of the remaining kerupuk crisps on the plate and added an appropriate shake of salt. But, I was surprised. Why was the oil's color greenish and its taste sort of bitter? To finish up all the rice I mixed the oil in with it anyway. But the dish wasn't as tasty as it had been. And my stomach was sort of queasy.

When Mother got up I asked her why the oil didn't taste very good. Mother said, that's not coconut oil, it's rat poison. I was shocked! Rat poison? But it wasn't a big problem because my body was much larger than that of a rat; I wasn't going to die from just that little amount of poison. At least, I cheered myself up by saying that.

Before seven o'clock I already had my clothes on. I had walking stick in hand (made of an umbrella shaft), ready to set off to the market. It already felt like I'd been walking to and fro forever out in the yard, but eight o'clock was still a long way off. Father had said I was allowed to go at eight o'clock. But I had no patience anymore. My feet were itchy to get to the market quickly. Everything I was going to buy I could taste on my lips already. So, what sort of plan could I put into effect?

Oh yes, better that I just turn the annoying clock forward! Because the clock was hanging way up high, I got a chair that Father usually sat on reading his sermon. At that moment it was exactly seven o'clock. An hour more to wait—I had no patience for that! I turned the long hand around till it chimed eight times. Well, now it's eight o'clock, I said. I went right off.

"If Father asks later, what time did you go, I'll answer eight o'clock."

Upon arriving at the market I found it wasn't crowded and busy yet. Not many market sellers had come. I bought whatever happened to be there first. By doing that, my planned program of last night was ruined. Seeing something, I'd want to buy it. Seeing something else, I'd want to eat it. My plan fell into disarray. Things I'd seen versus things I had not yet seen had different powers of attraction.

Between nine and ten o'clock was when things were busiest: everything had been brought to the market by that time. But my money had run out. I regretted the fact that I hadn't had much patience. Now there was lots of delicious food that hadn't been bought yet. Whereas, a while ago, things I didn't particularly need I had bought anyway.

Before twelve o'clock I came home, since my money had run out. Lots of friends were still at the market. Upon arriving back at the surau I lay down; my body was overtired from running all over the marketplace.

Not long afterward Father came along, with two friends of his. While they were conferring over something, Father happened to look over toward the clock and saw that it was already one o'clock. Although the mosque drum hadn't sounded yet? According to his watch it was only twelve o'clock. The sun had not yet sloped down toward the west: it could not be one o'clock. But the wall clock, which he took such pride in because it had never been wrong in twenty years, showed one o'clock. Was the watch wrong? He questioned his two friends. The two of them took out their watches from their pockets. One of them said five minutes before twelve; the other one said six minutes past twelve. The time was definitely twelve. Father stepped down into the yard and looked up into the sky. The sun was exactly overhead.

Seeing Father and his friends look up at the sky and glance at their watches, I began to get worried—would they find me out? Would Father launch an investigation into who had changed the clock, or would he just fix it himself without trying to find out who had altered it?

He was still amazed: what had caused it? Had there been someone who had changed the hour? One of his friends came up to him. The first thing Father asked him was what time did he have on his watch.

"Why, it's twelve-ten," he said.

Who could have changed it? It occurred to Father: "Oh, it must be Ridjal! Who else: no one else would be daring enough."

I was called in. I began to get scared: I'd be punished for sure.

"Do you happen to know who changed the time on the wall clock?"

"I don't know, Father."

"You, maybe!"

"No, Father," I answered, afraid that I'd get my ears boxed if I confessed.

"Confess it! Nothing will be done to you if you confess," Father cajoled me. "Who else could it be if not you?"

"It wasn't me. What would I need to change it for—besides, by hand won't reach up there."

"Maybe you were just playing. You certainly could change it by standing on the chair."

"I didn't change it, Father."

Dad began to get angry, and his hands started moving to smack me in the head. But, afraid he might break my head and brain, he got a stout palm leaf rib whose whip end was as thick as a thumb. He hit me hard several times on my back with it. I started crying from the pain.

"Confess whether you did it or not!" he scolded.

"It's true, I changed it," I answered.

"Why did you change a clock that was keeping good time?"

"Because Father said I was allowed to go to the market at eight o'clock. At seven o'clock I ran out of patience and then I went ahead and changed the clock."

"So why did you change the clock.[1] You could have left it at seven o'clock without turning the clock back," he said.

Father's words were true enough. I only just remembered! If I had gone at seven o'clock I'd be lying to say it was eight, but without changing the clock back surely Father wouldn't have gotten mad at me, because he wouldn't have seen me leave anyway. Ah, why had I been so stupid!

"I thought I had to leave exactly at eight o'clock."

"It didn't have to be eight o'clock. Seven or six o'clock would have been all right too, but don't you go disturbing the clock again, you understand!"

I got another beating and was told to ask for forgiveness and made to promise not to do it again.

"I promise I shall not set the clock back again," I said, sobbing.

"Now you go off and say the prayers and tomorrow start fasting—you're fully recovered!"

That was really an ill-omened day: after eating rat poison I got a beating to boot, and then I had to start fasting the very next day.

CHAPTER 7: ALL BECAUSE OF A BANANA

One time during the Fasting Month I almost wasn't strong enough to continue to fast until sunset. By four o'clock I was seeing stars and couldn't withstand the hunger. I was too afraid of Father to be open about this: he wouldn't allow it. And then, too, the rice wasn't cooked yet. And even if it had been cooked, Mother wouldn't have given me any anyway.

On Father's bookshelf there were six big king bananas[1] strewn about. Their peels were lovely like gold, shining brightly. Plump, fat bananas— ah, their insides would surely be sweet and delicious. A struggle ensued in my interior self: to eat them or not to eat them? If I ate them Father would find out. He'd get angry at me for sure. If I didn't eat them, then my hungry stomach would gnaw away at me. To eat . . . to not eat . . . to eat . . . to not eat . . . to eat . . . to not eat! That's how it went for several minutes. The bananas got lovelier, I rubbed them back and forth, they were all fresh and invitingly delicious there at my fingertips. And I kissed their peels. Oh, their scent! They're sweet inside for sure! . . . ?

Mother was out in the kitchen, Father wasn't around. Swiftly I picked one off, put it in my pocket and went straight out to the dark bushes in the back of the surau, where I ate it and threw its peel far away so that Father wouldn't happen upon it.

After I was through, that's when regrets arose. If Father found out, he'd punish me for sure, even though a single banana hadn't filled me up. Ah, why couldn't I have been patient! It was only two hours more. I hoped that Mother wouldn't find out, and if she did, she'd keep it quiet.

At five Father came back. Before this Mother was already aware that the bunch of bananas was missing one. She was certain it had to have been Ridjal who took it and ate it; who else!

She complained to Father.

That's the problem with having a stepmother. A real mother probably wouldn't have complained; she'd understand that her child was very hungry, and that it wouldn't do any good to punish him. She'd understand that her child was breaking the fast because he couldn't stand the hunger anymore. A real mother would forgive it: her great love for her child would press her to forgive him. If anyone was going to reprimand him, she'd be the one to do it, and not go and complain to Father. That would only increase the number of beatings.

A stepmother is just the reverse: she's pleased and satisfied to see her stepchild get punished. "Well, you didn't come from *my* womb," she'll say. For her, her stepchild's mistakes are a much-awaited opportunity to satisfy her hateful heart. Because of this she's always diligent, looking for mistakes on her stepchild's part. The naughtier the child is, the more opportunities she has.

My stepmother complained: "Ridjal stole the banana, to end his fast."

Not "took" but "stole." Well, sayings coming from a hateful heart differ from those coming from a loving one.

I was called in by Father and asked did I eat a banana from the bunch that used to have six bananas on it but now has just five left?

I did not confess it. "I was fasting," I said.

"If it wasn't you, who else could it have been? I was fasting, *you* were fasting you say—maybe your mother?"

"I don't know, maybe so," I answered.

"How could I ever have eaten a banana, I was fasting," said Stepmother.

"It's only three of us who dare to come into this inner room of the house and I did not eat that banana, because I wasn't in the house, and your mother's prepared to solemnly swear that she was fasting. So it was surely you who ate the banana. Where did you throw the peel to?"

"In the bushes," I answered, after being pressured.

Father got angry; throughout the fast he'd get angry very quickly. He went to find a wide napkin. Then I was tied to a house pillar. I started to cry and asked for mercy. He did not listen.

"The mosque drum hasn't even sounded yet and here you are ending the fast. Now, when other people are ending the fast, you must forgo food," Father said.

I was made to lean against the house pillar. My two hands were drawn together toward the back and they were tied at the wrists with the napkin. Then he went out of the house into the yard.

I sobbed and tried my utmost to free my hands, but they wouldn't come loose. I tried various strategies, all for nothing. While this was going on the mosque drum sounded. Mother set out rice and its many side dishes in front of me. Father and Mother ate together, chatting away, not looking at me, as if I absolutely did not exist. With a hungry stomach I was left to gaze at them scooping up the rice, eating fried fish and stewed meat and chewing on chicken thighs. My saliva began to drip. My stomach smarted and twisted in knots. Afterward, the two of them drank sweetened tea and ate the five king bananas. I watched all this with burning eyes, my body weak from hunger, irked and sad. This is how it is if you don't have a real mother. I was angriest at this stepmother; to go complain about a single banana!

I was left like that for two and a half hours, till my body got soft and hot from hunger and anger. I was only set free at eight o'clock. Upon Father's orders, Mother prepared some food for me, but I refused it.

Just as soon as I was free I went over to the house of my other stepmother. It was from her that I asked for some rice. I said rotten things about the mother who had informed on me—I said she was evil.

"That's so true," said the mother who had given me the rice. "She is a person with a rotten heart," and while saying this she gave me another big chunk of spiced meat. She was pleased to listen to me talk about her co-wife's wickedness.

"Now, you just keep on getting your meals here, from here on out," said this mother. "Moreover, I shall treat you like my very own child."

"Good," I answered. But I didn't really believe it. "Stepmothers really are all the same," said my inner heart, which had by now experienced so much bitterness.

That night I slept in her house, and ate the postmidnight meal there.

CHAPTER 8: FINISHING THE KORAN

When I was twelve years old, I came to the end of the Koran, which I'd been learning to read and recite in the surau for three years.

At the time I was learning how to read and recite the Koran, I did not know that the sentences had any meaning at all. I only knew that the Koran was in the Arabic language and had to be read by singing it, so that the reader would store up merit and later on would get into heaven. I did not know that if it were translated into our own language we would understand what God meant with all of these verses. However, though I had completed the reading of the Koran seven times, God had not said a single thing that I could understand, because it hadn't been interpreted for me.

The Koran must be read, recited, and sung, said the teachers. Each night for three years I wrestled with the manner in which it was to be read: a line over A, a line in front of U, a line under I; if there was a sloping line half a centimeter long, you'd read it in lengthened form, with three letter A's, AAA, III, UUU; if there was no such mark, you'd shorten a letter, A, I, U, and if you had the letter 'AIU, you'd have to drone out 'A, 'I, 'U. And if there was a mark looking like a backward brush, called a *tasjdid*, the letter underneath the brush would be read double.

We had to be very careful and cautious in reading the Koran, as if we were penetrating a road strewn with thorn bushes. For, the teacher said, if we read and recited it wrong (for instance, if *Islaaam* was read *Islam*), we would have committed a great sin and would be tormented in hell, whose fires were a thousand times as hot as those on earth. Or, if the voice was supposed to come out the nose and if it was supposed to be droned, but we read it with our voice coming out of our mouth (for instance, if we read 'A as A), our chances of getting into heaven were slim indeed.

I was much relieved once I had finished reading and reciting the whole Koran to read the very last verse of it. Our joy overflowed. If their level of expertise was about the same, students who had begun their studies at the same time would finish up at about the same time too; if their expertise differed, though, the difference in time would only be a couple of days. The ones who got there first would wait for all the others.

If seven or five students had finished the recitation at the same time, their parents would set to conferring about when, how, and how much they should spend to put on a big celebration for them. For the parents, it was a great joy and source of pride that their son had finished studying the Holy Book. And those who could afford it sometimes wouldn't begrudge the outlay of much money, just so long as the celebration was crowded and fun and quite splendid.

Our cohort consisted of five people. The decision was made at our parents' conference that they would all chip in together to buy a cow for the feast and they would make a big thing out of the whole celebration.

Our mothers and their relatives and comrades all gathered in a house near the surau to do everything that needed to be done, to shop at the market buying various and sundry stuff needed in the kitchen—several chickens, several half kilos of pepper, several big parcels of salt, dozens of coconuts, lots of spices and seasonings—all in lavish quantities.

The news spread through the whole village that a recitation graduation celebration was to be held, and everyone wanted to come to listen to the proceedings and to eat. Everyone could come to this celebration; you didn't have to be specially invited. All this became the main topic of conversation for two or three days beforehand. The theretofore quiet village became extremely busy; this was a veritable sensation for the villagers, and it made them very happy.

We kids who were about to be graduated from our recitation lessons chatted about the celebration cheerily, and about our clothes and the village processions and about whether or not we'd be panicky and quivering when folks heard our recitations and songs. For the recitation teachers from some of the nearby villages (the ones with good voices and great levels of expertise) were going to be invited. Half of us believed in ourselves, half of us were dubious. The only thing that made us anxious was our songs and our voices; we didn't have anything to fear about our techniques for reading the holy text because we'd been put through our practice drills for a long time now. But a voice and way of singing, well, that's really a talent given at birth. Most of us didn't have particularly melodious voices, except for one person, Djamin. He'd surely get some public acclaim.

We kept busy chatting and practicing as if there were no end to it, and the night before the celebration we got almost no sleep. Our hearts kept pounding away with alternating hope and apprehension—would we succeed or would we fail tomorrow when we were heard by all those hundreds of people? But alongside all this we got considerable entertainment out of our fine clothes and new shoes that we'd wear tomorrow. Moreover, our hair had been cut, too, and it looked quite smart; tomorrow we'd attract public attention for sure. And then, too, there was all that food and those rice delicacies that were going to be laid out on mats before us— since we were the ones the celebration was for, we'd doubtless get very special foods.

We woke up very early in the morning and our mothers ordered us to take our baths right away. This time it was with scented soap and special shampoo and lime rinses.

Father sacrificed the cow, although we five weren't allowed to accompany the other children who were out there having a good time helping folks cut up the meat into chunks. We had to get into our finery and stay calm and still as bridal couples do.

Because the celebration was a religious one and because Islam had originated in Arabia, we were all ordered to put on the national Arab dress: a long white sheath coming down to our ankles; over this a *sadariah*, or vest, in various colors such as deep red, brown, and blue, with yellow silk lace along the edges. And over all this a long robe that came in five colors, of which we could pick the ones we liked most. Then we wore some sort of head covering—some wore white haji pilgrim's caps, some wrapped their heads in turbans, some wore fez headgear like a Turk, and then there were others who wore head-scarf robes made of gold thread like those the sons of Arabian kings wear.

Our faces got powdered a bit so they would look nicer and then we were sprinkled with perfume. It looked in the mirror as if we'd all gotten better looking! The women who were helping to adorn us kept praising the fine way we looked, saying: "Maaasja Allah! Maaasja Allah!" [The will of God].

We spent two hours getting adorned, since these women were extremely exacting and they wouldn't allow anything to be off the slightest little bit. Clothes we'd already put on were stripped off again and we'd put on something else, and that too would be stripped off and then something else would be put on again, and it would go back and forth like this until they were totally satisfied. We just obeyed everything, having no way to refuse.

Meanwhile, lots of friends had arrived. Men and women villagers came, old and young, all done up in fine clothes. They'd sneak a look at us first, and laugh at us in a kindly way. They named us "Honorable Haji or Syech."

"Who knows, maybe they really will get to Mecca later on," shot back the women who were getting us properly outfitted. For them, going to Mecca was the very pinnacle of aspirations one could have in this world. Because we were still ignorant, we thought that going on the pilgrimage was a realistic aspiration for us, too, and that these women's faith was entirely appropriate.

In the surau yard, old women were boiling several cauldrons of rice and cooking spiced meat stew in three big frying pans. They were also preparing meat curry and jackfruit in three cauldrons, as well as a big earthenware pot full of chicken curry for the invited guests. Everyone was busily occupied; rattan mats were spread out in the big surau, and for the honored guests fine woven carpets had been laid out in the niche facing Mecca. These special guests were to be the jury to evaluate our recitation performance.

Before ten o'clock we put on our new shoes and took a turn at walking to and fro in the house to see if any of us might possibly cut a dashing figure. After all the women gained their satisfaction at viewing this, we were told to go on down out of the house into the yard, for the procession was soon to set off.

We went down the stairs, with everyone gazing at us and offering praise, most especially the old aunties who were cooking away.

"Oh my, you sure look fine! Seeing you helps heal my work-weariness," they said, fiercely pinching our cheeks.

The procession was put in order. We were placed right out in front and friends who had graduated from their recitation lessons before us sheltered us with parasols. Everyone—except those who had to cook and receive guests back at the main surau—went along with the procession. There were hundreds of them, singing religious songs, Arabic religious chants, and so on. As we passed by, everyone whose house was along the side of the road came out to take a look at us from the window, smiling.

After an hour of marching around in procession we went back to the surau. Meanwhile, the mothers pressed against each other in their room [their separate room in the surau]. All of them wanted to see the whole ceremony but they were hindered in this by the curtain. The hundreds of men sat down cross-legged in front of us in rows, awaiting us with their full attention, as we confronted this final test.

Then my father stood up and delivered a speech explaining the rationale for the celebration. And once he had asked permission of the honorable syechs about whether or not it was permissible to start, and once the jury had answered with a nod, we were told to read the final verses from the Koran, alternating with one another until we had come to the end. With apprehension and pounding hearts we set to reading. With the first recitation, luckily, there were no mistakes. The syechs, listening critically, nodded their heads, and when we saw them do this we grew bolder and we progressed through the test all the way through to the end. The recitation, our voices, and our songs were fully satisfying.

The joy of the mothers and fathers of the five in our group was beyond telling. Their eyes shone, radiating pride. Our mothers and fathers were the truly happy ones in that big crowd. Why, there were even two mothers who had tears flowing down their cheeks.

Then in incense burner with incense scattered on top was brought out and set before the Honorable Sjech Daud. He himself read a prayer, while those in attendance received his hand and pronounced: Amin, Amin, Amin! Then, as a supplement, Djamin—the one with the best voice—was asked to read the Joseph chapter. While reading, he raised his voice very high (and made it quite melodious), with the honorable syechs saying in accompaniment: "Taib, taib, Maaasja Allah!"

Then the foods were set out, with the most delicious ones for the honorable syechs. We didn't join in the meal since our food was all laid out at the minor surau, located alongside the main surau. We were told to go back down and go outside once again, since the mothers wanted to get another look at us. They acted as if they all loved us. An old auntie with a trembling voice said to me: "If your mother were still alive her happiness would just be beyond telling."

My tears flowed down my cheeks at this, at remembering my mother, and before my eyes images of the wide long leaves planted near her graveside also appeared.

While we ate, the women looked on, paying attention to our every move, chatting away animatedly.

We felt very lucky. It was only the Arab clothes that we regretted a bit; that was the only thing that dampened our feelings of joy and good fortune. We weren't allowed to get out of them until afternoon. We felt like actors in a stage show! To wear our own national costume would have made us truly joyful. And those clothes wouldn't have been any less fine looking than the Arab clothes.

But the adults were still in charge!

CHAPTER 9: THE VILLAGE PRIVATES STEAL A CHICKEN

Besides us recitation lesson kids, several near-adult youths were also staying over in the surau. There were also some "middle-aged" youths whom the villagers called the "foodstall privates." They didn't number more than ten. They didn't have regular jobs; they just existed by exhausting their inheritance from their wealthy maternal uncles. They weren't studying the religious texts anymore, but then, their parents hadn't given them permission to emigrate to the rantau either.

Every day they'd have no other work than just hanging around the foodstall, shooting the breeze, playing cards or dominoes, or walking about the village, walking out to the lakeshore, going fishing in the river, sleeping in empty suraus, and going home whenever they happened to get hungry. At night, while we'd all be doing our recitation lessons, they'd be shooting the breeze and playing dominoes in the foodstall. When it got time to go to sleep, they'd come over to the surau and use our mats and pillows. Their own blankets were just the sarongs they carried over their shoulders wherever they went.

Only one person from the whole group of them had his own mattress, pillow, and blanket—Datuk Mangkuto, who was their leader.

I've already related that grown young men in Minangkabau are embarrassed to sleep in their mother's house. Besides being made fun of by their friends who tell them they're still nursing their mothers, they're also embarrassed to be sleeping in the front main room of the house near their sisters' rooms (where the sisters' husbands arrive every night). They're embarrassed to be called the guardians of their sisters' rooms. Young men like this, not yet married, but not off in the rantau either, always sleep at the surau or the foodstall. Indeed, they're found wherever young village men normally gather.

Young men who think of themselves as fully grown often press their parents to let them emigrate to the rantau to make their own living, so folks will quickly ask for them in marriage for their daughters.[1] Otherwise, they'll end up staying in the village forever if their maternal uncle isn't wealthy enough and if they're not among the group of people asked for in marriage—maybe they'll end up being embarrassed, having a hard time of it, and people will take a very long time asking for them in marriage. And in truth, there are several of them in my village who never got married their whole lives.

Parents and maternal uncles also feel embarrassed that their son or nephew is grown but isn't yet married. So eventually they will let the young man emigrate to the rantau with several hundred rupiah in capital, to go work as a merchant in Tapanuli, East Sumatra, the Bangkahulu, Palembang, and the Lampung Residencies.

After two or three years of living in other peoples' lands, and once the young man had realized a profit from his work, he'd start to send money and also clothing back to his parents. And he'd return to the village wearing fine new clothes, new shoes, and maybe sporting a Shanghai suit jacket or a Bugis silk sarong. The villagers, especially the women, would crowd around these young men to talk to them at the marketplace, out at the bathing spot, in the surau after prayers, in houses—indeed, wherever it might be that women typically gather.

But my story has gotten sidetracked. To tell the truth, I don't want to talk about marriage celebrations, but rather about the chicken-stealing party.

One night, one of the "foodstall privates" named Rasidin proposed that I go steal a chicken from our neighbor, whose house was rather far from the surau, so that the chicken could be killed and cooked that night. Several of the foodstall privates had already decided to have a big meal out in the surau, which was located sort of on the edge of the village. This surau was one that was deserted because after the person who had owned it (a harsh and severe haji) was buried down under the space under the floorboards, no one had the courage to go pray there anymore.

Five of the foodstall privates had already stolen a can full of rice from their mothers. This came to some three-fourths of a liter apiece. And they'd secretly taken some spices from their sister's or their old auntie's house. So now it was just a matter of a chicken. And finding one was my task, according to Rasidin. Rasidin whispered to me that, look, I didn't have to contribute any rice, pepper, or coconuts, just so long as I'd go plunder a chicken from under someone's house.

I whispered to Rasidin (we always discussed things in whispers, even if we were far away from other people and no one could possibly hear) that I didn't want to steal a chicken. True enough, sometimes I would take people's fruit, but that was just playing and it wasn't really stealing. Stealing a chicken was stealing. It was a serious wrong and the punishment would be a heavy one if I got found out.

"I wouldn't dare," I whispered. "One time I heard from Father that a chicken thief in Tandjung Berulak was led off by the cops to Padang Pandjang and given three months in prison.

"You don't get punished for taking fruits because they're not worth much, not even ten cents, and besides, lots of folks take them. And moreover little wrongs like that can be forgiven," I added.

Because I didn't want to steal one, Rasidin said, well, I just wouldn't be invited to the big feast.

"Well, so be it," I answered.

My friends my same age, the ones well known to be naughtier than most (the ones like Djamin, Zainal, Dullah, and Bujung) also didn't want to go steal a chicken, for fear that they'd be put in prison for three months.

It appeared that one of the foodstall privates named Tjonat (who wasn't contributing any rice) was willing to go steal a chicken.

That night we went to peek after we'd all promised one another not to say the least little thing so as not to scare the big partygoers. We also promised not to cough or they'd think they had to invite us in to eat with them. Off we went very quietly to spy from the little gaps between the wallboards in the surau kitchen. We saw the five of them sitting there boiling rice and cooking two chickens into a curry; the four others, the older ones, sat deeper in the surau, shooting the breeze with one another, with one guy going out every few minutes to check to see if someone might be coming. In the pitch darkness he didn't see us.

Where they got the two chickens we didn't know, since no chicken squawk had been audible anywhere around our surau. The privates who were in there shooting the breeze would get up every second or so and go into the kitchen to see if the curry was done yet. None of them had the patience to wait; they could already sense those delicious chicken thighs between their teeth, especially Rasidin and Tjonat.

After the rice and curry were done they jostled each other to get firsts, though not to put on their plates because they didn't have any plates. Rather, they used banana leaves. They ate heartily and panted from all the hot spices. Some of my companions, doubtless, were salivating, but they just kept quiet, remembering our promise and also the fact that they hadn't taken part in the plot. None of the diners suspected that we were watching them.

They finished the rice and curry up without a trace left. Nothing at all was left over; in fact, they even managed to stuff all the bones into their faces. After they'd finished eating and all the banana leaves had been thrown away out back of the surau, they sat there and reclined, quite stuffed, talking over the delicious feast and trading jokes. One of them said, "It's really too bad that there aren't any bananas to act as an antidote to all that pepperiness."

While they were chatting, Si Udin proposed that half of them go out to a rice paddy plot outside the village to pull up some farmers' peanut plants and then boil them up and eat them before going to sleep. So four of them went out there in the pitch darkness carrying a broken old basket.

Meanwhile, we went back home from the surau with the intention of coming back later, about when the peanut pickers had gotten back too. Everything we'd seen we kept a secret, for we were scared of beatings and getting a sharp response from the privates, who were a whole lot bigger than we were.

When we came back to the surau the entire basketfull of peanuts along with all its roots, stems, and leaves had gone into a big cooking pot, for they hadn't had the patience to pluck off the nuts one by one. On the contrary, some of them were already eating the nuts half-cooked.

Once they were done, the peanuts were piled up in the middle of the surau and they all crowded around to eat them. Zainal couldn't bear watching and he whispered to me that he wanted to go on in. The other three did not agree because if we hadn't been joining in right from the start, we shouldn't want to join now.

The next morning we heard that those nine greedy consumers of that night's chicken and peanuts had gotten sick to their stomachs from overeating, or perhaps from gobbling too many uncooked peanuts.

Two days afterward a grandmother got into a tiff with her neighbor. She was missing two chickens . . .

CHAPTER 10: SUSPECTED OF EATING
FERMENTED CASSAVA

Even when we were really keeping the fast, grown-ups would suspect us anyway and think that we had drunk or eaten something on the sly.

They had also been young once, they'd say: they knew all the little tactics young people use. Back then, they'd also drunk water while swimming in the river, or climbed up a young coconut palm on an isolated farm and then pretended to the public to be fasting, making out that their bodies were weak and exhausted. They fully believed that we were using these same tactics too. About half their suspicions did prove true, but sometimes they'd be wrong, and one time I fell victim to one of these mistaken notions.

One morning during the Fasting Month while I was sleeping, Father called for me and gave me five cents. He told me to go buy some boiled yams at the marketplace for my little sister,[1] who was recuperating from an illness. I went around the market for two whole hours looking for the yam vendor, but no one was selling any. I asked my friends, thinking maybe they'd seen him; all of them said they hadn't run into him either. Finally I bought some fermented cassava as a substitute, thinking that my little sister would like to eat that.

It was already eleven o'clock. Halfway home, three friends of mine playing dominoes in a deserted surau called me over. They asked me to join in so they'd have four players for their game. And really, this was just what I was looking for: the chance to play, play, play!

One of them proposed that we all eat the fermented cassava so that the game would get even more fun, but I didn't want to since it was for my little sister. I put the cassava up on a shelf so it wouldn't tempt us.

We played with absorption for two hours. Then I asked to stop so I could go say the noon prayers. I went back to the surau. I only remembered the cassava when I saw Father. I wanted to go back and pick it up but too late! Dad had spotted me. He called me over.

"Why were you off buying boiled yams all this time? And where exactly are they?"

"Nobody was selling them, Dad. I took a long time because I was looking for them all over the whole marketplace and I kept waiting and waiting, thinking that someone would come."

"So if there weren't any yams, where's the money?"

"Since there weren't any yams, I used the money to buy fermented cassava root. I thought maybe—I was scared that maybe Father wouldn't accept fermented cassava."

"So where's the cassava?"

"It's over at the deserted surau, Father, I forgot to bring it."

"I don't believe it. You ate it for sure. Here you were ordered to buy yams but you get cassava and then you go and break the fast in the middle of the day with it. Accursed child!"

"I didn't break the fast, Father. I didn't eat that cassava—it's still there at the deserted surau."

"Go get it then! I want to see it, I want to see whether five cents' worth of cassava is really there. Don't let it be three cents' worth and the other two cents you use to break the fast, either."

I went to the deserted surau, but . . . God forgive me . . . only its leaf wrappings were left. The cassava had all been eaten up by my three friends and they weren't there anymore. They'd gone off to who knows where . . .

Coming back to the surau, I said to Dad with a scared, trembling voice that my friends had eaten up the cassava. Father absolutely did not believe it. His anger was incalculable. Not over the five cents' worth of cassava, but because I was suspected of breaking the fast.

"What did I say to you earlier? You're the one who ate that cassava and here you said it was your friends who did. So now where are they?"

"They've run off, Father."

"Don't say anything more. Your friends who polished off that cassava were the cursed devils nesting in your belly. You come here!"

I approached Father with my body trembling all over and he pulled me over to a house pillar in the middle of the surau. My two hands were tied in back; my shirt was taken off and I was left there just wearing short pants. I cried and begged for mercy for my carelessness and explained that I really had been fasting all along.

But I wasn't listened to.

Then Father went out in back of the surau. The jambak tree there had lots of red ants' nests in it. Father took a pole and stuck it into a bunch of nests, and after one of them had fallen down, he carried the nest (and its huge red ants swarming all over its outside) back up into the surau and deposited it on top of my head. After they'd only been on my head a minute, dozens of red ants spread out all over my shirtless body—all of them aiming to bite me too. Since my hands were tied up, I couldn't throw them off my back and chest. I shook my head and the nest fell off, but Father put it back on again. Being bitten by the ants wasn't as painful, though, as my fright at seeing Father's eyes burning like fire. I didn't have the courage to look him straight in the eyes.

I begged for mercy and vowed that I would keep the fast.

Luckily, at that moment, a close friend of Father's came along, Baginda Tanemas, who also happened to be exceedingly fond of me. He calmed Father down and untied my bonds and threw off all the red ants swarming all over my body. He was the only one with the gumption to do this. Other folks were afraid of getting mixed up in Father's dealings with his son. When Father got mad, everyone else kept quiet. And seeing Baginda Tanemas spring me, Father just kept quiet, and then went off to get some water for saying his prayers. In his heart he was actually glad that there had been someone who had pulled us apart.

After noontime prayers I went to sleep. My body was overtired from hunger, from wandering to and fro in the market, from playing dominoes, and from all that suffering of the last two hours. And then on top of that I kept getting yanked out of sleep hearing Father reprimand Mother, who (he said) had let him go and get furious at me.

"Why in the world didn't you come to Ridjal's aid? Did you want me to murder my child? Why didn't you break us up right away?"

"I was afraid of you," answered Mother.

"Even if you were afraid of being reprimanded, whenever you see me getting mad or punishing my child you must come to his aid."

When he was angry Father wasn't able to rein in his passions. He'd set to beating away on me or using the rattan switch or kicking me if there wasn't anyone to intervene and separate us. And then if we *weren't* separated, he'd turn around and get mad at the person who was supposed to be doing the separating. It was because of that that Father got really angry at Mother, because all the time I was tied up and being bitten by red ants she just kept quiet. If Baginda Tanemas hadn't come along who knows what would have happened to me . . .

Around afternoon prayertime, while I was still sleeping, Father came up to me real slowly and sat down beside me. He asked me if my body still hurt from being bitten by the ants. To cheer him up I answered, no, not anymore. This was a sign that he was trying to get back in my good graces. Apparently he regretted things. He gave me a quarter. "Maybe you want to buy some fire crackers," he said, to help heal my hurt feelings.

I cried, and he went away sulkily.

That night folks told my three friends that I'd gotten the ant punishment because I'd polished off a packet of cassava. My friends felt some regret at this. After the *tarwih* prayers [a kind of nonobligatory prayer performed during Ramadan], they called me over to the shady *kuini* mango tree in the surau yard and asked me to forgive them.

"You're just a bunch of devils," I said.

CHAPTER 11: FENCING LESSONS

Because I was growing up—and who knew? maybe I'd be emigrating to the rantau some day to live among foreigners who'd have aims and behaviors that might differ from or oppose my own, and maybe this would cause disputes and fights—Father thought I should study self-defense and fencing, so I'd be able to take care of myself.

"Sure, it's true enough that you aren't going to actually go looking for any quarrels," said Father, "but just supposing that some crazy person does come up and starts hitting on you first and challenges you to a fight, you'll have to be able to put up a fight. To rise to the challenge. No matter how much you might want to be peaceful, you really do need this skill as something to have in reserve."

Father chose four friends of about the same age as me, Bujung, Dullah, Zainal, and Kamal. They were all going to be given self-defense lessons too. That meant that when the teacher got tired of giving us examples to mimic and coaching us, the five of us could keep on practicing and the teacher could just watch over us. The ones who were going to teach us were Father himself, a renowned fencing master, and Uda Tjodi (that is, Older Brother Tjodi).[1] He was an expert fencing student, who'd serve as Father's stand-in whenever Father could not come to the lessons for some reason.

On Thursday afternoons, after sunset prayers, the five of us were told to go gather in a group in the minor surau. Father and Uda Tjodi were already waiting for us there. The seven of us burned some incense and said some prayers in the hope that these fencing lessons and self-defense exercises, soon to be given to us, would penetrate our bodies and souls, and that this skill would bring blessings, happiness, and good welfare to all of us. At the time, we had to vow that we would not use these fencing and self-defense skills for evil purposes, nor attack people arbitrarily. These skills could only be used for self-defense.

After evening prayers the five of us were called out into the yard to begin our instructions. The public sat around our fencing clearing and watched us, not joining in, but looking on from the sidelines. One by one Father instructed us.

Oh brother! Imagine how clumsy and awkward each move we made was. We wore ourselves out striving to imitate our teacher's arm movements and leg swings, but everything we did went awry. That night we were a most humorous sight.

This was especially true when Bujung stepped forward to center court: everyone would burst into guffaws of laughter. Some would emit little minor chuckles, while some would just yell and cheer. Indeed, there was a grown-up who ran right up into the surau, afraid he'd drop dead laughing if we looked at him, and caught his eye. Not a single one of Bujung's movements came out right. Every one of them was aslant and askew, far different from what the teacher had intended. And when he was ordered to turn his body around, he'd turn around his arms and upper body but he'd forget that his feet also had to turn. As a result, he'd fall sprawling to the ground. Everyone would yell and cheer. Our stomachs would hurt from laughing so hard.

We'd often seen people fence, and it looked quite easy to us. In fact, there were some among us (among us young kids, that is) who'd be so bold as to criticize a fencer if he made a misstep. But now, when it was we who stood there in the arena, we were confused and nonplussed. We felt the audience spinning around us, and whatever we did, nothing seemed to come out right. This was especially so if they'd start to laugh and we couldn't hear any of our teacher's admonishments and instructions.

Suppose there were girls in the audience who were watching us from the windows and that among them was someone we fancied. Well, to tell the truth we would have been happy just to be swallowed up by the earth at that moment. We felt really peeved: why didn't the ground we were trodding upon just have holes in it!

That's why we liked to take our instruction at night, after all the women had gone home. We didn't want to play in the daytime before we got really good at this.

Once in a while we would be told by the teacher to kick at each other or to go colliding into each other, and he'd watch us carefully with an air of derision. And after that he'd kick at us, but just in a make-believe way, not really hard (because if he did it for real, our bellies could easily get hurt by a bad blow). And we'd kick him back. If we didn't kick him enough, he'd point out how many times we should have actually done it. And in that way we would fight back and forth until our attempts to ward off blows were smooth, swift, and automatic.

The exercises were very wearying. After only a quarter hour of fencing and whirling around we'd already be panting for breath, thirsty, our bodies totally worn out. A good thing Mother had prepared a big bamboo tube full of coffee leaf-flavored water for us, as well as two or three coconut shells to use for glasses.

Father was tired, and we were being put through our exercises by Uda Tjodi. He was a sturdily built young man, a big guy, healthy, nimble, full of zest and hard to tire out. How many times we fenced with him and he never showed the least sign of tiredness! He'd fence for two hours straight and he'd still be strong; he'd still be challenging us one after another. With Uda Tjodi we felt free and unhampered, not hesitant and scared as we did around Father. We could kick at him as hard as we liked and his comeback would be strong in kind.

Eventually it would be the five of us who would give out of energy. Our exhaustion was indescribable. Our feet and knees wouldn't take any walking orders anymore. Zainal was stretched out on the ground, his breath coming in single puffs. The first night we went on for only three hours, until eleven o'clock. We went to sleep, after bathing late at night.

And that's the way it went, with us practicing three times a week.

After studying for a month and a half we had gotten a little skilled at all this, and we weren't embarrassed anymore for folks to watch us. On the contrary, now we wanted folks to pay attention to us and to watch and praise us. In fact, at any time at all we'd look for opportunities to show off our fencing mastery, like girls wanting to show off their clothes and jewelry. So if a coconut or a durian fruit[2] suddenly fell down with a great thump to the ground near us, or even a spine from a frond from an areca palm fell down, we'd deftly strike a defensive pose as if that coconut, durian, or frond was a kick from some evil-intended person. Our legs were ready to strike out, our feet were ready to kick.

If someone happened to say at such a moment, "Hey, you're good fencers now!" and then another chimed in, "Well, of course, his father's a fencing master, of course the son will also be a skilled fencer," I'd be exceptionally pleased. But I'd pretend to be embarrassed and say, "Ah, I'm not all that good yet."

Besides all this, we were starting to get aggressive.[3] We'd haul off and smack a friend who did something wrong or some such, to try to get him to fight. And this would be a great opportunity to show off our skills and really put them into practice. If no one wanted to be lured into a fight, though, we'd throw stones at the men who were walking by in our village, and when they'd get mad we'd hit them.

In short, each day we'd get into fights at least two or three times. And we wouldn't win all of them either—we got hurt and bruised from all our opponents' blows. But we'd sure be happy.

Our original aim and vow that these skills would be used only for self-defense was forgotten now, because we were fencing mad. Hot blood cultivated by all the fencing exercises heated up even more; our patient nature turned aggressive, reckless, and we forgot our original purpose and moral position. We'd challenge absolutely everyone, except our teachers maybe and a few fencing masters from Sumpur and other villages. We supposed that *we* were the fencing masters and the brave guys.

When we weren't fighting, we'd invite our other friends who couldn't fence yet to wrestle us: that gave us the chance to display all our great skills we'd studied. In our opinion, these pals were really ignorant and easy to beat up, since they weren't skilled or swift at kicking. They were persons who were going to lose in life's struggles, we thought.

After we had studied for three months, it could be said that we were adept at fencing, self-defense, and *randai*.[4] All the necessary martial arts theories had now been studied. The three-strides move, the nine-strides move: we'd memorized them all. We understood the attack moves and the defensive moves sufficiently well now. Father and Uda Tjodi delighted in our progress. We were very thankful about it all, too.

To celebrate the completion of our exercises, we held a *selamatan*[5] over at Bujung's house. This meal involved sǎcrificing a goat and three chickens. We invited lots of pals and all the santris who were going to pray over our selamatan.

Turmeric rice, roast vinegared chicken, and a goat head, cooked a special way: these were all prepared for our teachers, for Father and for Uda Tjodi—along with enough cloth to make new clothes for them to replace the old ones they'd worn out during all the time they'd spent giving us our lessons.

On that day the five of us wore new clothes: black Teluk Belanga shirts, wide Acehnese trousers (also black), batik caps and batik sarongs folded neatly into shoulder cloaks or draped at our sides from the waist. We also had heirloom daggers slipped into our waistbands. We were puffed up with pride, like rajas' sons.

Before eating, and as a kind of final event to close our fencing exercises, we did self-defense moves and slow-motion steps out in the yard. The whole populace, male and female, watched. The ceremony was an opportunity to show all that we'd studied. We fought (as was appropriate), not too long and not too hard, for we were afraid we'd get our fine new clothes all damp and dirty. The whole audience praised our skills. Our moves were indeed right on target.

Each one's family delighted in seeing their son or nephew so skilled at fencing.

Even though he didn't let it be known, Father himself was very happy: he was delighted to see his own child become a fencer. My friend said that every few moments or so Father would glance over toward me, smiling, with a look full of love and fondness, visible out of the corner of his eye. That day I was given a rupiah in pocket money, for sweets. To me, that much was just an extraordinary amount.

CHAPTER 12: THRESHING RICE

When the rice in the paddies begins to turn yellow, villagers rejoice, for in a few days they will be harvesting the fruits of their labor. They will be eating newly reaped rice and their granaries will be full. So they make their preparations to feed the people who will be cutting and threshing their rice for them.

People from our village (as was the case all through Minangkabau) did

not hire coolies to do this work. Rather, they relied on mutual cooperation leagues. They'd rely on these to cut down the rice with sickles (folks
would take turns at that), and for threshing the rice and carrying off the
rice of each person in the league. For example, say that thirty people de-
cide to get their paddy rice safely back into their houses; they agree to
work until the job's complete. On this one day, for instance, they'd be in
paddy A, threshing, while tomorrow they'd be in paddy B, cutting the rice
down, and the next day in paddy C, threshing. And that's the way it would
go on until all the rice of all those thirty people would be safely stored
back in their houses. Folks whose paddy rice was going to be cut or
threshed needed only to prepare food and drink; each person in the mutual cooperation league would bring his or her own sickle and threshing
cane.

When I sat on top of the steep riverbank, a spot called Tanah Runtuh,
looking down at the paddy fields spread out in the Sumpur Valley all the
way to the Lake Singkarak shore, I could sense the joy of the farmers during the cutting and threshing season. Out in the once-green, now yellow-
ing paddies, the grain swayed in waves and villagers zigzagged across the
terrain, going out to their respective fields. Women balanced big plaited
baskets of rice and curry on their heads.

Out in the middle of this valley were my father's paddies, three big wide
plots. In two days the rice would be cut down. While waiting for this, I went
over to the paddies of a friend who was threshing his rice. We weren't very
skilled at threshing yet. Because of this we kids only got to carry the rice
stalks back from the haystack[1] over to the thresher. We didn't particularly
put ourselves out working hard at this job; for us, what was really important was eating our meals out there in the fields. This was seven times
more delicious than just eating meals back home. Even if it was the very
same food we put into our mouths in both places, its taste was different
somehow. Maybe because out there we were getting to eat in a big noisy
group, and it was all going on out in an open field in the open air. And
maybe mostly because humankind simply loves change, as well as things
that differ from our ordinary, everyday customs.

Finally our turn to get our field rice came. I helped out with the cutting
job, too, but only for a little while: I was afraid of being bitten by leeches,
which hung about in great numbers in the damp paddies. Without your
knowing it these leeches would attach themselves to your feet and suck
your blood. Grown-ups weren't afraid; they thought of it as being just like
being bitten by mosquitoes. But I found it horrible and hideous to see
those ferocious black bodies. The grown-ups gave me jobs involving walking about so that the leeches wouldn't light on me—jobs like carrying the
bundles of rice stalks that had been harvested off to the haystack. Over
there were people whose job it was to tie them up into neat, tight bundles.

We were always cheerful as we worked. Cutting and threshing rice was an opportunity to celebrate, to play, to eat a whole lot, to consume stewed fruit and sticky rice, to hunt grasshoppers and roast and eat them, and then later on to go bathe in the river and chase each other around and finally to go on home, playing on flutes we made of rice stalks.

The haystack was round. The ends where stalks had been cut off were put facing toward the outside and the rice stalks were pointed inward. The rice would be gathered together in that way until it constituted a big globular haystack. The more time passed, the bigger it got, till seven plots' worth of rice was piled up.

Normally the job of cutting the rice down wouldn't take until afternoon, if the paddy fields weren't too broad and if there were lots of people doing the cutting. After cutting our paddy fields, folks would eat up on top of the haystack or sitting all around it, all in a big crowded group. After eating they'd smoke cigarettes or converse for several moments, to take a rest break; then they'd go to the fields of one of their members to thresh. There they'd work until afternoon and eat an afternoon meal. From there they'd go back home after making a decision: tomorrow they'd go to the fields of someone else from the same group.

At night, the haystack would have to be guarded. If it wasn't, there was a possibility that some of our harvested rice would be, shall we say, moved over to someone else's stack. True, this rarely happened, but there was no loss in being extra careful. Father and Mother told me to go guard it, accompanied by two friends. Dullah and Zainal (whose rice harvests were already in the storage house) were amenable enough to keeping me company. Bujung couldn't take me up on my invitation since he had to guard his own haystack in Sudut.

After sunset prayer time, off we went to the paddies, carting along mats, blankets, and a packet of rice and side dishes for each of us. On top of the haystack we'd fasten several straps made of coconut palm fibers, which we'd crisscross on top and fasten together. Then we'd cover this over with a big pandanus mat, and we'd cover the outside thickly with dried paddy stalk stubbles. In a quarter of an hour our simple but satisfactory tent was complete.

We spread out our mats underneath. That's where we'd sit around and go to sleep later on. We'd built this tent only for the possibility of rain.

Before going to sleep, we ate out there in the dark, our only illumination coming from the starlight and the sky. After eating we would chat comfortably and stretch out lazily, listening to the sounds of crickets and frogs in the drains, and to the hissing sound of the River Sumpur flowing not far away.

Other haystacks also had their guards. They had brought lamps from home and these could be seen flickering from afar. A dog could be heard howling, off in Batu Beragung, and to the south, behind pandanus grass clusters growing in rows, Lake Singkarak lay there clear and quiet, black and frightening, like a wild animal waiting for its prey.

"Zainal!"

"Yes?"

"When I look up at those animals way up in the sky, my thoughts soar way up high and I begin to want to emigrate to another land."

"I'm the same way," answered Zainal, "I want to emigrate to the rantau like our buddies. But I don't want to go really too far off. To Padang would be enough."

"For me, the farther the better," replied Abdullah. "I want to go to Sibolga, or to Bangkahulu, or to Lampung. Lots of folks from our village have gone there."

"But the pity is that the three of us are still tied down. Dullah by his mother and father, Zainal by his mother, and me by my father. Whenever will our parents be willing to give us permission to leave the village? Why do they find it so difficult to set us free?"

The three of us fell silent, coming to a realization of our respective fates.

Then I asked: "Why do you want to be in some foreign land, Zainal?"

"I want to go work as a craftsman. At first, I'd be a doorman at the Bioskop. That way I'd get to watch the movie every night. I used to go to the movies a lot with my father in Padang."

"Because I don't have any capital," said Dullah, "at first I'd become an employee of a big merchant in Pasar Gedang in Padang. Eventually, once I get good at commerce, I'd have my own store. And you, Ridjal, where do you want to go, what do you want to be?"

"I want to go to Java, and pursue advanced knowledge there. When I got back I'd be a clever person and I'd have a high position."

"But I don't think your father will allow that, just like my father won't allow me to go," answered Dullah, "because he wants you to become a religious scholar, a religious teacher just like him to replace him later on. Who's he going to pass his surau building on to, if not to you, his only son?"

"That's the rub. I don't want to be a prayer recitation teacher in the least and be tied down to the village and surau. I feel my world would be too cramped and narrow. I'd find that really hard to put up with! It would just be impossible for me to stay in the village until I die and never see other lands. That's the difficult thing—that my father's wishes aren't in line with my own. And we may not defy our parents' wishes: that's insubordination."

"My mother probably won't give me permission either," said Zainal, "but I'm going to fight her on that point, or just secretly run away."

"Well, Zainal can do such a thing since his mother's afraid of him," said Dullah, "but Ridjal and I don't have the courage to oppose our fathers."

As Dullah was saying all this I saw that there was a tiny fire coming from Sudut village. It was as if there was a torch over there carried aloft by someone running fast towards Seberang Air. It was going very fast. I was surprised, because a person couldn't possibly run that fast. And then, too, people from our village rarely ran along with torches in hand. The person wasn't visible, because it was so far away. It was just like a fire flying along the road at the foot of the mountain chain.

"Dullah, look over there, what's that fire?"

Dullah and Zainal, who had been lying down, immediately sat up and took a look. Both were surprised, as I had been.

"A fire carried by someone from Sudut going to Seberang," said Zainal.

"That's impossible," answered Dullah, "no one could run that fast, and what could possibly be chasing him? I think it's a ghost."

Zainal and I started to get scared.

"Incredible,"[2] we said, trying to console ourselves.

"It's true. Lots of people have said they've seen him from a distance. But the odd thing is that no one whose house is alongside the road between Sudut and Seberang has seen him. The fire keeps going downriver and then upriver. Look, now it's going one way, and now it's going the other way."

Zainal and I got more scared than ever. The three of us got face down, pushing our bodies close to one another. The flame kept flying along. It went out for a moment, once it got near Seberang, and then it went on and moved speedily downriver. We averred that there was no way that there was a person using a torch in such an uncertain, back and forth way.

"What if he comes over here, Zainal?" I asked.

"Hey, I'm scared," he answered, covering his head with a blanket so that he wouldn't be able to see the fire.

"If we go and ask Seberang people tomorrow, none of them will have seen it. It's got to be a ghost," said Dullah, who actually had seen it some days before.

The flame kept on running toward Sudut. Our hearts pounded. In Sudut it went out for a moment, then flared up again and rushed off upriver. After getting to Seberang, it went out and didn't come on again.

We did not understand what it was we had seen. We didn't believe in ghosts, but the village people would often say that there *was* a ghost that ran between Sudut and Seberang with a torch.

The three of us were afraid that maybe the ghost would come running from Seberang and pass by our rice paddy on its way back to Batu Beragung. We hid, pressing ourselves together under the tent, and we covered our heads with a blanket so that we wouldn't see it pass by. Whether he went by or not we didn't know because we were crowded together until we fell asleep. If we hadn't been upset by being afraid of ghosts, we certainly would have slept more soundly. We would also have played and talked far into the night.

Waking up in the morning, we went to Batu Beragung and bathed in the lake. We left our haystack unguarded, because no one would steal rice during the daytime. We got back to the paddy fields and lots of people were already there ready to start threshing. As our payment for guarding the haystack we were given one packet of sticky rice treats and fried bananas per person. Mother had wrapped these in strips of banana leaves. Our drinks weren't tea or coffee, but coffee leaf-flavored water. After we'd finished eating the sticky rice, we were told to take the rice storage bag back to the house.

Upon returning to the paddy fields, we saw the full complement of workers there. They set to doing the threshing, joking and jesting all the while so they wouldn't get tired.

Threshing means stepping on the ends of the rice stalks until the grains separate from the stalk. Threshing is done on top of a wide plaited mat. The rice stalks that aren't full of grain anymore are tossed out toward the edge. At that point they're called rice stubbles. The more time goes on, the more the rice separated from its stalk builds up in piles. When the pile is high enough and there is still a lot more left to thresh they move on to another mat. Carrying the rice over to the threshing spot and tossing out the stubbles was the work of us kids. We'd do it while we played, while we jumped up and down in a pile of stubble and threw stubbles at each other. We got itchy, but happy.

Ten women heated water along the side of the paddy field and warmed up the curry. In short, they got the food ready. They made a great racket talking about the curry, the special meats, the cooked rice and the field rice, and about how many hundreds of storage bags full of grain the paddies would yield this year.

By eleven the food would be served. The threshers would simply be invited to sit on top of the stubble piles to eat. There they'd sit facing an overflowing abundance of food: several basketfuls of rice, several big pans of meat curry with bamboo shoots, ten plates of spiced meat and ten, too, of stewed fish, and ten plates of buffalo milk curd and a branch of bananas broken into bunches. Seven bamboo tubes full of coffee-leaf water were there too. Everybody loosened their belts.

Oh man, it tasted so good to eat out there in the rice paddies, all together in a big group like that! That was true even if the food was quite simple. The folks in the kitchen always boiled too much rice. We kids always got criticized by the grown-ups: "Now, kids who don't know how to do threshing yet mustn't eat a lot."

And then the kids would ask their mothers: "Is that true, Uni?"[3]

"Yes, it is," Mother would answer, "but yesterday they guarded the haystack." We'd greedily eat up whatever happened to be put in front of us.

"We don't care!" we'd say to ourselves.

After eating and getting a bit of a rest, they went back and threshed again. The women began to sift the rice with the wind, since the breeze was beginning to blow. Wind sifting consisted of a woman taking a winnowing tray full of rice in its hulls and letting it flow down very slowly. The empty hulls would fly far away on the blowing wind and the full hulls would fall down near the woman's feet. Then the full hulls would be separated from the [remaining] empty ones. Full hulls would be put into a plaited bamboo basket and from there into a storage sack. As the sack was being filled, the number of baskets of rice in the harvest yield would be counted. This would be done until all the rice was in the sacks.

While all this was going on, we kids would be making flutes out of rice stalks and catching locusts to roast and eat. A person skilled at flute music would make a rice stalk flute (a kind of clarinet) and then he'd take some top leaves from a coconut palm, put them in the end of the rice stalk and roll them around in a spiral so that they'd have a big opening in the end like a trumpet. The sound would get even stronger than usual. He would entertain the threshers, the winnowers, and the folks filling the sacks with the moving sound of his rice flute. The workers would love this, and they'd cheer and work even more happily.

After the threshing work was done, the sun would be sloping down in the west. All the men would go to Lubuk Beriang to bathe and say their prayers. We kids would swim and splash in the water and chase one another around for hours. The grown-ups would have already gone back to the paddy fields, but we'd still be in there bathing. After we'd finally gotten our fill of this, we'd quit and go back to the paddy fields. The newly reaped rice would be waiting for us there, along with sticky rice treats and bananas and coffee. We latecomers would get the biggest share because Mother would slide over a basket of sticky rice and a pan of its cooking juice and a bunch of Ambon bananas toward us. The adults got jealous of us.

We also drank sugarcane juice, which was brought in by some women from Galogandang. They didn't charge us money for their cane juice. Rather, they insisted it be bartered for field rice. A half coconut shell of cane juice for a half coconut shell of field rice. The cane juice was really sweet. The women got lots of rice.

By about afternoon prayertime, the field rice had all been put into sacks. Big strong men, forty of them, picked up the bales one by one, putting a bale on each man's back. Then they returned home in a procession entertained by the flutist and by the *telempong* [percussion instrument] player. They didn't get tired, for they were happy and always jesting and cheering, even though they were climbing up an incline. Once they got back to the house, they put the field rice underneath the storage shed and there was sticky rice, stewed fruit, and coffee waiting there, too.

A big festivity was held that night in our houseyard to celebrate the rice's safe arrival and deposit in the storage sheds. The village people who were skilled at fencing, self-defense, slow-motion strides, and plate dancing were invited to come demonstrate their skills before evening prayer-time. Hundreds of people came to watch. The women could only watch from the windows.

The invited guests were fed while the rest of the audience was served sticky rice and stewed fruit. One after another, the skilled fencers, the self-defense artists, and the slow-motion experts strode out on the center stage; every one of them was wearing national dress. This consisted of black *komprang* trousers, black Chinese shirts, and Javanese *destar* head coverings.[4] The audience encouraged the players by clapping and shouting. The games were accompanied by rice flute, violin, and telempong music; the instruments played Minangkabau folk songs.

After serving rice delicacies and drinks to the guests, we young kids were asked by the grown-ups to show off our skills at fencing, self-defense, and slow-motion strides.

The next day people said that while folks had been busy with all this fencing that night, out in a thicket not far from our house there were two tigers fencing, in imitation of humans. There were folks who actually saw them, they said. That belief was widespread in Minangkabau: each time people fenced or did the self-defense arts at night, they said, there would always be tigers watching from afar and imitating it all.

Whether that's true or not I didn't know for sure.

CHAPTER 13: RECITING KORANIC VERSES AT THE PESANTREN*

One afternoon about three o'clock, while my friends and I were absorbed in playing soccer in Simpang Usang, Uda Tjodi called for Djamin, Nasir, and me.

"His Honor's calling you to the surau," he said.

"Oh boy, now what," I said to Bujung. "What have we done wrong now?"

When we got to the surau, a "Muchtasar" holy book was presented to each of us—a book as big as a world map and a book we had certainly never seen before in our lives. Its pages were all covered in extremely

*At the Muslim study-dormitory

refined Arabic letters. We couldn't read it yet, so it wasn't written at the same level as the Koran was.[1]

We had been ordered to go study it in the minor surau with Haji Daud,[2] my uncle.

Apparently our three sets of parents had come to the common decision to have us study the Arabic language, its grammatical rules, the *fikhi* [study of rules pertaining to ritual obligations], and the Muslim *syariat* [laws], all in as great a depth as possible. They were of the opinion that it would be better for the three of us to become religious teachers than merchants. And they'd be very proud if their children went on to become venerated religious scholars, *kiai*. All three of our fathers were hajis, not to mention the most prominent religious teachers in the village. And all of these men hoped that their sons would come to replace them eventually. Djamin and I did not agree, whereas Nasir was the exception. But we were forced to follow their dictates out of fear. After all, we could not fight our parents' wishes.

With sadness, because our ball game had been stopped, but also with some curiosity to know what that Arabic language was saying, we went on over to the minor surau. Each one of us was carrying the holy book under his arm. There we ran into Maskur, my paternal uncle's son (who also wanted to sell soap more than he wanted to do verse recitations) as well as several santris. They came from other villages and lived in the surau, studying religion. There were lots of other santris there, too, but they were already quite advanced in their recitation lessons. Only six started at the same time we did.

We sat cross-legged on the floor in a circle near a house pillar and opened the holy texts, which were rolled out on the floor. About half of the santris were pretty good by now at reading what they were going to study. For the three of us, though, everything was still murky. We did not understand a single word of Arabic. True enough, we were skilled at reading the Koran out loud, at droning it out, and we knew what letters to lengthen and which ones to shorten, but we didn't understand its content. We had been reading and reciting for four years, night and day, but we could not make sense of a single word of it. We couldn't take a single word of it to heart and retain it.

While I was still confused and nonplussed, not knowing whether I'd be reciting verses or going back to my ball game, my uncle came out of his room beside the surau. His body was thin, his face sour and rather pale from thinking too much and from studying inside the building too much and not getting any exercise. He always looked like he was going to get angry. He was always in his room, deciphering thick holy texts that he had carried home by the hundreds from Mecca. They were arranged along three walls of his room, absolutely covering them. He had studied the Islamic religion for eleven years in Mecca and because of that he was very fanatical.[3]

"Oh, so Ridjal is here too," he said, after gazing at us one by one. "Better that one recites Koranic verses than plays soccer during the day, or wrestles at nighttime—things which of course have no benefit whatsoever, and which only afford us such misfortunes as broken bones in our feet or hands. If you recite verses, besides storing up merit you will also become a learned, pious person. Now then, it's best that you simply quit playing soccer. Are you willing to, or not?"

I did not answer. I was surprised. I hadn't done anything and already he'd attacked me. I felt Uncle and Father had formed this study team of ten students so as to divert my attention away from soccer and divert Maskur's attention away from soap selling.

In my heart, I thought that no matter what, soccer is much healthier for the body and mind than verse recitation. To my way of thinking, a person with a red face, with sweat flowing down it—a healthy, well-built boy— was more attractive than a santri who's always sitting around cross-legged in the surau, pale and thin-faced, like a person who hasn't eaten in five days, sighing and looking peaked, and so on. But I didn't have the courage to voice that opinion since he was my uncle, not to mention a teacher much exalted by the public. He didn't address my companions but only observed them for a moment.

Before commencing, he prayed and we accompanied him with the appropriate hand motions. He asked God that our verse recitation studies might be lengthy and that all of us might become pious, learned persons and enter into heaven.

Then Uncle read: "Alkalamu hual lafzu murakkabu mufidu bil wadhi."

He translated this as: "As a beginning, there was the word and what was this beginning like? What was called the word was *lafaz*, which was composed, which provided a salutary benefit and a *wadahak*."

"Will of God!" I said to myself. "What does all this mean? Even though it has been translated, it still is pitch black."

What did he mean by "the word"? I only knew that that word was an instrument for writing the Arabic letters, made of a palm tree (rib) and sharpened at the end.

He continued further: "According to the Nahu people, those folks, a word is whatever, it *lafaz*, which isn't like the sound of the mosque drum, which provides some salutary benefit but has no letters to it nor is it like the *wadhak*."

This didn't make it any clearer at all, just murkier. When he mentioned the *nahu*, I remembered a certain woman in Seberang Air whose name was Nahu. Her house was along the Sumpur River out in back of the surau of the Honorable Imam Muda. Perhaps she was an Arabic grammarian. And why did the Indonesian passages used for the translation here have to twist and turn so much and be so repetitive, with half of the words in Indonesian and half in Arabic but the sentence structure absolutely, totally in Arabic? Only later on, three years afterward (once I'd studied Indonesian and Dutch grammar), did I come to understand that the meaning of the holy text was the following:

"A sentence is a composition of words which can be coherently understood and purposefully pronounced."

If he had only said that, we would have understood!

Or if he had gone on to say, "According to grammarians, *lafaz* are the voiced sounds that can be written out with words and whose meanings can be understood," we could also have understood.

But after reciting for some two hours, listening to his murky explanations, which repeated themselves and twisted and turned like a snake's armpit, half in Arabic, half in Indonesian, I was still totally confused. So were my friends.

Moreover, I was surprised: Why didn't we understand a single word of Arabic? Why didn't we know the words for things around us, like house, surau, school, door, window, kitchen, to eat, to drink, me, you, and him or her, in Arabic? We'd been taught the grammar and we'd been taught explanations of it in an unspeakably exalted[4] form of Arabic—which we'd have to keep mulling over again and again and asking, does each letter have to be read with an A or a U or an I? Grammar was the science of the types of words there were, and the ways to join them together into compositions—but as yet we didn't even know the words *themselves* which those types and compositional rules would apply to. So what were we supposed to be joining together into sentences?

We barely had any acquaintance at all with the Arabic language when our heads started to spin with its grammar and with all these rules that we had to memorize and know by heart. Even though we had just started to study the science of reading, we weren't allowed to make any mistakes when reading aloud from the grammar text.

I was taken aback. Had we been born in Mecca, had we been speaking Arabic since we were little? Was it because of that that we had to be corrected with grammatical rules?

At five o'clock we were allowed to go home. Thanks be to God, but we were told to come back the next day at three o'clock, just when we'd all be in the middle of playing soccer.

"And you, Ridjal, don't you play ball anymore!" said my uncle as I was standing up. And then he went into his room.

"If he doesn't want to play ball himself, he shouldn't go forbidding others to," I said to Djamin, grousing. "I don't go preventing him from reading his Arabic holy texts, do I? Why does he forbid me to play ball? He's permitted to read Arabic books to his heart's content, but as for me, I don't need to read Arabic at all!"

Once we got to the Upper Surau we tossed our holy texts onto a chest that was set over against the wall, and we all ran off to Simpang Usang to play ball again. Running around the field was more refreshing and healthful than studying Arabic grammar, which just made our heads spin.

I was much happier going to school [elementary school] than I was reciting holy verses. Both the teaching method and what was taught there were in accord with the character and aims of my life. And these lessons could be *understood*; they made sense, and your mind would accept them.

But what was a mind, anyway? Besides school to prepare us for life in this world, Father forced me to go to recitation school, as preparation for the life hereafter.

The next day at three o'clock we didn't get the ball and go out to the field. Rather, we got our holy texts that we'd tossed down yesterday and went over to the surau.

Uncle ordered me to read aloud what I'd studied yesterday. Of course I didn't know it and I made lots of mistakes reading it. Was he angry! This situation derived from the fact that all my thoughts were directed toward soccer, he said.

Actually it wasn't because I was always thinking about soccer but rather because I didn't understand things. And the reading method had to be just like what he'd been saying yesterday: repeating and twisting and turning around. In short, I was supposed to use a language system that I had not studied from the time I was little and that I was not studying at all in school. How in the world could I understand it if I wasn't given examples to show similarities and differences with the grammar of my own language? We were forced to study, read, and memorize what we absolutely didn't understand or feel. And if we didn't know something, he'd get mad at us.

Imagine how long those two hours felt. The cheers of my pals playing out in the field could be heard echoing through the surau. My feet itched to kick that ball. Uncle kept right on repeating and repeating his explanations.

After our recitation lessons, once again we tossed our holy texts onto the wooden chest of one of the santris who stayed there in the surau. We immediately ran off to the field, to play soccer until it got dark.

And that's the way it went every day. Mornings I'd go to elementary school, afternoons I'd study Arabic in the Lower Surau, and at night I'd recite verses from the Koran. And almost every day I'd get criticized by my uncle because I'd only pick up the holy text when I was in front of him and wouldn't read it at all once I'd finished my recitations.

Even though I was so lazy, he couldn't really reproach me, because whatever he asked me about a lesson that we'd already studied I'd be able to answer adroitly enough, even if I didn't really understand what it was I was saying. Djamin was the same way. He had a sharp intelligence, though his laziness and love of sleeping exceeded even mine.

Apparently Uncle was still not satisfied; his face was always sour.

Every time I would come in, Uncle would ask:

"So, how do you do, Tuan Goal Keeper? No broken leg yet?"

I knew that this bit of ridicule did not come from someone who really cared. But, the more I was condemned and mocked, the more I wanted to go play soccer. Really early in the morning we'd be playing before the sun had appeared. And, at night when there was a full moon, we'd play far into the night.

Uncle thought Father still let me run wild. So, he proposed that I be ordered to stay right there in the Lower Surau and not be allowed to go out, except to go to elementary school from eight o'clock to one in the afternoon. After eating at home I'd have to come to the surau to memorize my recitation verses and then I could go home for the afternoon meal. After that I was to come back to the Lower Surau to wrestle with Arabic grammar until nighttime. I wouldn't be allowed to play anymore with my friends, and most especially I wouldn't be allowed to play soccer. The friends I'd have to associate with would be the santris, who had good conduct and character, he said. He made clear to Father that in such a way I would emerge as a pious, religious scholar in quite short order, in just five years.

And Father swallowed Uncle's suggestions.

One accursed day I went over to the Lower Surau not just clutching the "Muchtasar" text under my arm but also balancing a mattress, pillow, and blanket on my head. My uncle was delighted. He was satisfied now. He pointed out a bed alongside Juanin's, a santri from Katjang. Juanin was going to become my tutor because he was three years ahead of me in his recitation lessons.

Before doing my verse recitations, I thought things over, sitting there on my rolled-up mattress, contemplating this fate of mine—this fate of being put in jail and separated from my friends, from the soccer ball, and from the playing field. For sure, I wouldn't be getting to bathe and swim much either, or go splashing around and swimming in the Sumpur River and the lake. Here I wasn't free anymore; I was always under my uncle's supervision. And he rarely left the surau. He examined my every move.

I was amazed. Why was he like a person who was maliciously jealous of me? And one who would use any and all tricks to limit my freedom, as if the condition of my heart (always free, happy, full of laughter, dashing here and there, wrestling and always playing ball, bathed with sweat, red-faced, strong-bodied, healthy) was painful to him.

Starting that day I began to follow the lessons of the santris, who were three years ahead of me. In the afternoons, I'd have to study Arabic grammar from the "Muchtasar" text and the Muslim laws from the "Fathul Karib," and after evening prayers until twelve midnight, I'd have to study Koranic exegesis, and Arabic language morphology (the science of the types and forms of Arabic words). This was all way too heavy for me. My brain was still too young for all this. Moreover, I had to go to elementary school. But Uncle didn't care a whit. It was as if he had become my guardian, for his main aim was that I would not have any time left over to remember games and freedom—his aim was that I would be diligently memorizing away day and night, without any time to do anything else.

I didn't find anything taught to me there to my liking. I just couldn't take any of it in. First, because it was forced on me, and second, because it was not in accord with my abilities and character. It was the same way for Djamin. He actually wanted to emigrate to the rantau to become a merchant in Muara Aman or Bangkahulu with his maternal uncle. Maskur paid more attention to how much soap got sold than he did to linguistics and Koranic exegesis. Every Monday and Thursday his maternal uncle would let him sell soap, blue bleach, cigarettes, and so on at the marketplace.

Only Masir was diligent. Indeed, he actually *did* want to become a religious scholar, but even though his aspirations leaned in that direction, because his brain was rather dull he was always falling behind us—we who didn't pay any attention at all to our lessons. He'd often say to us that he wanted to go on the haj to Mecca and then come back wearing a turban.

In the surau, so like an internment camp, I associated with a group of santris who came from several villages around Lake Singkarak. Some of them had done their recitations for some five, four, and three years over there. All of them slept on the floor: those who were well-to-do, on mattresses, and those whose parents were not wealthy, on rattan mats. Early in the morning these mattresses and mats were rolled up and piled in the corner because the room was going to be used as a place for prayer and recitation.

The surau's upper story was four sided and large. It was used as a sleeping spot for the santri group, not just as a place to call people to prayer, as is usually the case. When the room down below was full, about half the santris would be up there on the top floor, which could hold twenty people. At first, I had wanted to have my bed there, but Uncle would not allow this because he would not be able to watch my every move.

The surau was set in a little hollow about a half kilometer from the Upper Surau. Out back was a stream with clear, pure water in it and a water jet where women would take baths and fetch drinking water. This is what livened up this surau. The sloping land all around had been made into a cemetery, which made us very scared to come to or leave the surau at nighttime. If there weren't lots of friends around I'd be scared to sleep there; the hair on your body would bristle up if you heard anything. But all the time I was there, nothing strange ever happened, even though among those buried there were some who had killed themselves or had been murdered.

The person who commissioned the surau, I was convinced, was not a person who loved life in this world. All he must have cared about was having a place of shelter! For him, a good building was of no consequence whatever. None of the pillars were firmly placed in their sockets; all of them were wobbly, and the floor was not even or strong. The floorboards didn't meet—it was enough if they were just joined together any which way—and they weren't made of strong wood. When we walked on them the whole surau would wobble back and forth. At first they were going to build the walls of masonry, but because they didn't have enough money, they only did the front wall that way, and didn't continue it all the way around. The men's hall and the women's hall were separated with boards, not a screen of unbleached cotton, like the one at the Upper Surau. So people couldn't peek into the women's hall.

In front of the surau there was a hard, but it was too small and cramped. Over on that same side was a big water reservoir for bathing, fetching water for prayers, and for washing the rice. The water was rarely changed, so it got greenish and putrid. At first I found it hideous to bathe there but because I got used to it (and because I was forced to use it) eventually I didn't find it all that revolting. The water jet in the back was only for the womenfolk. Near this reservoir stood a shed made of zinc siding, which served as a kitchen for the santris. They'd take turns boiling their rice out there.

There were about one hundred santris living there in the surau. About half of them (the ones with mattresses) had definite places to sleep. At night the others rolled out their mats wherever there happened to be a spare spot. Usually it was those who were still in the lower classes at school who'd be moving hither and yon.

In Minangkabau santris were called "siak people": folks who had emigrated from their home villages to take recitation lessons and pursue knowledge at the surau of the renowned syech. Normally they'd be young kids whose parents had ordered them to go pursue religious knowledge so that they could become religious teachers in their villages, or at the very least, so that they could become pious people. For, at this time, religion teachers were still held in very high regard, and the public would praise those who were pious and devoted to their religious duties. Consequently, the aim of Minangkabau people was to live a life devoted to religious duties—and especially to get into heaven. So they'd be really pleased if their children were skilled at reciting their verses, providing exegetical commentaries on the Koran and reciting chapters of the Koran to the village populace.

When a certain syech was famous (because he had performed some miracle or other) and if his students had gotten much praise and appreciation (that is, if they were highly respected by the populace), parents would tell their children to go take recitation lessons there. Syechs' villages, which were once lonely and unknown, would eventually become quite crowded from the many santris crowding in from villages far and near in Minangkabau.

There were many famous recitation spots in Minangkabau, such as Silungkang, Parabek, Batu Hampar, Djaho, Mungkar, and so on. Thousands of Minangkabau youths would come to these villages, urged on by the hope of becoming learned devouts. All the time they were taking their recitation lessons they'd be called "siak men."

From their home villages they'd bring mats, pillows, blankets, two or three sets of clothes, several kilos of rice, a bit of cash, and a stock of delicacies as was appropriate for presenting to his honor the syech. Normally this would be all the provisions they'd have; the majority of them couldn't hope to get a package or contribution from their mother or father if they weren't very well-to-do. Wealthy kids would get money contributions from the village each month; the nonwealthy ones would have to endeavor to eke out some sort of a livelihood some way. "Obtain knowledge, obtain a livelihood."

Every day off, each Friday, all the santris who didn't get contributions from home would go begging for rice early in the morning out in the villages rather far away from their surau. In the syech's own village they'd be embarrassed to go around asking for handouts of rice, because these villagers would come to the surau every prayer time and surely they would recognize the mendicants who'd come to ask them for rice.

To go begging like this the santris would wear special clothes, all in white. The hat, shirt, pants, and the sarong they'd carry over their shoulders would all be white; so would the knapsack where they'd put the rice. All the clothes would normally be made of rough material, for instance, of Merekan, or unbleached cotton. Lots of them carried canes, which also were white.

At each house that a mendicant came up to, to start with he'd stab his cane up and down on the foundation stone under the house ladder. Then he'd cough softly for a bit and then in a low, touching voice he'd say: "Please provide your humble servant with an alms meal so that there will be provisions enough for him to recite the prayers!"

Not long afterward, a woman would come out of the house, and if she truly did wish to give alms (according to the Ulamas, if you give on a Friday that means you store up ten times as much religious merit as you would on a normal day), well, she'd pour the rice down into the knapsack. Normally this would be about three-fourths of a kilo or more. If she didn't intend to give alms, she'd say, "I'm very sorry, siak man."

Sometimes, she'd happen to want to call in a siak man to say some prayer. Then the mendicant would be asked to step up into the house to eat a meal and to say prayers, after the woman had burned some incense on the burner. In his prayers the mendicant would ask God that the lives of the woman and her family might be lengthened, that their means of livelihood might come quite easily to them, and that they be comforted in this world and in the hereafter.

When he was getting ready to leave, the mendicant would be given rice grain and some cash, to buy his provisions, to support his recitations. As the mendicant took his leave, the woman would feel very happy to have done good to a person who was pursuing knowledge. Then the mendicant would go on to another person's house. He'd get rice grain there, too, and sometimes a meal. A mendicant once told me that he had eaten seven times, just from morning to noontime prayers.

Because he'd come every week, eventually he'd find a woman who liked to give alms and who was a soft touch. She'd become the regular source of support for the mendicant. When he'd come over to the house he wouldn't have to cajole her in touching tones—it was enough just to cough a little and then he could come right on up into the house. The woman of the house would have prepared food, and after he'd prayed, there would be piles of uncooked rice at the ready. Some mendicants had as many as fifteen supporters.

A mendicant with a supporter would already know for sure, once he left the surau, that he'd be getting enough rice grain to last an entire week. So he'd just have to ask for rice grain to sell, on top of this basic supply.

When it got on toward noon and he'd gotten ten or fifteen half-kilo measures of grain (in short, more than a week's provisions, which was not more than six half kilo-measures), the mendicant would go home to his surau. The excess rice (over what he needed until his next begging day) he'd be able to sell to well-off friends or to the village people. He'd save the money that he got from the sale. Once he had enough, he'd buy a shirt, a book, or other necessities. Sometimes they'd be able to send some money back to their parents in the village. "Knowledge he's gotten, yet the parents receive aid to boot."

At night, after saying the sunset prayers, the santris who'd been begging during the day would get their worn-out feet massaged, since they ached from walking so far. All their friends who'd also been out begging would be there. While they were sitting there massaging their feet, they'd relate all their experiences from the day and praise the goodness of their supporters. Afterward, after evening prayers, they'd recite Koranic verses or memorize their lessons.

That night, in the surau at issue, several little knots of santris would sit in a circle around the light or a wall lamp, diligently reading the holy text and memorizing it, watched over by an older tutor, the syech's assistant. The surau walls would rebound with the great hubbub of noise as the people recited from the Koran and memorized Arabic grammar rules. Underneath the roof of the surau people would get playful when doing their memorizations; they'd say daraba, darabaa, darabu, darabat, darabata, darabna, darabta, darabtuma, darabtum, darabti, darabutma, darabtunna, darabtu, darabnaa. The smart ones would just lie back comfortably on their backs while doing their studying.

They'd only go to sleep once it was far into the night. They wouldn't sleep apart but would all be lumped together. There on the floor they'd sleep side by side, sometimes crowded tightly together.

Eventually Uncle also proposed to Father that, like the other santris, I should bring rice and dried fish from home, sufficient for a week's food. That way I would have to go back to the house only once a week. That would be to ask for rice, dried fish, and pocket money, because (he said to Father) when I'd go home to eat two times a day, often I'd play halfway home with the Village Privates (that is, with my old companions from the past).

To me, he said, "You must see the one kilometer distance between your parents' house and the surau as a distance of one hundred kilometers, and you must think that you are far off in the rantau, and you must not remember your desire to go home every moment or so. In short, all of your attention must be focused upon your religious lessons and on the life hereafter."

Little by little my connections to the outside world lessened. I would rarely run into my old playmates, such as Zainal, Bujung, Dullah, and so on. They played with one another while I associated only with the santris. I wore white clothes and *pelekat* sarongs[5] like they did, I behaved and talked like the santris—that is, I always acted modest and viewed myself humbly and was pale faced and always bowing my head when I talked to women, since santris weren't allowed to see women's faces. And, when out taking a walk, I wasn't allowed to look up but always had to keep my head bowed down toward the ground. Those were the teachings in the surau.

We'd take turns cooking meals. Eight santris, for instance, would buy a large cooking pot, then each would pour a cup of rice into the pot and one person of the group would cook it. After the rice was done, the one who boiled it up would ladle it out onto the plates of the eight people in equal amounts. Then each person would eat it, using his own side dishes.

Rarely would anyone eat meat; the usual thing to have was dried fish with hot red pepper sauce. The fish would be fried or cooked with coconut milk so that it would last for a week or two. After that, someone else would take a turn cooking the rice. They'd keep taking turns, back and forth in that way, until all eight had had a turn. If a tutor happened to be among the eight, he was freed from the obligation to cook rice because, after all, he was helping them in their studies.

In that way I pursued my recitation lessons there for almost a year. Every Friday, vacation day, we'd set our blankets and mattresses out to air in the sun and we'd search for lice in our trousers, shirts, and sarongs. We'd brush our hair to get rid of the fleas and we'd kill the bedbugs that nested in the gaps between the floorboards. (Our lice and fleas were numerous. In fact, beyond counting.) The bugs would pick up and move from one person to the next because we slept all mixed together.

When the blankets were set out to sun and they got hot, dozens and dozens of loathsome lice would come creeping out. We'd kill the whole lot of them off. Tomorrow there would be more of them.

Many of us had scabies from bathing every day in dirty water, in that water from the tub that never got changed. These folk would always be scratching their bodies because they were itchy from sweat or because they'd been bitten by lice, which made nests in every little fold of our shirts and pants.

I myself got scabies, for three months, on my feet and arms. Its pain, dirtiness, and itchiness were unbearable. If you wanted to go to the polyclinic, you couldn't: there wasn't any such thing as a polyclinic in my village. So we were forced to try village doctoring. Uncle said this was all a result of a Koranic curse, which came from holding the holy text without using prayer water first. He went on to say, scabies is a test from God, a sign that he loved us, as with the Prophet Job in ancient times. I myself did not believe it was a test. Scabies results from nothing other than dirtiness.

The number of books I was studying grew to eight in all: I had four during the day and four at night. Afternoons we studied from two to five o'clock, and in the evenings from nine to eleven, though sometimes until two o'clock. It was like that every day, except on Fridays. We'd read with the aid of a tempel lamp [wall lamp]. The lessons got harder and the conflict between them and my soul became sharper, conflicting as these lessons did with the books I was reading in school. These two sorts of reading materials continuously caused a conflict inside me. The one told me to believe and accept on faith whatever the ancient syechs had taught, while the other broadened the intelligence and urged me to actually think. The one taught that the earth was flat and was carried on the shoulders of a cow, while the other said the earth was a globe. The latter was the one that my mind could accept.

One day, while he was teaching about the sky and the earth, my uncle explained that the first sky was made of copper, the second sky was made of silver, the third of gold, and the fourth of diamonds. And that atop these diamonds the sun revolved, pulled by thousands of holy angels on a golden chain. According to what he said, the sun went around the earth, not the earth around the sun as they taught us in school. Each of the skies was as thick as a foot trip taking five hundred years.

"Please give me leave to inquire, Your Honor," I said to Uncle, for there was something that I didn't understand yet. "Your Honor said the first sky is made of copper, which is as thick as a foot trip of five hundred years. All right, for now let's just discuss this first sky and put the second, third, and fourth ones off to the side for a moment. What I don't understand is how can copper as thick as all that be penetrated by the sunlight, whereas the sunlight doesn't shine through roof tiles of just one centimeter thickness?"

"Because God *intends* that the copper sky as thick as all that will be penetrated by the sunlight, while he does *not* intend the same for the roof tiles," answered my uncle.

"Oh, so the difference doesn't depend on the quality of the things at hand but rather upon the will of God? All right, then! Let me go on to ask, why does God's will differ in that he wants the sunlight to come through in one case but he doesn't want the sunlight to come through in the other case, although the rays that pour out of the sun are exactly the same in both instances?"

"That is God's own will and we are not allowed to question it. God does not want the house roof to be penetrated by sunlight, so that the people inside the house won't get too hot."

"Well, all right! But if, say, we make roof tiles out of glass and not clay, why is it the will of God that the sunlight goes through the roof? Why would it be God's will that the clay tiles not get penetrated but the glass ones do, even though the two roof tiles might be placed right beside each other?"

My uncle was about to lose all patience at this point. His answer was that it was *all* the will of God and we weren't allowed to ask any questions.

"If you speak thus, you do not believe that the first sky is made of copper and is a five-hundred-year-long foot trip thick?" he asked me.

"No, I do not believe it! And the same goes for the silver sky and the gold one and the diamond one. I'm totally sure if all that were true, we couldn't see the sun. Why, roof tiles as thin as this aren't penetrated by the sun—that would surely be all the more the case with copper, silver, gold, and diamond skies, two-thousand-year-long foot trips thick."

"Now, you must be very careful here! If you say that one more time and purposefully cast doubt on the teachings of religion, you will be an infidel . . . an apostate . . . a polytheist . . . a criminal, and will burn in hell for thousands and thousands of years. You must pronounce the Confession and ask for God's forgiveness."

"I don't feel I'm being insubordinate to God," I answered. "It's just that

I don't understand all this yet and I'm asking for further clarifications. And if everything is the will of God, might not my desire to find out all these things be an action of God, too?"

He didn't answer. His face just reddened and he said to the other students: "Now, *this* is the cause of so many young children becoming lost souls today. It's all because they base their faith on their intellect. They do not have a firm faith because they lack a complete belief in the prophets, the caliphs, and the ancient Ulamas."

I didn't feel lost; I just wanted a satisfactory explanation of how the sunlight could come through the copper! I hadn't suspected that I would get called an infidel because of this question, for, in my opinion, the intellect is an instrument of inquiry that we must make use of, and what we accept must be in accordance with the intellect. And, I averred, God would not have given us an intellect if it wasn't to be put to good use. And what's wrong with measuring everything we're taught in terms of our intellect, so we'll know which parts are true? Because maybe the teachings are not true, and then too, sometimes it just might happen that our intellect might make a mistake.

Upon hearing his pronouncement, half of my companions agreed with me while the other half were of the opinion that in matters of religion, no doubts could be countenanced, and we must not ask any questions. Our teacher (who had spent eleven years in Mecca) knows more than you do, they said.

Starting that day, I began to be seen as an apostate child, and my own heart flagged at my efforts to do the recitation verses, since I couldn't accept any of it. How could I find any satisfaction at this? What use was religion's recitations and teachings if they told us to live with our eyes closed, if they wouldn't let us look at the things all around us, and if they wouldn't allow us to discover our true character—and if religions' recitations and teachings wouldn't tell us to think, but only to believe in a totally reckless manner and follow the pronouncements of some syech or imam?

Once we spent almost a whole month studying and memorizing the *tayamam* theories, that is, the ways to get prayer water out of the desert and how to clean off our feet and hands by rubbing them against the house pillars or trees when there wasn't any water around.

I proposed to my uncle that we just skip the tayamam chapter or just take from it what we really, really needed, (that is, the core essence of it), so we could just finish it all in a day or so.

"All this tayamam business, in my opinion, is important in Arabia, with its vast deserts, where it's real hard to get water. This matter can be explained at great length for the Arabs, down to all its tiny details. But for us Indonesians, who live in a country rich in water, where the waterspouts overflow and the fish ponds, rivers, and lakes are very numerous—just look at Lake Singkarak and the Ombilin River—we don't really need to study these tayamam matters very intensively, wasting a whole month over it."

"But that is what's written down in the holy book and we are not allowed to skip it. Tuan Syech, who composed these passages, knows better than we do about what we need to know and what we don't need to know!"

"I think we don't need to study everything that's been written down. What we study must be in line with our own situation and our own self-interest, among our own people and in our own native land that we inhabit. We don't have to recklessly follow whatever such and such Syech happens to have written down from its beginning to its end—even if we do acknowledge the learning and piety of the Syech and the fact that he's smarter than we are."

"So it's your opinion that here in our country, there's lots of water, right? Well, what if we happen to be up on a mountaintop and we want to say our prayers, what can we do then?"

"In Indonesia, if there isn't any water on a mountaintop, there certainly will be some down in the valley, and we can just go down there for a moment and fetch some."

"And if there is no water in the valley?"

"So don't pray right away, before you can happen upon some water! And you don't have to make an easy matter so difficult. God, I think, will not force us to pray if he knows there is some obstacle in our way."

"I have reminded you time and time again," said my uncle with a growl, "do not use your intellect. That's the work of the devil. You're being an apostate, like Abu Djahal. How many times have you said words that veer away from the teachings of religion? You must ask God's forgiveness and read the Confession. If you speak that way one more time you will become an infidel and will burn in hell for a thousand years. I shall tell all this to your father!"

In that way, my desire to know and to analyze anything with the intellect and with healthy thinking was discouraged. It was all abruptly cut off by his saying that I was an infidel, and by his scaring me with the torments of a thousand years in hell.

I believed that God would not be that cruel! God knew more about what I was feeling in my heart—maybe God caused all of this uproar, who knows!

One other time, on a Sunday morning, because I didn't have to go to school, I attended a class of the real brains, the ones whose books were as thick as bricks. For more than two hours they debated the matter of whether or not some prayer water would have to be invalidated as unholy if it were stumbled over by a guy who happened to be walking along and a little piece of his penis, which had been chopped off his body, happened to be lying across the highway.

Half of them said yes, it would have to be invalidated. The other half said it wouldn't be. Each of them set forth various proofs and reasons that they had taken from the holy books they'd read, or that they had excerpted from the teachings of Imam Sjafei or Imam Maliki or Imam Gazali—but none of which represented any brain work of their own.

And a second question: must a little piece of penis be prayed over, like a corpse, or not? Must it be wrapped in a holy shroud, or not?

For hours and hours they debated this, but they never came to any conclusion. Even my own uncle was unable to give a satisfactory answer.

At first I had just kept quiet. Finally, I got bored listening to them, and I thrust myself into the middle of the discussion.

"Listen, all of you! I would ask to speak. In your entire lives have you ever encountered a piece of a human penis rolling along the middle of the road?"

"Never."

"If this never happened, why do you make it into such a big deal, and one that wastes so much time and energy?"

"We're only talking it over and making a case of it, just supposing it *should* happen."

"Why should we waste time talking about something, 'supposing it should happen,' while there is lots for us to study that really *has* happened and demands our full attention? Aren't there really a great many things which are real and very much more pressing, which we must bring to some satisfactory end? The whole matter is really simple for me: if it gets stumbled over, we'll just go and get some more prayer water. What's wrong with having to work a bit—there's lots of water around. And then, too, why do we want to go and bother ourselves so much whether to pray over it or not? If we really ran into a piece of a man's penis along the road—something that very rarely happens in the course of a hundred years—what would be wrong with digging in the earth for a moment and burying it in a little hole? To touch it we could wrap up our hand with a banana leaf, for instance. That's a very easy matter. It isn't necessary to hem and haw over it for so long a time or to keep cracking open the ancient Ulamas' holy texts!"

"But we have to be capable of answering this question if there happens to be a person who asks such a thing when we are dispensing religious advice for the multitudes."

"I think that the Indonesian people are healthy enough in their thoughts and will not be so crazy as to ask such a thing, even if they *don't* know how to recite the Koranic verses," I answered.

My uncle got angry again, called me impudent, and told me to go on off, because I was just sowing disorder. I went on off . . . My pals were asking me to go bathe and swim in the healthful, refreshing lake.

But things were not destined to be that much fun, splashing and swimming around in the water! Halfway to the lake we were asked by an old woman rushing toward the surau if we would be willing to go recite verses over an old man who was about to die. He was in fact at that very moment in his final death agony. The five of us were confused; we trembled and just looked at one another. All of us were afraid to see a person who was actually going to die. The old woman urged us on, while crying: "If you're willing to do it then I won't have to go on to the surau," she said, sobbing.

We were still looking at one another, confused and stunned as if we had just been hit on 'ne head. None of us had the courage to make a decision. To go see a person die? That was an event that we had not yet experienced. Once, we'd seen a person who had already died, who was covered over with a long cloth. But even that scared us, and here we were going off to see a person whose last breaths were coming out one by one?

But to refuse her wouldn't be very appropriate either. The woman urged us fervently to do it and pulled on our arms. Udin, who was rather bold, came to a decision:

"Come on, let's go!"

The four of us followed along once someone had made a decision. But oh, it felt so heavy to pick up our feet! Our hearts pounded. Out in the houseyard, people noisily reading the Surah Jasin [37th chapter of the Koran, read when someone is dying] could already be heard. That was what was normally read right before and after a person died. At that time it was twelve noon. The sun was straight overhead, and toward the north, not far from the house, a hawk keened movingly, in an uncaring way. The sound was touching, hair-raising. "This is not a good spot to be in," my heart said.

One by one we climbed up the stairs. Our feet got even heavier. In the front room I saw an invalid stretched out on the mattress with two men on his left and right holding his two hands, and fifteen men and women sitting all around him, reading the Koran. In the midst of all this clamor, the sick person drew in short little breaths, one by one. His chest was evidently closed and tight, so that he wheezed. They passed out one Koran per person to us and asked us to sit down. We sat down near the wall, a bit distant from the invalid, while opening the holy book. Back inside, in back of us, the sobs of about half the women could be heard, and the other half had red, weeping eyes, at seeing this person in his death agony.

I could not focus my attention on what I was reading, because what I saw and the whole atmosphere of the house was very frightening. The others would look at their books for a moment, then they'd take a look at the invalid for a moment, who was kicking his two legs and thrashing his two arms about at every faction of folks gathered around him. All the while he was drawing short, difficult breaths, one by one. His eyes, wide open, looked upward; he did not hear or even care about the requests of those beside him that he start pronouncing the Confession. (According to the beliefs of Muslims, when the final words of a person who is dying are "la ilaha illallah," he or she will get right into heaven.) The invalid just kept pulling up violently, even though the men at his side were trying to calm him down. His chest rose and fell furiously; his mouth gaped open.

I did not have the strength to look at him.

Two of my companions had already gone down out to the house in turn, saying that they had to go pee. I had thought I was the most scared of all of us, but apparently they were even more so. Eventually, I saw that the limbs of the man's body (from the knees on down) were not moving anymore. He lay still and stiff, his eyes were open, still staring upward. (At that time, old folks said, a person who was about to die would see the Angel of Death descending the stairs that extended from the doorway of the sky to the soles of the feet of the person who was going to die.) I trembled even more. In a few minutes more would the Angel of Death stand in the midst of this gathering of Koranic reciters and pluck away the soul of the person who was going to die? Would I get touched on the shirt by the Angel of Death, who'd be standing just three meters from me? Or might he look toward *me* after pulling out the soul of the sick person? Oh—maybe he's already standing right there in front of me and he's just invisible!

Disturbed by these frightening thoughts, I quaked with fear even more. I whispered to the person sitting next to me that I was going to step down out of the house for moment to go pee. I stood up and went on down. On the stairs I met the Datuk nobleman, the younger brother of the man who was going to die. I said with a trembling voice that I was in a real hurry to go pee. But he was so sad and panicky, he hardly heard my words anyway. Thank God, he didn't hold me back any longer!

At first I walked along kind of slowly, with the scene still hovering in front of my eyes. Once I got to a turn in the road, and the people in the houseyard couldn't see me anymore, I ran just as fast as I could toward the lake. It wasn't far from the house, and my friends were waiting for me there. Apparently we all felt the same way and each of us was just as scared as the other.

"He hasn't died yet?" they asked.

"Not when I stepped down," I answered.

While we were talking, two more friends came up, running fast.

"Why did you leave us behind?" they asked, panting and out of breath.

"How in the world could we invite you to come along in front of all those people? We were really scared. Had he already died when you left?"

"Almost. The longer it got, the more horrible it was, and we told the householder that we were going out to pee."

"So, it was the same trick for all of us then," said Udin. "Well, let's all just go bathing in the lake and forget what we just saw."

But even though we tried to forget, we kept remembering the scene. Indeed, as we dove down into the water, the man with his breaths coming out one by one kept hovering before our eyes. Even though we didn't talk much about it, it hung in each of our imaginations.

Upon returning from the lake, we heard that he had passed away.

"Well, luckily not in front of us," my buddies said.

In our village—when I was still really small—when someone died the whole family and especially the women would sing mourning laments. That is, they'd cry hard and mention various good deeds done by the deceased, as well as that person's behavior, disposition, and how deep and close the lamenters' love had been for the person. A short-form life story of the deceased starting from A going to Z would be related in a softly moaning voice. It would greatly move the listeners. They'd moan out laments, sitting all around the corpse of the deceased, all the while lashing themselves on the body, beating their chests, or rending their own garments, or rolling about on the floor moaning and screaming. No one would be able to calm them down. The women who'd lament would adjust the lament's intensity according to the size of the family of the deceased, and according to how close the lamenter was to the deceased. Or the lament's intensity would depend on the person's wholesomeness over the course of his or her life. From the intensity of the laments, it would be evident whether folks loved the person who'd died or not. Men did not lament; they'd just cry with pouty faces.

The neighbor women would normally be the ones to calm the lamenters down and restrain them from lamenting and shouting too much so that they didn't go so far as to bother the one who had died. I myself once saw some lamenters go to excess, in fact. They went on and on for two days past the burial of the deceased.

Little by little over the course of ten years, thanks to the teachings of religious teachers (who explained that religion strictly forbids lamenting, or crying with words), the custom of lamenting decreased. They still cried in great sobs and that was allowed, but it wasn't with words anymore. The Ulamas said that when the living lament, the tranquility of the soul of the deceased will be bothered and the dead people will think back, more than they should, toward the world they have left behind. The living should be willing to let their loved ones move on to eternity, so they can depart with tranquility, and so their quiet won't be disturbed, said the Ulama.

If a person died, the neighbors and the women from the village would come into *mendjenguk*, in the local word: to bring a half-kilo measure of rice or two, as a contribution for the people who had been afflicted by hardship. This they could cook and offer the folks who came to help with the burial.

After a person had breathed his last and the public had finished reading the Surah Jasin, the body would be laid out in the middle chamber, covered with a lovely cloth. The guests would come to formally declare that they were among the grievers, and they would sit down around the body, talking and whispering about the illnesses or the well-being of the deceased throughout the course of the person's life. If he had done small, insignificant wrongs now and then, those in attendance would remember those wrongs with contented smiles and look upon them as instances of sweet naughtiness. The atmosphere there in the house would be dark and blurred, rather quiet and desolate, with a kind of moving, dull sadness.

But out at the cemetery it was just the reverse. After stopping for a moment or so at the house, the village men would go out to the graveyard to dig the grave. Out there, everyone would be happy, and laughing in loud guffaws and joking and jesting uproariously. Not a one of them was grieving. On the contrary, the family of the deceased, when they got out there, would smile hazily, listening to the jokes and pleasantries of some certain guy who'd be playing the clown.

Often I've noticed that in every gathering of human beings there is a clown, even if that wasn't the person's particular gift since childhood. There will be someone among those in attendance who's natty-looking and whose behavior and speech make people laugh. And without their meaning it to, everyone's attention will focus on the clown. If there isn't any clown, the crowd will surely not be so cheerful. But there are always clowns around, even in graveyards.

There was another adat custom in my village. If a person fell fairly ill in his wife's house, everything possible would be done to take him over to his mother's house. He wasn't allowed to be seriously ill while still in his wife's house. Because, according to public opinion in my village, it would look as if his siblings and close family didn't care anything about him and didn't want to take care of him. And this would disgrace his mother's family. Even more so, if he actually died: it wasn't at all proper that he be brought down the steps, that final time, at his wife's house, when his corpse was being carried to the grave. No matter how great his wife's love and devotion for him was and no matter how much she wanted to care for him, his parents' and siblings' rights were greater than hers.

His wife was permitted to go along over to her husband's mother's house. If the invalid happened to have two or three wives (something quite common in my village), all of the wives would take care of their husband in their parent-in-law's house. A person might ask, well, don't they fight? I also asked that and wanted to witness such fights, but the situation had never happened, to date. Apparently they just didn't think of fighting because their mutual distress so strongly suppressed their hatred for their co-wives—even though we can certainly imagine what feelings might actually be running amok, hidden down deep in the recesses of their hearts.

If the husband died, all the wives would cry, and sometimes they'd compete fiercely with each other at this. Because in their opinion the louder their sobs were, the greater their love for the deceased. Who loved him the most? The one who cried the loudest!

When the corpse had been washed off and prayed over, he was carried out to the grave. At the moment he was about to be carried down the front steps, the whole family and all of the relatives would start to sob all at once, because the deceased was leaving and wouldn't ever come back. They all would escort him out to the grave, reading and reciting the *zikir* [the first part of the Muslim Confession of faith *la ilaha ilallah*]. After the body was put into the grave and buried with clumps of earth, the *talkin* was read and recited—that is, the advice for the dead about questions that must be answered when the two angels Munkar and Nakir came to interrogate him.

According to Muslim people's beliefs, when a person had been put into a grave and the escorts had all gone back home, along would come two angels, Munkar and Nakir, carrying poles as big and as long as coconut tree trunks. These would be flaming like torches. The dead person would be asked who God is, who God's prophets were, what the holy book was, what religion was, and what sorts of things had the person done in the world. If he didn't answer or answered in the wrong way, the person would be pounded with this big pole until he was beaten down into the seventh layer of the earth. And the angel would scrape him with his long fingernails and beat him again and then scrape him again and then beat him again. He'd keep being beaten and scraped on until doomsday. Not a single person knew how many more years that would be!

The *talkin* readers would instruct the one down in the grave what his answers should be.

But the Modernists[6] in Sumpur Bawah had eliminated the *talkin* reading. A dead person, they said, wasn't going to be listening anymore, anyway. If he had been a good person in the world, he'd give the right answers.

Usually, the people who worked out at the grave a while beforehand were formally given a meal of rice and chicken curry, contributed by the women. But this custom of providing a rice meal had been eliminated too by the Modernists, in their circle: according to them as long as the corpse was lying there stretched out in the middle of the house, folks shouldn't be making a big racket, boiling rice, grating coconuts, chopping up chickens and cooking curries out in the kitchen. All attention, rather, should be focused on the funeral ceremony and the atmosphere must remain tranquil. As long as the folks in the house are still sad, they shouldn't be bothered with some obligation to offer big festive meals to their guests, said the Modernists.

That night, people who had suffered the death would call on several santris to read from the Koran, to pray for the safety and good rest of the deceased in the afterworld. The Surah Jasin was what was always read, though why I don't know. And after praying, they'd all eat. On the way back to the surau they'd ask the santris if they could come over to the house for the next six nights to read and recite and say prayers—a request that the santris always greeted with good cheer and glowing faces.

But, the Modernists had also cast off this reading and recitation custom. A Modernist house that had suffered a death would always be quiet and lonely and tranquil, and I noticed that this quiet and loneliness increased the sadness of the house's occupants. I don't really know which is the right approach, of the two options offered by these two groups. But what I do know is that people who called in the santris to read and recite weren't all that sad since their house was noisy and crowded and this constituted a form of entertainment, which deflected their attention from their sorrow. The same was true of folks who had the person in the death agony prayed and recited over, in a big noisy crowd; that way the attention of the one who was going to die wasn't directed one hundred percent toward his or her illness. In the din and uproar, the dying person's concentration would be broken a bit, and amid all these goings on, without knowing it, he or she would just appear in the World Hereafter. The sufferings would be very severe and frightening if the person's room were quiet and still, and if all those in attendance had gloomy faces. In my opinion, all that noise does have its purpose, especially if a few drums are beaten and there are a few cheery *mars* songs [marching tunes] sung.

Because I was in the santri category, oftentimes I was called in to do recitations. I didn't yet understand everything I was doing because I wasn't allowed to investigate it carefully. However, I just followed along and did it anyway. All of it amazed me—an amazement that I did not understand the cause of. And could I make this amazement disappear? A tutor of mine said philosophy can eliminate amazement. But because I was still small, I didn't know any philosophy yet.

Because I was not yet fully acquainted with the study of philosophy by this point, what I relate below once happened:

One night, after doing recitations at a house of folks who had suffered a death, we were about to go on down out of the house when suddenly it began to rain really hard. In a book I had read: "Rain poured earthward from the skies." That night the rain could be said to have been almost like what was written in that book. The surau was a kilometer away from there, and we didn't have an umbrella along. We hadn't thought that it might rain, and the people in the house there, by happenstance, also didn't have an umbrella.

We waited a long time there on the front stoop but the rain showed no sign of slackening. According to all indications, the rain was going to last for a long time—maybe until midnight. Because the cloud cover was very thick, the whole sky was pitch black. The householders did not go back inside. They just looked at us from the door and the windows, pitying us.

Eventually, we (eight of us in all) became quite embarrassed. The householders weren't going to go back inside before we left. We made the decision to take shelter for a moment under the eaves of the neighbor's house, who had already closed their door and windows. We dashed over there and held another meeting to determine how we were going to get to the surau, because it was getting near the time for the night classes, and to run through rain coming down that hard meant our clothes would get soaking wet for sure, and about half of us didn't have a change of clothes.

Finally, we just decided to go stark naked. We santris (who had just a while ago been acting so polite and virtuous back in the people's house) now shucked off all our clothes in a dark spot and wrapped them up into the smallest bundles possible. Luckily, no one from the house saw us. If there had been anyone who did, their faith in our santriness would surely have faded a bit.

Clutching our clothes packets to our chests, we ran off fast in the dark in the rain. It was good we ran into only a few folks along the road: just three women coming home from the surau carrying torches. The women were startled to see eight black shapes running along in the dark. So that they wouldn't recognize any of us, the naughtiest one of all of us kicked out their torch. It shot skyward. And the one who kicked it flipped and fell on the ground himself and all three women screamed.

"Help, help, a ghost, a ghost!" they cried.

People in the nearby houses opened their windows and doors and looked outside, but we were already far off. The next day, all the village people fully believed that it had been ghosts who had run along bothering the women.

Under the eaves of the surau's roof we put our clothes back on, and inside we became good, pious santris once more.

The seventh night, the householders killed a goat and some chickens. Normally people in my village would hold a selamatan on the seventh day. Holding a Seventh Day ceremony, it was called. Rich people would kill a water buffalo, while folks who weren't rich would buy some meat (rather a lot of it) in the market. Lots of santris and other guests would be invited over for that night. Father and my uncle attended. That night they read not only the Surah Jasin but the *salawat* [invocation, short prayer, usually made of Koranic verses] too, a prayer passage whose contents we didn't know. People said it was packed with praise of the great beauty of the Prophet Mohammad. And a little bit of his life story, too. When they'd read the part about the Prophet emerging from his mother's womb, those in attendance stood up and read the "Marhaban," saying "Welcome, Welcome." All except the Modernists, that is; they just sat there. They didn't believe that the Prophet was really in the house at that moment. By contrast, the Traditionalists[7] actually did believe it.

After we ate, a tutor who had been sitting next to Uncle moved over to sit next to me. And after chatting about other matters for a while he asked: "So, does Ridjal believe that the Prophet Mohammad came to the house a while ago, when folks were reading that part about him emerging from his mother's womb?"

The tutor had to have been put up to this by Uncle.

"Please tell my uncle that if the Prophet came in his actual physical body, no, I did not see him, as I don't have the right sort of faculties for seeing him. So there's nothing that has to be believed in here."

I kept waiting for some bit of ridicule to issue from Uncle the next day. I wondered if I was going to get called an infidel again.

While everyone was sitting around smoking cigarettes, from around back came a person carrying a tray full of yellow rice and little leaf packages. He placed one in front of each of us. The package for Uncle was bigger than all the rest. And then another man came out and gave each of us a religious alms meal, and the tutors got a quarter apiece, and my uncle got half a rupiah. All the santris were pleased and merry, at getting some yellow rice provisions and a dime or so, too—and all that after just having eaten a big meal.

Off we went back to the surau, our yellow rice packets swinging from our hands. When we got back, our friends who hadn't gone along all crowded around and tried to get some food from us, since they hadn't been invited. About half of the stingier santris hurriedly stuck their yellow rice into their wooden chests of drawers and locked them shut.

A month later we were invited out to the same place for the Fourteenth Day commemoration, and three months later for Hundreds, and three years later for Thousands. Most of the animals sacrificed for the feast turned out to be buffaloes, or cattle, too.

For a year and a half I lived in the Lower Surau, isolated from the outside world. We lived in our own little world, with a view of life that differed from that of most people, who struggled on the practical plane of life.

We lived in an age of five or six hundred years ago, thinking in the way the ancient Ulamas we were studying had thought. We planned to make the outside world conform to plans set down by these Ulamas, complete with the very best forms of social organization—because those forms had emerged from the brains of syechs who had risen to the crowning, topmost part of religious scholarship. When we all returned home to our individual home villages, we would doubtless be spreading these medieval views to the Minangkabau people.

When I say "we" here, I mean the majority of santris. I myself was always rebelling; I'd opposed the whole lot of it, seeking freedom of thought. I was always worried that if I stayed there a long time, associating with these santris who were thinking like human beings living in the thirteenth century, I'd surely be influenced by them. My spirit would be extinguished, and after that I would have no use whatever for living in this real world. My hopes and the aspirations whose flames still burned in me would be cloaked and vitiated by a darkness that would simply kill them.

For one and a half years I studied Arabic, and I memorized a great many grammatical rules (whose books were of a thickness we could take pride in). But we didn't know how to talk yet! How to say, for instance, "A coconut fell from its tree, rolled swiftly into the river, and got washed away toward the estuary." We had no idea how to say this! It wasn't just us, either: our tutors, who had been reading and writing for seven years now, couldn't chat along in Arabic among themselves. They were really adept at reading aloud from an open book, but if that book was closed then everything disappeared from their memory. The life spirit of the language had not penetrated our souls.

One time I asked Djaunin, one of my tutors, what was the Arabic for "The day before yesterday, in a friend's rice paddy, I ate some really yummy stewed breadfruit, sticky rice, and newly harvested rice." After thinking a long time, he didn't know what it was and he just stood there confused. And if you went to look for "stewed fruit," "sticky rice," and "breadfruit" in the text, you wouldn't find them, because the holy texts were crowded with nothing other than matters of praying, *tayamam, zakat,* fasting, going to Mecca on the pilgrimage, marriage laws, the divisions of inherited goods, major sins and minor sins, and so on and so forth.

After that I became even lazier about making any effort to waste my life studying a language that would never get used in human society. Even though the holy text may be big and thick, everything you read really has to be translated first into your own language and only then can you understand what it says. If you just read it through once all in the Arabic language, you sure won't understand it.

To improve our comportment—as if our comportment all this time hadn't been good enough—to our eight books we had added yet another one, the "Tarikat Muhammadiah." This one was filled with advice and models for good conduct, like that demonstrated by the prophets. This text taught us how to be afraid. Whoever was the most afraid would be the very one most praised and loved by God.

The prophets would sometimes sweep out the floors of their houses. So every morning and afternoon we ourselves would be ordered to go sweep the surau yard and floors, so that we'd be humble just like the prophets.

The texts also told how the prophets would carry their own sandals in their hands rather than having some follower carry them. This was also a sign that the prophet was humble. We were told by my uncle to carry our sandals in our hands when we were coming home from some selamatan, in imitation of the prophets.

I asked the tutor (saying that I didn't understand this at all) why we were asked to carry our sandals in our hands when we could just wear them? And moreover, for us normal people, I said, it's not a sign of glory when we sweep out the yard and carry our sandals: the general public will see that as just an ordinary sort of thing to do. For the prophets, as very important personages, that sort of humble behavior is praiseworthy, but for us who are already humble to start with, there isn't much left to lower us even farther down.

But the tutor did not agree with me.

We were taught hundreds of prohibitions to rein in our inclinations and movements. Hundreds of "don'ts": don't lust, don't be jealous, don't be angry, don't be insulting, don't think obscene thoughts, don't be lazy in saying your prayers, don't be gluttonous, and so on, until they mounted up to hundreds and hundreds of them. There were more prohibitions than there was time and ability to carry out all these taboos in the first place. I was confused: what was left that we were allowed to do?

Don't do this, it's a sin. Don't do that, it's a sin. We were also taught lots and lots of theories about goodness. This thing here was good to do on a regular and customary basis. This thing here, though, should be done every minute. This prayer was good to read; that prayer had to be read two thousand times—yes, there were hundreds and hundreds of good prayers and supplications, but we didn't have the energy and time to do them. To do them all, a thousand-year-long life wouldn't be enough.

This one here was good to read each night so you'd get into heaven. That one there was good to recite each morning so that you wouldn't go to hell. This one's good, that one's good, and so on—until finally not any of them got done at all!

These theoretical teachings piled up in heaps, all mixed together haphazardly and all running wild in our young minds. It got so our heads felt very heavy, as if they were going to explode. To put all of these rules into practice—we had only two hands and just two feet! There were hundreds of holy verses and deeds of the prophet that we had to memorize, all of which told us to do thus and so, or prohibited this or that, but what we actually did every day was just read, sit, eat, sleep, and shoot the breeze with one another.

What we filled our heads with each morning and evening until two o'clock was not in accordance with what was actually put into practice. And certainly not with what was *going* to be put into practice in the future.

I was very, very worried that if I kept going the way I was, after seven or ten years in recitation school, after using up all of mother and father's money as well as my own time and energy and ruining my eyes and health, I'd be about as clever as my tutors. There would be no difference whatever between us.

And this wasn't what I hoped for!

Moreover, I didn't have even the slightest, tiniest desire to become a syech.

A syech, a recitation teacher, would usually make his living from the alms given him by his students of the village people, if he didn't own rice paddies or garden land. His weekly income was quite uncertain. Sometimes it was just a little, but usually it was more than his needs. In fact, there were some honorable syechs who were rich and who could afford to build two or three houses from their followers' alms and donations. Their students would not allow the teacher to work for his livelihood by being a merchant or farmer, so he could concentrate absolutely all of his time on teaching.

However, to support their families, the small unknown teachers were forced to work paddy land and farmland since the income from alms was not sufficient. They didn't have many students; their names weren't famous yet. But in the rice paddies and on the farm the students could help the teacher out, and they'd just get paid in food to eat.

Once they'd gotten the title of syech, religion teachers (especially if they were hajis) were held in very high regard and were greatly respected by the village people. In fact, there were several syechs who were thought to be outright holy men, like Syech Silungkang, Syech Batuhampar, Syech Lima Pulah, Syech Malalo, and so on. Sometimes this feeling of respect would get excessive and would overstep proper bounds. For instance, the syech's followers would fight mightily over the leftovers of his meal, and they'd drink the water where he'd bathed his feet, so they'd gain a clear mind when reciting.

In Malalu, the water that fell from the floor where folks had been washing the corpse of the honorable Syech Lima Puluh was caught by people in dishes, glasses, and basins and they drank it to receive his holy blessings.

Because of the great respect these honorable syechs had in the eyes of their followers, they had lots of wives. Their followers very much wanted to receive blessings from their teachers' great religious scholarship, holiness, and sacredness. Even if the teacher already had three wives, there'd still be somebody who would get lucky and get the opportunity to seek the teacher as a son-in-law. They'd feel very fortunate indeed when the honorable syech would have the pleasure of going up the stairs into their house and sleeping there. Because of that they wouldn't feel burdened at all to surrender their young daughters to the syech, who'd usually be quite old. A man would do this because he believed that in the world hereafter the syech would help save his wife and relatives from the fires of hell, and would carry them all into heaven.

The people of his own village and of other villages wanted to have a syech as a son-in-law. But according to Muslim law, devoted followers of the religion may not have more than four wives. So in order that all the others would get a share (and be able to get the much-sought-after syech as a son-in-law), the syech would be forced to divorce one of his wives. And then if there was yet another person who came to seek him as a son-in-law, he'd divorce another one of them so his total number of wives would always stay at four. But it was a pity about the women he divorced. Rarely would anybody else want to marry this widow, since they feared a curse. A great many syech's former wives never did marry again.

According to the story told by a certain santri who once did recitations in the Payah Kumbuh area (and who was now continuing his recitations at the Lower Surau), over in the Lima Puluh domain lived a syech who had more than one hundred former wives, and numberless children. The honorable syech didn't even recognize his kids if he happened to meet them going along the road. Even though he was seventy years old, there were still folks who wanted to surrender their virgin daughters to him in order to get his blessings for as long as the syech happened to live. This was so he could help them out in the hereafter a bit later on.

In addition to being skilled at recitations, the honorable syechs knew witchcraft, or how to cure the sick. Sometimes one of them would have to protect his high position with witchcraft, since, to be frank, not everyone really loved him. Someone who hated him would put a witchcraft spell on the syech, or play with him with magic so that he'd fall ill or crazy, or so that he'd actually die. But if he *didn't* get injured after all that, then people would acknowledge the syech as a very sacred person.

To frighten people: that's why syechs would often mention magic in their conversations with their followers. They'd say it was all part of the secret knowledge of the West they had pursued in Mecca. The aim of all this was that folks would not try to test or challenge the syech.

CHAPTER 14: MASKUR FALLS IN LOVE

For Maskur (my uncle's son, two years older than I was), the falling-in-love season had apparently arrived. All of a sudden he'd fallen in love with a girl named Dasima. Word was, she was beautiful. This girl was only fifteen years old, rather plump, of normal height, with skin the color of light yellow *langsat* [round, yellowish-skinned fruit]. She had a face that sloped downward in an oval shape rather like a lovely betel leaf. She had long hair, which was thick and abundant when she undid it and let it hang loose.

Maskur was really crazy about her. He got scatterbrained; his mind over-heated; finally, he just wanted to pour out his heart to someone. But right before the Fasting Month all the santris had gone back home to their own villages and Maskur was left there all alone with just his father and mother. Because of that he asked me to stay in the surau with him to keep him company. Because I didn't know anything about what was going on, I accepted his invitation.

His mother and father themselves didn't know that their child already wanted to take a wife. I had almost no time to ponder my own situation since Maskur was always wanting to chat about his love, about his sweetheart's great beauty, about his intention to marry this girl, and about his soap business. And because he kept talking all the time, I was forced to listen constantly to him, until my head hurt and my body ached from weariness. After talking along for a while he'd ask my advice and guidance about what he should do.

Maskur only knew how to talk, not how to write. He was a person with a flair for business, not one to become a religious scholar as his father wanted. So he asked me to write some love letters and to get the responses back from his sweetheart. Yes, that's right, like his secretary. Because I did know a bit about writing letters, and since I knew hundreds of love verses by heart, I began to put Maskur's totally disjointed thoughts into orderly language. What I wrote was exactly in accord with what he felt in his heart, he said.

But when I wrote these letters, often I'd quarrel with Maskur, who had a real old-fashioned way of thinking and who certainly took a strict religious view of things.

He wanted each letter to begin with, "Bismillahi Rahmani Rahimi" because every virtuous endeavor must always begin with *bismillahi*, and only after that could come, "my beloved little sister."[1] And every line had to start with "Furthermore." I said that that style was outmoded now. Love letters nowadays were much simpler and didn't use *bismillahi* and "furthermore" any longer. Just go read novels nowadays and see, I said. Eventually he agreed.

But he did insist on putting verses from the Koran and all sorts of exemplary deeds of the Prophets into his letters—ones in accord with the condition of his heart at the time. This was so he could strengthen his love argument to Dasima. I said, you also don't need those.

"Don't go mentioning God's holy name every few seconds—you'll distract his attention from the really important things he has to think about, like keeping the stars and the sun and the earth in their proper courses. You don't have to keep dragging him into little matters like this love affair. We ourselves have to keep charge of that."

Maskur kept being stubborn anyway.

"As a Muslim," he said, "in all matters, we must rely on God's guidance, and the same is true in my love for Dasima. We must ask his guidance and mercy so that he can foster my actually getting married to that girl."

While I was hard at work thinking about how to compile the most beautiful letter possible, Maskur kept leafing through the Koran and the book of *Buchari hadis* Muslim traditions, searching for verses and exemplary incidents that he might slip into his letter.

No matter how much I'd argue with him, he was always obstinate—so the letter became crowded and full of the most diverse things: quatrains, verses, exemplary deeds from the Prophet, proverbs, and two types of alphabetic letters—Latin ones and then Arabic ones.

Once the letter was finally ready, we turned it over to a little girl and she delivered it to Dasima.

When the response came back, the two of us read that letter for hours. We read it over and over again, debating, analyzing and interpreting what the girl might have meant and pulling out what might be hidden in all the concealed parts. Maskur's joy overflowed its bounds. He kissed the letter, fastened it to his chest, and closed his eyes blissfully.

And I just looked on. I didn't really understand it yet because I had never fallen in love. I only knew about love in books.

The letter was carefully put away so his father wouldn't find out about it, and he asked me to write a response. I asked for a full day to write a letter of four pages in length, since I wasn't all that fast at composing yet (and so that Maskur would have time to look for his verses and exemplary deeds).

When I was finished I read it to Maskur and he liked it very much indeed, especially the quatrain verses and the *Hadis* interruptions [traditional collections of stories about exemplary deeds of the Prophet]. He asked about how impressed Dasima would be when she read the letter. I answered that her love would deepen for sure. Maskur laughed cheerfully and his hazy eyes imagined the body of the plump Dasima and her cute little mouth with its enchanting, faint, knowing smile.

When every once in a while Dasima would send over some little delicacy as a love token (something like sticky rice treats, fried bananas, fermented cassava, sugar and coconut creams, a bunch of bananas, or other stuff), he'd ask me to join in and eat some, as my payment for writing all the letters. And Maskur would ask whether or not his sweetheart's gifts and cooking tasted good.

"When Dasima was making these cakes and treats, do you think she was reminded of me or not, Ridjal?" Maskur asked, pretending not to know.

"Certainly she was," I answered. "Your shape and appearance was reflected there before her gentle loving eyes."

"Do you believe, Ridjal, that she returns my love?"

"Well, why not! If she doesn't, she sure wouldn't want to go to all this trouble cooking cakes and stuff."

"Maybe there's some rich guy, old and senile, who's going to steal her away from me and ruin my life?"

"I don't think so. Her mother and father have a great deal of respect for your father and surely they'd like the idea of having a religious scholar's son as a son-in-law."

Maskur cheered up on hearing this and then went over and lay down on his back on a mat, reclining comfortably. He closed his eyes and smiled to himself, hugging a bolster pillow. He opened his eyes a moment but they weren't shining but rather looking upward in a daydreamy way, like those of someone not really paying attention to the things he was seeing. And then he heaved a long sigh, closed his eyes, and smiled a discontented smile.

I was dumbfounded looking at him there, and I asked myself, is it possible that sometime in the future I myself will act as crazy as he is?

Sometimes when Dasima would bathe in the water jet out in back of the surau, Maskur would go up to the second story to spy on her through the gaps in the wall. And he'd invite me up to peek out too. He wanted to show me how beautiful his sweetheart's figure was. Dasima was bathing with a sarong on; it covered her body from above her breast to her knees. Her sarong went down a bit between her two breasts, which were just beginning to blossom. They had a lovely shape. Her skin was radiantly yellowish tan and her upper chest was decorated with a gold chain hanging from her neck. Her hair was long, reaching all the way down to her knees; it was radiantly black. Her lower arms were plump and decorated with gold bracelets, which made them even more attractive. She was so enticing!

Maskur's eyes burned like fire and he looked at her passionately in total infatuation. His breathing was constricted, his hands trembled and his thoughts were chaotic, like a mountain about to erupt.

"Look, Ridjal, isn't she cute!"

"Yeah, she's really enchanting. You'll be a real lucky guy if you can make her your wife."

"I shall strive hard until I die just to get her. Is it really true she returns my love? Do her parents want to take me as their son-in-law? Ah, I think maybe her parents want to have a rich merchant as their son-in-law. Take a look at that gold chain on her body—seeing that, we just get more infatuated, don't we?"

"Yeah, well, the sarong she's using as a bathing cloth really does match her light tan skin. I suppose you're going to have to buy her several sarongs even prettier than that!"

"Sure, sure, I'll buy her a whole wardrobe full."

Maskur and I kept on peeping.

"I'll bet her body smells sweet, Ridjal, even though it's not scented with powder or soap or perfume!"

"Yeah, real sweet and soft and smooth."

"Oh, if only our skins could touch!" Maskur sighed, and then he laid down and stretched out on his back and closed his eyes blissfully. "Oh brother!"

Meanwhile, Dasima finished bathing. Maskur got back up and started sighing again.

"Is it true she really loves me, Ridjal?" he asked with a concerned face. "If her father forces her to marry someone else, what will I do?"

Then when Dasima went on home, we followed her with our eyes until she disappeared behind the underbrush alongside the road. Then Maskur asked me to write a letter that would pour out everything running amok in his heart at that moment—a letter that had to be sent to Dasima immediately, and one which asked her not to obey her father if he forced her to marry a merchant or a *datuk* nobleman.

Once the letter was finished it was sent, and while waiting for the response and waiting for the mosque drum ending the fast to sound, we fell asleep on the floor near the gaps in the wall . . .

I helped Maskur out for twenty days, doing his correspondence and listening to his sighs, his exclamations of praise, his cries of hopelessness, and watching his face as it changed expressions from desire to discontent to joy.

Suddenly, Father called me home. One of Dad's friends who apparently knew about our situation and our conduct had told him that I was acting as Maskur's clerk, writing his love letters for him and getting paid with no more than a half plate of sticky rice, five bananas, and some half-sour fermented cassava. And he'd lodged the further complaint that Maskur and I—even though it was the Fasting Month—were spending our time from morning to afternoon peeking at women taking their baths out at the water spouts.

My father, who was a real stickler for upholding standards of respectability, got extremely angry at hearing that his child had become a clerk for his younger brother's son—and especially at hearing that I had been peeking at women bathing.

"What's the use of me turning you over to study verse recitation if you're going to go off and become someone's clerk and peek at women bathing? Haven't your holy texts taught you that such activities are sinful, especially during the Fasting Month?" Father scolded. "Starting this very day you are not allowed to go there anymore. You'll just have to stay here in your own surau and play with your old friends from before."

After that I was not permitted to go to the Lower Surau. I was delighted. This was *exactly* what I had wanted. So—I didn't have to do recitations anymore. My pals were happy, too, at seeing me come back to them.

How Maskur's love affair came out, I don't really know. I had wanted to find out how it all ended, but Father wouldn't allow me to see Maskur anymore. I only knew what I heard from other people. Maskur was always very downcast and got more and more heartbroken: adat did not allow him to go meet Dasima and be with her, and he wasn't any good at sending letters either. He didn't want to keep on with his recitations. His desire to pursue a life of market selling got stronger and stronger.

Eventually, after the festivities ending the Fasting Month were over, he did go to Padang to become a market seller there. But before he had amassed enough money to take a wife (even though he worked extremely hard at this day and night), Dasima married someone else. It turned out this man really wasn't much wealthier than Maskur, but he happened to be Dasima's father's nephew.

CHAPTER 15: WALKING AROUND LAKE SINGKARAK

Once after we had gotten tired swimming, we were just sitting around the lake shore, resting and lying there in the sand. I was looking at the edge of the lake as it wrapped all around us, and a desire to walk around the whole way occurred to me. I relayed this idea to the others, asking who wanted to go along to help celebrate my being sprung from the pesantren [Muslim study-dormitory]. Four of them wanted to go. That is, Sjarif, Djamin, Zainal, and Dullah. So we picked Sunday as the day to depart and agreed to ask our parents' permission as soon as we got back from bathing in the lake. That way, maybe they'd give us some traveling money.

Our trip was bound to be a long one and very tiring. It might even take three days, but we all wanted to have a go at it anyway. We wanted to experience new situations; we were bored with what we'd seen, heard, and experienced in the village from the time we were little. We wanted to launch out into some sort of variation of our normal experiences; we wanted change of whatever sort, just so it would provide some kind of freshness for our inner selves. In addition to fostering healthy bodies, of course.

Our intentions were OK'd by our parents. They understood that their kids were beginning to get bigger and wanted to get out into a widened world. Father gave me a *ringgit* [two and a half rupiah] in pocket money. The others were also given sufficient funds to buy food along the way.

Sunday morning at five o'clock we set off, carrying one leaf packet of rice provisions per person. We weren't wearing shoes: village kids normally didn't wear shoes as city kids did. We took the road to Malalo, going along the west side [probably the west side of the lake]; this was the road without the railroad tracks on it, because on that first day we certainly weren't going to get exhausted enough to have to hop a train. Once we got to Singkarak at the southern end of the lake, well, if we weren't able to walk anymore at that point then we could catch the train back to the village if we really had to. But we were going to try as hard as we could not to use any vehicles and to keep going on foot.

We walked along cheerfully, warmed by the rays of the sun. It shone above the fields around Simawang and shone onto the surface of the lake, dazzling our eyes. None of us could sing; we hadn't been taught to do so from the time we were little. That was a major loss. As a substitute for that we just joked around and made fun of Zainal, who was always so droll. Luckily, he never got angry if we bothered him.

All the way to Malalo there was a road that was passable by pony carriages or autos, but after that, we had to go by village pathways on to Penjinggahan.

At ten o'clock, after we'd passed Malalo, half of us began to get hungry and wanted to eat. We couldn't resist the temptation of the rice packets we were carrying along in our hands. It would be better just to carry the rice in our stomachs than to get our hands tired carrying it, we said. So we agreed to find a clean, quiet spot near the lakeshore, and we sat down in a circle on the big rocks.

It was delicious to eat a meal there. There wasn't nearly enough rice, even though we had more than the normal portions. While we were eating, over on the other side of the lake we saw dozens of train cars full of coal coming from Batu Tebal, headed toward Singkarak, following the eastern edge of the lake like a big snake. All of us watched the train till it disappeared from view at Singkarak.

At Bajing village the road was rather far from the lake's edge but the view was still extremely lovely. That was the first time I heard the beautiful songs of the shepherd children. I had never heard these in my life. I had thought that shepherds weren't particularly good at singing (as was the case with the shepherds in my own village, who always just kept mum).

The kids who were singing were sitting up in orchard trees with their legs dangling off the limbs, taking turns singing songs and answering each other back and forth. While this was going on, some of their water buffaloes were wallowing in mud holes in a nearby rice paddy. Other beasts were soaking in a creek, while others were standing quietly under a shade tree munching on corn stalks. We listened to the kids a long time and our thoughts wandered far away to who-knows-where. We hid so we couldn't be seen; if they saw us they would stop singing out of fear and embarrassment.

My friends were also very moved, for we had never heard these songs in our village. Their songs were not sad or pathetic, but cheerful and full of life, love, and joie de vivre, as if the children had been inspired by the forest gods hovering close by. Even though they lived in isolation in a quiet and lonely village, they inhabited a world that was quite lovely to them, and they adored the natural world surrounding them.

It is a great pity that it did not occur to us to want to learn these songs from them. Think how good it would be if we had made the time to study these songs, which we could have then carried along with us everywhere, when we grew up and moved away to the rantau—so that other people could hear the spirited songs of Lake Singkarak. These are the most beautiful of all the Minangkabau songs I have ever heard.

From here we walked slowly to the south, going through paddy fields, farms, dry rice fields, and underbrush. And when we came to a river, we would wade through it, since there were not any bridges there yet. Even though we were starting to get tired, we were still happy, for everything we were seeing was brand new to us. The village people we passed were absolutely amazed to see us. They rarely saw anyone pass by there. Some of the small children got scared and sped off back home to go cry in their mothers' laps. If they were scared just to see us, imagine how terrified they would have been to see the Dutch or some soldiers come along. Old and young alike hid in their houses, with the doors locked. In fact, some of them even crept up under the ceiling.

At three o'clock in the afternoon we got to Penjinggahan. There we stopped at a foodstall to drink tea and to eat some sticky rice wrapped in banana leaves, some bananas, and so on. Since it was very hot, I took off my hat and put it on my knee. I wiped off the sweat on my brow with my sarong. I probably had had my hat off for no more than three minutes when a man in the foodstall turned a fierce look of anger on me. I immediately put my hat back on. I had thought that as long as I was in the foodstall resting a bit, people would allow me to go hatless.

After we finished our drinks, I asked the others if we could leave. In fact, if we could just get out of that foodstall immediately. My friends understood the situation too.

Among the villages that surround Singkarak, it is only Penjinggahan where folks will not let you take off your hat, especially if you are out along the main road in public places. Anyone who is so rash as to do that will get called impudent, and the crowd will beat him up. People in the other villages also get angry at folks who walk along hatless, but these people will not go so far as to actually beat you up. They will only slander and insult you and say you have no manners. People in Penjinggahan are renowned for liking to beat folks up. The day before we left home the old people back home had warned us not to take our hats off out on the main roads, especially in Penjinggahan. People could take their hats off there only for bathing and sleeping and if they were in their houses and no one was around to see.

In a village called Muara Pingai the rain came down extremely hard, and we took shelter in a water-driven rice mill. Once the rain let up we started walking again, till five o'clock, when we were at Sanimbakar. We were able to say our afternoon prayers on the verandah of the village mosque there.

Here, the interior part of the mosque was open only on Fridays. On the other days people would pray out on the verandah. For us in Sumpur, the surau was open all the time for praying, reciting verses, sleeping, eating, drinking, and playing. Sometimes we would play dominoes at the surau. In short, for us there really was no sacred ambience and sense of quietude in the place where people paid homage to God. To have folks chatting away companionably right next to a devout paying homage to God as he said his prayers was a normal sort of thing for us.

Because it was still light, we planned to spend the night in Sumani. In Sanimbakar we did not have any acquaintances to spend the night with. Along the shore of the river flowing through the village we paused a moment to rest.

We were being watched by a young girl wearing a veil, maybe a student home on vacation from the Diniah School in Padang Pandjang. We kept asking each other, Which one of us she was evaluating so carefully? She just kept looking at us with her smile. My heart pounded, for her eyes were on me, there was no mistaking it. Did she perhaps love me, as I went about my wanderings? I recalled the books I had read, the totally unexpected encounters between two people who eventually become marriage partners.

"So, what do you say, Ridjal," asked one of my companions. "Do you want to be harvested as a son-in-law by one of these Sanimbakar folks? Apparently there is someone who likes you here!"

"It's their child who likes him—remember, her mother and father haven't committed themselves yet!" answered Dullah.

The girl went back inside. We left too. However, when we glanced back she was waving her hand from the window. We waved back, once we checked to see that there were no boys from the same village passing by.

We would not have suspected that there were any mischievous types among the Diniah School students. Well, their faces and hair might be veiled, all right, but their God-given womanly hearts certainly could not be covered up.

It was nearly twilight when we got to Sumani. Here we pondered the problem of where we could spend the night and who might be willing to have us in their home for a night. If we slept in the surau, doubtless we would become public entertainment for all comers. As we were pondering this and sitting there in a foodstall in the marketplace, along came a bus looking for passengers. Tickets were cheap: just two thin dimes per person from Sumani to Solok. Sjarif proposed that we go to Solok and sleep over and eat dinner in the house of his maternal uncle, a photographer.

"Tomorrow we can just catch a bus back here and from here we can go on around the lake on foot. That way, see, we won't be violating our agreement," Sjarif said.

All our companions said all right, since this way we would get a pleasure trip to Solok, which at the time we considered quite a big city. We were going to Solok? . . .

We were delighted to be able to look at the scenery out the left and right sides of the bus. We got to Solok at six-thirty and went straight to the house of Sjarif's maternal uncle. By happenstance his uncle was not at home, because he had gone to Kota Enau with his children and wife. We were taken in by his servant who was watching the house.

This servant just could not figure out our arrival. He was quite surprised to see us and I too was surprised to note his attitude. But he was a city person, after all. I thought, maybe that sort of behavior is normal for them.

That night we did not eat there as Sjarif had imagined we would, but in a dark foodstall out back, behind the marketplace. The people sitting there eating looked like ghosts, in the faint light of a little torch and the fire from the hearth. After eating we walked all over town, which was very large and simply amazed us—and we looked upon all the city people as most famous personages who had to be greatly respected. In fact, we paid our proper respects to the kid sitting out in front of the store he worked for. He was considerably loftier than us villagers.

After we had our fill of walking around we went to a movie. At 0.10 florins for third class it was really cheap. Fl. 0.20 was enough to buy the best seats in second class. We ended up buying first-class tickets for fl. 0.30 apiece. But imagine how startled we were when the film started to roll and we found that we five were the only ones sitting in first class. Second and third class were jam packed—and everyone was looking at us. We felt like big shots, but we were a bit nervous.

The film was a story about Tom Mix and a bunch of bandits. They were all fighting over a picture of a lady, but the picture was already all torn up. We did not understand what the point was. The thing we liked best was the fights, and how good Tom Mix was at riding his horse.

Coming back after watching the movie we slept at Sjarif's uncle's house. The odd servant gave us one wide, single-layer mat to sleep on, along with two pillows. Our own sarongs had to serve as our blankets. That night we discovered how tired all our joints were, especially our knees. My calves were swollen and hard. They felt really heavy when I tried to raise them. I thought, tomorrow I will not have the strength to start walking again.

The next day, true enough, I was not strong enough to walk. We took the train from Solok to Singkarak. We got off there and walked on foot to Katjang. We spent the night in a foodstall in that village, while eating our fill of Katjang oranges, renowned for their sweetness.

The next day we walked again. Because we were so over-tired, we did not pay much attention anymore to what was along the road. We just wanted to get back home and sleep. It was night before we got back to the village. We had gone around Lake Singkarak in three days.

We were pleased to have demonstrated our perseverance. With this experience, we had strengthened our will, in addition to seeing new vistas.

For us, this was a performance to be proud of. But after getting back home to the village we were sick for two days and did not even have the strength to go outside the house and play.

CHAPTER 16: A SIDETRIP TO OMBILIN

We wouldn't always be guaranteed of getting new clothes and shoes every Lebaran holiday [the day celebrating the end of the fast]. One time, a week before Lebaran Haji [a holy day in honor of pilgrims] in 1926, Father did not plan to buy me any new clothes at the Pitalah market, even though there were not any more market days left before the holiday. Probably he just didn't happen to have the money, because he had already bought clothes for my younger brothers and sisters.

This situation did not especially annoy me, because I could figure out what was happening, but it did make me very sad. On the day when all my friends were wearing new jackets, sarongs, caps, and shoes, would I just be wearing old ones, which had only been washed and pressed? Everyone would be looking at me, and what, I wondered, would be in their hearts . . .

Of all my friends, only Zainal was not going to have a new change of clothes. That was because (in my estimation of things) he did not have a father anymore, and his maternal uncle was not very well off. When just the two of us happened to be alone, I asked him what he planned to do on Lebaran day.

"I haven't made up my mind yet," he answered.

Even though I did not say a word about the clothes problem he knew what was inscribed in my heart. And with a knowing smile he asked me if I would like to go on a little trip with him to Ombilin that day. I said fine, just so long as we don't have to be home in the village. We agreed to set off at 5 A.M.

Fair to say, the night before Lebaran we did not sleep very soundly. We were afraid of over-sleeping. Supposing we had gotten up as late as seven in the morning: the sun would already be shining, and, well, what could we say . . . ?

Luckily we awoke at 4 A.M. and started to boil our rice right away, while our friends were all still sleeping contentedly. If they had gotten up, too, doubtless they would have dashed right out to the mosque drum and started beating it till daylight, and they would have asked us, "What's the use of boiling rice when there's going to be a great big meal later in the day after prayers?"

Once the rice was done we wrapped it up in leaves, along with a few chunks of spiced meat. Zainal had gotten these from his older sister yesterday.

In the dark we walked on foot upriver along the Ombilin River toward Lake Singkarak, which was seven kilometers from Sumpur. We did not have a cent in our pockets. Not a single one of our friends knew about all this; the night before we had not spoken to them. We had kept quiet, with gloomy faces, but our very closest pals had apparently sensed what we were concerned about. It was a pity, but they had no way to help.

When we got to Ombilin we saw folks headed off toward the surau and mosque to go say their Lebaran prayers. None of our acquaintances were among them; if we had known anyone they surely would have asked what we were doing there so early in the morning.

In a quiet spot out in back of the bushes along the lakeshore, we sat down on some rocks and talked about all our friends who were having such a good time back in the village. And we talked about Father, who surely would be asking about me when he noticed I was not there. After we had run out of things to say (especially since they were all so sad), we lost all desire to chat, and I just sat there musing dejectedly . . . watching the ripples that rolled in toward the shore in a rough and tumble fashion . . .

At that moment I recalled the advice Lebai Saman had given me three months earlier: "You kids who cannot take the long-range view yet; you're always so quick to blame your parents if they don't give you what you want. And you accuse your fathers of being stingy and of not loving their children. Or if the father has lots of children from two or three mothers, you'll say for instance that he's not playing fair with you. But often Father won't give you money or buy you clothes because it happens that he just doesn't have any money at the time, or there are other needs more pressing at the moment—needs you don't know about."

My thoughts swung around for a moment to a train that thundered by. It was packed with passengers, most of them little kids and youths on pleasure trips celebrating the holiday. They were all wearing new clothes, cheering gaily, and waving their hands at who knows whom. As the train disappeared from sight the words from Lebai Saman's mouth whined complainingly: "But you kids just don't understand yet. You're so cocky: you think your fathers are just big storehouses packed with goods and you assume he will always just be there and has to fulfill your every wish by doling out money, which you imagine he has tons of. You just figure things have to be there. What you don't know is how hard your father works to make a living for his family, and how heavy his responsibilities are day and night. You will only realize all this when you start to make your own living, and when you have kids to boot. Only then will you be aware of all this. But that awareness will come too late, after you can no longer make up for the wrongs you have done to your parents."

I got sad, thinking of all the hard responsibilities Father perhaps bore but never let show, since he was a real man who always hid his sorrows. Because of that I did not pressure or blame him. Going off to Ombilin was not to grumble or just sit there and be irked, but rather it was to avoid embarrassment.

Zainal too kept quiet and mused . . .

Were we thinking the same thing? The experience was just the same, but the reactions we had inside our souls differed . . .

At ten we ate, but it didn't taste all that good and the meal really wasn't all that much fun.

After that we slept under the sky . . . we woke up, bathed, ate again, talked some, slept . . . and woke up again and it was already four in the afternoon. It wasn't night yet, though. Think how long it was taking to get here. We had no patience, but we didn't have the courage to go back home yet, when it was still light.

To make our peevishness dissipate a bit we started walking, though we really had no desire for it; then we just stood on the long iron bridge, watching the swift Ombilin River current flow by. For hours Zainal and I stood there like statues, waiting for the sun to set . . .

Our feet were very heavy as they carried us home. We got back to the village and folks were already saying the evening prayers. Our bellies were starved. We went into the house and asked Mother for some food. She asked where I had gotten to earlier in the day. On hearing that I had gone off to Ombilin, she was quiet, understanding what had concerned me.

She set out roast chicken in front of me, and marrow stew, and spiced dried spleen, and so on. Altogether there were seven little side dishes she set out, everything that I loved.

"Your father kept all this aside for you specially," Mother said. "He just kept thinking about you earlier."

Hearing that, I knew Father understood why I did not spend Lebaran in the village, and I realized that he was sad about it too.

That whole night I did not encounter him.

The Sunday after that Zainal and I went over to Pitalah to buy clothes. Father had given me some money and Zainal's mother had given some to him too.

I bought the material for a jacket and a length of batik for some pants, and a cap and some sandals. Zainal bought some tricot cloth for trousers and a T-shirt, a glaringly bright red one. I never ceased to be surprised that he picked that color. It positively hurt your eyes. With the rest of the money we bought some sweets. Our sadness in Ombilin was forgotten, and the only unsatisfactory thing was that we got our new clothes after Lebaran was over.

CHAPTER 17: EARTHQUAKE

The next day, June 28, 1926, the four of us were playing jump rope out in the surau yard. Zainal was wearing his bright red T-shirt. It tickled us to see that; we were all laughing and kidding him.

The village was deserted and the natural world around us felt quiet and lonely.

All of a sudden at exactly ten o'clock we heard a rumbling, thundering, terrible noise, and at that very second the ground got wobbly and began to shake fast and hard. The surau, the village houses, the trees, and the coconut palms all shook and rocked back and forth in the most frightful way.

Earthquake! Earthquake!

We were staggering around and couldn't stand up! It flashed across my mind that a planet had surely collided with the earth over in the continent of America, and that America had been crushed and totally pulverized by the planet's impact, whereas Sumatra had only been pushed up into the air unexpectedly by the collision.

Losing our heads, we all ran up on top of the minor surau, searching for shelter. The surau was rocking back and forth very hard. Its suspended lamp was tossing here and there, its wall lamps swayed and fell, and after running up there we staggered around on the floor, not knowing which way to go. A santri who had been reading the holy texts went pale in the face and said continuously: "La ilaha ilallah! La ilaha ilallah!" We started doing this too and pronounced the first sentence of the Koran along with him, for according to Muslims' beliefs, whoever happens to die while saying this sentence will go directly to heaven. With death drawing near we were truly scared of going to hell. We started pronouncing that sentence right away! What enthralled our souls was fear, fear, fear! We fully believed this was doomsday.

The first quake lasted for two minutes. We trembled all over; cold sweat oozed out of us, our lips were pale and bloodless, and we couldn't catch our breath. It was coming in uncertain fits and starts.

Not long after that, the second quake came and it was also dreadful. We went and hid in a dark corner, not brave enough to see all the things wobbling around. After the second one had stopped, the third one came.

Was this what the end of the age was like? Many of the village people had gathered in the surau yard. They wanted to ask Father for an explanation of what all this meant. Fear, apprehension—that's what was reflected in their deathly pale faces and in their trembling lips. The latter kept repeating phrases over and over again.

One of them said to us that when there is an earthquake, don't go hide inside a house. Rather, you should go running out into an open field so that nothing falls on you and pins you down.

Well, that's the first that we were aware of that. We had not known about it, for we had had no experience with quakes. It was lucky the minor surau wasn't built of stones.

Then the fourth earthquake came, and it wasn't any weaker than the others. Everyone said at the same time: "La ilaha ilallah! La ilaha ilallah!"

Father arrived, accompanied by Datuk Mangkuto and three other villagers. Later on people told me that when the first quake hit, Datuk Mangkuto, who had just been sitting around at his mother's house, jumped out of the window and started running straight for the surau. Halfway there he ran into my father and asked him, out of breath:

"Are you all right?"

"There is no more hope," Father answered. "It's the end of the world!"

Datuk Mangkuto didn't want to stray too far from Dad; he wanted to die together with him.

The people who had gathered in the surau yard immediately all crowded around Father asking him what the quake meant.

"We must simply trust in God," answered Father. "The world will be ending in several days. There are a great many evil human beings and God is punishing us because of that."

We all trembled for we believed that he was a religious scholar who of course knew everything. He was our leader here in this world as well as in the hereafter. He told us to start saying the prayers and to await death and destruction with patience and trust in God.

"Our sins have been too numerous," he went on, "and because of this, Allah is furious at us."

We were reminded of all our sins at that time. I asked forgiveness from all the people I had stolen things from: rambutan fruits, dukus, mangoes, and jackfruits.

"Yeah, yeah, I forgive you," said the owners. "Listen, I'll just give it to you as religious alms. You don't have to pay for it in the hereafter."

I felt very relieved. Suddenly there was another quake. But this one was gentle.

"Now that's five times."

We all uttered, "La ilaha ilallah!"

Then Zainal took off his red T-shirt.

"Maybe this is what's bringing all the bad luck," he said. (As far as I know, for three months afterward he still didn't have the nerve to wear that T-shirt, fearing that the earth would suffer another quake.)

People had spread out rattan mats in the surau courtyard and they sat there all together awaiting whatever was to occur. All of them believed that they were surely awaiting the hour of death. Quakes came continuously, some strong, some gentle. At noon prayertime a very great number of people came to pray. The surau was jam packed, like it was Lebaran; it was rarely like that at a normal noon prayertime. Folks who never prayed or who were lazy about coming regularly this one time bowed down their heads before God, for they would be dying not long afterward. In the afterworld only two places awaited: if it wasn't heaven it would have to be hell. And if you want to enter heaven, you have to pray. That was the belief planted in their hearts from the time they were very small.

The really scared ones didn't have the courage to pray up in the surau; they were afraid of having a beam or a house pillar fall on them. They just followed the prayers from out in the courtyard.

People had only just finished their prayers and had not yet stood up from their seats when another quake hit. This one was more terrible and harder than the one at 10 A.M., and it lasted for three minutes. At that time, I was sitting out in the yard. It seemed that the Upper Surau would crash down; it kept cracking and creaking. The ground swayed, shook, and thundered. Everyone ran, pushing each other to get out into the courtyard. One person fell into the washtub used for washing your feet.

At that moment we heard a person scream not far from the surau. Guru Junus's wife (he was the one who fell in the tub) fell to the masonary floor and lost consciousness. People ran over to help her. Everyone got more scared; the quakes just kept coming and closer together. Hundreds of people gathered in the surau courtyard looking at one another; they were asking questions with their looks, but none could answer back satisfactorily. Some of them neglected to eat or they lost their appetites.

The trains weren't running in the downstream direction from Padang Pandjang or in the upriver direction from Solok. The tracks were surely ruined in several spots. The village felt extremely quiet and desolate, because no locomotive whistle was to be heard. Nor were there any train noises as the engines moved away. Everywhere we looked we saw people whose faces were pale from fear. No one laughed or joked around.

The old folks said that earthquakes came from the cow (who was holding up the world on his shoulders) being bitten by a mosquito. Those of us who went to school did not believe that anymore, the notion that the earth was flat and underneath a huge cow held it up.

It continued in that way all afternoon. Every half hour a quake would come. At five o'clock another really hard one hit. From several directions came the rumor that later that night, at twelve midnight, the very hardest one yet would come and make all the houses collapse. Where that bit of frightening news came from no one knew, but whatever the case, it moved swiftly from mouth to mouth. The frightened village people were very quick to believe it and eventually no one at all was willing to sleep inside the houses.

That night hundreds of people slept out in the rice fields on the edge of the village. Those who were anxious about leaving their houses unattended slept out in their front yards. We boys slept on top of mats that had been spread out on the rice stubbles, the sky serving as our ceiling. About half of the children fashioned simple little field huts out of rice stubble stalks, using coconut palm fronds as support posts. They slept under there, all crowded and pressed together. When a quake would hit, their hut would come tumbling down. The ones who didn't have the nerve to go back home to eat would be invited to eat with families who had brought rice, fish, and kitchen utensils out to the rice fields.

Every few moments a quake would come, but they wouldn't be too hard. Everyone was apprehensive waiting for twelve midnight.

That night the highway connecting Padang Pandjang and Solok was very crowded. Many people were going up- and downriver. They all wanted to get back to their home villages and wanted to die with their own families. People in the Solok area living in Padang Pandjang went back to Solok and the reverse was also true: Padang Pandjang folks living in Solok wanted to die with their children and wives in Padang Pandjang. All of them, men and women both, were carrying all their valuables and everything they could cart along on their backs. This switch of residences was turbulent and funny looking. We would have laughed gaily to witness it if we hadn't been quivering so much with fear at the time.

Sumpur folks who had gone into the Padang Pandjang market earlier in the morning to sell things or to shop, walked back home on foot that night. They're the ones who related that the entire town of Padang Pandjang was now level with the ground. All of the stone houses caved in thanks to the 1 P.M. quake. Hundreds of people died under the rubble because at that hour lots of folks happened to be at home; schoolchildren had just come home from school and were still eating their meals. The marketplace was in an uproar, what with the majority of people in town rushing around to see if their houses were still there or to check whether their families were buried under the rubble. Women were sobbing that their child or man had gotten buried under the rubble, and they kept asking for help so that they could be dug out quickly, but all the people were concerned only with their own immediate difficulties. Later on, luckily, soldiers came; they had been mobilized to help the people who had been buried under the rubble. The unlucky people who no longer had any houses slept all in a heap out in the field in front of the normal school.

(Those who died under the rubble surely would have thought that the whole world ended on that twenty-eighth of June, 1926, along with them. They didn't know the world and humankind just kept right on living. It was just they who saw the end of the world.)

Until daylight, quakes repeatedly shook the rice fields and everyone woke up and started uttering prayers. The stars in the sky just kept on twinkling, as if watching what was happening on earth. I got tired trying to think about whether or not the stars sensed the sufferings of humankind on earth. If, say, we should all die, destroyed by this great disaster, and our bodies got totally pulverized (like those hundreds of folks who were buried under the rubble in Padang Pandjang), would the stars all just keep on twinkling along clearly without directing any pity toward the earth?

I looked at the stars for a very long time!

In that manner we stayed out in the rice fields for five days and five nights. The quakes weren't so very frequent now, but each day there would be at least ten of them. For those five days the trains did not run and there were still lots of people out on the highway going back to their home villages. The pace of this didn't let up; in fact, the number returning to their home villages actually increased.

Everyone was saying their prayers. Men, women, everyone. White cloth, which women would use as prayer veils, and Silungkang woven sarongs (which men would wear to the surau) were really hot items at the marketplace. In short, all throughout Minangkabau folks became more devoted to religion. In a great disaster everyone remembers God.

Kids didn't go to school because their still-nervous parents wouldn't let them. The schools were forced to close temporarily. Various stories about conditions in Padang Pandjang emanated from that town.

Finally we started to joke around and kid our pals. Especially Zainal, so that he'd put on his red T-shirt again. But he didn't want to anymore. "That's an unlucky T-shirt," he said.

Eventually we got used to the quakes. We began to get the courage to sleep at home again. Quakes came continually for two months, but as time passed they got rarer.

All the time the quakes were occurring, we had a way to tease our friends. When they'd be sleeping in a little dorm cottage or in the minor surau, the four of us, for instance, would all start to rocking the pillars so that the whole cottage swayed back and forth. Our sleeping friends would wake up, utter "La ilaha ilallah," and bound outdoors. We'd burst into laughter. Sometimes they'd do the same thing to us. Often we'd get fooled thinking it was a real quake.

Gradually normal conditions returned and the prophesied end of the world did not happen. Folks began to stop praying so much. The surau, so busy when the quakes were raging, went back to normal. It was only the devoted and the devout who came each day. Little sins got committed once again, like playing cards, betting on cockfights, and slandering other folks. Only a while before, during the quakes, folks had lived holy lives like angels.

The terrible quakes that violently shook the interior spiritual lives of all humankind in Minangkabau did not return. Mount Merapi had erupted and expelled lava for several days; the earth's angry abscess had erupted now, and henceforth was no longer a threat. But people who believed in superstitions were still nervous because they said that this quake was a forerunner of a great confusion and commotion that would happen in the future.

The Minangkabau populace's soul was no longer shaking violently back and forth, although a bit of a tremor remained.

CHAPTER 18: THE FASTING MONTH

The Fasting Month is almost here!

Just three days more!

We kids eagerly awaited the arrival of Ramadan with great merriment, because the Fasting Month was really special. It was always packed with a freedom and youthful happiness unequaled any other time.

First off, we didn't have to go to school during this month. Every day we could play as much as we wanted to, day and night, setting off firecrackers and bamboo cannons. In the villages it was quite a custom to set off Fasting Month firecrackers.

True enough, our parents would always be telling us to fast and to do the *tarwih* and *tadarus* prayers, but that was not all that hard—it was just a little diversion, a sort of change of pace from the usual run of things, after eleven months of eating a midday meal every day. We'd fast all day long, do tarwih as fast as lightening, do tadarus until the midnight meal. We'd do all three gaily, like a sport, not a duty. Particularly since we did it all together in a group, these religious duties were easily borne. They were a kind of game.

True enough, during normal months we were mostly happy, too, since the only work we did was studying and playing every day. But our happiness during the Fasting Month was doubled. That was because there were more things to make us cheerful during the fast.

Everywhere folks would be crowded around, talking animatedly about the fast: in the coffee stalls, at the surau, in the houses, and along the road. In short, wherever people happened to sit down in groups, the fast would be the main topic of conversation. The marketplace would be extraordinarily crowded and busy, jam-packed with people buying and selling all the necessities for the Fasting Month: food, cakes, clothes, dates, firecrackers, shampoo, and so forth. Young guys and girls and those who would normally rarely come to the market would flock there in droves, wearing beautiful clothes.

Everyone would walk along with radiant faces, fine smiles playing on their lips in the shining, lovely morning in Sumpur valley. Everyone took great pride in going around discussing Fasting Month matters, or talking about what particular day was truly Day One of the fast, because a few Ulamas hadn't come to any agreement yet about that. After a few moments they'd get back to joking and jesting and laughing merrily, and the road to the marketplace would be tumultuous with talk.

Young guys would follow along after sweet-looking girls, admiring the prettiest one and praising her skill at dressing and the enchanting way she swayed her hips. And this girl would often glance sideways at these young guys, who were handsome, cocky, and finely turned out.

However, they didn't have the nerve to go up to each other and actually talk. For, according to Minangkabau adat, it was indecent for a girl to talk right out there in the middle of the open road to a young man who was not her *muhrim* [a man and a woman are *muhrim* if they have a close enough degree of consanguinity to associate in public but not to marry]. They could only greet each other for a moment, flirting with their eyes. But even though their mouths were locked shut by the rules of public decency, feelings and love and deep desire burned not any the less hot. These feelings ran amok inside; in fact, they flared up even more. And because they were so restrained in these ways, the flames of love flashed out in the shining eyes of the adolescent boys and the blushing cheeks of the girls.

Ah, imagine how happy those young guys were! Walking along slowly with the girls, matching them stride for stride, joking and jesting, teasing each other politely, laughing cheerily, caught up in the Fasting Month atmosphere, the Fasting Month that had almost arrived.

Two days before the Fasting Month began, as had long been the custom every year, the residents of my village would kill some cattle and water buffaloes. Between sixty and one hundred of them would be killed. Normally the slaughter would be done in a big, festive way out on a large coconut farm laid out along the Sumpur River. This massive meat slaughter was done to celebrate the arrival of the month of Ramadan by having a big feast for two days before the fast began. Before the point at which they weren't allowed to eat during the daytime for thirty days, the Muslims would indulge the desire to eat to its very fullest.

Very early in the morning, the dozens of livestock would be driven out to the farm. We young kids would be tagging along after our fathers or maternal uncles so that we could help cut up the meat and bring it home later. We'd do all this while getting in a lot of playing, too. A large segment of the village populace would be gathered out there on the coconut farm; the women would be back in the houses preparing the ground spice mixtures.

On this day a man's wealth or poverty would be evident to all. The rich ones, like merchants, would order lots of meat to be carried off to their wives' houses—sometimes as much as twenty-five to thirty kilograms of it. If a man had two or three wives, the meat would be divided up evenly. The half-wealthy ones would have ten or fifteen kilograms, while the outright unwealthy ones would have only five kilograms. But that day, everyone had to carry home some meat. If one did not do so he would be embarrassed in front of his wife, his parents-in-law, and especially in front of the people of his village. Several people had gone in together for each head of live-stock that was slaughtered. For instance, eight or ten people would go to-gether to buy a cow or buffalo and then would divide up the meat accord-ing to how large or small each person's contribution had been.

At that time many people in my village were rich. In fact the whole vil-lage was prosperous, for many folks had migrated to the rantau to go into commerce, and these merchants would send money and goods back to their families and home village. They could afford to buy dozens and doz-ens of heads of livestock and to show off their wealth once a year: that is, by carting off several carrying handles weighted down with meat to their wives' or parents' houses. Those who carried off a very great deal of meat would be lavishly praised, respected, and admired by the village people.

In the course of these two days the people of my village ate their fill. In fact, some of us young kids ate as many as ten or more times in a single day or night. Not in their own homes, though: they were invited in by other people, or their friends had them over. This was especially true of the santris; for these two days they were rarely at the surau. From morning to night, and then the next day, too, they'd be going down out of houses and then up and back into other houses, constantly invited in to eat and pray. They weren't able to say no, even though it might be only one small handful of rice that they could manage to put into their mouths—they'd have to eat something, whatever the case. After eating, the santris would be sitting there in the midst of billowing clouds of incense smoke in the front room, and they would beseech God that the residents of the house might be safely seen through the fast, that they might be graciously re-ceived by God, and that they might have a long life and a prosperous livelihood.

Then they'd go down out of the house and climb the stairs right back into another house. Sometimes the santris would have only gotten to the first step when someone from another house would be waiting there to in-vite him directly over. Could he refuse?

During this time we'd truly get to eat what we wanted to, all sorts of foods: hot curries, stews, roasted kidneys, spiced heart, brain curry, and so forth—and all of it cooked in delicious ways. Over these two days we filled our bellies until they were bloated, until there wasn't any more room in there at all. After all, after these two days, we'd go hungry for sure, since we wouldn't be allowed to eat at all during the day.

There was rarely any meeting of the minds among the religion teachers about what day the fast should actually begin. Some held firm with the

Almanac, while another group of them wanted to go see the moon with their own eyes; that is, they'd follow *Rukjat*. Normally the main ones in disagreement would be the Modernists and the Traditionalists. The difference in determining what day the fast should begin would often cause quite a quarrel. It would be a fight; an outright state of hostilities would break out between the people of these two groups. Sometimes people in the very same house would start the fast on different days. Even though they wouldn't come right out and refute each other's stand, they'd silently mock each other. When the Modernists talked among themselves, they'd slander the older generation by mocking them and sending insulting looks at them out of the corners of their eyes.

The reverse was also true.

My father, who was part of the Traditionalist faction, always wanted to check the moon's phase first. So when the fast was to start the next day, we'd all be rounded up to go out to the mountain peaks to observe the moon. But the pity was, every time it was nearing the Fasting Month the sky wouldn't be clear. Off in the west the sky would be covered over with clouds. We'd have to wait patiently until the wind chased away the clouds. It would be near sunset but the moon would not have appeared yet. The clouds would be thin and beginning to turn red, but they still covered the sky. The new moon was very hard to discern because it was too small. Then, too, over on Sumpur's west, the mountain chain was too high. Maybe the moon was behind the mountains, but it wasn't visible to us.

To get an absolutely certain answer, a good tree climber would be told to go shimmy up a tall coconut palm. But he said he still couldn't see it. So because the moon wasn't visible, Father just relied on the almanac. It wasn't because the moon hadn't been there but because it had been covered with clouds or mountains that we could not see it. If our village had been near the sea, like Pariaman, the moon would have been visible for sure.

Father told us to beat the mosque drums for hours so that all the residents of Sumpur would know that tomorrow had been determined to be the first day of the fast and that that night the tarwih prayers would begin.

As it got on toward evening prayertime, people would all walk toward the surau, one after another, both men and women. The surau would be busier than usual. Women with torches swinging in their hands would come from every direction. Their torches would be made from dried coconut palm leaves tied into little bundles, used to light their way. The men didn't carry torches (if they weren't carrying flashlights); they'd just walk along normally there in the dark.

For those of us who had been living in the village since we were small, walking in the dark was not so hard. The roads were paved in asphalt, and we'd also know where the rocks and holes were. Half of us could even run fast in the dark without stumbling, slipping, or falling down. Even if our eyes could not see too clearly, our nerves were sharp enough to guide our way so that we didn't slip or stumble.

Usually the surau was lit with oil lamps, but in the Fasting Month we had gas lamps. It was we young fellows who pumped the tank and got the lamps going. Two gas lamps were sufficient to light the whole surau and its courtyard. Everyone was cheerful and diligent at saying their prayers, even though the tarwih prayers had a great many repetitions in them to do.

Those of us who were going to say the tadarus prayers after tarwih and sleep in the surau had brought provisions from home: a dinner pail of cooked rice and all its side dishes. We could eat the rice after the post-midnight meal, after the tadarus prayers. Reminding ourselves of our rice and side dishes awaiting us, we encouraged ourselves to pray and do the tadarus.

Tadarus consisted of us reading a page of the Koran one by one, taking turns. After the tarwih the village people would go home. The gas lamps would be damped down and replaced with hanging lamps, and just those of us who were going to sleep over at the surau would be left there, along with a few old grandfathers who had brought along food provisions too. Those of us who were going to do the tadarus would sit in a circle, about thirty of us, each of us with a Koran in front of us, placed on a bookstand, a seat, or a pillow. There would be an elder tutor there, that is, the eldest and most adept of all the tutors, who would correct all our reading errors. The first night Father was there, listening along attentively, but after that he'd just come over when he wanted to, or to inspect us to see if we were being faithful and obedient at doing the tadarus.

The Village Privates who had come in to do the tarwih prayers would go on off to the coffee stall when folks started the tadarus. They'd come back again when people were eating their postmidnight meal, and after eating, they'd fall asleep in the surau. While waiting for the postmidnight meal, they'd play dominoes, checkers, *kim* [a gambling game, resembling bingo, in which the numbers are called out in rhymed verses], or they'd just chat and shoot the breeze.

Zainal, Djamin, and I did not join in and do the tadarus, for we were part of the group that was no longer fully obedient and submissive to the discipline of the surau. Father let us get away with this; perhaps he knew that I didn't particularly like tadarus. While we waited for the postmidnight meal, we'd run all over the village, playing and chatting, or conversing with the comical Lebai Saman and hassling him.

We were a bit put out because we didn't have many playmates: all of them were doing tadarus and we weren't allowed to invite them to come join in the fun with us.

While Zainal played, every few moments he'd think fondly of his rice meal, which on one such night happened to include side dishes of spiced heart and fried chicken—and me, too; I'd want to eat right away and wouldn't be able to wait until one o'clock. But we'd be embarrassed in front of our friends to eat at ten-thirty. And then too, if we ate too early, we'd get very hungry during the day. Lots of fellows ate their postmidnight meal at 4 A.M. so that they wouldn't get too hungry during the daytime. We had to admire their patience at fighting off rice and curry temptations for four whole hours.

By one o'clock people would be through with the tadarus, and we'd beat the mosque drum to wake up the villagers. The ones who had just said tadarus would take up their food provisions and their dinner pails or banana-leaf wrappings, grab a bottle of tea, and start in. Just how noisy it was with all these thirty people and more eating their meal can be imagined, especially ʿince they kept talking and arguing as they ate. Some of them exchanged their side dishes. For instance, a person who had some meat might want to eat chicken, so he'd exchange a chunk of spiced meat for a little piece of fried chicken. The piece of chicken would be smaller because it was tastier. There were also a few among us who were soft touches; they'd agree to give a piece of meat away without expecting anything in return. We'd be in luck if we got to sit next to folks like these. Normally they'd be wealthy people's kids who had lots and lots of rice and side dishes, so many that they couldn't even finish it all by themselves.

We did not take long to eat. In fact, some of us were really greedy: we'd swallow the rice down without even chewing it first. A person who ate slowly would be made fun of; he'd get called a toothless old gramps.

After we'd finished eating we'd toss the banana-leaf wrappings from the rice out the window. We wouldn't wash the dirty plate and dinner pails right away. We'd just wrap them up with handkerchiefs and put them along the edge of the wall to wash them tomorrow, during the day. Those who wanted to chat and smoke would sit there in small groups. Those who were drowsy would go to sleep.

The zealous and energetic among us would go all through the village waking people who hadn't gotten up yet and weren't cooking their rice. We'd knock on their door and walls ceaselessly until they answered. Once they'd awakened, we'd go on off to someone else's house who was still sound asleep. They wouldn't have heard the clang of the mosque drum.

We didn't do this to get thanks, praise, or to store up religious merit in the hereafter. Rather, we did it out of simple glee; it was all a game to us. After the villagers in each and every house had been woken up, finally we'd go back to the surau.

Those who had been chatting and smoking a while ago would be getting drowsy, too. They'd damp down the lamps by closing off the chimneys, and the surau would go completely dark. We'd sleep soundly, tired and full.

The next morning at eight o'clock half of us would be awake but still lazy about actually getting up to bathe and say the dawn prayers. We'd be still contentedly lying down; we'd go back to sleep.

Father would have arrived by then. He would have gathered the females together for their tadarus; a few girls would already be sitting in a circle in the woman's hall. We couldn't see them but could hear their voices—they were still busy finding their seats and conversing softly.

Without the agreement of the other interested party and totally on the sly, we guys had already picked out which of these girls were our sweethearts. Djamin loved Hasjah, Bujung loved Djawanis, Dullah had Nurdjannah, and I had Jusna, and so on. Hassling one another about this had become a daily pastime for us; the one who got hassled would pretend to get really mad if it was said that he was closely connected to a certain girl (who he actually did love), but in his heart he'd actually be quite pleased to be teased like this. The girls didn't return our love yet. But because they'd often smile very sweetly at us, we figured they must already have the same feelings that we had for them.

For us, those smiles were signs of love. For instance, on a lovely morning, when a certain girl that we loved smiled at us, our whole day was made. We felt exceedingly lucky. We'd jump here, leap there, and punch our buddies standing next to us—then we'd ask to be forgiven. Our buddies would understand that the guy who was jumping and leaping about and punching him out was madly in love. They weren't angry or hurt, for when it came to their turn to fall wildly in love they could pound away on us, too, and they'd be allowed to pour out their hearts to us.

While we'd be lying there on our backs, we'd hear the voices of our sweethearts singing passages from the Koran. The fellow whose sweetheart would be reading would be boundlessly happy. All of us would look at him and sometimes he would bite the edge of his pillow and hug it like it was his sweetheart.

"She's my love and you aren't allowed to take her," he'd whisper.

We'd converse in whispers, afraid that Father would overhear us. But for our part we didn't want to take this other guy's sweetheart whatever the case because each of us already had a special girl who was a fair match for everyone else's.

Of all of us it was Udin who was the craziest. When he'd hear his sweetheart recite from the Koran he'd show his lovestruck bliss by hugging his pillow, rocking it in his arms, singing to it, crying over it. But his voice wouldn't really come out: just his mouth moved. We wanted to laugh but we kept it all inside. If we couldn't help but laugh out loud, we'd press our pillows up against our mouths so Father wouldn't overhear us.

By ten o'clock it was getting hot and the surau would be bright as day, since the fellows who had gone off to bathe and pray had opened up all the windows. We'd also go bathe and pray, while our pals mocked us for saying the dawn prayers after the sun was already high in the sky.

"Are you saying the noontime prayers or are you saying the dawn ones?" our buddies would tease.

We wouldn't feel too good, as was normally the case after we'd eaten the midnight meal. We'd just keep sleeping. We would be hot, apathetic; our thoughts would be all confused and tousled. We wanted something to drink but it was the fast. We kept asking ourselves, whatever would we do until afternoon? To just stay there in the surau snoozing and listening to the girls do their tadarus recitations would begin to get boring after a while.

The older kids would go over to the coffee stalls to play dominoes or chess. And the five of us who didn't want to play dominoes would go take a walk along the edge of the lake. Maybe we would feel more refreshed if we could nap alongside the lakeshore, fanned by breezes from the calm lake.

On the walk we had our regrets, too, for our conversation didn't go very fluently since we had no set destination. We tried to be cheerful, but after a short while we got tired and thirsty. At seeing the clear water in the lakefalls, our dry throats started to work uncomfortably. On one of these walks before going to Batu Beragung we went to Kubu Gedeng, to Father's coconut farm.

While we were pausing for a while in the stand of coconuts, one of the fellows challenged us to simply break the fast right then and there and drink some young coconut juice. We might have accepted this challenge if any of us had happened to be any good at climbing up coconut palms. We were embarrassed to try telling an adult farmer to go climb up there for us and then paying him with two mature coconuts—and then, too, we were afraid it might get back to Dad.

We went straight on to Batu Beragung. Seeing the blue lake all fresh and rippling before us, we could not resist going for a swim. We shucked off our clothes and in a wink of an eye jumped into the cool water. Whether one of my friends might have taken a drink while diving, I don't know. But I think bathing a long time does tend to abrogate the fast.

We spent two hours bathing, splashing about, swimming, chasing each other around, and diving down into the water. One of us who was good at rowing a boat borrowed a canoe from a sailor there. And after we got our fill of swimming we rode out to the middle of the lake.

"You aren't allowed to bathe for a long time, your fast will be violated," said each sailor or old auntie bathing there along the edge of the lake.

"It won't be abrogated since we're not drinking anything," we answered. But we believed that we had indeed violated it for our bodies felt refreshed; even though water didn't go into our mouths and noses, it certainly penetrated our pores. That's what refreshed us.

Having gotten our fill of bathing, we went on home, walking along very slowly. And when there happened to be a grassy field sheltered by trees along the side of the road, we'd stretch out there to wait for late afternoon. Some of us even fell asleep.

To tell the truth, if we had had some musical training at that time, we could have sung songs or played flutes and sung shepard songs, or whatever. These might have cheered us up and banished feelings of regret. But because the Ulamas had forbidden the study of music and the public considered singing an insolent sort of thing to do, we were forced to just keep quiet when we weren't conversing. Moreover, musical feelings had already died inside us because they had not been nurtured by our ancestors. They might have left these to us as an inherited treasure. So—what was there for us to sing!

That afternoon the whole world was weak and sluggish, I noticed. The sun took a long time to go down in the west. Its hot, white rays dried out the leaves. The sky was clear and dark blue and a few clouds gathered there above the mountain chain. The heat made folks even more tired and hungry and thirsty. There was no activity whatsoever in the village. Few people were even out walking. Most of the men were asleep or playing dominoes or conversing. And the women were in the kitchen cooking. It could be said, in fact, that throughout the Fasting Month the women were the only energetic ones.

During this exhausted, empty time, when nothing was undertaken or thought about in any positive, definite way, daydreams were more active than was normally the case. They got wilder and flared up much more violently than usual. Daydreams that rarely occurred to us (ones we considered indecent, for instance) cropped up repeatedly during this time. Sometimes they would take control of us for an entire hour. If they were put aside they would just crop up again. A young woman with an average sort of face would become a princess in our eyes: her whole body would attract us, her hair, cheeks, chin, chest, waist, thighs, and calves—all of these enchanted us.

We young fellows—who had gotten such a strict education based on purity of body and moral decency, who were shackled by adat and religion, who were not ever given an opportunity by society to lighten the natural urges coming from inside us by having an appropriate romantic life—we would become extremely confused when we were beset by such romantic daydreams. We hadn't conjured them up on purpose; they were just gifts from the natural world and our physical existence. During the fast our appetite for food was indeed reined in. However, in reaction to that, romantic daydreams and youthful desires ran wild, unrestrainable. Oftentimes we felt as if we were deep inside a cave that had no hole from which we might climb back out. I asked myself, wasn't there a way or a mode of life in this land which would be in closer accord with human character? So that perhaps these natural desires that were so much in motion inside us wouldn't be suppressed forever—something that could ruin our entire souls?

This question was still blurred in my mind and its answer was darker and more obscure still.

So in that way we lay there on our backs and fantasized under the shade trees with the hot wind from the north blowing on us. At four in the afternoon we got up and continued our walk home at a very slow pace. And we thought that when we got to the surau the mosque drum would be about ready to sound. When we arrived at the surau we washed our dinner pails and plates from the day before and all went home to our mothers' houses.

Before the mosque drum sounded and we broke the fast, we all got reprimanded by our mothers because we had spent the whole day playing and not helping them by buying this or that which they needed in the kitchen. But we didn't really pay any attention to what they said, for all our attention was on the lavish variety of food laid out before us and on delicious, sweet stewed fruits. By this point I'd already spooned out a full plate of rice and whole plateful of stewed fruit too. I had ladled out the latter specially since I was afraid I might not get a big enough portion later on.

The mosque drum had barely boomed out the first time when I pounced on my plate of rice and greedily gobbled it up very, very fast. I felt it a real shame that my mouth was so small when what I wanted to put inside it was a very great deal and I wanted very much to get it all in. Seeing all that food set out there, I became doubtful about how to choose the dishes, and about which food to pick first. Every type of food had to be put into the stomach. No matter how much Mother tried to make me have some patience, I didn't listen to her. After I'd finished off the rice I struck into the stewed fruit. And after that I drank a glass of coconut milk and then had three king bananas.

My belly was full within ten minutes and I got a bit out of breath from being so stuffed. I could hardly stand up. Now that I had ended the fast I hadn't gotten any stronger; rather, all my limbs had just gotten more exhausted. I went over and leaned against the house pillar in the middle of the room. I loosened my belt so the digestion of my food would not be hindered.

Mother had prepared a dinner pail of rice and another pail of side dishes for the postmidnight meal, later on, along with a bottle of tea. I went over to the surau, running into no one on the way over. It was all quite quiet and deserted, as everyone was back at their houses eating their meals. I was the only one who had finished eating. Once I got to the surau I pumped the gas and put the lamp on. Father had appointed me the one to do this job every time we ended the fast.

Gradually more people came to the surau to say tarwih.

Several of us young guys just didn't have the strength to pray the tarwih with its *twenty-one* repeated recitations in the middle. Our bellies were still packed full. We got tired after only ten repetitions, but if we didn't keep praying Father would surely get mad at us.

Father was the imam, and when he stood up, all his followers stood up, too, and we did the same thing. Before the *takbir* [recitation of laudation, "God is great"], Father had glanced over to his right to see whether I was praying or not. Upon seeing me standing there ready to do the takbir, he was pleased, and he began reading it. When he had just begun the takbir, my three pals and I immediately sat back down, leaned against the wall, and stopped praying. Father didn't know this since people who are praying aren't allowed to look up. But when the repetition prayers were almost over and Father was getting ready to read *assalamu alaikum* [peace be unto you] and to look to his right, my friends and I immediately bunched together like folks who were actually praying. He glanced over, saw that I was turning to the right and reading *assalamu alaikum* and wiping my face with my right hand.

And in that way we kept arching our backs again and again [bending over, to pray] until the tarwih and *witir* prayers were finished. The grown-ups who were sitting next to us knew about the deception but they simply laughed.

"I'm just too tired, I ate too much," I said.

They nodded their heads. None of them told on us to Dad. But if they had, he would have taken a rattan switch to us for sure.

After tarwih the village people went on home and the young guys did tadarus. Those of us who were not joining in would just go to sleep and wake up for the postmidnight meal, if we weren't going to play dominoes or watch people play cards. It would go like that every night.

The old grandpas who were sleeping over there would pray *sunat* or *zikir* [repeated chanting of sections of the Muslim confession of faith, often done in unison], after tarwih, before the postmidnight meal. Their incentive in doing all this was their awareness that they were nearing the grave. They filled their time with religious services so they'd be tranquil and happy after dying.

One night, when the public was doing tarwih, Zainal and I found ourselves confused about what sort of thing we could possibly find to do. We were real lazybones about praying. We wanted to eat, but if we ate up our own rice provisions, what would we have to eat for the postmidnight meal?

On the sly we quietly took an old grandma's dinner pail—and by happenstance her son was a wealthy heir. We ate up all the rice and its unusually delicious chunks of spiced, dried meat. These were really tasty because they had been fried in butter.

After that we went over to the food stall to play dominoes. It was only when she got ready to eat her postmidnight meal that she discovered that her dinner pail was totally empty. She just kept mum, though, for she was a very pious and patient person and didn't want to make a big disturbance. She asked us which boy would be willing to go over to her house (which wasn't very far from the surau) and fetch some new rice for her. Zainal said he'd go. Smiling, we carried along the empty dinner pail (which of course had been emptied out by the two of us) and asked for some rice and side dishes from the grandma's daughter. The latter was astonished because the dinner pail had been quite full when her mother had carried it over. Zainal said that the old grandma had given its contents away as alms to a santri in the surau. The daughter was satisfied now that she understood.

One matter that really drew my attention in the surau throughout the Fasting Month was a husband and wife pair who had come to the surau together and who'd go home together.

After ending the fast at home, this man (a merchant who'd just arrived from the rantau), would go to the surau along with his wife. In the surau they would separate, with the man going to the men's hall and the woman going to the woman's hall. They'd part for a moment happily, knowing that a moment later, after tarwih, they'd be back together again. At times the wife would be wearing the printed pattern sarong her husband had worn the day before. That was a sign of pride, and a sign that she was in love with her husband. Just look at them sharing the same sarong! From that, all the women praying the surau knew that the two of them were very much in love with each other.

And this was really quite a sign of things if the husband happened to have two wives. Wearing her husband's sarong was a weapon that a woman could use to stab the heart of the co-wife she was jealous of. Several of the women at the surau would tell the co-wife that yesterday the other one had been wearing her husband's sarong.

It was not two co-wives married to the same man that attracted my attention this time, though, but rather a pair of lovebirds who had only been married three months. They were at the peak of happiness. After saying tarwih the village people would not go straight back home. Rather, they would stay around and chat awhile, at first in small groups consisting of three or four people, while smoking cigarettes. Waiting for their husbands, the wives would be out in the woman's hall, chatting among themselves. Even though these two halls were divided by an unbleached cotton screen, this wife would know, or at least she would sense, that her husband was already standing up, ready to go home. Sometimes the husband would cough a bit so his wife would know he was suggesting, "All right, let's go home!" The wife would stand up and excuse herself from her companions, with a knowing smile. In her heart she was saying, "We'll go home and go to sleep . . ."

At the foot of the surau steps the two would put on their slippers and sandals and go on home. The woman would be holding her veil and her folded, printed sarong, walking along with sweet, swaying motions, while the man would be holding the flashlight, illuminating the way in front for his wife to walk along. They were not holding hands like Europeans do. Indeed, that was not accepted custom and the public didn't really approve of it.

In Minangkabau, holding hands irritated other people. If they saw a husband and wife holding hands, Minangkabau people would say in derision, "They go on as if they're the only ones who are in love with each other. I love my wife, too, but I certainly don't want to show it off to the general populace. Showing it inside our room is quite enough!"

Because of this there were no husbands and wives who held hands in Minangkabau. If they were out walking along the wife would go on before the husband or she'd walk along in back of him. Rarely would they walk side by side, except in the big cities.

Minangkabau people would usually find it peculiar if a man displayed his love for his wife. In fact they'd condemn him for it. They'd say this man had been love-hexed.[1]

Seeing this intimate pair going on home that night, my thoughts wandered off toward the future. Three or four years from now, once I'd emigrated to the rantau and was engaged in commerce and when I had amassed a good deal of profit, surely folks would come asking for me to be their son-in-law. I'd be married to some certain pretty girl in my village. And after tarwih I, too, would be going home with my wife. She'd still be sort of shy and embarrassed and wouldn't have the nerve to look me straight in the eyes yet; she'd always just bow her head and glance at me sideways. I'd look at her with increased passion. And I'd be carrying the flashlight.

When the mosque drum for the postmidnight meal sounded she'd get up and go off to the kitchen to help her mother cook the rice and get the food ready. After the side dishes were set out she'd awaken me with a soft, intimate voice:

"Older kinsman [Uda], try to wake up now, the food's been set out!"

And I'd wake up and rub my eyes and stretch. I'd stand up, brush my teeth, and then we'd eat our meal together out of a single plate. She'd sit there in front of me smiling, still kind of shy. I'd give her the other half of a chunk of spiced meat I'd already bitten in half. But at first she wouldn't want it. It's disgusting, she'd say, but then she'd eat it anyway.

Often such thoughts would drift around inside. The desire to emigrate to the rantau would get even greater, and so too my wish to become a rich merchant.

Dad would often be angry all through the Fasting Month. This had become part of his character. Maybe because his belly was hungry, you always had to watch that you didn't get on his nerves. He'd get hot and mad if someone did the least little thing wrong, and if it was me who had made the mistake, he'd smack and beat me. Because of this I kept my distance from him during the Fasting Month, trying to encounter him as rarely as possible. I'd reduce my naughty behavior. However, even though I'd try keeping away from him, if he hadn't seen me for a long time he'd call for me anyway. He would ask what I'd been doing all this time that he hadn't seen me. He'd ask me whether or not I was keeping the fast.

One night after tarwih, Father was still sitting there conversing with several merchants who had returned home from the rantau. (If there were people conversing, we wouldn't do *tadarus* because they would be sitting there, right in our recitation room.) While waiting for them to go home, I asked my companions to play touch tag.

We played tag very energetically, making a huge amount of racket. All of a sudden one of Father's martial arts students, Tjodi, stepped down into the courtyard and told us to stop making so much noise.

"His honor forbids it," said Tjodi.

Absorbed in playing and in a joking way, I answered, "Well, I'm 'his honor,' too."

Tjodi reported this to Dad. "Ridjal says he's an honorable sir, too."

"What did he say!?" snapped Dad, jumping up and running down the steps out of the house. "Where is this honorable sir?! I would like to make his acquaintance!" he said with a scarlet face and voice. We players dashed off in every direction, going wherever there happened to be an escape route.

"If you're really an honorable sir, why are you running off?" he called out. And we could still hear him from far away.

That night we didn't sleep in the surau but rather in the coffee stall. After midnight we delegated two buddies to go get some food provisions for us from the surau, on the sly.

The next day I supposed that Father would have forgotten the incident from last night. Before the Friday prayers began, those of us who had been playing tag were lying around and sleeping at a deserted food stall near the surau. Because the weather was really hot we weren't wearing shirts.

All of a sudden Father, who had just finished bathing, came into the food stall carrying his bath sarong, which he hadn't wrung out yet.

"Now, so here are yesterday's honorable sirs, are they?" he said angrily. He hit me as hard as he could with his bath sarong and then he hit my pals. But he hit me the most times because I was the leader who wasn't willing to run away. The others dashed off in a big hurry, holding their shirts. Father was really angry since his honor as an estimable sir had been violated by my insolent remark.

Because I had gotten beaten I was irked. But I didn't have the nerve to actually fight him. Besides, religion did not allow it. To get back at him I did not do the Friday prayers, and I also went over to the house of one of my stepmothers. I asked her for some rice and I ended my fast right then and there.

"So why are you ending your fast?" Mother asked.

"I'm mad at Father because he beat me."

"Yeah, well, that's what I'm always telling you. As long as it's the Fasting Month, you just have to keep away from your Dad," Mother said, getting me some water to drink.

One day, also in that same Fasting Month, Zainal and Bujung and I were playing out in the bushes between the houses, looking for silver coins that had maybe been tossed out there—or who knew, maybe there was a lump of gold someone had buried out there in the past. And because it had gotten rained on all this time, its hiding place might have gotten washed away. We had read in books about a lucky kid who'd found some buried gold. Who knew? Maybe we'd find a buried treasure that we could divide up three ways as capital for our commercial enterprises in the rantau.

Out in the bushes we'd investigate anything at all that happened to catch the sun's rays and glint. Unfortunately, most of the things we saw were chips of porcelain or glass fragments. We walked around and around for three hours, not finding anything but a worn-out old plate made of brass, and a watch chain that had turned green and rusty. Money and gold were not anywhere in evidence.

Bujung was delighted to find this plate. Even though it was thickly tarnished, he polished it with salt and sand very diligently, for a long time, until it shone bright yellow and looked slick, almost like brand new. But it still smelled rusty and rancid. Bujung had the intention of eating off the plate at dinner that night. As Bujung was occupied with this, I was polishing the brass watch chain so that it shone, too, and so that it was as yellow as newly gilded gold. Because I didn't own a watch, I put it on my ankle so that I would have an ankle ornament.

That first day I was still sort of embarrassed to wear the anklet, afraid that people would laugh at me. But at night, from twilight to morning, the ornament would not be stripped away from my leg for a moment.

That night before tarwih, Bujung, Zainal, and I made some fruit compote from oranges, tubers, cucumbers, and mangos, all mixed together with ketchup [a soy, pepper, tomato mixture] and hot pepper. We ate it in a normal plate but Bujung wanted to use the brass one. We wanted to restrain him in this, just in case there might be come invisible germs or dirt on it—after all, how many years had it been tossed out in the bushes there? But Bujung was determined to use it, so we just let him! The compote was only half finished when his stomach started to feel queasy. His belly felt like it was turning upside down, and then he threw up again and again. Finally, not just the compote came out but also all the food that had gone into his stomach a while before, when we had broken the fast. Those of us who were using regular plates didn't throw up: a sign that it wasn't the compote that was at fault.

Other friends of ours (who'd come over in great numbers) laughed and laughed and hassled Bujung about his brass plate. They also made fun of me because I was wearing an ankle bracelet, but I didn't want to take it off. Gradually all the guys got used to this new sight and didn't make fun of me anymore.

I wanted to discover whether or not I would have a weird dream when I slept with that ankle bracelet on. That night, though, there wasn't any extraordinary dream at all—no syech or goddess who came and visited me or anything. Apparently that watch chain had no special history to it.

The next day at nine o'clock, my father was busy listening to the girls say tadarus. We were still lying down; he ordered us to get up and bathe. We were lazy about going into the water tub but eventually we did go.

The eight of us stripped off our clothes and put them down on top of the wall around the tub, which was over a meter high. We bathed without sarongs since we were all about the same age and there wasn't any need to be embarrassed around one another—and then too, we members of the younger generation wanted to violate customs every once in a while. It was very refreshing there in the cool water since we'd just gotten out of our hot beds.

Eventually we stopped just bathing and started diving into the water and immersing ourselves, splashing each other, chasing each other, and shouting as loud as we possibly could. We did this when someone who was chasing us caught us. The tub water was muddy because the muck that had settled down to the bottom got all stirred up. The tub was a great tumult of us shouting, yelling, and crying out. We were gleeful.

All of a sudden my head got hit, and one of my companions got hit hard on the back—we had been struck by the end of a pole, a long, bent bamboo pole that someone was working from outside the wall around the tub. It appeared that Father was striking out at us with that pole, and because it was bent at the end, it would hit the front end of the tub and whoever happened to be swimming there would get struck.

The girls had had their tadarus halted. They all came out to the windows and door to watch us being hit.

Finally we couldn't stand to stay there anymore in the tub. Lots of us had been hit and we were afraid that Father himself would come and slap us on the sides of our heads. So we seized our clothes and without even putting them on (because there wasn't an opportunity to) we ran out the door from the tub enclosure, and dashed as far away as possible. All the girls and women standing at the windows and in the surau courtyard screamed and laughed when they saw us—a bunch of guys between fourteen and seventeen years old, stark naked. Their screams and laughter rose in intensity when they saw me running naked holding my bundle of clothes with my shirt, my trousers, my cap, and . . . wearing my ankle bracelet. I was extremely embarrassed, but, well, consider: I didn't have time to take it off when I had to get out of there!

That whole day I didn't have the nerve to put in an appearance in front of the womenfolk who had seen me naked, in my ankle bracelet. I was very embarrassed in regard to a certain girl I considered my sweetheart, who had been smiling along with the rest of them. What were her thoughts when she saw me in such a state? Maybe she fell more in love? Or did her love perhaps start to fade when she saw the proof that I was an insolent, bad kid? One who went in for wearing ankle bracelets? Would her estimation of me be lowered? What would happen if the girl's mother and father found out? Would they still want to take me on as a son-in-law? Maybe the girl's love would shift over to someone else, to a merchant's son, for instance?

Such questions tortured me all day long, until it got so I forgot I was fasting. Without my anticipating it, the mosque drum sounded.

Starting that day I did not want to wear my ankle bracelet anymore; I just stored the watch chain away.

After doing tadarus for ten days we would come to the end of the Koran. And that was usually a cause for celebration. But you wouldn't slaughter a cow or a goat as people did when they finished studying how to recite the verses of the Koran; normally you'd only eat rice delicacies and have some drinks. Two days before the ceremony was to be held, the kids who were doing tadarus would go tell their mothers to get some sort of rice treats ready, and the teacher would divvy up the verses that each one of them would have to read as their part in the final ceremony.

The whole village knew, when that celebration was going to be held. Besides the mothers of the tadarus kids, there would also be other mothers who wanted to help out, and they'd make little rice treats as their contributions or give them as religious alms for the celebration. That night the mothers would come crowding in carrying their containers of stewed fruit, fried bananas, sticky rice treats, rice porridge, Ambon bananas, *ondeh-ondeh* treats,[2] gelatin snacks, pancakes—yes, and lots more things. All these delicacies would be piled up in big basins, one basin per type of treat. And there would be an unusually large number of people praying tarwih. They were just there in droves, men and women both, all present to show their interest.

We young guys were delighted at all this—especially to see the girls, who on this night were all decked out in very special clothes. One moment we'd set off a firecracker, the next moment we'd ask the old aunties for some rice delicacies that they were supervising. When we were doing the tarwih, we absolutely didn't think about God; our thoughts were all disarrayed: we thought about the rice treats, about girls, about firecrackers, about bamboo cannons, about playing tag, and about eating stewed fruits. All of these things crawled through our heads.

After the tarwih we sat in a circle in the main part of the surau ready to recite the *juz* [a section of the Koran] verses, which came at the end of the Koran. Everyone was able to hear clearly, and the ones with the best voices were beaming with pride. They got a good deal of praise for it—and then, too, their sweethearts gathered farther back inside could hear them clearly.

Then the rice treats were set out in front of the people in attendance. Everyone was lined up in a big long row. Spoons were not used to eat the stewed fruit because there weren't enough of those for the more than two hundred guests. Rather it was eaten with a coconut palm spoon—that is, young coconut palm leaves cut up into short lengths. Stewed fruits, sticky rice, and porridge would all be mixed together and eaten in the same plate, and four people would use that one plate. Because there weren't enough cups either, one cup was used for two or three folks who'd take turns.

Even though a very great number of people came, there were still too many rice treats, and the old aunties who had taken care of the food gave the leftovers to us in the surau. After all the guests had gone home we ate our fill again of stewed fruit and sticky rice. We got enough, and then later, at the postmidnight meal, we ate again. Before that [late meal] we didn't really need to go to sleep since it was nearly one o'clock anyway. Some of us weren't very patient, though: at eleven o'clock those folks had already greedily attacked their postmidnight meal, and then they went right to sleep.

"I don't have to be woken up again," they'd say.

A week afterward it was the ladies' turn to graduate from tadarus. Their ceremony was almost the same as that related above, only it was even more joyful and brilliant because their clothes were extraordinarily pretty.

Then, too, their voices, when they read the Koran, were more melodious and softer than the voices of us males. Each of us paid great attention to his respective sweetheart, to her clothes, the styles she wore, to her voice, and we'd continually be trying to peek at her through the little gaps in the partition or when she would descend from the house. If she wasn't accompanied by her grandparents or her mother, we'd want to escort her home.

But that wasn't the custom in Minangkabau.

Speaking of tadarus, I recall a contest out at the big mosque in Baruh.

In my village, at that time, there were two religious strains of thought: the Traditionalists and the Modernists. Upper Sumpur was dominated by the Traditionalist group, Lower Sumpur by the Modernists; however, in Upper Sumpur there were also some Modernists, who were sympathetic toward the folks in Lower Sumpur. And during the Fasting Month they would say the tarwih prayers at the Baruh mosque, and the reverse was also true. Many of the older people in Lower Sumpur were in agreement with the conservative stream in Upper Sumpur. Usually they were close friends with Father and my uncle.

The Traditionalists were very diligent in their religious duties. They'd carry out whatever the syechs and the holy texts said to do without thinking about it, or without inspecting it first or weighing its merits. They believed in a totally reckless way, for, they'd say, in giving birth to these syechs God made them smarter than other people were and people had to simply follow the syechs' dictates. They'd do a full twenty-one repetitions when doing the tarwih and the witir, while the Modernists would just do seven. They prayed the tarwih very slowly, not fast as lightning as the Modernists did.

The Modernists wanted to use their brains a bit, but really just for seeking an easy way out in religion. Actually, they weren't searching for truth, but for an easy way to do things.

At that time the conflict between the two factions was really terrific. Wherever I'd look or listen, adults would be disputing each other over these matters, or having a falling out, getting their feelings hurt. Sometimes they'd even get into actual fights; mutual insults and mockery were now the general run of things. Wherever people would gather in groups they'd quarrel over religious matters, as if all of them were great experts. Not rarely people would break off friendships and long relationships of camaraderie because they differed over some small, difficult point of religion, which did nobody any good to quarrel over in the first place.

I myself, I didn't take sides at all. First because I was still young. I respected the Traditionalists, because I loved Father, who was their promoter. But I respected the Modernists, too, because I myself was a young soul and I knew that this newer strain would be the common position in the future.

But I didn't agree with their efforts to always find the easiest way, which they pursued out of laziness and nothing more.

Moreover, for me, this Modernist faction was actually already old-fashioned, while my own understanding of things was more progressive. If I uttered that, though, doubtless the public would think me an infidel.

I didn't agree with the Modernists when they reduced the number of repetitions in their prayers—lightening religion's obligations for sure, but using the time they gained by shortening the religious services for such things as gossiping at the coffee stall, playing dominoes or checkers, or slandering other people. In my opinion it would be better just to go pray than to do all these things. I would agree with them if they would use the time they gained from reducing the number of prayer repetitions to go hoe in their rice fields, say, or study; sure—to do something that might have a concrete outcome. I was not in agreement with the Traditionalists, who were of the opinion that religion was the most important thing in the world and that all humankind must live for religion, neglecting the world.

In this matter, then, I was neutral. I understood the position of each side and recognized the narrow-mindedness of each, and I remained friendly with both groups. I just didn't want to expend time and energy debating matters of religion. I felt this was futile. I didn't want to go looking for hostility in religious matters. I felt that somehow there was something far more important which I had to do, but at that time I still did not truly know what it was. It was still all hazy—maybe because I was still too young.

One night during this particular Fasting Month, a Koran-reading contest was held at the Baruh mosque. The ones who had the best voices and the best songs and who made the fewest mistakes would get prizes, consisting of such things as a printed, patterned sarong, a towel, a handkerchief, and so on. Our surau had three contestants, chosen as the most highly skilled among us.

With pounding hearts we set off. We were worried that the Lower Sumpur people wouldn't be fair because we were their opponents.

We prayed the tarwih at that mosque. Before saying the prayers we ate some sweets, because out in front of the mosque there was a person selling various sorts of light foods. It was a pity that I had only five cents; I was only able to buy three sorts of treats, since the best-tasting ones weren't one cent apiece but two cents. We felt the tarwih prayers were taking a really long time, maybe because we were used to doing them quick as lightning. There in the Modernists' mosque, there was a fellow who prayed as many repetitions as they did in Upper Sumpur.

After tarwih, the ones who were going to be in the contest were told to gather into a group. Six people were chosen from among those in attendance to be the jury. They were supposed to be the great reading and reciting experts. Everyone sat down with their legs crossed, except for those (the jury members) who sat on chairs facing a long table. This table had paper and pencils on it for noting down our reading mistakes. All the members of the jury thought themselves very important. They set their faces into serious expressions and settled their bodies down in their chairs, portentously, like real big shots.

Whenever it was someone's turn, he would go sit facing a Koran, which was lying on top of a pillow. The jury would listen to the reading, paying close attention to the highness or lowness of the person's voice, how long or short the sung phrases were, how many phrases were pronounced, and how the verses were droned out. Their evaluations would show in their faces.

When it was one of our friends' turn to read, one of the members of the jury would shake his head and another one would furrow his forehead. I asked myself, were they only putting on all this or pretending? Because, after all, they thought they were such big shots: shaking your head or furrowing your brow was a sure sign that you were an important person.

"We don't have much hope," a companion whispered into my ear.

"Aw, look, they're just putting on airs," I answered, beginning to figure out their motives. I was surprised. Might not the job be done better if they weren't shaking their heads and furrowing their brows so much?

Finally the contest was over. Our surau received a towel, second prize. Some of us weren't satisfied with that and suspected the Baruh folks of not playing fair—for the Upper Sumpur people were convinced that their pals had done better-sounding readings than the others and, after all, had made only two mistakes.

I just laughed. Why make such a big deal over such a small matter? That night and the next day all this was the sole topic of people's conversations in Sumpur, as if their lives depended on whether the Koran was recited rightly or wrongly! Why didn't they try to understand what the Koran actually meant, and maybe compete with each other to find its profound and hidden meanings.

Oh, humankind, still so blind! Only the outer skin of things is viewed, paid attention to, and adored!

When people weren't saying tadarus, the surau was rather quiet and deserted, because after tarwih most fellows would go over to their parent's house to go to sleep. If everyone else had gone home and if they didn't want to play dominoes or *kim*, the ones staying over in the surau would just sleep straight through till the postmidnight meal. And then after eating they'd fall asleep again.

However, the closer it got to Lebaran, the more people would sell firecrackers. This is what made things entertaining and what certainly served to liven things up a bit. Pocket money our parents gave us would be used to buy firecrackers, which we'd set off in tremendous blasts—or we'd buy oil, to set off bamboo cannons. We'd be even happier if our blasts got responses in kind from the cannons of other suraus. In that way our cannons would go off and answer each other until the postmidnight meal, or at least until our oil ran out.

Starting on the day of 20 Ramadan (to the extent we were able to, at least), we'd wait up for morning—watching for *Lailatul Kadar* night. According to the Ulamas, Kadar night would come on the odd nights between the twenty-first and the twenty-ninth: on the dates of 21, 23, 25, 27, or 29. But because we really didn't know for sure which day it would fall on—after all, had we really begun fasting on the exact, correct first day of Ramadan?—we had to get up every night, odd or even, so we wouldn't be fooled. From sunset prayertime to dawn, every few moments we'd go and check the trees to see if the leaves were bowing down or whether they were withered yet.

According to the Ulamas and our recitation teacher, on *Kadar* night, the door of the sky would open and thousands and thousands of angels would come down to earth. And all the trees would bow down to God. At that moment the whole earth would go deathly still, no dog would bark, no stream of water would flow, and everyone would get sleepy. That was what spurred us on: the fact that everyone else would be sleeping. At the moment that the trees bowed down, God would give us whatever we asked for. Whatever we happened to be holding in our hands, we could just ask that it be turned into gold or diamonds, and, why, that would happen in the wink of an eye.

During these final ten nights Bujung and I—who wanted to propose certain requests to God—isolated ourselves from our friends who weren't paying any attention to this Kadar night business and who were more interested in sleeping than keeping watch. After tarwih, the two of us stealthily climbed up into the upper story of the surau, which in Minangkabau was called the *lenggek*, the spot where people call you to prayer. We brought along an unshucked coconut, which we had wrapped in a sarong so our friends wouldn't see it. This upper story didn't have any walls, so we could see all the trees surrounding the surau. We purposely didn't bring any mats or pillows so there wouldn't be any temptation for us to go to sleep.

So that we wouldn't get tired, we took turns watching, all the while holding this coconut. If the leaves and branches on the trees all of a sudden seemed to be bowing down, the one who was awake was to wake up his companion and both of us would ask God to turn the coconut into gold. Bujung proposed that we ask that it be turned into a diamond, but I didn't agree with that because a diamond as big as a coconut would be too expensive, and we'd end up being too rich, and when other people saw the huge stone they'd get real jealous and rob us. But a lump of gold as big as a coconut could be cut up into little pieces and hidden in your pockets. Our plan was to divide this gold in two, equally, and sell it in Padang and use the money for capital to set us up in commerce, so we could get married.

Supposing that the coconut did turn to gold, a little chip of it would be used in the meantime to buy shirts, sarongs, shoes, handkerchiefs, perfume, watches, and firecrackers, which we'd use on Lebaran. All our friends would be surprised to see us dressed up in such fine clothes, but Bujung and I vowed that we would not tell anyone where we got all this wealth. Bujung and I had agreed to bury the gold temporarily, out in back of the surau, in the middle of the night. We had shaken hands on this and had vowed we would not act deceitfully when it came time to divide up the gold two ways.

Three days in succession we stayed up all night, fighting sleepiness and heavy eyelids, defying the nighttime cold. But none of the leaves ever did bow down. We ate our postmidnight meal out there in the dark, too, for if we had gone down to the lower story our buddies would have wanted to come back up with us and later on, maybe they would have wanted to join us when we were standing there under the bowed leaves.

The fourth night, there we still were, staying up all night. Even though we were exhausted and could hardly keep our heavy eyelids up, we steeled ourselves to keep awake. In the middle of the night, while I was on watch, suddenly I heard a magpie warble and then a squirrel chirp. According to the old folks, this was a sign that there was a tiger around, who would be given to coming into the villages when there was a pregnant woman there. By happenstance, one of the women over at our neighbor's house *was* pregnant just then.

I began to tremble, my body to shiver. In the dark out in back of the surau, underneath a jambak tree, a certain black form was visible. It had two shining red eyes. Even though I was high up in the upper story, which was a full ten feet above the ground, I was still scared that the tiger might be able to jump up there. I wanted to wake Bujung up, but my mind didn't have any power in it at all; my tongue stayed mute. I covered my eyes with my two hands and I dove face downward beside Bujung so the tiger wouldn't be visible anymore.

I stayed that way until I fell asleep. And when I woke up it was already light. I related the whole story to Bujung, but he didn't believe that a tiger had come into the village.

I began to get worried. Maybe the *Lailatul Kadar* had come when we were asleep last night. My hopes grew thin, especially since my eyes were real drowsy. I began to doubt that it was really true that God would want to change a coconut into a big lump of gold, a thing that surely wouldn't do two young kids any good—kids who didn't know how to handle a lot of money yet anyway. The Ulamas always said that God was wise and astute and knew just exactly what his creatures needed. These were the sort of considerations and doubts that cropped up to weaken what had once been certainties. And this was especially true when I heard that the old folks in our village had never seen this particular incident happen. Nor had they ever seen anyone's request to get rich fulfilled.

I told these doubts to Bujung, and his passion began to flag, too, since a half a night had passed when no one had been watching. Maybe the *Lailatul Kadar* had happened during that time.

Finally we abandoned all hope and didn't keep watch, right up until it was Lebaran . . .

Going on about asking God in this stupid way to make us rich, I am reminded of an experience of mine a year before this, also during the Fasting Month, when I was very much in the need of money to buy Lebaran clothes. Because I had to depend on whatever Father might happen to give me, my clothes were never good or abundant enough. Sometimes he'd just buy a jacket and a sarong but no shoes or a cap. Of course our joy was incomplete if we had a new jacket and sarong but our cap was all worn out and encrusted with dirt and our shoes (leftover from last year's Lebaran) were way too tight. We were embarrassed to wear a sad, old, worn-out cap—we preferred to let our friends see a bare head.

Pressured by such hardships, I kept turning over a copy of the "Mudjaradat" book, which was filled with hundreds of most efficacious prayers that were vouchedsafed by a number of syechs in Arabia, I was told. Inside the book I came upon a certain prayer, which, if it was read twenty thousand times, whatever you asked for, God would bring to pass.

"Now, there is a good opportunity," I thought. "I'll go ask God for some money."

After I had memorized the prayer, I hid the book so my friends wouldn't be able to know about any of this. For two days I isolated myself, sitting there all by myself up in the *lenggek*, living as an ascetic, day and night, coming down out of the building only to end the fast and to eat my postmidnight meal. I sat there cross-legged on the floor with a bottle of unboiled water in front of me.[3] This I intended to drink after saying the prayer those twenty thousand times. Maybe some extra blessing would come of that!

After I had read the prayer ten thousand times I asked God to bestow ten thousand rupiah on me for buying clothes, shoes, a bicycle, and a watch. Also with this same money I was going to go to Padang and buy a tuna fish as big as ten normal ones, which I was going to fry in a pan (but not with pepper). And I was going to savor it all by itself, without having any rice alongside. And I asked God please not to give me bills in big denominations because people would be suspicious and think that I had stolen the money. Just make it a thousand ten-rupiah bills, tied up with a string.

I began to put this request into the middle of the prayer so that while I was finishing reading the other ten thousand prayers God would be getting the ten thousand rupiah ready, which perhaps he would withdraw from a bank and which he would shower down on me from the sky (later on when I finished reading the full twenty thousand times).

After I recited the prayer the full twenty thousand times, I drank the unboiled water in the bottle, breaking the fast. And I repeated my request. And there I waited, full of hope, my heart pounding, for a parcel of cash to fall from above. But it didn't. Every moment or so I would look up to see where the money might be falling from, but it was all futile! I closed my eyelids tightly together—maybe God was shy about people seeing him when he was dropping money from the sky—but nothing could be heard falling. I made my request again, with my tears flowing down. My hopes were beginning to be dashed: it wasn't here, was it? Hadn't God heard? Impossible! Why, it wasn't just things that were uttered aloud that God knew about: He even knew what was inscribed in our hearts. Was it maybe that God didn't want to listen to a prayer that had been said in Indonesian? Maybe it should have been in Arabic? I was very concerned! All that asceticism for two whole days for nothing!

"But maybe later on, after ending the fast in a little bit, I'll just take another look," I thought. "Probably God doesn't like for people to see him. He'll be sending that money down all right."

After eating my meal I went to the upper story to see if maybe God had put the money there while I wasn't around. There in the dark I felt all over the floor, going this way and that: who knew, maybe there would be a roll of money there, but . . . there still wasn't!

My body was weak and tired, I was heartbroken and sad. I was shattered with disappointment. It appeared that I would not be wearing fine clothes on Lebaran after all, and that I would not be eating that delicious big tuna with all its layers of fine fish flesh!

"Why is God so stingy?" I thought. "What does ten thousand rupiah mean for him, who's already made the earth and the sky, the sun and the stars? I feel God has abandoned me like Jesus on the cross when he called out in complaint: 'Eli, Eli, lama sabachtani?' (God, God, why have you forsaken me?)."

Because God didn't give me any money, I didn't have a new cap for Lebaran. Also no new shoes, only leather sandals, which Father had bought me along with a jacket and a sarong. But a worn-out crummy old cap didn't exactly go with brand new clothes. I was forced to wear a white wool cap that Father usually wore when it rained. It was not only hot but also way too big; I folded it down two or three times but it still swallowed my head. All my friends were taken aback. Why in the world was I wearing a wool cap on so hot a day as that? They didn't know the burden of bitterness I was carrying, nor that the wool cap was a tragic result of a difference of opinion between God and myself about ten thousand rupiah.

Like the year before, this year too I had terrible luck. The coconut did not turn into gold! I looked at Bujung, grieving, and felt pity for him. I was already experienced at these things and could soothe myself. Oh well, it must not be our fate yet to get that gold! The Lebaran that both of us were going to celebrate so brilliantly became just a normal sort of holiday. Well, so be it! Bujung and I didn't have the strength to keep staying up all night anyway. The hope that the coconut would turn to gold was destroyed by the belief that this thing was just impossible. And so from Hindu Heaven we fell headlong all the way to the ground. It wasn't our bodies that got shattered but our hearts . . .

CHAPTER 19: LEBARAN

We rejoiced as it got closer and closer to the Fasting Month, and the same was true when Lebaran approached. Five days before the big day, villagers would be busy getting ready, buying new clothes and various and sundry sorts of foods. The marketplaces at Sumpur, Pitala, and Batu Tebal would be crowded and bustling; many people would be selling all sorts of cloth for making clothes, as well as firecrackers, cakes, and sweets. The tailors and barbers were busy, without letup (after all, everyone had to get a shave), and the same was true of the laundrymen. All the clothes had to be finished one day before Lebaran; naturally, the starch had to be a bit stiffer this one time. And even if that was a little more expensive, folks didn't mind. Package after package of firecrackers were bought, both small ones and large ones; these were safely stored away for Lebaran day.

For this Lebaran my Father bought me a cap, a jacket, trousers, and shoes. No need for dismay; my friends wouldn't show me up this time. The cap was black velvet, the jacket was white and like a goalie's jacket. The trousers were made of batik, the shoes were black with blunt-nosed tips. Mother was going to borrow a batik sarong for me and I'd have perfume squirted on me before I went to say the Lebaran prayers. Older Sister[1] was going to borrow a handkerchief for me. So: everything was complete.

Three days before it came, the joyful atmosphere of Lebaran could already be felt. People's faces were glowing; the hunger of the fast almost wasn't felt anymore. Folks whose fast had not "sprung a leak" felt very lucky. Those who had broken the fast regretted it, for that showed that they were still weak in the face of their desires and that they had been tempted by food and drink. Their hearts hadn't been strong enough to stick it out to the end, whatever all their good intentions might have been.

As for us young kids, we overflowed with merriment. Our chests felt like they would crack open. If we hadn't been a bit shy about it, we would have yelled and shouted hard all day, all along the road. We felt we wanted to grab ahold of Lebaran and pull it toward us so that it would come faster; what we really wanted was to eat during the day and wear all those fine clothes, which were still being sewn together, or were in storage. But if we set off the firecrackers right now, what could we set off later at Lebaran?

It was really strange: the last day of the fast we got extraordinarily hungry. The temptations were great but we just stuck it out whatever the case, until sunset. After all, isn't it just this one more day, we'd tell ourselves? Throughout the village residents were busy. The mothers were in the kitchen continuously. Wherever we'd go, when we'd pass by a kitchen, fragrant, delicious foods could be smelled—especially since Sumpur folks were famous for being great cooks.

Our parents told us to go clean up the house, sweep the yard and pull up the excess grass outside. Then we cleaned up the surau, all together, throwing out the spider webs. We cleaned until it was all spick-and-span and pleasant-looking. And the strings on the drumhead in the mosque were tightened so tomorrow the sound would be even more piercing.

Girls helped their mothers in the kitchen.

After finishing in the surau, each of us would go to the graves of our datuks, our grandparents, or out to our parents' graves if they had already departed this world. I went to Mother's grave and cleaned it off. I pulled up the grass that had grown there, while praying that she was happy in the hereafter. Then I went to the grave of my datuk, on the slope of the mountain. This ceremony was to show that in this happy moment we had certainly not forgotten our ancestors.

All of these tasks were done cheerfully, even though hunger gnawed at us.

That night, even though they weren't actually saying tarwih, the young guys all slept at the surau. After ending their fast, they all came over and talked animatedly about firecrackers, clothes, and the big feast tomorrow. From the start of the evening prayertime, we took turns beating the big mosque drum and setting off bamboo cannons as well as a few firecrackers. We planned on not sleeping that night; there'd be a lot of merit in that, old folks said. Our clothes were stored carefully away, perfumed with a medley of flowers; our shoes were polished as shiny as could be; our caps were brushed off, so that absolutely no dust remained on them at all. And everything was folded up very, very neatly.

Bamboo cannons were continually set off, and cannons from the other suraus answered in turn. The firecrackers started popping one after another, and all the while we'd steal a glance at our new clothes every moment or so. We had an extremely strong desire to put them on right now. Ah, daybreak took so long in coming! That whole night our eyes weren't drowsy at all and our brains grew feverish with high hopes for the next day, which would surely be glorious and brilliant. Our hearts pounded like the mosque drum that was being beaten incessantly.

Everyone rejoiced, perfectly blissful. All had smiling faces: the old folks, the middle-aged people, the youths, and the little kids. Their chests swelled with joy. No one remained sullen or bore a grudge. People who had hated each other all this time, who hadn't been talking to each other, damped down the fires of hostility on this one night and started to chat comfortably—in fact, they were much friendlier than they were normally, and they laughed all the time. Everyone was garrulous and wanted to chat—and any and everything became the subject of gossip. Agus, whose character it was to be a taciturn person, who rarely laughed, and who was always sitting there pondering things morosely, on this night would converse at great length. He'd take a turn at beating the big mosque drum and laugh heartily with all of us. But admittedly, his mouth would look sort of awkward laughing! This night everybody was really hassling and annoying each other, but nobody got angry, nor did anyone get their feelings hurt. A blanket of good cheer protected all.

Really early, at five o'clock, about half of us went out to bathe and work lime juice through our hair, while the others beat the drum and set off firecrackers. These burst noisily in the morning air, normally so quiet. Both men and women villagers came to the surau in ever greater numbers to bathe and shampoo with lime, and to pray and to say the takbir. Peals of merry laughter boomed out in waves from the surau's water tub. And when you listened to folks reading the takbir all together, the Lebaran atmosphere truly cloaked the village.

The sun appeared and half the fellows spread out mats for folks to do the Lebaran prayers on later, while the other half set off firecrackers and beat the drum nonstop. Mother fixed banana treats, a kind of sweet which every house would normally have for Lebaran. It was made of king bananas and rice flour densely packed together, made into little balls like the full moon, and fried—but not really cooked all the way through. You have to leave a little undercooked part down deep inside.

The day got sunnier, hearts got merrier, the golden rays of the sun scattered outward from the peak of Mount Galogandang and lit up Sumpur village. Little by little a great many people came into the surau. All of them wore new clothes of various colors—to cheer themselves up. My friends and I got all decked out too. We had been restrained for five days from putting on these new clothes but this craving was finally satisfied. However, I couldn't wear the batik trousers yet because we had to go pray first. After we got all neatly decked out, Mother sprinkled us with perfume; when I borrowed a handkerchief from my older sister, my joy burst its bounds. Every moment or so each would look at his own shirt and then at those of his friends. With his inner voice, each praised his own clothes and his own appearance when he glanced in the looking glass. Our caps were set at an angle; they looked even more attractive. Then, once we went down the steps into the courtyard, we'd set off firecrackers with the other guys, and beat the big mosque drum. Meanwhile, the women would come in by the dozens and dozens carrying trays on their heads, filled with cooked rice and all sorts of side dishes.

Girls in lovely clothes would also come to pray, but before they'd go up in the surau they would flirt with their eyes with us—this bit of enjoyment added to Lebaran's splendor and happiness. They'd come with their mothers, acting shy. They'd glance out of the sides of their eyes while casting faint, knowing smiles at us. We didn't converse; that would seem peculiar according to adat! My sweetheart was among them; that was the most important thing. I asked myself, would she be attracted to my fine clothes here? Well, I sure had been dashing and fine-looking there in the looking glass just a while ago! Would her heart pound to see me looking so stylish this day, as I had been so deeply moved to see her own splendor and loveliness? . . .

She went up into the surau . . . . I had no reason to stay below in the courtyard now. I also went up, thinking I would join in the takbir. There were already lots of men sitting there lined up in columns. Haji pilgrims were there in Arabic dress, wearing big turbans and fine robes of various colors, like martyrs who just arrived from Mecca. Of all of them, Father's turban was the biggest.

Everyone prayed, some fiercely and some submissively, trying to be deeply engrossed despite the fact that their thoughts were actually always on the food sitting in its trays, lined up in rows out back along the wall. After the prayers, Father read the sermon, and when he came down from the pulpit, everyone rushed up to shake his hand. This was because according to the beliefs of Muslims, whoever is the first to shake the hand of the one who delivers the sermon when he comes down from the pulpit on Lebaran is doing the very same thing as shaking the hand of the Prophet Muhammad himself. I joined in too, and shook his hand and asked forgiveness for all my wrongdoings. But I came right at the end of the line. Father also asked me to forgive him because he'd beaten me. Tears flowed down my cheeks.

The surau resounded with the clamor of people greeting each other with handshakes and asking each other's forgiveness, everyone rejoicing. All slights were sincerely forgotten and all who had been enemies made peace on that glorious day. Each and every person was as pure as an angel on that day: all were good, patient, sincere, and the sort who loved each and every creature of God. On that day people who usually criticize folks and ridicule and slander others were really good-hearted; they'd laugh ceaselessly and only say good things. No sharp or biting comments could be heard.

After all the mutual greeting and handshaking was over, those in attendance sat down facing each other and the delicious food was laid out. They all feasted; everyone got full. A moment had been spent as angels, but once they saw all these various foods, people's greed came fiercely to the fore. Their eyes were like those of cats seeing a mouse pass by. A haji pilgrim, I saw, greedily stuffed two chunks of spiced meat at once into his mouth. He asked for some roast chicken that was lying on my own tray, a full meter away from his seat, and it was flung onto his plate from that distance.

The Traditionalists still kept the custom of eating a meal in the surau after Lebaran prayers. According to their teachers' dictates, good Muslims must put on a big meal that day. The women of Upper Sumpur felt that providing a meal for folks after they'd finished praying afforded them an extra measure of religious merit; they thought it was just the same as inviting people over to their own house to eat. The Modernists in Lower Sumpur had abandoned this custom. They'd just invite several close friends over to their house to eat.

To add to Lebaran's splendor, before all the guests left for home a performance of fencing and the martial arts was held in the surau courtyard. Every single person who was skilled at fencing was asked to step forward into the center. For us young guys who had had the requisite training, this was a great opportunity to show off our skills, our loveliest hand and feet movements, and the rhythm and high standards of all the martial arts strides. All was done in strict accordance with the guidelines of the art form. We wore our new batik trousers for this performance. Our sweethearts watched from the windows, whispering to one another. What exactly were they whispering?

When the martial arts performance broke up, we put on our new shoes, which were still tight. Their leather was still fragrant. We put on quite a cocky show walking around. We felt that everyone was sneaking a peek at our shoes and admiring them. Our pride increased when we heard the shoes' clickety-clack noises on the ground. We ourselves would often look down, admiring our footwear and watching that we didn't stub our toes on a rock. It would be such a pity if our shoe tips got scratched the least little bit!

I got a rupiah in pocket money from Father. Now that was really a lot for us. But what was distressing was that rich people's kids got five rupiah.

We went over to Seberang on a pleasure trip, taking pony carts both ways from Seberang to Tjintuk around the edge of the lake. This was a distance of two kilometers. This was the ultimate pleasure trip for us.

The pony carts (which were all owned by Malalo people) were all old and always squeaked as they rolled along. And if one of them ran over a big rock, the cart felt like it was going to split into pieces. Our bodies hurt from being bumped from one side to the other, but that didn't lessen our merriment or our pride in the whole endeavor. After all, this was the one sort of vehicle we could afford to hire, by all chipping in together. At that time only rich folks would hire autos, and even they couldn't afford to buy one.

We all smoked cigars that had little paper rings on them. Father would give us these only on Lebaran and we'd use the fire at the ends of the cigars to set off our firecrackers, which we'd toss at passersby. We kind of looked down on people who walked on foot—and we'd especially look down on their crummy clothes. This category of people were not sporting any new clothes.

When we happened to come across a person who was wearing crummy clothes and a crummy sort of sarong, we'd look at one another and ridicule him. We'd curl our lips downward and hunch our shoulders up, as if we'd seen something loathsome. After seeing such a person, we'd automatically look at our own clothes, to admire them, and if there was any dust on them, we'd flick it off and be very, very careful that the ironed pleats didn't get messed up.

In Tjintuk, folks were already milling about in large numbers. Some were bathing in the lake, others were just watching. Lots of young guys and girls from Malalo were strolling around. Every one of them, without exception, wore dark glasses.

"Do they have some sort of eye disease?" I asked our pony cart coachman. "No, it's just something to make them look smarter," he responded. "In town in Malalo nowadays almost everyone wears dark glasses—young men, girls, grandfathers, oldsters, and little kids. It's become a Lebaran custom over there. Right before Lebaran dark glasses are the thing that sells the most at the market. Just look, tomorrow is going to be the busiest time over there because it just so happens that tomorrow is marketday."

Indeed it was so! When I went there, almost everyone was wearing dark glasses. And not just that, hundreds of people were wearing tin watches (these normally were just children's toys and had their numbers and hands stamped onto tin of various colors; these watches showed just one time, which never varied).

The cost of the pony cart from Sebarang to Tjintuk was just five cents, and the round trip was ten cents. We were able to take several rides that way and eat *gado-gado* [vegetable salad with peanut sauce] and drink sweetened coconut milk and eat other kinds of sweets in Tjintuk and Sebarang.

The rich kids ate as many as three platefuls of *gado-gado*, but this was a contest that we weren't able to participate in.

More than twenty pony carts went back and forth between Tjintuk and Sebarang carrying hundreds of kids. When the carts would cross each other's paths the kids would all cheer and throw firecrackers at one another.

Having gotten enough of pleasure trips, enjoying ourselves immensely (but also having run out of pocket money), we went on home, with the sun inclining toward the west. Our feet hurt and were all blistered from the new shoes, but we were embarrassed to take them off and carry them along in our hands. The pain was unbearable, but we just kept toughing it out. Some of us, though weren't embarrassed to take our shoes off, because their wounds hurt too much when they kept them on. It's better to be embarrassed than to hurt, they said. For the other half of us, it was better to hurt than to be embarrassed.

Once we got back to our respective houses, our feet were all wounded and our heels were blistered and peeling; we didn't wear our shoes anymore at all. We were tired, our eyes were sleepy. Before falling asleep I heard a boy (who was only eight years old and was standing at the top of the surau stairs) say to a friend of his of the same age, who was passing by in the yard:

"Hey, Amir, who has the best-looking clothes, you or me?"

His pal didn't answer. But, I don't know the reason, it was *my* heart that was stabbed in pain. This child had let a feeling slip out that most adults keep carefully hidden inside them: a feeling that you're secretly comparing other people's clothes to your own. The boy's shirt wasn't very nice; it was just made of rough cotton, but he felt that it was really first-rate, so much so that he started to challenge his buddy about whose clothes were best.

I was embarrassed, embarrassed for myself. It was as though this boy had held up a mirror to me, one which showed everything going on down in the dark hollows and curves in my deepest inner self, feelings that were obscured from view or which I myself had hidden away. True enough, I myself had never uttered such words—I was never as crazy as all that—but still, hadn't a voice of pride whispered away in my heart (which others didn't hear, but which I certainly did) that my shirt was better looking than my friends' shirts were? And didn't we secretly feel more fortunate than others? And when we were about to go to sleep weren't we still smiling and reminiscing about that little bit of happiness? . . .

That night the surau felt really quiet and lonely. It was very moving. For a whole month it had been crowded and busy with men and women praying and with young guys and girls doing tadarus; now only four people had come over there, and they were really old, to boot. The surau was lit by an oil lamp, a weak one. How very lonely it was! All the folks who had crowded in there earlier, making it so busy and fun, were all back at their own houses, sleeping. After all that overflowing good cheer and all the festivities of Lebaran, I felt that I had entered a desolate ravine, which was all dark inside and which made me melancholy.

This loneliness and desolation was very deep and left a strong impression in my heart. Could I perhaps go pay a visit to a friend of mine to forget all this, and to distance myself from the quietness and isolation? But this friend had gone back to his own house with his mother, his brother, and his grandparent. Well, maybe I could just go some other place, perhaps to the food stall: wouldn't there be folks gathered there? No, there weren't! The whole village was quiet, lonely, and dark, as if all the residents had just died from a plague. So where could I go?

This shift from great festiveness to a state of loneliness and quiet had been very fast, and it stabbed my emotions. In consequence I became confused and sad. After every Lebaran I experienced this loneliness. I almost started crying to see Father serving as imam; he was saying the sunset prayers with no more than two men following along, plus two gloomy-faced old grandpas. And the surau was all quiet, even though that morning there had been dozens of cheery-faced people here. Caught up in this sadness and loneliness, I fell asleep by myself in the surau.

The next afternoon, folks held a boat race in Batu Beragung. It was called a "pacu biduk" in the Minangkabau dialect. Hundreds of people came to watch. They lined up all along the edge of the lake, or sat with their legs dangling down on the big rocks. They came from all directions in Sumpur. Parents also let their girls come watch, and among them was my sweetheart, Jusna.

Along the edge of the lake there were thirty small craft that were going to join in the race. A friend of mine and I were going to compete. We were fully aware that we weren't going to win, because we weren't really very skilled at rowing boats, but we competed anyway to make it all more festive and to attract some public attention to ourselves. If we competed, we figured, the girls would respect us more than if we didn't join in. At the very least we would become a topic of conversation for them. Surely their thin, red, pretty lips would speak our names numerous times—and our names would come out of their mouths right along with their sweet breaths.

We had competed three times and hadn't won a thing. Unfortunately everyone's attention had been focused on the winner. Only he gained esteem and admiration. Even Jusna's eyes were on him. So, what to do? The fourth time I totally lost hope and turned my little boat back and suddenly the two of us fell right into the lake and got soaking wet! Everyone cheered and shouted; there was a tremendous clamor that sounded as if it would never die down. The attention of the hundreds of audience members was no longer on the winner, but on us. Our faces reddened a bit from embarrassment, but the payoff was becoming the center of attention.

When I got to the edge of the lake, Jusna came up close to me, smiling, and the glow of her soft eyes reflected love.

"Why did you flip over? Had Uda [Older Kinsman] gotten dizzy?" she asked in a soft voice.

"Yeah," I answered, and my heart swelled out as if it were going to explode with happiness. There was no telling what I might have said at that moment.

"Go home quick and change your clothes so Uda won't get sick," said Jusna, with an even more enticing smile.

I went home, chilled, walking along for two miles—but happy. If that incident had not happened, there would hardly have been the chance to converse like this with Jusna.

CHAPTER 20: A TRIP TO SULIT AIR

Lots of Father's pupils had come from Tandjung Alai and Sulit Air. For years they had taken recitation lessons, studied fencing, the black arts, and so on from Dad. The ones who had completed their lessons would go back home to their villages and then they would always be replaced by new ones. And that was the way it would go, on and on.

One time they invited both Father and me to come visit their village because they were going to have a huge celebration there.

At that time it had become an adat custom in Sulit Air for the people who had emigrated to the rantau all throughout Sumatra to come back home for the Fasting Month. All the money they had saved in little increments during the other eleven months they'd squander all at once during the fast. They would blow it all—they'd buy beautiful clothes, new shoes, dark glasses as well as regular eyeglasses, and boxes of firecrackers. They'd go make money in other lands and safe it, to throw it all away during the Fasting Month, back in the home village.

This had long since become quite the custom. Whoever didn't want to join in (that is, whoever didn't want to put on royal airs during that set, determined time) would be deemed poor—someone who hadn't had any luck at all in his commercial endeavors or in his job. And folks who didn't come home to the village for the Fasting Month would become the subject of rumors among the Sulit Air public: folks would say that they were just wandering around in the rantau, afraid to come home. The people called this great waste of money "badunie," that is, having yourself a great time, enjoying the various amusements, and competing with one another to show off your worldly wealth.

For Sulit Air folks this operated as a strong pressure to work hard to make money. So it's no surprise they were very thrifty. In fact, some over-stepped the boundaries of this. Lots of them economized on food, not eating meat, fish, or eggs all during those eleven months. They'd just eat vegetables, salty side dishes, and hot red pepper sauce atop their rice—just so long as the money saved could be used to buy boxes and boxes of firecrackers, which would go bursting off in the houseyards back in the village, later on.

Three days after Lebaran, Father and I got on a train to Singkarak. When we got there, the pony cart of the village headman of Tandjung Alai was already waiting for us. He had ordered it to come meet us. From Singkarak, the road kept going upward for a distance of about six kilometers. All during this trip, the coachman kept telling us about how tremendous the celebration would be that night, out in Tandjung Alai. I was all agog to sit there and listen to him, for all of this was still new to me. In Sumpur we sure didn't have customs like this. Father just kept quiet; he had already seen many celebrations like this. He was pleased to see me all amazed like this, for that was a sign to him that what I would be seeing later on would very much attract me.

"You go on off and take a look for yourself. Dad has lots of other business to attend to," he said.

On one incline up a hill, I noticed that the horse was having a very hard time pulling our cart. I got down so his load would be lighter.

"Why did you get down?" asked Dad.

"My legs are stiff from sitting so long; I wanted to stretch my arms and legs a bit by walking."

Father smiled. He knew that I pitied the horse.

The village headman and over thirty of Father's students and former students were waiting in Tandjung Alai. After greetings all around and handshakes and everyone asking each other's pardon in the usual Lebaran way, we were taken off to the village headman's house. There we were offered food and drink.

Then we talked comfortably about doing recitations, and about fencing and the black arts. In this conversation one of them asked Father whether or not he had passed on all his knowledge to me yet.

"Later on, in future days, surely Ridjal will replace you to become our teacher—isn't that so, Honorable Sir?" asked Haji Saleh, the village headman's son-in-law.

"This is indeed my own aim, but Ridjal thinks otherwise. Kids are difficult these days. They don't like to do what their parents want. He wants to become a train engineer," Father said with a smile.

"A train engineer? Ah, but surely it is impossible that Ridjal would want to be shiny black, like a lump of coal! Isn't it better that he become our teacher, to guide us in our recitations?"

I only laughed and didn't answer because that's what the older folks had told me I should do. You weren't allowed—it wasn't polite—to talk back and speak strongly in the midst of a gathering of adults. The whole group of them agreed with Haji Saleh, and they all nodded their heads.

I was just plain surprised: who had told Father that I wanted to become a train engineer? I had never told him these aspirations. What he had said was actually true.

I *had* wanted to be a train engineer from when I was little. The game I liked best of all was pushing a row of matchboxes or benches along, like a train. I was fond of seeing those big, black, strong locomotives. If I didn't see a locomotive in any two days, my life would be empty. I didn't have any entertainment; sometimes I would even get sick. Seeing a locomotive pushing along dozens of train cars full of coal, while the smokestack exhaled billows of smoke like folks panting from the exertion of carrying a load of rice on their shoulders—that, for me, was a wonderful, wonderful sort of entertainment. I found the locomotive a very congenial thing, especially the sixteen-wheeler, which pulled the train from Solok to Sawah Lunto. One time I had the great good fortune and pleasure to be pulled by this big locomotive when I went to Silungkang with Father. If one of these big locomotives happened to stop at the station in my village, I'd always keep looking and looking at it until it left again. I'd even forget to eat.

I wanted to become an engineer so that every day I would get to pull a long, long train and would get to associate closely with that big, dashing, black, strong friend of mine.

At three o'clock in the afternoon, we could hear the dozens of drums, *rebab*s [two-stringed instruments], flutes, clarinets, and crash-banging firecrackers. These were all accompanied by the voices of the shouting, cheering crowd.

"The procession is about to begin," said Haji Saleh.

Father gave me permission to go look, escorted by one of his students who would accompany me and who'd provide explanations.

We went over to a certain house in whose yard had gathered those who were going to be in the procession. The ones up in the house were all getting decked out in their finery; they were putting on powder and making up their eyebrows and lips. Ten of them were dressed in women's clothes. These men had wrapped their head coverings (which women let just hang loose) very tightly around their heads, so that their short hair wouldn't be visible. There was a boy who looked like a girl. I was surprised, for in my village we didn't have any such thing.

Tonight the village faction was going to have a competition with the mountain faction, they said. The Tandjung Alai houses that were gathered there on a flat area were named "The Village." The ones spread out over the slopes of the mountain were named "The Mountain." These two factions of residents were going to have a contest over who was the most extravagant. The villagers averred that they would be the ones to win. They had boxes and boxes of firecrackers, and many of their games were really odd and peculiar (and so consequently, most attractive). Their clothes were also very beautiful as well as varying greatly in style, they said.

I just stood there and listened, not understanding a single thing.

After everybody got all decorated and turned out, they lined up in rows, and headed toward a field located between the mountain and the village. Only two hundred people had come; the other formation had not yet arrived. The ones who were all decked out so finely were wearing eyeglasses, some with clear glass while some wore dark glasses; some just wore the frames. And then some of them were wearing masks as well.

The firecrackers hadn't been set off yet, because they were being kept in readiness for nightfall, later on.

I accompanied them from the side and attended to their every movement. I was very attracted by all of this, even though I couldn't experience its full joy like they could.

Lots of people were out in the field from the village faction and the mountain faction, but their smaller divisions within each faction were kept separate. In one formation the mountain people were dressed as soldiers, and in another formation the village people were dressed up as sailors. Mountain people were dressed as Arab soldiers and had big headdresses on in another formation, while the ones standing just opposite them were the boys dressed as girls, mentioned earlier. A great deal of money had been expended to buy these clothes. The mountain divisions were being taught how to line up in rows by one of their leaders, a former soldier. They looked smart and stylish, like genuine soldiers, but their posture and movements were stiff and clumsy.

I went over to stand in the midst of the mountain faction. I had been invited over there by one of Father's students whose house was in the mountains. He said the mountain faction would surely win. They had a very great number of firecrackers all stored up in readiness, he said. There were even several mountain people who had sold their water buffaloes to buy firecrackers. And he asked me not to talk about any of this to the village faction.

These two factions appeared to be jealous of each other, and they didn't want to mingle during the contest. The village faction stealthfully glanced over at the mountain assembly, noting what advantages they enjoyed, what deficiencies they suffered, and what their odd, special, quirky performances might be. And the reverse was also true. The drums were beaten noisily and flutes and trumpets answered each other in turn, all played under the direction of the clear voice of a commander.

At sunset, they went home to pray. Later on, at nine o'clock, they'd be reconvening in the courtyard out in front of the Adat Hall in the village.

Before nine o'clock it was very, very crowded and busy in the village. People came from all around. Dozens and dozens of torches lit up the extremely dark roadways. All the village's factions were ready; and they waited for their opponents, they headed out of the village in procession.

Everyone (the men, the women, and little kids) wore clothes of various styles and colors. The prettiest clothes they had in storage came out this night. The prettiest jewelry and ornaments got displayed, too, especially by the women. They shone brightly with diamonds on their chests, fingers and ears. If a woman happened to have five or six rings, she'd wear them all. If she had three necklaces, she'd put every one of them on. At that time there weren. t any thieves. The village women and also those from the mountain were going to have a real contest over clothes, jewelry, and appearance. Too bad none of the women were very good looking, except for the village headman's daughter. My eyes were always fixed on her.

The mountain faction could be heard shouting and cheering from far off, from the time they started to descend to the time they got near the hall. The village procession turned back so they would encounter their opponents in front of the hall. The meeting was something to behold—a really gratifying sight. Those hundreds of torches were like a huge *Naga* serpent [a mythical dragon-snake] whose back was all alight with fire. The two sides yelled and cheered as loudly as they could.

Firecrackers were set off, big and little ones, who knows how many hundreds of strings of them. They were tossed up into the air with ear-splitting bangs. All the drums were also struck as hard as possible and the two-stringed *rabab* violins were scraped as hard as they could be. The flutes were blown as fervently as possible—in short, everything had to ascend the highest peak. All those hundreds of people cried out as one:

"Here come the opponents! The enemies have arrived! Here come the opponents! The enemies have arrived!"

The village faction ridiculed the mountain faction and vice versa. The village faction thronged in along the right side of the road while the mountain faction came in along the left side. In between these quarreling parade lines the road was empty for about a cubit; people weren't allowed to be in there except for the village headmen and the cops, who kept the peace.

The village faction continued straight on to the edge of the village on the east side while the mountain faction went on to the western edge. Then the two of them turned back and met in front of the hall. The entry of the two sides were kept orderly by the village headmen and the cops, so that the parade lines wouldn't crash into each other and start fighting. The open field in front of the hall was divided in two; one half was for the mountain faction and the other half was for the village faction. The border was a gravel path leading from the main road to the steps of the hall. The village headmen was standing there on the gravel path. In his capacity as headman, he wasn't allowed to venture into the area of one side or the other, because maybe then he could be accused of favoring one over the other.

The village people all watched their faction, and the mountain people did the same. Then they fought with lots of games; these involved lots of firecrackers and weird oddities. All the fervent shouts heated up the blood of each side. The longer it went on the more heated it all got.

A leader of the men dressed as women strode forth into the center, clasping an atlas. This happened to be the one book they had in that village, beyond the Koran. He said he was a Resident [a high official] from the country of Who-Knows-Where. He had not neglected to sport his dark glasses there in the gloom of night. He went to sit down as if to sit on a chair, but because there wasn't any chair he squatted down like a dog about to defecate—all the while opening his atlas and reading it as if he were reading out important acts and ordinances. He called in his faithful adherents, one by one, to mete out punishments to them. The leader who was reading this atlas was actually illiterate in the Latin letters. The only ones he knew were the Arab letters he had studied in the surau.

I found this really funny and I just laughed and laughed inside. When about half of the onlookers asked me what I thought about it, I'd always say that I liked it a lot and that in my village we didn't have anything like it.

I did this because earlier, in the train, Father had advised me that whatever I happened to see (even if I didn't agree with it inside) I must not come right out and condemn it. And especially (he said), don't get overheard saying such things by the villagers, while we were their guests. If we say frankly what our opinions are they'll feel hurt and will lose all respect for us (in their opinion, after all, we are personages of very high character). If anyone happens to ask, just say you like it, Father said.

All the time I was in the village I followed Father's advice. Because of that, all the time I was there the village people were quite content with me. Actually the oddities really *were* appealing, so I wasn't lying.

The martial arts demonstration, the fencing, the *randai* performances, the plate dances, the Sempaya songs, and Entjik Siti songs were all things that I could understand. But there were lots of other games that emerged from the brains of these mountain people which I didn't understand at all. Probably I was too young to understand them. The longer it went on, the more boisterous and heated it all got. When lots of folks switched over to look at the mountain people's games, they said the villagers would lose. But the reverse was true too. Firecrackers were set alight constantly, boxes and boxes of them.

By one o'clock at night I was very drowsy and I went off to go to sleep. The games continued on, energetically, till five o'clock in the morning.

When I woke up, I heard that the mountain faction had won: they had had more firecrackers. By four o'clock the village faction had run out of them; they hadn't had any stockpiles.

The firecrackers of the mountain people kept going off and thundering away till morning. In fact, they were still hauling new ones in from the mountain. Even though they were still grousing about it, in their hearts the village faction had already acknowledged their defeat. Many of the mountain people had emigrated to the rantau. They had a lot of money and livestock that they'd sell off in great numbers to buy their firecrackers with.

All day long the Tandjung Alai people gossiped heartily about the festivities of the night before; such talk never left their lips. The mountain people were cheerier. A few of their young guys invited me to go sightseeing with them up into the mountains, so we could also (they said) get to eat sticky rice cooked in bamboo tubes, sugared rice chips served with buffalo milk curd, *penyaram* [some kind of snack], bananas, *dodol* [a taffy made of sticky rice, coconut milk, and palm sugar], and a bunch of other delicacies they mentioned. I accepted their invitation and off we went, up mountains and down, dropping in on the houses of each one of these guys. Each home was located far from the next. And that was the first time that I got to drink cow's milk that had been squeezed right before my eyes. And bee's honey.

I was brought to Ngalau, a cave inside a long, large rock face. The rock was shaped like a ship that had run aground on the slopes of the mountain. According to their story, the stone mountain had once been a ship, owned by a child who had rebelled against his mother. It was exactly like the story of Malim Kundang.[1] Seeing the shape of that rock (which really was like a ship), I almost believed this story too. This was especially true since there were lots of things normally found on ships there. But they had all turned to stone. Some of them were like folded cloth, some were like boxes, and some were like sailors who were sitting there musing quietly. And their small rooms were there too.

I went into the cave. Its ceiling was absolutely black from thousands of tiny bats that hung there, squeaking noisily and fluttering back and forth in the dark cave. I wanted to keep going down into it but the guide prevented me. He was afraid there might be snakes inside.

The inhabitants of Tandjung Alai really believed that that rock had once been a ship.

We climbed up a certain mountain, from whose peak we could see all of Lake Singkarak. It was lying there like a big lens, with the mountains all around, looking like a big eyeglasses frame, painted in several colors. To

its south were the rice paddy flatlands from Singkarak all the way to Solok.
And in the middle of it a train was crawling through, like a snake.

The next day I went to Sulit Air. This village was located at the foot of
Mount Papan, and it was one of the very largest villages in Minangkabau,
with a great many houses and inhabitants. Its houses numbered in the
hundreds. They were all closely pressed together on the slopes of two
mountains, between which flowed a tributary. They didn't have any rice
paddy land, their garden lands weren't very fertile, and water was scarce—
consequently it had been named Sulit Air [Scarce water]. Rice had to be
imported from Singkarak and Talawi. Because of this, many, many of the
inhabitants had emigrated to the rantau.

One of these many houses was as much as one hundred meters long,
four times the size of a normal Great House in Minangkabau. We could
even play ball in the front hall. It had hundreds of occupants and four
stairways. When I visited there, this longhouse had been divided in two.
This constituted Sulit Air's only oddity.

We looked around until nightfall. This place was more sensational and
fine than Tandjung Alai. That afternoon they also held a soccer match.
The number of firecrackers they lit at night was incalculable. Their fireworks stockpiles, accumulated carefully over eleven months, all became
smoke and ash. But they liked to revel in the sound of all of them going
off. The clothes, jewelry, and games were five times more numerous and
sensational than the ones in Tandjung Alai. They really and truly were simply throwing away money, burning it. No matter, they'd say. Later on we'll
just go out and get some more.

CHAPTER 21: STUDYING BLACK MAGIC

Black magic is an instrumentality for seeking revenge, or for putting a love
spell on someone. People who aren't shy will just come right out and have
a fight with each other when they seek revenge. They'll just want to beat
their opponents up or challenge them to an outright fight, or murder them
with a sharp weapon.

But Minangkabau people rarely used such forthright, inelegant means.
Fighting brings embarrassment and lowers people's respect for a person.
The feeling of shame and embarrassment is very strong among the Minangkabau. They cannot bear another person's contempt for them; to violate
public opinion is a very discordant and awkward sort of thing.

Because of this, many of them use a subtler way; that is, they use black
magic. They go on off to a skilled *dukun*,[1] and provide him with a big bribe.
The dukun will put a spell on the victim, deep in the night. That night, or
perhaps the next day, the one who's been bewitched will fall sick or go
crazy.

Besides this, there are spells for making people fall in love with you. In Minangkabau most men have more than one wife, so the wives are always competing with one another to ensnare the man's fancy and to control his love. But Minangkabau women (if they're not all that adept at taking a man's fancy because they are not such great housekeepers or cooks, or they don't watch their figures) oftentimes will just employ subtle means to accomplish their task. That is, they'll use love spells. A woman will go to a dukun and ask for a potion for the husband to drink so that he falls in love with just her and no one else. The potion is usually a "chanted-diarrhea" spell. That is, a very, very filthy sort of potion.

A great many men who drink these potions do indeed fall sick or at least their bodies feel ill. They cough and feel tired at intervals. In the long run, usually such a man will begin to act quite desperate and distraught, and he won't want to live anymore. He won't want to work and he'll just hang around his wife's house, musing and pondering morosely; he also won't be raking in much profit from his trade, as had been his custom beforehand. In truth, the woman will come out the loser to have a husband who's acting retarded like that.

Moreover, not rarely the husband will grow afraid of his wife. Whatever his wife orders him to do, he'll just do it. If he's told to go sweep the floor, or wash the kids' clothes, or go over to the shop and buy some oil, well, he'll just do it. A man who had once been a wealthy heir, full of life and highly skilled at commerce, has now become his wife's retarded servant boy. Every day his wife will keep abusing him while his parents-in-law and his brothers-in-law ridicule him slyly.

I've already related that Father knew a great deal of esoteric lore and that I was his only son. He very much wanted to pass his knowledge on to me, so that his knowledge would become a precious heirloom, passed on to his child, and then from his child to his grandchildren. Even though many people might come to him and study his esoteric lore, Father didn't want to give them all of it. He laid the most important parts aside for his child.

But he really regretted that I never asked him to teach this lore to me and that I paid very little attention to it. At that time I believed only in the demonstrated laws of nature, the ones which strongly influenced the lives of humankind. And I was a free-thinking sort, as was normal for young kids at their first time up at bat. Magical and mystical knowledge weren't attractive to me. In fact, I considered them superstitions. My faith in my own self was very much at its apogee.

Father was always trying to cajole me so that I'd ask to be taught all this stuff. Sometimes he'd tell some close grown-up friend of mine to advise me so that I'd want to learn the lore and so that I would take it upon myself to ask to be instructed.

Finally Father himself gave me some advice: "Look, even if you're not going to actually use this knowledge, there is nothing wrong with just keeping it in readiness. It's like carrying along a blanket: if you don't need it, you don't have to use it, but if you happen to feel chilly, say, then use it. You don't have to attack other people with this knowledge—and that's not even allowed, after all—but it's just for defending yourself later on. Here in this world, Father's experiences have shown that not everyone loves us; half of them hate us even if we've never done anything foul to them. They want to bring misfortune to us. And it's as preparation for confronting just these sorts of people that we must have something in readiness to defend ourselves."

"But Father, I don't go around looking for hostilities in this world," I answered. "I'm a peaceful sort. If people want to bring misfortune on me when I haven't done anything wrong, well, that's just up to them; I'm not going to render myself invulnerable so that I can endure attacks. If I'm in the wrong, well, what I suffer I shall just view as my fit punishment. And supposing that I die: well, I'm agreeable enough to leaving this world behind. And, after all, God himself has protected our bodies from all sort of outside attacks. Moreover, I'm worried that if I acquire all this esoteric lore I'll get cocky and arrogant and take to going around attacking people, just like I did when I first learned how to fence."

"Well, Father cannot agree with your position. You're still young. You haven't had much experience associating with people in society and you haven't felt much of life's bitterness yet. Father knows that in later days, when you've gotten a bit older, your position will change. You will regret this later, if you don't learn it now, just as Father regrets the fact that he didn't follow the advice of your datuk. You are going to lament: Why didn't I follow Father's advice? When you encounter dangers or hardships, that is.

"And then, too, even if you are skilled at fencing and the martial arts, these skills are not enough to fully ensure your safety. A person who can't bring you down with martial arts kicks will use magic formulas and put spells on you. Even though his foot may not make contact with your belly, he'll still leave an impression on your body with his witchcraft. So listen, just study it, please. Even if you have no intention of using it. Father, who loves you, doesn't want you to have deep regrets later on."

Because I loved Father, my only intimate friend in the world since Mother had died, I didn't have the heart to make him sad. So to make him happy I explained to him that I did want to study the lore and was ready to begin.

He was very glad. He made me vow that I would not use this knowledge for evil ends.

In addition to studying the techniques of fencing and the martial arts in more depth than before (things he had never taught other people), I also studied several magic formulas. There were formulas to heal the sick; formulas for self-defense; love-spell formulas so that women will fall in love with us; hate formulas so that some certain woman will hate some certain man; formulas to give a bellyache to someone who has humiliated us; a formula directed at a newlywed who's going to run off and marry our own sweetheart so that he's always gassy and needs to pee; a formula that will ensure that the rice being cooked at the wedding of our sweetheart will not get done no matter how many dozens of bundles of firewood might have been stuffed into the fireplace—and still more formulas after that.

Well, within three months I had acquired quite a large store of knowledge. Father was happy, but I had my doubts. Was all this stuff really going to work in practice? I didn't know if I'd have to do something first to make all this lore work. Or would I just have to wait for someone to attack me?

At that time, by happenstance, I had fallen in love with a young woman whose husband had been away for a year, as he had emigrated to Medan. She was plump and pretty, with a cute bosom and a big rear end. All this made me desire her, especially when I could see her shapely figure beneath her clothes as they clung to her body. She often smiled sweetly at me. So wasn't this a sign that she wanted to be with me?

One night in the moonlight, during the Fasting Month, she was walking home all by herself from the surau. I followed her from behind.

"May I escort you home?" I asked with a quaking voice—you know how it is, I was just a young unmarried kid.

She smiled in understanding. My body trembled, going hot and cold.

It was lucky we didn't encounter anyone along the way. But if there had been anyone, folks would not have been suspicious anyway. They would have thought it was just an older sister with her younger brother. All along the way I admired the shape of her lovely body, which would go under the shadows of the trees for a moment and then would come out into a clearing. My heart pounded, desiring her all the more. Suddenly, I grabbed hold of her hand and my right hand embraced her slender waist. My hand trembled all the more to touch her thin, scented lacy *kebaya* jacket.

She started in surprise, rebelling and getting angry at me.

"Oh, so she doesn't love me, it seems," I thought.

I turned around and ran back to the surau: disappointed, sad, cross, and afraid that she might complain about all this to Father.

I was irked: she didn't love me back.

The next day I didn't even want to see her. That whole day I spent searching around for a rough-skinned orange, some incense, a long string, and an incense burner. I was going to put a spell on her so she'd fall in love with me; if she didn't want to fall in love with me, I would just slam her with a magic charm to drive her wild.

That night, at twelve o'clock, when everyone in the surau was already asleep, I got up. I heated up the coals of the incense burner, I tied the upper end of the string to a crosspiece. Its end had a needle on it and I'd brought this over and put it atop the incense burner. Atop the live coals I scattered chips of incense. The smoke billowed upward.

I stole a look: no one had awakened.

I pricked the rough-skinned orange in my left hand with the needle, while reading mantras and imagining in a vision that the thing I was pricking was not an orange, but the heart of the woman who had rejected my love. I pricked away at her heart with the needle. Then I rolled the orange (which was on top of the hot incense burner) with the palms of my two hands like it was a top. In my vision it was the heart of the woman I was twirling around. I read the mantras over and over again. "I love so and so, but she doesn't love me in return. She must fall in love with me. If she doesn't, she will get sick, thanks to the Prophet Muhammad, the messenger of Allah. La ilaha ilallah!"

I spit on the orange after each time I read the mantra.

But I could not concentrate my thoughts; a healthy mind was not going to believe that that orange was a person's heart. The orange had just stayed an orange, my mind said. The vision got hazy, its images all mixed together. I was the one who was conjuring up the vision, but I myself didn't believe it.

After a quarter of an hour, the witchcraft spell-casting ceremony was over—a quarter of an hour full of conflict in my confused, chaotic thoughts. I put all the devices away. I wanted to see the proof of the ceremony's efficacy tomorrow. Was she going to smile sweetly tomorrow and return my love and not get mad again when I hugged her? While mulling these questions over I fell asleep.

But the next day the young woman was just as she always was, still healthy, not sick in the least. There was no trace that her heart had been twirled around. And she also hadn't started loving me to any greater extent. It was just like it used to be: she regarded me as her friend and apparently she had forgiven my badness.

I was surprised. Hadn't yesterday's witchcraft spell been effective at all? Why not? Had my mind's concentration lacked force, or was it that the woman had a very strong soul? I was afraid Father would be mad at me if I asked him about it. Why were his prayers effective whereas I had barely started out and had failed already? Had I perhaps attacked someone? But no, I certainly hadn't, right? I was only defending myself because my own love had not been returned.

After that I didn't want to put witchcraft spells on anybody anymore. If anyone happened to be in love with me, well, thanks be to God for that. But I wasn't going to force some girl to love me with my occult lore. I was lucky that none of my friends had known about any of this; that goes for that young woman, too. If I do not write it all down here, the secret will remain hidden inside me, and maybe I shall just carry it to the grave without any other person ever knowing about it.

But what's the need to carry it into the grave? It's better to leave that insane story right here in the present world.

CHAPTER 22: ASJIAH GETS MARRIED, AND I . . .

Very rarely would people from my village get married out of love. They'd always marry a person who wasn't their own choice. It was the parents who would go find a marriage partner for them. If the parents made a good choice—that is, if he was a suitable sort for her to fall in love with—then the two of them would be fortunate; if not, then they would suffer a great deal. The feelings of their child (who was going to spend her whole life with this person, whom she didn't know) were unimportant, in the parents' view. A child has to obey. Mother and Father know better than a child does who is a good choice for their child. Love? Unimportant! Love would develop of its own accord after they were married, after the young fellow and the girl have kept company with each other for a few months. That was the opinion of the elders.

Most folks suppose that an adolescent girl will be miserable to be married off to a middle-aged man. I thought so at first, too, particularly after reading lots of novels. I had supposed that from that point on she would be living a life in hell.

That might indeed be true if the girl has had some schooling—and doubtless it is true if she has been to middle school. Girls like that have already met and gotten to know some guys they like, and they'll want to make their own choice. If luck is with them, they can go ahead and marry him.

But country girls who've not been to school, well, the complications of life are not as clear to girls like these as they are to their friends who are attending middle school. A girl probably will have a strong inclination toward some special young guy, but if she hasn't had any strong association with that fellow yet her longings will just stay rather quiescent. If she's forced to marry some other man, even if her heart rebels at first, sooner or later she'll simply surrender to her fate and she'll be devoted to her husband. Especially so, once she's had children. Her world will be just her household, and she'll forget all about her earlier sweetheart.

I've seen many young women who certainly do not feel like they are in hell to live in the same house with a middle-aged husband. When these women have needs and desires, why, these are met. They've got a house, lots of clothes, they have jewelry, enough to eat, and if sometimes they can have more than what the neighbor women or their friends have, well— okay, they're content. All those castles they built in the air before they got married have totally dissipated.

We're the ones who are always exaggerating these female sufferings. We imagine that they are miserable, disappointed, without hope. But according to my past experiences, there isn't any of this. Whichever man happens to be given to her she'll just accept. That's exactly what I saw in my village and in other villages in Minangkabau.

Asjiah, my Dad's niece, was going to be married. She was sixteen years old. Two years older than I. For months before, her mother and the folks in her house had been getting ready to receive a son-in-law: they had bought an iron bed, a mattress, pillows, mosquito netting, clothes, and all the various and sundry newlywed needs. Asjiah joined in to help sew clothes, crochet lace for silk pillows, and make the decorations for the bridal bed. And besides all this, she learned how to cook.

For the three months before getting married she was kept in seclusion and wasn't allowed to go outside the house. This was so her skin would be white and soft because it hadn't been out in the sun. At seeing her mother make all these preparations it dawned on her that she was to be married. But she did not know to whom. The scheme was still in her mother's head; the woman was forever whispering back and forth with her maternal aunt and her grandmother. And Asjiah wasn't allowed to know what they were whispering about. She was worried, embarrassed, yet pleased about being married. Pleased to be becoming a complete woman with a husband, like her friends who had preceded her in this, but distressed, since she didn't know who she was going to be paired with. Would the man be nice? But because she had to follow her parents' wishes, she kept quiet.

In Minangkabau, it's the woman's side that does most of the elaborate marriage preparations, because she is the one who is going to receive him in her house, in order to form a household and family. To receive a bridegroom everything must be in complete readiness. If it's not, they'll be embarrassed in front of the villagers. It's the woman's side that must swallow a lot of the costs. They have to arrange for a big feast, for slaughtering a cow or a water buffalo, and they must invite hundreds of people to the ceremony.

The man's side only buys the man's newlywed clothes and pays for a small feast at his parents' house, as well as several suits of clothing for his future wife, as a first marriage gift. And then there's the support money that they give to the woman's side as their contribution toward the big feast. There's also a box of big cigars. However, the man does have to have a strong means of support and some definite source of income. And he has to be skilled at commerce off in other people's lands, and he must have made a lot of money. If not, he will not be sought out as a son-in-law in the first place.

The one who was going to become Asjiah's husband was Hadji Rasul, my stepmother Ami's older brother. He was already forty-five years old, four times married. And he already had seven children. He was a cloth merchant in Bangkahulu. He'd had a store there for ten years now, and each time he came home to the village he brought lots of money and gifts, things that he had bought for his wife and kids and his brothers and sisters. Each time he came home, he'd be escorting a wife who had been with him for a year. And after a month's vacation back in the village, striding to and fro, showing off his wealth, he'd haul off yet one more wife.

He had two wives at that time, one in Baruh and another in Batu Beragung.[1] Because he could afford to support three wives, Asjiah's mother and maternal uncle had a meeting with my father about seeking out Hadji Rasul to become Asjiah's husband. Then my father whispered stuff to my stepmother, and asked her to go check out her older brother, Hadji Rasul, to see whether or not he would be willing to take on one more wife—and marry the sweet Asjiah, who's so meek and submissive and such a good cook, and a good seamstress to boot. In short, who would be a wife who could deliver satisfaction. My stepmother whispered with her older brother, aided and abetted by her other brothers and sisters who joined in in praising Asjiah.

"Just accept her, Hadji," they whispered, "so we won't be embarrassed toward His Honor, our brother-in-law. After all, it was he himself who came asking for Older Brother in marriage."

Hadji Rasul did accept the proposal. I knew that it wasn't just because of the respect he had for Father. There was an additional reason, a more urgent one . . .

When he went on back to Bangkahulu he surely had to have a new young wife in tow.

I was allowed to attend all these whispered conferences because they thought of me as still quite young and green . . .

I had already read *Siti Nurbaya*[2] and felt very sorry for Asjiah. Here it wasn't Datuk Meringgih but Hadji Rasul. I loved Asjiah, a love of the sort a younger brother would have for his older sister. And Asjiah loved me too. She had only gone to school as far as the third grade. Her mother and her maternal uncle had yanked her out after that. She didn't really understand when I read the book *Siti Nurbaya* to her. She was quite assiduous in doing her recitations and praying; in fact, she's the one who helped me when I had just started to study how to read and recite the Koran. Later on, when she herself was studying the *fikhi* [Muslim laws], as a payback to this I helped her with the parts she didn't understand yet.

Because she was studying the *fikhi,* every night I would come over to her house and sleep there. I'd sleep alongside her on two rattan mats that had been put together on the floor. When we were ready to go to sleep we'd turn down the lamp. Her mother and maternal uncle weren't discomfited by any of this because I was only a younger brother with his older sister, with Asjiah. And actually, that's what I thought, too. We had no intention of becoming husband and wife because she was older and I wasn't a trader yet. Mother, Father, and Maternal Uncle viewed me as a kid.

Every night after doing our recitations, when we were getting ready to go to sleep, we'd converse in a very free and friendly way, opening our hearts, secrets, and experiences to each other. To me (whom she considered her little brother) she poured out the contents of her heart. She'd say all this in a slow gentle voice so her mother wouldn't hear. I would listen, full of interest; all of my attention would be directed toward her sweet lips. She was cheery, quite happy and content with me. Whenever she would cook some treats, of course she would give some to me. If I happened not to come over to her house she'd put the food aside till I got there. If I didn't come over for two or three days, she'd be angry. Every night I was supposed to come by and keep her company while she was in seclusion, before her wedding.

If it had been a rainy day and it was cold in the middle of the night, she'd put her body up close to mine and we'd feel hot. I could feel her soft scented body and could hear her orderly breathing as her chest went up and down.

"Can you hear it raining, Ridjal?" she'd whisper.

"Yeah, it's really pouring down. The thunderclaps are also loud and scary," I whispered.

"It's cold, isn't it?" she'd whisper, moving a bit closer to me.

"It sure is. Too bad my blanket is so thin," I whispered, drawing my body close, pulling up the blanket a bit and scrunching up the pillow. She was silent; I could feel that she was happy.

"Older Sister's hair smells so sweet," I whispered.

"Go to sleep. It's almost daylight!" she whispered and went right to sleep.

When it was full morning, her grandmother got up and Asjiah would distance herself from me. And during the day she'd act as if nothing at all had happened. We'd still be like two siblings.

In reality it was already time for her to want a man, but she was still scared and shy. Because I was the one who was free to associate with her, for the moment, with me she had the nerve to satisfy her desires by being friendly, by loving me, and by protecting and teasing me.

Asjiah would be married in one more week. The water buffalo had been bought; the kitchen now had a new addition made of bamboo, as a place to be used later for preparing the spices and seasonings. All the preparations and supplies were there in sufficient quantities; in her house folks were already hard at work assembling decorated mattresses, pillows, putting up the mosquito net, and getting the bridal bed in order. Out in the kitchen people were making numerous little cakes and sweets. I was allowed to taste everything they made. A delegation from Asjiah's house had gone over to Hadji Rasul's house, carrying the incised metal betel box as a formal sign of the marriage proposal.

It was only that day that Asjiah's mother and maternal uncle told her that she was to be married to Hadji Rasul. The adults just informed her of that. They didn't ask what Asjiah thought of it or ask her for a decision about whether she agreed to it or not.

Asjiah was crying. I could not fathom her feelings at the time. Even though she was friendly and frank with me, much was still obscure to me. She cried, but not very hard.

Her mother and her maternal uncle cajoled and flattered her and praised Hadji Rasul as a good person who wouldn't neglect Asjiah. They also told her that she had a fine chance of winning out over her co-wives, who were already getting sort of old and had bunches of children—oh yes, they told her lots and lots of other reasons to keep her chin up.

Asjiah didn't agree to it, but she didn't refuse it either. How could she refuse it when she had never really loved a young man? Her heart was still vacant. If she was going to love anyone, certainly it would have been me, because I was the only male she knew. But all this time she just loved me as an older sister loves a kid brother. But then, how was she to simply accept it all? Only this last year she had happened to get a glimpse of Hadji Rasul and had noted that he was already kind of old and had a long mustache, and that his hair was white, his body skinny—not at all cocky and dashing—and that he was sickly. The soul of this simple country girl, who was so devoutly religious, who had never opposed her parents and in fact would be afraid to do so, didn't know what it meant to rebel—she simply cried and didn't say anything. Her mother left her alone to cry and went off to work on something else. And also went off to a dukun to get a fortune told about whether or not Asjiah and Hadji Rasul's constellations matched, and whether they would make a fortunate pair.

According to the dukun's secret lore, each letter of the alphabet had its own numerical score. For example: A=1, S=4, R=5, and so on. The scores from the name of the girl to be married would be added up and then added to the total score from the name of her future husband. Then the sum from the two scores would have 5's subtracted from it in sequence. If it didn't come out even, of course there would be something left over, 1 or 2 or 3 or 4. If it came out perfectly even, that was a sign that their union was an exceedingly auspicious and good one. If 1 was left that meant good, 2 meant average, 3, not so good, and 4, really rotten.

If the total from the two names had 5 subtracted from it and the remainder was three or four, often the marriage would be canceled. Or, if it was undertaken anyway, the woman's name or the man's name would have to be changed. If it wasn't changed, they'd live a life of poverty and dishonor.

When the remainder left over from the sum of the names Asjiah and Rasul had fives subtracted from it, it showed that the marriage wouldn't be so good. Asjiah's mother was worried. She asked the dukun what could be done to evade this misfortune. The dukun proposed that Asjiah's name be changed to Alimah. That was because the score for the names Alimah and Rasul when added together and when 5 was subtracted from that, would have a remainder of 1. That was good. They would have a life of good fortune, it would be easy to make a living, they'd have many children, and the public would respect and honor them.

Upon arriving back at the house, Asjiah's mother announced to all assembled there that starting that very day, Asjiah's name would be Alimah. And she asked all the people in attendance to announce that fact to the entire village society. The village people well understood why Asjiah was changing her name, because they themselves had often done such a thing. Only the children, who weren't grown up yet, did not understand. To make Asjiah and her mother happy, after that day I called her Uni Alimah, even though in my heart she was always Asjiah.

Two days before the festivities even more people had come to the house. Out in the kitchen people were busy grating coconuts, crushing pepper, and getting the spices and all the various seasonings for the curries ready. They were also grinding the seasonings for the spiced dried meat dishes, the roast meat, the stews, and so on. People put up a curtain in the middle of the room along with a multicolored velvet canopy that had hanging partitions on it and tassles. The elaborately sectioned mosquito netting for the bridal bed was decorated and scented with perfume and floral petal medleys. Asjiah began to rinse her hair with lime and she was bathed and powdered so that her body would be fragrant. I wasn't able to get close to her anymore.

The next day, Asjiah's maternal uncles and Dad assembled all the names of the people to be invited and they told Saini and me to go run all through the village inviting all those folks. There were more than two hundred of them. I felt both sad and angry to be ordered to do this. I was very sad at the loss of my friend Asjiah, and now to be ordered to go help carry out a humiliating thing (that is, to go approach those more than two hundred people with the proper amount of respect)! I wasn't allowed to protest, for according to adat, as *Anak Pisang* [relatives subservient to the bride's family], I was obligated to come to the aid of my father's close family. The other Anak Pisang had their own special tasks to do.

Saini and I rearranged the list of names of those who had to be invited, according to the location of their houses, so we could do it all in one trip. If we hadn't done it this way things would have gotten hot and tiring—going to one house very far away, then coming back to square one, to the house nearby that we had just invited beforehand.

After everything was all organized and after we had been instructed in how we must issue invitations to people, off we went. I carried a sack full of betel quid, and Saini held two sheets of paper with our list of invitees on it.

When we'd come to a house of a person to be invited, we'd cough a bit at the foot of the stairs and then the householders would ask: "Who's that?"

"Me."

"Well, come on up!"

Up we went, and upon arriving at the head of the stairs we asked: "Is his honor Sutan Such-and-Such at home?"

"He is," answered his wife. "Do sit down!"

We sat down on the mats.

"So, who's that?" Sutan Such-and-Such asked his wife. He was still in a side room.

"Ridjal and Saini, messengers from Baginda Sati, Asjiah's maternal uncle," answered his wife.

Sutan Such-and-Such would emerge and we would stand and shake hands with him and then the three of us would all sit back down again. Then I would begin the ceremony.

"Please take some betel quid, Honorable Sutan," I'd say as I pushed the betel sack forward.

"Thank you."

"Well, and so, we have come here, having been ordered to so by Maternal Uncle, Baginda Sati, to invite the Honorable Sutan to come to his house, on Thursday evening after the prayers. He's holding a modest selamatan meal. The Honorable Sutan's presence is much hoped for."

"Oh, so Asjiah's getting married this Thursday, tomorrow, is she?"

"Yes, Honorable Sutan."

"Insya Allah [God willing], I'll come," he answered.

"We ask your permission to leave, your honor."

"Yes, thank you," he'd say as he escorted us to the door.

Over one hundred houses were approached in that same way, all with this same ceremony.

If we happened to encounter an invitee there in the middle of the road, we would say to him that we had planned to go over to his house to have a conversation with him. Then I would ask respectfully that since we had already run into each other if I might simply be able to converse right there on the road, or would that be lacking in respect or adat?

"It's all right, it's no problem at all," he'd say.

So we'd all go over and sit on some big rocks along the side of the road and we would present our betel quid to him and after that the ceremony noted above would ensue.

The invitees weren't always at home; some would be off gossiping in the coffee stalls, others would be fishing in some water hole, others would be saying the noontime prayers and we'd have to wait till they got done. Others would be arguing with their maternal uncles, others would be off crushing lice in an empty surau, some would be hoeing their fields, others would be up a coconut tree, others would be out daydreaming along the lakeshore, and so on.

Some among them were willing to help us out. If he saw on our list of names that two or three of his friends were going to be invited, he'd say to us that we didn't have to go tuckering ourselves out to go to all their houses; he'd just convey the invitations himself to his friends. We'd thank him for his help.

Doing all this inviting took up a whole day. When we got back to Asjiah's house we were worn out, hungry, and thirsty.

I went to take a look at Asjiah, who was having her hair combed and embossed with fragrant oils. She smiled a bit and my exhaustion vanished.

"Where were you all day, Ridjal? I didn't see you," asked Asjiah with love and sympathy. She felt she had lost her pal.

"Inviting everyone from the whole village."

"Did you finish them all?"

"No one got left out."

"So, eat something! You must be hungry."

That's what she said, but there was more that she didn't say. I was moved to see Asjiah. We conversed more with our eyes than our mouths. Asjiah's feelings were reflected there in her eyes and thrust sharply into my heart. I could feel these. But . . .

The next day the house was crowded with women. The water buffalo was slaughtered very early in the morning and the men set to chopping up its meat into chunks. Large cauldrons and pots were being fired up out in the yard. Middle-aged women were busy cooking delicious foods for the guests and the bride and bridegroom, as well as decorating the house. Asjiah got fitted out with the adat bridal clothes and the costly gold headband with spangles and spikes. It weighed four kilograms. Asjiah just sat there with her head bowed down. I had less and less opportunity to talk with her.

After some of the curries and spiced meat dishes were done, several fancily dressed women acting as messengers carried some of it over the house of Hadji Rasul's mother. Out in front walked a person carrying a betel box.

Near noon prayertime, in came some young women and girls all dressed up in finery; they were all daytime invitees. All of them had come to take a quick look at the bridal chamber and to praise Asjiah at being so lucky as to get Hadji Rasul as a husband. Only the ones who had gone to school and had read stories about girls forced to marry senile old guys felt sorry for her. But they didn't do anything, as they themselves had once experienced or would experience such forced marriages.

When it was crowded and boisterous like this I got confused and felt awkward and didn't know what I should lay hold of and start doing. This didn't satisfy; that didn't please me. Finally I was just bothering people. I went over to the surau to be by myself for a while. There I saw several men gathered in front of the *kadi* judge [marriage official] to carry out the wedding ceremony, according to religion. His Honor the Kadi was holding Hadji Rasul by the index finger. Adat did not allow Asjiah herself to come, so she was represented by her father.

I went up to the peak of Mount Four Houses to daydream and to cry, recalling Asjiah's and my fate. I was all alone on the mountain peak. Because they were so busy, other people and even Father had forgotten all about me.

That night the house was bright and shining, as gaslamps had been set up from end to end of the structure. After the evening prayers people started coming in one by one, or the invitees would come over in small groups. The front hall was almost totally full. The spot right in front of the bridal chamber was left empty because it was waiting in readiness for the bride and groom and their attendants.

The bridegroom had to be formally called for. That was what the ceremony stipulated. That was the first time that people thought about me. Zainal and I were ordered to go over to the groom's house carrying a betel box, which was covered over by a wide velvet handkerchief. Its edge was embroidered in gold thread.

I felt humiliated again. How could it be that I was going to be the very one to call for the man who was going to make Asjiah miserable—the man who didn't love my good-hearted older sister. But Father's orders could not be protested. Oh Father, you don't know how shattered your child's heart is!!!

All along the road I kept fantasizing. Should I just toss the betel box off to the side of the road? No, don't try it, Father will be mad. Oh, if only I was grown and skilled at a trade and had a lot of money, then surely folks wouldn't order me to go call for the bridegroom. Rather, I *myself* would be the bridegroom and I would be Asjiah's husband. She wouldn't look on me as her kid brother but as her husband, her life companion. She'd live a fortunate, happy life, with me, without any doubt. She certainly wouldn't be sad like she is now. But, fate dictates . . .

At the bridegroom's house, the house of my stepmother, I was well and properly received for the ceremony. After that cursed ceremony Step-mother called me inside the house and dubbed me a sweet kid. Oh, sweet? Sweet? She didn't know what ran amok in this young boy's heart.

I didn't want to be a sweet kid; I wanted to be a bridegroom. My step-mother didn't know; she saw me as young and green.

At ten o'clock the bridegroom made his exit from the decorated room. Astaga, I thought he was an Arab![3] He was done up in a huge red turban and a white inner robe and a blue outer robe down to his ankles, and he was carrying a gold-knobbed cane and smoking a cigar with a big paper ring on it. His face had been shaved smooth and his mustache had been fancied up so that he would look younger and more dashing. All the women in the house sang his praises. My head was spinning. Oh, Asjiah! Your husband is Hadji, Hadji Mustache! My tears flowed down my cheeks.

The bridegroom stepped down from the house escorted by some twenty men. I asked Zainal to hold the betel box. I didn't have the strength anymore.

"What a pity Asjiah is marrying an old guy," said Zainal, remembering *Siti Nurbaya*.

"Yeah," I answered. He himself didn't know how shattered my heart was at the time, for I had never told him how intimate my feelings were for Asjiah.

Upon arrival at Asjiah's house, the bridegroom and his escorts were asked to sit down in the hall outside the bridal chamber. The womenfolk out back pushed against the door into the main part of the house to see what the bridegroom looked like. All of them declared him appropriate enough, not too terribly aged and still dashing enough. And most espe-cially, he had lots of money! The bridegroom sat next to the layers of mat-tresses and rows of silk pillows facing a tray of rice and a tray of various sorts of specially prepared goodies.

Then the dishes of food for the three hundred guests were brought out and set down in two rows from end to end in front of the four rows of at-tendees. The rice was set out in big plates for four people apiece. And be-sides that there were plates of curry, a cup of stewed jackfruit, a plateful of spiced meat, a plate of simmered fish, and a bowl of water for washing your hands.

After all this was set out, an official speechmaker stood up, represent-ing the maiden bride's side. In a long speech he inquired why the bride-groom and his retinue had come over to the house like this. This speech was chock-full of flowery words, aphorisms, and old sayings, as well as nu-merous veiled allusions and quatrains. After speaking for a half an hour he stopped and sat down. The orator the bridegroom had brought along stood up and explained at great length the aim of the groom's arrival and asked that they be well received. He was answered by another speech, also of a full hour's duration, from the first speechmaker.

Meanwhile, the rice and curries were getting cold and about half of the guests were dozing off. The ones who were sitting cross-legged found their legs were getting tired and stiff, but they couldn't change their sitting position without making a little speech asking permission to do this from the people who were sitting to their right and left. So, little whispered speeches were murmured back and forth in the midst of all the fiery main orations. The ones who wanted to pass gas or go pee also had to ask permission when they were going to step down into the courtyard. Half of the attendees hadn't eaten a meal back home and their eyes were fixed on the rice, curry, and spiced meat. They were getting fed up because the speeches had not ended yet.

After the first orators' speeches were over a second pair took over for one and a half hours. Although the speechmaker tried hard, he couldn't defeat the bride's faction with the adroitness of his tongue nor the sharpness of his thoughts. He ended his speech and the bride's faction gave yet another hour and a half speech. Meanwhile, it was getting to be five o'clock in the morning. Many of the guests were getting totally fed up with the whole situation. They were dozing off; they were passing gas and going outside to pee. Neither one of the speechmakers was willing to wind up the loser.

Finally a neutral datuk stepped forward to break them up, explaining that both orators were absolutely first rate and both were champions—and the guests were respectfully asked to begin eating. Like a flock of ducks fighting to get at the rice bran in the trough, the guests attacked the rice and the curries (which were of course cold by now). Four people ate out of one plate. The spiced meat, the curry, and the stew all got mixed up together with the rice, to become a single dish. Four hands competed with each other in the same plate.

If all the hands were clean it wouldn't have been much of a problem. However, if it happened that we had to share a plate with someone who's hands were all full of scabies sores that stank and were suppurating and oozing blood, well, we could hardly choke our rice down. Greedy people put in an appearance, too, when it was time to eat. We'd barely taken two fingerfuls of rice, but each one of these folks would already have stuffed in five. There'd be four chunks of spiced meat in the side dish, one for each person, and he'd grab two of them and the others would be left with just the gravy and leftovers.

The bridegroom was not eating. He just looked on.

After eating, the oldest one of the four of us would get to use the finger bowl first. We young ones would get dirty water since the ones who got to go first would plunge their hands right into the bowl. They weren't going to wash up just any old way! And if the oldest one among us happened to have scabies sores on his hands, well, we'd be forced to step down in the courtyard and ask for a little water from the women heating the cauldrons of water for the kitchen.

That night the bridegroom did not meet the maiden. At dawn everyone went off and the groom and two of his escorts went to bathe in the river. After this he and his escorts came back to the maiden bride's house to drink coffee. His damp towel was set out to dry on the windowsill. This was a sign that a new bridegroom was inside the house.

Asjiah was very tired. She had been wearing the four-kilogram gold crown all this time and now she could barely hold her head up. Her heart pounded as she confronted her new life. Her only hope was that she really could beat out those other two co-wives, since she was still young and more beautiful than they were.

At midday the bridegroom came back again with ten escorts, this time wearing a gold robe and a blue turban. After eating and chatting for two or three hours he went on home. Over these three days he had not had the nerve to go over to the houses of his two other wives. He was afraid of seeing their eyes radiating the fire of anger and hurt.

The second night he arrived with five escorts, done up in a black robe and white turban. After eating a meal and talking a very long time with the men and women at Asjiah's house (who asked him about how things were in the rantau), he was asked to go on into the bride's room.

Hadji Rasul pretended to be shy, and declined:

"Oh, in a moment or so, I'm not sleepy yet."

This, even though he very much wanted to go back in there.

He was invited to go in two times and finally did, sitting down on a thin mattress spread out near the bed. The room was heavily scented with flowers. He hadn't been sitting there long when fearful Asjiah, more dead than alive, was urged to go on in. She glanced out of the corner of her eye and saw Hadji Rasul sitting there; she started in fright and kept her head bowed. She was formally married by an old woman, acting as Village Messenger. This old woman was the one who introduced them to each other and who urged Hadji Rasul and Asjiah to chat. Then she served them sweets, yellow rice, and roast chicken; third, she set out some drinks. The Messenger kept up a continual stream of small talk, trying to get Asjiah to open her mouth. Hadji Rasul pretended to be shy. Actually, he was beginning to desire the lovely Asjiah.

The dishes were cleared away, and Asjiah was escorted out to take off her gold headdress and change her clothes. Then she was told to go back inside the room by herself. She was pushed along by people in back of her, and inside the room Hadji Rasul awaited her.

That was the first night for Asjiah, who was entering a new life . . .

I had lost a friend I had loved dearly all this time. I felt lonely, extremely lonely! I went to the surau and went to sleep by myself up in the second story, sad, lonely, without hope. I could not be entertained or diverted by anything. My beloved friend had disappeared . . . forever.

Three days later Asjiah was escorted in a big happy group over to the house of her husband's mother to be acquainted with her mother-in-law, who was now ninety years old. This is called "Assailing the Enemy" in Minangkabau. I kept my distance, not wanting to see or be seen.

Two weeks later, in the middle of the day, I came over to her house to chat with her. I had thought that her husband wouldn't have arrived by that time, but he and Asjiah were in her room. They were laughing, joking—very cheerfully. Asjiah was happy. It was as if my heart were being sliced with a knife. She did not know I had come over. But if she had known, she would have seen to her husband first anyway. Ridjal can just wait. Her mother asked me if I'd like something to eat, as if eating meant anything to me at that moment. I declined the offer. I didn't need to eat, my heart said, I needed to see Asjiah. To see whether she was still the same as before and hadn't changed.

But she was already a great success with her husband. There, she's laughing merrily, again!

I had lost a friend . . . forever . . . and until we died and turned to earth in our graves, it would never be like it was. Perhaps she didn't remember me anymore.

A month later her husband took her off to Bangkahulu; lots of people escorted them out to the station. My father was also there. I looked on from a distance. Would Asjiah remember to ask her friends where I was, as they stood alongside her under the *puding* tree[4] at the station? Maybe not, really, maybe not. She'd have forgotten.

CHAPTER 23: A SMALL KID IN THE VILLAGE, AN ADULT IN THE RANTAU

Sooner or later, of course, I had to leave the village! To follow Father's wishes and stay there forever, to share the fate of the majority of villagers who never journeyed more than fifteen kilometers from Sumpur from the time of their birth till their death—for me that would have been an absolute impossibility. This would have meant killing off my sturdily developed longings and damping down the aspirations burning inside me. If these two things were killed off, that would have meant a sort of suicide. Everything that I had read, studied, and heard from other people would have all gone for nothing.

My knowledge, growing little by little about life in the future and about other regions (knowledge that I'd gotten by reading books and listening to market sellers, who'd returned from the rantau), added at every moment to my desire to start my own wanderings, and to go see how things were in other lands. I began to be dissatisfied with just reading and looking at pictures and hearing other people relate their stories. I wanted to see things for myself! What did these storytellers have that I didn't? If they were able to go there, why couldn't I? Didn't I have energy and brains as they did? If they had advantages over me now, wasn't that all just a matter of time? In several years wouldn't I, too, be able to go wandering just as they did?

Wouldn't God also be affording me, like my friends, the good fortune to go into commerce in South Sumatra? My friends were already associating with the peoples of Lampung, Pasemah, and so on, peoples who had lots of money but who didn't know how to spend it since their needs were so few. What form did those wide pepper fields of theirs take? Those fields which provided a sizeable income each week, so that they had virtual fistfuls of rupiah bills to spend? Was it true that because of their stupidity they were always getting fooled by clever Minangkabau traders, so that the latter derived extraordinarily large profits from business dealings with these South Sumatran hicks?

Wouldn't I be fortunate like those folks who'd gone off to Java, who were seeing all the odd and remarkable conditions there? Who were making the acquaintance of the inhabitants there, and noting all the progress, clothes, adat customs, foods, and ways of life they had which differed from those of the Minangkabau people?

The bigger I got, the harder I worked at interrogating people who'd just come back from the rantau. I'd do this till late at night and not get drowsy: I'd be totally absorbed in listening to and taking in each and every word that they uttered. Everything that they portrayed with their stories was pictured with great clarity in my thoughts. Sometimes I'd ask myself in my heart, why couldn't my body just fly off over there so I could witness all this for myself, so that I could see everything that they were talking about—all these fellows who were so fortunate as to have seen and experienced these places? Oh, why was Father still tying me down to this village and not letting me leave as long as I lived? Within several years would my heart continue to be scorched by the desire to go wandering—till I died from the suffering?

From my birth till I came of age I had traversed absolutely every nook and cranny of the whole village. I'd climbed the steps into all the houses, I'd seen every bend in the road, and I knew every person in the village. I had had enough and it was all boring to me. I wanted to see whatever was outside the Lake Singkarak region. I'd traversed all the villages around Sumpur. I'd been to Solok and Sawah Lunto, and I'd been to Sulit Air. I had been to Payahkumbuh and Padang, I had slept out in the forest and out in the middle of the rice paddies; all the mountains surrounding the village I had climbed, and there were no more valleys left to assail. Yet I wasn't satisfied. Outside of this region I had walked through so thoroughly, surely there were many other ethnic peoples whose adat customs and habits and souls it was fitting for me to study, so that I'd really get to know about them in detail.

In that way, every day, the desire to emigrate to the rantau came to dominate my soul more and more. A large portion of my thoughts came to concentrate on this matter alone. And at night, when all my friends were sleeping, I would often sit by myself on a bench in the courtyard of the surau. I would look up at the sky, looking at the stars twinkling above the tapering roof of the surau. I grew sad and subdued: why was I still bound to this village? Why wasn't I free like other people who could move about from one place to another? I would listen to people relating tales of Java, Bandung, Solo, and Malang. Would it be that only these *stories* would come into my brain, and I would have to live on these tales in the village till I got old and was put into my grave? With my own eyes never seeing what these stories were about?

One by one, all my playmates from the surau emigrated into the rantau. Of the sixteen that there were before, only six were left; the others were scattered all through Sumatra and others had gone to Java. Some were working for their fathers, some were learning commerce from their maternal uncles, while others were working as employees for a merchant in Padang while accumulating some capital. The six fellows just mentioned were beginning to say that they couldn't stand staying in the village any longer; they were searching for a way out.

When we had a friend who was leaving for the rantau, those of us staying behind would all go together to escort him to the station. And when there would be someone who was coming home from the rantau we'd wait for him at the station and welcome him back cheerfully and go all together over to his parents' house, all the while asking him about his experiences off in other people's lands.

But there was another group of our friends who used to play with us, two or three years older than us, who had started to hold themselves aloof from us after they'd been off in the rantau, as if they weren't part of our faction anymore. They'd associate with people who had gone off to the rantau with them, who'd gone upstream and downstream with them, and they'd converse with these new friends of theirs. They almost didn't pay any attention to us anymore.

We were quite sad to lose one friend after another. In the past, before they'd set off, they had promised that they would not forget us.

On market day, the fellows who'd come back from the rantau would sit on the long benches at the station talking and joking among themselves. They wore great clothes. We were standing sort of far off and even though they could see us, they didn't invite us over to join their gang. When our gazes would meet they'd smile a bit for purposes of politeness, so as not to hurt our feelings too much. Actually, they had begun to be rather averse to associating with us.

This was especially true of the ones who already had wives. They were even more aloof—it was impossible that they would want to be close with us as they had been before. They considered themselves most important people now, and it was appropriate for them to associate only with market-sellers who were also already married. When we'd approach them and we'd question them a bit about something, their answers would always be brief and given without their full attention or friendship. Perhaps they thought we were going to ask them for money.

Every marketday a peddler would come from Padang Pandjang selling saté [chunks of roast meat on skewers] that was famous for tasting so good. The fellows just back from the rantau would race to buy it from him. Some of them would ask for two katupats [leaf packets of rice] and twenty sticks of saté; others would ask for three katupats and thirty sticks of saté, and some would even ask for four katupats and forty sticks. After that, they'd drink a couple of bottles of lemonade. From a distance, we'd glance at them out of the corners of our eyes; if we had wanted to join in and buy some, too, we only had ten cents in pocket money, enough for one katupat of rice and five sticks of saté and a glass of coconut milk with syrup. It would all just start to get good when we'd run out of katupat and saté.

None of those fellows invited us over. And even if one of them had wanted to buy us some, we probably would have refused them because we'd be embarrassed in front of the others. At that moment our pain intensified our desire to go make some money in the rantau, like those fellows had, so that we too could buy five katupats and fifty sticks of saté at a throw.

It wasn't because of a shortage of anything that young guys from my village emigrated to the rantau. Their mothers, maternal uncles or fathers had already provided them with all the food, clothes, and so on they might need. And in fact they wouldn't be left high and dry anytime in their entire lives. Rather, it was a feeling of embarrassment which pushed them to leave the village. If they just stayed right in the village, even if they had everything they needed, girls' mothers and fathers wouldn't be rushing in to ask for them as husbands. This not only embarrassed the young men but even more it embarrassed their mothers, maternal uncles, and fathers.

These three would be very embarrassed indeed when a young man the same age as their child got married and their child hadn't yet. It was as if their kid wasn't marketable, no matter how much noble blood flowed in his veins and no matter how much religious lore had been packed into his head. For, as long as young men stayed right there in the village, the fathers and mothers of girls much preferred to go seek young men working in commerce in the rantau as husbands for their daughters.

There is a history of this practice of going to propose marriage to a man.

According to the story the old people told me, during the age when the Minangkabau Kingdom was still in its glory and the aristocratic class still held the reins of government and still was powerful and influential in society throughout the villages in all of Minangkabau—Sumpur certainly not being an exception to this—mothers and fathers with daughters would fight for the chance to ask for someone from the nobility to become their sons-in-law. They'd be proud if their child's husband were a datuk or a sutan, and so on. That way, their grandchildren wouldn't be just anyone. The son-in-law didn't have to provide his wife with a living—it was enough just so long as he wanted to come over every night; or if he had more than one wife, just so long as he came over when it was this girl's turn. During that age, economic conditions were good, and people's means of support were quite satisfactory—this was especially true of the nobles, who had much inherited wealth and wide rice paddy lands and gardens. The son-in-law's family would also be heirs and they themselves would be quite rich. So this marriage would not be based on sheer economic calculations but rather on matters of social honor and getting descendants. The mothers and fathers were only hunting for social honor so that their social position among their aristocratic social circle would be nice and high. The nonaristocratic group, it's true, would also manage to get wives, but they'd only get the ones who didn't sell well to the aristocrats (because they weren't all that good looking, for instance).

Even if a datuk or sutan was old and worn out, pockmarked or crippled, for instance, the mothers and fathers who were social-status crazy would not find it in the least burdensome to surrender their pretty daughter to him. In such a case the satisfaction gained from bowing down before the aristocrats didn't have to heed other feelings.

That's the way things continued until the age of the rise of the religious faction. That is, once the Padris gained control in the beginning of the nineteenth century. This paralyzed the adat group's governing powers and adat's influence. In the years after this, little by little, public respect turned away from the aristocrats toward the religious faction. This was particularly true after people had been taught by the religious leaders that their faction would have great influence later on, in the world hereafter. The *kiais* [religious scholars] would be able to help people they favored, and they'd be able to spring them from hell. The general populace (which was afraid when they heard that they'd burn in hell for thousands and thousands of years if they rebelled against the religious leaders) fought one another to get in line to play up to the santri group. One means for doing this was to come asking the santris to be their sons-in-law.

One of these *kiais* once told his followers: "My wife shall not be going to hell at the moment she is crossing over the *Siratal Mustakim* bridge in the hereafter, because she is allowed to hold on to the end of the cloth from my turban." In other words, he meant: "Unfortunate are those who don't have a kiai to help them out."

It's because of that that many kiais have four wives or even more. Everyone wanted them as a son-in-law, though there weren't all that many kiais at this point. And, so that everyone who came along proposing marriage to them would get an equal share, quite happily and in full sincerity a kiai would divorce his senior wife so that the resultant vacancy could be filled with the girl who had just been proferred—a fresh one.

The girl's mother and father figured that if their child was going to be kept from the fires of hell, the kiai certainly wouldn't forget to come to the aid of the two of them as well, as his parents-in-law. Beyond such calculations connected with matters of security after death, it was a distinct honor and source of pride for them that they would have a syech, in his big turban, in his long flowing robes, climbing up the stairs into their house— just as they would have felt fortunate in much the same way decades earlier to have a datuk in his big kerchief, wearing his golden dagger, come up into the house.

The adat group's price had skidded, so people weren't fighting over them anymore.

Noting that it was the religious group, hajis or syechs, that Minangkabau society values more highly, the young men raced each other to study religion. And the ones who could afford it would go off to Mecca, so that when they'd come back to the home village they'd be wearing a turban, a robe, eating dates and shortening, and so on, and they'd occupy a high level in society.

Their calculations hadn't been wrong either, because as soon as he arrived back in the village, the man would be invited to come over to eat here and to eat there because everyone wanted to hear him tell tales about Arabia. Several days afterward some mothers and fathers would already be having whispered marriage conferences, and two or three days later along would come someone carrying the incised metal box of betel leaves to the mother of this new haji. After he'd been married only two or three months another person would come along and propose marriage again to him, and please, please do not turn down this proposal, the petitioners would say, because, for lo, all these many years this girl's mother and father have had a pure, holy intention to have him as their son-in-law—yes, from before the time he went to Mecca even, they'd already had this notion.

(This wasn't true! If he hadn't been a haji but only an ordinary farmer they wouldn't have wanted to lay eyes on him. It was the turban that lured them in!)

It was because of that that so many people wanted to become hajis in Minangkabau during that time. Every year, hundreds of them. Many of them were just hunting social position and public respect, although a few sincere ones really did want to serve God devotedly.

But several decades afterward, religion's influence gradually ebbed away. Many folks knew its economic system wasn't strong. Religious leaders had based their influence on fear and the obedience of their followers. The general public began not to give so much credence to religion's teachings, since these teachings didn't increase people's prosperity and riches. The lovely promises about what it would be like later on in heaven, and the threats about burning in hell, no longer flowed through the hearts of the people who emphasized material wealth over all things. The public no longer fought over who was going to propose marriage to hajis first, with the exception of a man who was truly a syech—rich, very influential, or very sacred.

Their retreat was quickened by the rise of the merchants. A while before, they—and the majority of them were the sons or nephews of the adat group—hadn't been very strong competitors of the religion group. Now, though, the merchants emigrated to the rantau in Padang or other towns in Sumatra, going into trade there with capital they had brought with them, or becoming employees of merchants who were already rich. There were even some who became stable boys at first. However, thanks to their willingness to work, their neatness, and their skills, many of them were able to go into trade themselves and to own stores and to get rich. When one or two of them would come back to the village, he'd be carrying several suitcases full of clothes, jewelry, and lots of money. And he himself would be wearing a wool jacket, a silk Buginese sarong, beautiful and costly European shoes, a gold pocket watch, and a costly velvet hat, and smoking a cigar as big around as his big toe. When they'd return home from Padang, they'd also be carrying *salak* [snakefruit] and pineapples by the basketful, as well as a basket of mangoes. And a line of five coolies would be strung out along the road from the station to his parents' house, carrying all these things along for him. The village people, particularly the women, would just stand there and gape, flabbergasted. They'd inquire among themselves, Who's that carrying so much stuff?

Several days later he'd return to Padang. People would come up to his mother to propose marriage to her newly rich son. Two months later he'd have a pretty girl as his wife, a girl who earlier would have gone to the datuks or the kiais.

In the long run people came to prefer merchants as sons-in-law because they had a great deal of wealth, and they were able to fulfill the desires of the women, who were weak-willed when they got a glimpse of luxuries. The adat group (which had boasted of its high aristocratic standing) and the religious group (which had boasted of its great influence in the world hereafter) weren't paid much attention to anymore. And because of that the majority of young men wanted to go into business and become merchants. They dreamed of their future riches, and the number who wanted to do Koranic verse recitations decreased.

In the long run there wasn't much room for new traders in Padang. So many of them tried their luck in Sibolga, Medan, Bangkahulu, Tjurup, Bintuhan, and Kroe in the residencies of Palembang and Lampung. They traded in cloth there and peddled housewares. Kids who'd just reached the age of consent (who were just out of elementary school and still studying recitations in the surau) would be ordered by their mothers and fathers to emigrate to one of these towns just mentioned above, so that the boy could quickly get married like his pals who had been trading for two or three years.

When the young man had been in the rantau for two or three years and had sent back lots of money and clothes to his mother (and the villagers had gotten wind of this), without fail some mothers and fathers would want to come propose marriage to him. So his mother and father would order this young man to come back home, and in the letter to them he'd be told to go get some wedding clothes and buy the various supplies for the bridal ceremony. The young man would understand everything perfectly and would be indescribably delighted. But oftentimes he wouldn't know who his future wife was. Usually she was not the one he had been in love with back in the village before.

The young traders would swagger about boastfully, striding to and fro on the village road, changing clothes four times in one day, so that everyone would know exactly what he had stored away in his suitcase. Some of them even wore formal dance shoes on roads with lots of rocks and sharp gravel, and others wore raincoats out in the blazing heat. This was because the guy had already waited for several days for it to rain, but none had come. He really wanted to show off his newly bought raincoat to people, so he was forced to wear it out in the hot sunlight, using as his excuse that he didn't feel very well and had chills. One who had a new gold ring with diamonds on it would be talking in the food stall, and while saying (for instance) that the weather was really hot, he'd wipe his forehead every three minutes or so, so that people would see his diamond ring and gape in admiration.

His cigarettes would be Westminsters, from a can. Or he'd be smoking a cigar with a beautiful ring around it and a fragrant smell. One with a gold watch would pull it out of his pocket every ten minutes or so to check the time repeatedly, as if he had an appointment or something was rushing him, as if his time was very valuable. He'd say that he needed to go meet so and so at Polan's house at such and such an hour, whereas actually if he and Polan didn't meet for five days it wouldn't really mean anything. His real reason was to boast about his watch.

Half of them had gold teeth. Every few moments they'd laugh. Sometimes, when there wouldn't be a reason to laugh, they'd laugh; just so long as their lips wou'd part and the gleaming gold teeth would appear.

There was even a trader named Rasidin who'd laugh to himself on a deserted road. I saw this myself, when Bujung, Zainal, and I were lying down in the shrubs by the side of the road to Lower Sumpur one very hot afternoon. People who'd pass by couldn't see us, but we could see them. When we saw a man laughing to himself, looking up toward the sky, laughing again, bowing his head to look at the ground, laughing again, the three of us just looked at each other, inquiring with glances whether this man was sane or not.

It was Zainal who said: "Presumably he's remembering joking around with his wife last night."

But what's the use about talking about other people when I haven't put my own business in order yet? It's best that I just return to my own situation, which is more important.

Already I had loved two girls who had married other people: Asjiah and Jusna. Both were snatched up by traders. Now I was beginning to fall in love with a third girl, but I was convinced she'd also be taken away by a trader so long as I was still living in the village. Because of this, if I truly wanted to have her I would have to emigrate to the rantau first for two or three years. So long as I was a santri, I would come in last in the race.

True enough, Father was wealthy enough to support me and a wife, but I would feel heavy-hearted at that. I wanted to have the wherewithal to earn my own living and not have to depend on my parents. I wanted to have my own income to support my own household.

But in reality this consideration of wanting someone to quickly come asking me to be their son-in-law didn't particularly influence my desire and decision to leave the village. I must admit that I certainly had some small wish to be married and have a house of my own, like my friends. But the wish was still quite hazy and hadn't become the main pressure. No, what always pushed me on in all this was the sadness and loneliness of being left behind by my friends. Gradually, I thought, all of my fifteen friends would leave and I would be left all alone there in the village with kids younger than me.

What really, strongly pushed me to leave was the longing to add to my knowledge and life experiences in other regions that I didn't know yet. To exchange my tranquil, secure life in the village for a life of struggle in the rantau. Sumpur had nothing more to give me. I already knew everything about it. In fact: more than enough about it.

Because I couldn't stand it any longer, finally I got up the courage to tell my wishes to Father, along with all the reasons I could possibly think of. I accompanied this with attempts to explain several opportunities open to me in other lands. As might be imagined, at first Father did not agree to any of this. He didn't want to be separated from me. He was already old, he said, and because of that he was worried that when I was far off in the rantau, if all of a sudden he should die, we wouldn't be able to meet again before we parted forever. And moreover, he wanted me to replace him as a teacher in the Upper Surau. In short, he didn't like my going.

I started crying—I was extremely sad. When Mother told me to go eat, I didn't want to. I had no desire to eat, my throat having been locked by my unrequited longings. My heart was shattered when I thought about Father's firm hold on me. Why didn't God soften his heart so he would give me permission to leave? If he really loved me, surely Father would be happy to see me making preparation for my life in the future! After all, isn't it always the future that mothers and fathers hope and plan for, for their child, in accordance with their child's true inner desires, talents, and wishes? Wasn't my father misplacing his love, like other fathers who ordered their children to always live near them until the child just becomes dull and stupid? Wasn't it possible that in the future the building he had thought was so fine and good for me would turn out to be a fragile cardboard carton? And that way, wasn't it possible that I wouldn't have any shelter from the difficulties of life in days to come?

This is what I was always worried about. Because Father was not a holy angel, not a saint, perhaps his view of the future did not actually extend any great distance. So wouldn't I have to suffer the consequences if he had calculated wrong?

Isn't it better for mothers and fathers to just let the child shape his own future with the two of them giving guidance and comparative examples, since they have a good deal of experience—and for the two of them not to force their desires harshly on their child? Isn't that harshness wrong-headed, because the mother and father can't be absolutely convinced that they're not making errors? And if they do stubbornly aver that they're right, might not this conviction be based on stupidity and lack of clarity? Did they really like to see their child miserable year after year because he's been forced to bow to the harshness of his mother's and father's decision? Or wouldn't they prefer to see their child living a fortunate existence, following his own desires, even if those are in conflict with their own wishes?

I was abundantly aware of the fact that the ancestors of the Minang-kabau people were illiterate and their descendants were ignorant and foolish. Many of them didn't want to go to school, and because of that they didn't know or understand what had happened and would happen in the world and in their land. And wouldn't it be true that we young kids would be ignorant and foolish later on, too, and that we would be miserable if we simply obeyed the wishes of adults who had no sense of understanding in this life? What would we become, we young fellows, if we followed the guidance and teachings of the kiais in the peasantren—as I once experienced for two years in that dark period of my life? What would we young fellows become if we followed the advice of our maternal uncles and datuks, who among other things didn't know any geography—men who told us that Berlin was close to Mecca, because in the World War, Germany had come to the aid of Turkey? We already knew that Berlin was far away from Mecca, but our datuks kept stubbornly saying that these two cities were located very close to each other. Hmmm, we sure have savored a lot of life, they would say to us snidely. Could we possibly, possibly surrender our lives and fates to people who were mired in such darkness?

After a month-long period of my asking, cajoling, and pressuring—and after my bluffing that I would just run away from home some night without telling anyone where I was going, if I wasn't allowed to leave—little by little Father's heart did soften and he gave me permission to go. But not all that far away as yet, only to Padang; and not to go into commerce but to go to school.

For the meantime, I accepted it. Being allowed to go to Padang was already a stroke of luck. For me at that time, that was already quite a distance away, and I saw this as my first step. The most important thing was getting out of the village and going to the city, for I wanted a big change. And in Padang I could put some of my ideals into action. There, there were various types of human being to be found, whom I could approach, get to know, and study. There were Niassians, Indians, Chinese, Arabs, and so on, whose adat customs, character, and entertainments held much attraction. Life in the big city would doubtless bring a good deal of enjoyment and happiness each day.

The next day I was going to set off. That night I could hardly sleep, my thoughts were heated, I dreamed wild dreams. Other people were already sound asleep while I was still imagining what I would be doing in the city of Padang. This was a great event and a major change in the life of my soul. The blood of adulthood was starting to throb and flow throughout my body. The blood was hot and powerful and provided the strength and courage to attack a new life full of struggle, difficulties, failures, and victories. The waves of life thundering in the wide world had begun to roar in my heart, and like it or not, I had to jump into the roiling waters.

The bright moonlight through the skylight came into the hall where we sprawled about, sleeping. The room was lit up a bit because of this, and the sleeping forms around me were slightly visible. I was going to be separated from these friends. Such were the desires of life; my tears flowed down my face. The clock on the wall ticked in its orderly fashion, introducing its disturbing sound in the surau, which was deathly still, inside and out.

My thoughts flew farther and farther away. What were Bandung, Solo, and Malang [cities in Sunda and Java] like when it was a moonlit night like this? If I could take walks there, surely I'd be surrounded by beautiful, natural scenery and my heart would be refreshed, bathed in its beauty. When exactly would I be able to go to those places?

Hearing the wall clock strike two times, my thoughts came back to Sumpur and the surau. I found that I was just daydreaming, and sorrow flowed through me when I thought of being separated from the village. I could feel how deep my love for Father was and for the surau, the place where I'd lived both happily and sadly for fifteen years—and for Mount Four Houses, and the Sumpur River and Lake Singkarak, where I'd splashed about. But I was going to leave all of it behind because I was now an adult and such were my life's pursuits and aspirations. How very sad I was that all I had loved all this time must be left behind. Life in the rantau was calling to me.

It was if my heart were being torn to pieces by an internal struggle: the struggle between love for Father and village, and love for my aspirations.

But I knew these ties to the village were just the bonds of feeling, and that sooner or later these would be snapped by my relentless, heedless life desires. And I simply could *not* base my character and life outlook on feelings alone, if I did not wish to become a mere ball in a game between nature and the world around me.

Life in the wide world was beginning to call to me; its voice was blurred, like softly rumbling thunder, audible from afar.

Tomorrow I would begin, and attack this life . . .

NOTES TO *VILLAGE CHILDHOOD*

Chapter 1

1. Oldest man in a clan or lineage, in some Malay-area societies; "nobleman" in another usage. Radjab uses the Minangkabau term, apparently, to mean ceremonial leader in his lineage, a sometimes elected post. Radjab uses the word here without

further elaboration, although its meaning may well not be self-evident to Indonesians of other ethnic backgrounds. In this translation I shall forthwith use *datuk* without always giving an English kinship term afterward.

2. As readers discover later in the translation, the boy's family is intimately connected to esoteric *silat* lore and self-defense practice. Minangkabau men are famous throughout Sumatra for their skills at the martial arts.

3. A fruit with a smooth, yellowish-tan skin. The color is much admired in many Indonesian societies, especially for women.

4. Minangkabau great houses once served as the residences for compound matrilineal households, consisting of an old woman, some of her sisters, and their daughters. These women's husbands would sleep in the house too, although their "own houses" were with their mothers and sisters.

5. The *rantau* is the geographical and social realm outside a Minangkabau person's close-to-home domain. In this translation the word will be retained in its original form.

6. The author uses the term *aesthetika* here.

7. That is, Ridjal's father was set to make the pilgrimage to Mecca—a public demonstration of his great devoutness to Islam, and to his family's considerable wealth and prestige.

8. The notion that returning *haji* pilgrims come home to Minangkabau laden down with dates is a common assumption in many Muslim parts of Sumatra.

9. In everyday family conversation in many places in Sumatra children will often use kin terms of address in place of a simple "you" when talking to their parents. For instance, a child might say to the father, "Will Father take me along to the market?"

10. Engku Sutan, with an extra honorific.

11. The author has switched from "stepmother" to "mother" here. Later in the narrative he often uses "Ibu" (Mother) as his term for referring to his stepmothers.

12. Banyan trees are reputed to be the abode of large populations of spirit beings.

Chapter 2

1. From the small Muslim recitation-school, dormitory, and prayer mosque.

2. Radjab does not specify if this school fee is for a month or a week or what.

3. In Arabic, in the text.

Chapter 3

1. That is, to sleep with their wives (the group of sisters living there in the great house with their mother and aunts).

2. *Nenek-nenek*. This word is not marked for gender and could also mean grandfathers and grandmothers.

3. This phrase resembles oratory passages used throughout Sumatra, to laud the unitary nature of important social groups.

4. By our *sifat* and our *suara hati sendiri*: our qualities, features, looks, characteristics, and the voice of our hearts.

5. Another evocation of oratory, similar to that in note 4.
6. Tapanuli here could mean Toba, Angkola, or Mandailing.
7. *Dialek Minangkabau.*
8. A *dukun.*
9. Another section of the Arabic prayers.

Chapter 4

1. *Hilalang* grass.

Chapter 5

1. *Jambak* is a sort of fruit (*Eugenia jambus*). Jambak-jambak refers to fruits like *jambus,* or roseapples.
2. *Sunat* means circumcision, and sunat prayers are special ones for that ritual occasion.
3. *Sembayang* and *zikir* in the original.

Chapter 6

1. The author uses no question mark here.

Chapter 7

1. King bananas (*pisang raja*) are great delicacies in Sumatra. Their skin is deep yellow, and their meat is sweet, fragrant, firm, slick, and juicy.

Chapter 9

1. In Minangkabau, young men living off in the rantau (the precincts outside their home villages) who are already established as promising merchants are considered much more attractive as husbands than are young men "left behind at home." Young merchants typically receive handsome money gifts from their new in-laws; they add luster to their bride's family line.

Chapter 10

1. The word for sibling here, *adik,* is not marked for gender so it is uncertain whether this half-sibling was a girl or a boy. The author does not mention a half-brother anywhere else in the text, however.

Chapter 11

1. *Uda* is a Minangkabau kinship term of address, which the author then translates into an Indonesian near-equivalent.
2. *Durian* is a pungent-smelling, soft-fleshed, creamy colored fruit covered with a spiky green or tan rind. It is hugely pupular in Sumatra.
3. "Aggressif" in the text.

4. A style of mannered high-stepping used in Minangkabau martial arts.

5. A *selamatan* is a communal meal designed to give thanks for important events, and to secure continued spiritual blessings for the assembled participants.

Chapter 12

1. *Lungguk*: a "haystack" of cut rice stalks.

2. *Mustahil*, a word borrowed from Arabic, in common Indonesian usage.

3. A respectful term of address for older female lineage relatives in Minangkabau.

4. *Komprang* pants are a sort of bell-bottom trousers. A *destar* is a Batik cloth head covering, suitable for ceremonial occasions.

Chapter 13

1. Islamic theological writing in Arabic is phrased in different texts at different levels of difficulty and abstruseness. At this point in their studies, the boys did not control much of the more esoteric writing.

2. *Haji* means that the uncle has made the pilgrimage to Mecca.

3. The usage here is "fanatik."

4. Literally, in a form of Arabic of such a high level that it cannot even be written about.

5. *Pelekat* is an ornate, heavy cloth, sometimes shot through with fancy metallic threads.

6. The *Kaum muda*, the Younger Generation.

7. The *Kaum tua*, the Old Generation.

Chapter 14

1. *Bismillahi*: "in the name of God" in Arabic. Often said as part of grace before beginning a meal. "My beloved little sister": *adindaku yang tercinta* in the text. The sibling terms *adik* and *kakak* are often used between boyfriends and girlfriends in the formal prose of Sumatran letter writing.

Chapter 18

1. I am uncertain of the translation of this difficult idiom ("termakan tjirit berendang").

2. *Ondeh-ondeh*: rice flour cakes filled with sweetened, mashed mung beans and sesame seeds. It was fried and sold on market day or made at home on holidays.

3. Minangkabau townspeople and villagers typically boil water for drinking, as unboiled water is considered likely to cause diseases.

Chapter 19

1. "Older Sister" here could refer to any of a number of older female relatives.

Chapter 20

1. The story of Malim Kundang is a familiar one throughout Sumatra. It concerns a young man, Malim Kundang, who curses his mother and is immediately turned to stone as a supernatural punishment.

Chapter 21

1. A *dukun* is a folk healer, diagnostician, spellcaster, and spell remover.

Chapter 22

1. Apparently Haji Rasul had divorced two of his four wives, giving him the opportunity to marry a young, new one.

2. Marah Rusli's novel *Sitti Nurbaya* (Radjab uses the spelling *Siti Nurbaya*) concerns a young Minangkabau girl who falls in love with a boy her own age but is forced by her family to marry a rich merchant, Datuk Meringgih. The novelist argues that such "hidebound" family practices laid waste to young people's lives.

3. *Astaga* is a common Sumatran exclamation of surprise, one with an Arabic, Muslim tone to it.

4. That is, under the croton plants. Note Radjab's mention of these plants in relation to memories of his mother, in chapter 1.

REFERENCES

Anderson, Benedict. 1979. "A Time of Darkness and a Time of Light: Transposition in Early Nationalist Thought." In *Perceptions of the Past in Southeast Asia,* ed. A. Reid and D. Marr, 219–248. Singapore: Asian Studies Association of Australia.

———. 1983. *Imagined Communities: Reflections on the Origin and Spread of Nationalism.* London: Verso.

Benda-Beckmann, Franz von. 1979. *Property in Social Continuity: Continuity and Change in the Maintenance of Property Relationships through Time in Minangkabau, West Sumatra.* Verhandelingen van het Koninklijk Instituut voor Taal-Land-en Volkenkunde, 86. The Hague: Martinus Nijhoff.

Bowen, John. 1991. *Sumatran Politics and Poetics: Gayo History 1900–1989.* New Haven, Conn.: Yale University Press.

Datoek Besar, R. A., and R. Roolvink, eds. 1953. *Hikayat Abdullah.* Jakarta: Djambatan.

Drewes, G. W. J. 1951. "Autobiografieen van Indonesiers." *Bijdragen tot de Taal-Land-en Volkenkunde* 107 (2–3): 226–264.

———. 1981. "Balai Pustaka and Its Antecedents." Papers on Indonesian Languages and Literatures. *Archipel* 13:97–104.

Drewes, G. W. J., trans. 1961. *Hikayat Nakhoda Muda: De Biografie van een Minangkabausen Peperhandelaar in de Lampongs.* Verhandelingen van het Koninklijk Instituut voor Taal-Land-en Volkenkunde, 36. Gravenhage: Martinus Nijhoff.

Errington, Shelly. 1979. "Some Comments on Style in the Meanings of the Past." In *Perceptions of the Past in Southeast Asia,* ed. A. Reid and D. Marr, 26–42. Singapore: Asian Studies Association of Australia.

Foulcher, Keith. 1977. "Perceptions of Modernity and the Sense of the Past: Indonesian Poetry in the 1920s." *Indonesia* 23 (April): 39–58.

———. 1980. *Pujangga Baru: Literature and Nationalism in Indonesia, 1933–1942.* Flinders University Asian Studies Monograph, no. 2. Adelaide: Flinders University.

Fox, James. 1979. "'Standing' in Time and Place: The Structure of Rotinese Historical Narratives." In *Perceptions of the Past in Southeast Asia*, ed. A. Reid and D. Marr, 10–25. Singapore: Asian Studies Association of Australia.

Fox, James, ed. 1990. *To Speak in Pairs*. Cambridge: Cambridge University Press.

Frederick, William. 1974. "My Childhood World." *Indonesia* 17 (April): 112–135.

Freidus, Alberta Joy. 1977. *Sumatran Contributions to the Development of Indonesian Literature 1920–1942*. Asian Studies at Hawaii, Monograph Series 19. Honolulu: University of Hawaii Press.

Graves, Elizabeth E. 1981. *The Minangkabau Response to Dutch Colonial Rule in the Nineteenth Century*. Monograph Series no. 60, Modern Indonesia Project, Southeast Asia Program. Ithaca, N.Y.: Cornell Modern Indonesia Project.

Grijns, C. D., and S. O. Robson, eds. 1986. *Cultural Contact and Textual Interpretation: Papers from the Fourth European Colloquium on Malay and Indonesian Studies*. Verhandelingen van het Koninklijk Instituut voor Taal-Land-en Volkenkunde. Dordrecht, Holland: Foris Publications.

Gungwu, Wang. 1979. "Introduction: The Study of the Southeast Asian Past." In *Perceptions of the Past in Southeast Asia*, ed. A. Reid and D. Marr, 1–9. Singapore: Asian Studies Association of Australia.

Hamka. [1951–1952] 1974. *Kenang-Kenangan Hidup*, 3d ed. Jakarta: Bulan Bintang.

Heider, Karl. 1991a. *Indonesian Cinema*. Honolulu: University of Hawaii Press.

———. 1991b. *Landscapes of Emotion: Lexical Maps and Scenarios of Emotion Terms in Indonesia*. Cambridge: Cambridge University Press.

Johns, A. H. 1979. "The Turning Image: Myth and Reality in Malay Perceptions of the Past." In *Perceptions of the Past in Southeast Asia*, ed. A. Reid and D. Marr, 43–67. Singapore: Asian Studies Association of Australia.

Josselin de Jong, P. E. de. [1951] 1980. *Minangkabau and Negri Sembilan: Sociopolitical Structure in Indonesia*, 2d ed. Leiden: IJdo.

Kahin, Audry. 1979. "Struggle for Independence: West Sumatra in the Indonesian National Revolution, 1945–1950." Ph.D. dissertation, Cornell University Department of History, Ithaca, N.Y.

Kahn, Joel. 1980. *Minangkabau Social Formations: Indonesian Peasants and the World Economy*. Cambridge: Cambridge University Press.

———. 1992. *Constituting the Minangkabau: Peasants, Cultures, and Modernity in Colonial Indonesia*. Providence, R.I., and Oxford: Berg.

Kartini, Raden Adjeng. 1911. *Door Duisternis tot Licht*. Semarang, Soerabaya, and 's Gravenhage: G. C. T. Van Dorp and Co. (*Letters from a Javanese Princess*, translated by Agnes Louise Symmers, edited and with an introductory essay by Hildred Geertz [Lanham, Md.: University Press of America, 1985].)

Kato, Tsuyoshi. 1977. *Social Change in a Centrifugal Society: The Minangkabau of West Sumatra*. Ph.D. dissertation, Cornell University, Ithaca, N.Y.

———. 1982. *Matriliny and Migration: Evolving Minangkabau Traditions in Indonesia*. Ithaca, N.Y.: Cornell University Press.

Kipp, Rita S. 1990. *The Early Years of a Dutch Colonial Mission: The Karo Field*. Ann Arbor, Mich.: University of Michigan Press.

Kipp, Rita S., and Richard Kipp, eds. 1983. *Beyond Samosir: Recent Studies of the Batak Peoples of Sumatra*. Athens, Ohio: Ohio University Papers in International Studies, Southeast Asia Series 62.

Kuipers, Joel. 1990. *Power in Performance: The Creation of Textual Authority of Weyewa Ritual Speech*. Philadelphia: University of Pennsylvania Press.

Lewis, E. D. 1990. "A Quest for the Source: The Ontogenesis of a Creation Myth of the Ata Tana Ai." In *To Speak in Pairs*, ed. James Fox. Cambridge: Cambridge University Press.

Liaw, Y. F. 1985. Review of Sweeney, 1980a. *Journal of Southeast Asian Studies* 16 (1):167.

Maier, H. M. J. 1982. "The Failure of a Hero: An Analysis of Pramudya Ananta Tur's Short Story 'Sunat.'" *BKI* 138:317–345.

———. 1987. "Chairil Anwar's Heritage: The Fear of Stultification—Another Side of Modern Indonesian Literature." *Indonesia* 43 (April): 1–29.

———. 1988. *In the Center of Authority: The Malay Hikayat Merong Mahawangsa*. Ithaca, N.Y.: Southeast Asia Program, Cornell University.

Manafe, Minggus. 1967. *Aneka Kehidupan di Pulau Roti*. Jakarta: Balai Pustaka.

McKinley, Robert. 1979. "Zaman dan Masa, Eras and Periods: Religious Evolution and the Permanence of Epistemological Ages in Malay Culture." In *The Imagination of Reality: Essays in Southeast Asian Coherence Systems*, ed. A. L. Becker and A. Yengoyan, 303–324. Norwood, N.J.: Ablex.

Muis, Abdul. [1928] 1974. *Salah Asuhan*. Jakarta: Balai Pustaka.

Niessen, Sandra A. 1993. *Batak Cloth and Clothing: A Dynamic Indonesian Tradition*. Kuala Lumpur: Oxford University Press, Oxford in Asia Series.

Peacock, James. 1968. *Rites of Modernization*. Chicago: University of Chicago Press.

Pospos, P. 1950. *Aku dan Toba: Tjatatan dari Masa Kanak-Kanak*. Jakarta: Balai Pustaka.

Pramoedya Ananta Toer. 1952. *Tjerita dari Blora* [Stories from Blora]. Jakarta: Balai Pustaka.

Quinn, George. 1983. "The Case of the Invisible Literature: Power, Scholarship, and Contemporary Javanese Writing." *Indonesia* 35 (April): 1–36.

Radjab, Muhamad. 1949. *Tjatatan di Sumatera* [Notes on Sumatra]. Jakarta: Balai Pustaka.

———. 1950. *Dongeng-Dongeng Sulawesi Selatan* [Some Sulawesian folktales]. Jakarta: Balai Pustaka.

———. [1950] 1974. *Semasa Kecil di Kampung (1913–1928): Autobiografi seorang Anak Minangkabau* [Village childhood]. Jakarta: Balai Pustaka.

———. 1952. *Toraja Sa'dan*. Jakarta: Balai Pustaka.

———. 1954. *Perang Paderi* [The Padri Wars]. Jakarta: Balai Pustaka.

———. 1969. *Sistem Kekerabatan di Minangkabau* [Kinship system of Minangkabau]. Padang: Center for Minangkabau Studies Press.

Reid, Anthony. 1972. "On the Importance of Autobiography." *Indonesia* 13 (April): 1–4.

Reid, Anthony, and David Marr. 1979. "Preface." In *Perceptions of the Past in Southeast Asia*, ed. A. Reid and D. Marr, vii–viii. Singapore: Asia Studies Association of Australia.

Reid, Anthony and David Marr, eds. 1979. *Perceptions of the Past in Southeast Asia*. Southeast Asia Publications Series, 4. Singapore: Heinemann Educational Books (Asia) for the Asian Studies Association of Australia.

Rodgers, Susan. 1979a. "Advice to the Newlyweds: Sipirok Batak Wedding Speeches—Adat or Art?" In *Art, Ritual, and Society in Indonesia*, ed. Edward M. Bruner and Judith Becker, 30–61. Athens, Ohio: Ohio University Papers in International Studies, Southeast Asia Series 53.

―――. 1979b. "A Modern Batak Horja: Innovation in Sipirok Adat Ceremonial." *Indonesia* 27 (April): 103–128.

―――. 1981. "A Batak Literature of Modernization." *Indonesia* 31 (April): 137–161.

―――. 1983. "Political Oratory in a Modernizing Southern Batak Homeland." In *Beyond Samosir: Recent Studies of the Batak Peoples of Sumatra*, ed. Rita S. Kipp and Richard Kipp, 21–52. Athens, Ohio: Ohio University Papers in International Studies.

―――. 1984. "Orality, Literacy, and Batak Concepts of Marriage Alliance." *Journal of Anthropological Research* 40, no. 3:433–450.

―――. 1986. "Batak Tape Cassette Kinship: Constructing Kinship through the Indonesian National Mass Media." *American Ethnologist* 13, no. 1:23–42.

―――. 1988. "*Me and Toba*: A Childhood World in a Batak Memoir." *Indonesia* 45 (Spring): 63–84.

―――. 1990. "A Sumatran Antiquarian Writes His Culture." *Steward Journal of Anthropology* (University of Illinois, Urbana) 17-1 and 2 (1987–88, Special Issue on Literacy and Literature): 99–120.

―――. 1991. "Imagining Tradition, Imagining Modernity: A Southern Batak Novel from the 1920s." Bijdragen tot de Taal-Land-en Volkenkunde, KITLV, 147, 273–297.

Roff, W. R. 1972. *Autobiography and Biography in Malay Historical Studies*. Singapore: Institute of Southeast Asian Studies (Occasional Paper 13).

Rusli, Marah. 1922. *Sitti Nurbaya*. Weltevraden: Balai Pustaka.

Salmon, Claudine. 1981. "Literature in Malay by the Chinese of Indonesia: A Provisional Annotated Bibliography." Editions de la Maison des Sciences de l'Homme, Etudes Insulindiennes. *Archipel* 3 (Paris).

Sherman, D. George. 1987. "Men Who Are Called 'Women' in Toba-Batak: Marriage, Fundamental Sex-Role Differences, and the Suitability of the Gloss 'Wife-Receivers.'" *American Anthropologist* 89:867–878.

―――. 1990. *Rice, Rupees, and Ritual: Economy and Society among the Samosir Batak of Sumatra*. Stanford, Calif.: Stanford University Press.

Siagian, Toenggoel P. 1966. "Bibliography on the Batak Peoples." *Indonesia* 2:161–184 (Cornell Modern Indonesia Project, Ithaca, N.Y.).

Siegel, James. 1977. "Pramoedya's 'Things Vanished,' with a Commentary by James Siegel." *Glyph* 1:67–99.

―――. 1979. *Shadow and Sound: The Historical Thought of a Sumatran People*. Chicago: University of Chicago Press.

Singarimbun, Masri. 1975. *Kinship, Descent, and Alliance among the Karo Batak*. Berkeley and Los Angeles: University of California Press.

Siregar, Merari. 1958 [1927]. *Azab dan Sengsara: Kissah Kehidupan Seorang Anak Gadis*. Jakarta: Balai Pustaka.

Soetomo, R. 1934. *Kenang-Kenangan*. Surabaya: Kata Pendahoeloean.

Steedley, Mary Margaret. 1993. Hanging without a Rope: Narrative Experience in Colonial and Post-Colonial Karoland. Princeton, N.J.: Princeton University Press.

Sutan Iskandar, Nur. 1928. *Salah Pilih.* Jakarta: Balai Pustaka.

———. 1948. *Pengalaman Masa Kecil.* Jakarta: Balai Pustaka.

Sutherland, Heather. 1968. "Pudjangga Baru: Aspects of Indonesian Intellectual Life in the 1930s." *Indonesia* 6 (October): 106–127.

Sweeney, A., and N. G. Phillips, trans. [1872] 1975. *The Voyages of Mohamed Ibrahim Munshi.* Kuala Lumpur: Oxford University Press (Oxford in Asia Historical Memoirs). [First Malay printing, 1919.]

Sweeney, Amin. 1980a. *Reputations Live On: An Early Malay Autobiography.* Berkeley, Los Angeles, London: University of California Press.

———. 1980b. *Authors and Audiences in Traditional Malay Literature.* Berkeley: Center for South and Southeast Asian Studies, University of California at Berkeley.

———. 1987. *A Full Hearing: Orality and Literacy in the Malay World.* Berkeley, Los Angeles, London: University of California Press.

———. 1990. "Some Observations on the Nature of Malay Autobiography." *Indonesia Circle* 51 (March): 21–36.

Teeuw, A. 1967. *Modern Indonesian Literature,* Vols. I and II. The Hague: Martinus Nijhoff.

———. 1986. "Translation, Transformation, and Indonesian Literary History." In *Cultural Contact and Textual Interpretation,* ed. C. D. Grijns and S. O. Robson, 190–203. Dordrecht, Holland: Foris Publications.

Thomas, Lynn L., and Franz von Benda-Beckmann. 1985. *Change and Continuity in Minangkabau: Local, Regional, and Historical Perspectives on West Sumatra.* Athens, Ohio: Ohio University Papers in International Studies, Southeast Asia Series 71.

Tickell, Paul. 1987. "The Writing of Indonesian Literary History." *Review of Indonesian and Malaysian Affairs* 21, no. 1 (Winter): 29–43.

Vergouwen, J. C. 1964. *Social Organization and Customary Law of the Toba-Batak of Northern Sumatra.* The Hague: Martinus Nijhoff. [Translated from *Het Rechtsleven der Toba-Bataks,* by J. Scott-Kemball, 1933].

Watson, C. W. 1972. "The Sociology of the Indonesian Novel, 1920–1955." Master's thesis, University of Hull, U.K.

———. 1986. "Pramoedya Ananta Toer's Short Stories: An Anti-Poststructuralist Account." In *Cultural Context and Textual Interpretation,* ed. C. D. Grijns and S. O. Robson, 233–245. Dordrecht, Holland: Foris Publications.

———. 1989. "The Study of Indonesian and Malay Autobiography." *Indonesia Circle* 49 (June): 3–18.

———. 1991. "Religion, Nationalism, and the Individual in Modern Indonesian Autobiography: Hamka's Kenang-Kenangan Hidup." In *Variation, Transformation, and Meaning: Studies on Indonesian Literatures in Honor of A. Teeuw,* ed. J. J. Ras and S. O. Robson, 137–162. Leiden: KITLV Press.

INDEX

Abdoelgani, Dr. Roeslan, 71–73
Aceh, historical thought, 33–34
Address usage, in Pospos memoir, 82, 94, 95, 113, 127, 135, 142 n.5, 143 n.4
Age at school entry: in Pospos memoir, 83; in Radjab memoir, 158
Anakboru (Toba wife-receivers), 13; in Pospos memoir, 92
Anderson, Benedict, 6, 37, 41–43
Angkola and Mandailing, in Pospos memoir, 115, 145 n.1 (for chapter 11)
Audience for the memoirs, 25–26, 29
Autobiographical writing: in Southeast Asia, 26–28; in Indonesia, 28, 37; in Malaysia, 37–41; in the memoirs, 65–66

Balai Pustaka books, 9, 23, 36, 51; in Pospos memoir, 105. *See also Sitti Nurbaya*
Birth, infancy, in Radjab memoir, 149–153

Christianity: in Toba, 60–61; Toba Christmas, 61–62; German mission personnel, 62; Toba New Year, 62; in Pospos memoir, 82, 84–86, 93–100, 106–107, 140
Circumcision, 23; in Radjab memoir, 179–184
Clothing, in Radjab memoir: going naked, 176–177; at circumcision, 179; on finishing the Koran, 188–189; Lebaran clothes, 244, 280, 282–283
Cooking and food: in Pospos memoir: 82–83, 87, 120–122; in Radjab memoir: nursing, 153; eating eggs, 154, 158; fruits, 158, 173–174, 178–179, 267; snacks, 160–161; eating outside, 169, 239–240; at circumcision, 180–181;

during Fasting Month, 181–182, 184–186, 194–196, 253–254, 261–262, 268–269; stealing food, 190–194; during harvest, 206–207, 302, 304; for mendicants, 217–218

Death and death scenes, in Radjab memoir, 223–225
Djojopoespito, Soewarsih, 74
Drewes, G. W. J., 7, 9
Dutch people, 19, 52, 65; in Pospos memoir, 98, 108, 114

Economic conditions: poverty in Sumatra, 50–53; in Pospos memoir, 81, 115–116
Ethnic insults, 29, 51
Examinations, in Pospos memoir, 133–137

Fasting month, 23, 61, 64; in Radjab memoir, 239, 252, 266
Fathers: father-son relationship, 16, 21, 45–47, 50, 56–58; in Pospos memoir, 82, 84, 92–93, 94, 138–140; in Radjab memoir, 149, 154, 177, 196–197, 200, 246, 265, 318
Feasts: in Pospos memoir, 116; in Radjab memoir, 253–254
Feelings. *See* Longing; Love

Games and sports: in Pospos memoir, 88–89, 96–97, 127–128; in Radjab memoir, 172–178, 207, 223, 259, 284–285
Girlfriends, in Pospos memoir, 103–104, 107–108, 110, 115, 121, 124–125, 130–133

Designer:	U.C. Press Staff
Compositor:	Prestige Typography
Text:	10/12 Baskerville
Display:	Baskerville
Printer:	Haddon Craftsmen, Inc.
Binder:	Haddon Craftsmen, Inc.